ELECTRONIC SPEECH RECOGNITION

ELECTRONIC SPEECH RECOGNITION

Techniques, Technology, and Applications

Edited by

Geoff Bristow

McGraw-Hill Book Company

*New York   St. Louis   San Francisco
Montreal   Toronto*

Library of Congress Cataloging-in-Publication Data

Electronic speech recognition.

   "Follow-up of Electronic speech synthesis." — Foreword.
   1. Automatic speech recognition.   I. Bristow, Geoff.
TK7882.S65E43   1986   006.4'54   86-20921
ISBN 0-07-007913-7

First published in Great Britain by
Collins Professional and Technical Books 1986

Chapter 4 © Controller HMSO London 1986
Chapter 13 and the Glossary are not subject to copyright

1234567890   DOCDOC   8932109876

ISBN 0-07-007913-7

Printed and bound by R.R. Donnelley and Sons

CONTENTS

v

FOREWORD

The current volume on *Electronic Speech Recognition* is a much welcome follow-up of *Electronic Speech Synthesis*. Together they serve as a major introduction to the growing field of speech technology. The emphasis is on fundamental concepts and practical applications, including VLSI realisations and ergonomical considerations – how does speech recognition compete with or complement other modes of man–machine interface?

Whereas speech synthesis is by now a fairly well established field, speech recognition aiming at speaker-independent large-vocabulary performance remains a major challenge. Will a 'talkwriter' ever substitute a skilled office secretary? Of course not, but it could become a valuable assistant. Limited performance systems will surely find their way in many application areas and we have already reached a high performance of speaker-trained limited-vocabulary systems.

Far-reaching objectives call for long-range investments in a broad field of supporting science. Computer technology has developed at an almost explosive rate but our basic knowledge of human speech communication processes, including language, speech, and hearing, remains the bottleneck. Advanced signal-processing technology, dynamic programming and statistical approaches, such as hidden Markow models and Boltzman machines, are important tools but cannot substitute an acoustic-phonetic-linguistics knowledge base. We cannot leave it entirely to computers to attain an implicit knowledge of the speech code. We should approach the problem as though discovering and learning a new language, the speech code, in a narrow sense, of the language of visible speech. Advanced development systems for speech recognition thus become images of our concepts of the entire communication process with all its components, including production and perception, and our established rules for text-to-speech conversion.

High hopes are attached to national and international speech technology projects, such as the US DARPA, the British Alvey project, the French GRECO, the European ESPRIT and COST and, in the background, the large Japanese investment in the fifth generation of computers.

It is my hope that *Electronic Speech Recognition* will contribute to the main prerequisite, that of developing a fifth generation of speech technology scientists.

Gunnar Fant

PREFACE

Electronic Speech Recognition is a companion volume to *Electronic Speech Synthesis*, which was first published in November 1984. Each book stands alone and can be read without any previous knowledge of its subject, but readers of the synthesis book will find this new work familiar in style and layout.

Each book is intended to be light enough to serve as general reading on the subject of man-machine interaction, and yet complete and accurate enough to form an introductory text book of speech science. A simple 'Readers' Plan' assists navigation through the chapters for readers with different backgrounds.

Electronic Speech Recognition brings together between two covers an introduction to the principles and methods of speech recognition (*Techniques*), an overview of the state-of-the-art devices and systems available in the market (*Technology*), and a collection of design experiences written by groups who have already applied the technology (*Applications*). Further reading ideas are suggested in each of these sections.

As Professor Gunnar Fant has indicated in his *Foreword*, the implementation of voice interaction between man and machine requires a new breed of designer – a *speech scientist*. Such people cannot start out with perfect credentials – what is required is a training in linguistics, an appreciation of ergonomics, *and* an engineering background! *Electronic Speech Recognition* is designed to introduce all three of these important topics without the need for previous knowledge.

My thanks go to all the authors, many of whom are known as the pre-eminent experts in the fields about which they have written. Each has accepted the challenge to treat a complex topic in a straightforward way.

Once again, I am indebted to my family for donating my Sunday afternoons to a book.

Geoff Bristow
March 1986

ACKNOWLEDGEMENTS

Chapter 13, *Assessing the Performance of Recognisers* is a reprint of an important paper on this subject written at the US National Bureau of Standards, reflecting contributions and discussions with many speech professionals from around the globe.

The paper was originally published in the *Journal of Research of the National Bureau of Standards*, volume 90, number 5, Sept –Oct 1985, pp. 371–387. It has been reprinted with permission, and is not subject to copyright.

AUTHORS' BIOGRAPHIES

Brantingham, Larry
Currently Speech Program Manager for Texas Instruments at their headquarters in Dallas, Texas, Larry has held a number of senior posts in the speech world. He holds 27 patents, most of which are in speech and include the invention of the first single-chip LPC synthesiser. (*Chapter 7*)

Bristow, Dr Geoff
Currently Director of Network Products for ICL, Geoff was previously Marketing Manager for the North European Semiconductor Division of Texas Instruments. He holds a PhD in speech science at Cambridge University, and invented a speech training aid for the deaf which is now in use around the UK. (*Chapter 1 and Editor*)

Fisher, Mike
Currently Technical Director of Voice Systems International in the Cambridge Science Park, England (previously Voice Input Systems), Mike has spent the last 5 years designing systems for voice input and output. Before co-founding Voice Input Systems he was a freelance consultant. (*Chapter 14*)

Ivall, Thomas
Now a freelance writer on technical subjects, Thomas has been working with acoustics and electronics for more than 30 years. He started his career in the BBC research department, and was editor of *Wireless World* from 1973 to 1982. He can now be heard discussing electronics on the BBC World Service. (*Chapters 9 and 10*)

Jones, Dr Martin
Currently Technical Director for Kelvin Hughes Ltd, Martin formerly held the same post for Neve Electronic Holdings Ltd. His specialism in physical and electro-acoustics began with a lectureship and doctoral research at the University of Manchester Institute of Science and Technology. (*Chapter 12*)

Lea, Wayne A.
Probably one of the best known names in Speech Recognition, Wayne

has been a Director of Voice Control Systems of Dallas, Texas, and now runs Speech Science Publications in Minnesota. He has written several books on the subject, including *Computer Recognition of Speech, Trends in Speech Recognition* and *Selecting, Designing and Choosing Speech Recognisers. (Chapter 3)*

Magnusson, Lars-Erik

Currently President of Infovox, Stockholm, Sweden, Lars-Erik has a background in telephony and high technology project management. He has worked for Ericsson, Philips, Standard Radio & Telephone, and the Swedish National Development Corporation. He holds a Masters degree in Electronics. *(Chapter 18)*

Meisel, Dr William S.

Currently Bill is President of Speech Systems Incorporated, Tarzana, California, a company which he founded in 1981 and has grown to a workforce of 52. He published original work on Computer Pattern Recognition as early as 1972 and holds a PhD at the University of Southern California. *(Chapter 16)*

Moore, Dr Roger

Currently at the Radar Signal Research Establishment at Great Malvern in England. Roger has been a prominent speech researcher for more than 10 years. He holds a PhD at Essex University and has also held a research post in speech processing at University College London. *(Chapter 4)*

Nolan, Dr Francis

Currently a lecturer in phonetics at Cambridge University, England, Francis mainly researches into techniques of synthesising different voice qualities and into the causes of speaker variability in speech recognition. He is author of *The Phonetic Bases of Speaker Recognition. (Chapter 2)*

Pallett, Dr David S.

Currently David is a Physical Scientist at the Institute for Computer Sciences and Technology at the US National Bureau of Standards in Maryland, where previously he has been Chief of the Acoustical Engineering Division. His PhD was in Engineering Acoustics, and he is a leading campaigner for worldwide standards for Speech Technology. *(Chapter 13)*

Peckham, Jeremy

Currently Managing Consultant (Speech Technology) at the Cambridge Technical Centre of Logica, Jeremy has 8 years' experience in the speech field. Prior to Logica he spent 8 years with the UK Scientific Civil Service, and his original work includes a study of the ergonomic design of speech systems for pilots. *(Chapter 6)*

Quarmby, Dr David
Currently David is Director of Research of Loughborough Sound Images Ltd, a company which he founded to specialise in the application of high speed digital electronics in speech and sonar systems. Previously he conducted research at EMI on visual pattern recognition, has lectured in signal processing, and he is editor of *Signal Processor Chips.* (*Chapter 8*)

Rigoll, G., Kornmesser, B., and Faehnrich, K. P.
These authors represent Europe's largest independent research organisation, the *Fraunhofer Institute fuer Arbeitswirtschaft und Organisation* (IAO). The IAO is based in Stuttgart, West Germany, where G. Rigoll is responsible for the speech laboratory. K. P. Faehnrich is the head of Department for Advanced Information and Communication Systems. (*Chapter 17*)

Taylor, Mike
Currently Mike is Principal Engineer and Section Leader of the Speech Technology Section at Smiths Industries Aerospace and Defence Systems, Cheltenham, England. He has designed several real-time isolated word recognition systems, one of which has been built in more than 10 countries. (*Chapter 15*)

Tecosky, Jeff
Currently researching at Harvard in the field of computer-aided learning methods, Jeff was previously involved with speech compiler development at Dragon Systems Inc. in Newton, Massachusetts. He holds a Bachelors degree in Maths at Harvard and a Masters at the University of Columbia. (*Chapter 11*)

Viglione, Sam S.
Currently President of Interstate Voice Products, Orange, California, Sam has been involved with speech and pattern recognition for more than 20 years. He has published more than 100 articles and has chaired several professional groups. Previously with McDonnel Douglas, he left for Interstate in 1976. (*Chapter 19*)

Young, Dr Steve
Currently a lecturer in Computer Speech and Language Processing at Cambridge University, Steve's involvement with speech began with doctoral research at Cambridge on automatic speech output from semantic input. His recent research has related to voice-operated systems and Artificial Intelligence. (*Chapter 5*)

Towards a world where machines learn how to communicate
with humans, rather than vice-versa.

INTRODUCTION

This book is about man's desire to speak and his ability to design machines that can respond to his voice. It is entitled *Electronic Speech Recognition* because it describes the way that electronic circuits can be made to recognise speech utterances that have been captured by a microphone.

The importance of voice input technology may be masked in the reader's mind by images of toys that exploit the novelty of man-machine communication, or even by futuristic views of robots that appear human. However, there are many worthwhile activities that will only be made possible by using voice input systems, some of which are already feasible today because of the technology described in this book.

The ability to enter data into a computer without using one's hands has been proved to be of direct financial benefit in many situations – in inventory checking, for example. In the military environment the usefulness of speech input is beyond question, because any enhancement of the efficiency of a pilot under combat, for example, must be exploited. Many physically handicapped people are able to use their voices to control equipment, and so on.

Electronic Speech Recognition aims to give the reader an appreciation of what is possible, what will be possible, and what is a sensible way in which to use this powerful communication medium. This is achieved by dividing the subject into a small number of key topics, each one being treated in a separate chapter. The 'Readers' Plan' shows how these topics may be selected or omitted according to the background of the reader.

Part 1 provides a thorough grounding in the *techniques* of speech recognition. This starts (Chapter 1) with a short history of the subject, and a comparison between its complexity and that of speech synthesis. The elements of phonetics are described (Chapter 2) and the principal methods of speech recognition are introduced (Chapter 3). The mathematical models in common use for automatic speech recognition are then covered in depth (Chapter 4).

The *Techniques* section is concluded with a brief 'appetiser' on the influence that artificial intelligence will have on our ability to understand the meaning of speech utterances (Chapter 5), and an introducion to the human factors aspects of speech system design (Chapter 6).

Part 2 introduces the reader to the main silicon technologies having an impact on the type of speech recognition products that can be made (Chapter 7), and goes on to describe the state-of-the-art silicon devices in use (Chapter 8). A survey of the 'ready-made' products on the market is offered, giving emphasis to the techniques that have been employed (Chapter 9). The reader is then referred to a list of vendors from whom to obtain the latest product information.

Since most recognisers are actually used in conjunction with a computer system of some sort, Chapter 10 indicates how the recogniser and computer may be linked together. Chapter 11 discusses the expected emergence of a standard interface for this purpose. The problem of capturing the data, including the choice of microphones, amplifiers and room acoustics, is then covered (Chapter 12), and Part 2 concludes with a discussion of how the designer should tackle the comparative assessment of available products (Chapter 13).

Part 3 presents a selection of application examples, written by designers who have already learnt the techniques described in Part 1, and have experimented with the technologies summarised in Part 2. The application areas chosen for this exposé include those where the usefulness of speech technology is beyond doubt – for example, in aids for the disabled (Chapter 14) – as well as some where there is considerable controversy, such as with the speech recognition typewriter (Chapter 16).

The book ends with a review of the product history to date, and some views as to the future of the industry, in the eyes of the president of one of the major speech recognition manufacturers.

Reader's plan

Part	Chapter	Short title	Prerequisite chapters	Non-technical interest in speech revolution	Casual interest in speech electronics	Training in speech systems design	Speech researcher looking for update
Techniques	1	Fact and fiction	—	●	●	●	
	2	Nature of speech	—	○	○	●	
	3	Elements of recognition	—		●	●	○
	4	Computational techniques	1, 2, 3			●	●
	5	Speech understanding	1,2	○	○	●	●
	6	Human factors	—	●	○	●	○
Technology	7	Silicon breakthrough	—	●	●	●	●
	8	Silicon devices	7		○	●	●
	9	Commercial recognisers	—		●	●	●
	10	Linking to computers	—		○	●	○
	11	Interfacing standards	10			●	●
	12	Audio and acoustics	—		●	●	○
	13	Assessing performance	6	○	●	●	○
Applications	14	The disabled	—	○	○	●	○
	15	Aerospace	—	○	○	●	○
	16	The 'Talkwriter'	—	○	○	●	○
	17	Computer systems	—	○	○		○
	18	Personal computers	—	○	○	●	○
	19	Past and future	—	●	●	●	●

● = Strongly recommended reading plan.

o = Optional extra reading plan.

PART 1

TECHNIQUES

CHAPTER 1

THE SPEECH RECOGNITION PROBLEM

Geoff Bristow

In this chapter, the problem of speech recognition is introduced and compared in scale to that of speech synthesis.

1.1 *Fact and fiction in voice I/O*

THE TOOTHPASTE TUBE

A well-known adage amongst speech scientists is that the problem of speech technology is like handling a toothpaste tube – speech synthesis is like squeezing the toothpaste out of the tube, and recognition is like trying to put it back in again.

This is not in line with the common perception of these two associated problems. Science fiction has conditioned us to believe that there will eventually be machines that can understand any utterance from any person in any dialect, whilst at the same time the reader may be forgiven for believing that robots will only be able to talk with monotonous, 'mechanical' voices. The authors tend to depict it this way so that the audience is left in no doubt as to whether the robot is human or mechanical, and at the same time they do not wish to limit the dialogue of the human speaker.

However, the toothpaste tube analogy leaves us in no doubt that the situation is in fact quite the reverse. In this chapter, and in the rest of the book, the reader is shown the reasons that make speech recognition such a tough nut to crack. At the same time, the reader should hopefully become ever more optimistic as he or she works through the book and realises how much can actually be achieved within a tightly bounded application area by following good system design principles.

3

SOME FACT

Speech synthesis

It is possible now to add an automatic synthetic voice to any kind of machine, for a cost of less than $10 per unit (assuming reasonable numbers of the machine are produced). That voice can sound as natural as a human being, provided that the vocabulary to be spoken is limited (a few hundred words only).

Speaking machines can talk in any language with any accent, provided that someone has already done the work to capture the essence of the dialect in an appropriate numerical model. They can also speak from textual input with very large vocabularies, although in this case they will probably sound rather less human.

The machine that is given the voice can be anything from a door-bell to a robot. However, a machine that already contains some form of microcomputer (as do most major domestic appliances) can be rather more sophisticated if the program in the microcomputer is so modified – for example, the character of the voice can be adjusted automatically according to the day of the week, temperature, or number of times the appliance has been used. The voice could also be either male or female, or could change its sex according to the sex of the speaker who is talking to it!

Speech recognition

It is also now possible to add to a machine the capability to listen to a human voice and detect (*recognise*) when certain words are uttered. This again can be for a moderate cost (perhaps less than $100, according to capability required and number of machines made). However, the number of words that can be recognised in this way will be limited, and the full list of possible words must be declared in advance.

If it is required that *any* speaker should be allowed to approach the machine and speak utterances (known as *speaker-independent* recognition), the vocabulary that the machine will be able to recognise will be severely limited. Ten very different words could be recognised with confidence, but 100 would give a much more erratic response.

If, on the other hand, only a small number of people are to address the machine, it is possible to register who is speaking at any one time and a much better performance can then be achieved. In this situation, which is known as *speaker-dependent* recognition, vocabularies of hundreds of words can be recognised correctly (provided the speaker does not have a cold, and there is no loud traffic going by!).

It is also possible, with today's technology, to make a reasonably accurate judgement about which of a list of potential speakers is

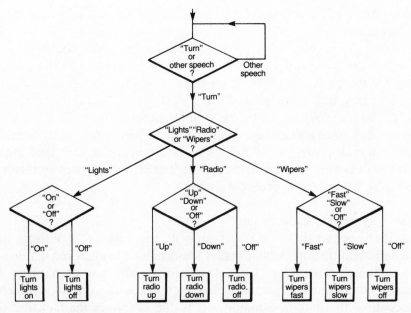

Figure 1.1 Example of use of an artificial language grammar in a car application.

speaking at any one time (*speaker identification*), or whether a speaker is indeed who he says he is (*speaker verification*).

As with speech synthesis, the presence of computing power in the machine that is to be given the recognition capability can be of great benefit. An example of the extra capability that can be added in this case is that the recogniser can be asked to be sensitive to different sets of words at different times – this can greatly increase the vocabulary that is being used effectively by the system. For example, a recognition system in a car may first be checking for the word *turn*, after which the active vocabulary may be changed to include only *radio*, *lights* and *wipers*. After successful recognition of one of these words the active vocabulary may be changed to include only the words *on* and *off* (see Fig. 1.1). By such techniques, very high recognition accuracy can be achieved at the expense of having to use a very artificial and restricted sentence structure.

SOME FICTION
Natural language programming
A popular misconception is that advances in speech recognition mean that there will be less need to use programming languages to program computers. Whilst it is true that research into natural language

programming is taking place, this is a different subject to that of speech recognition.

Speech is a way of transmitting messages that could also be transmitted in writing, in free-hand, or by typing into a keyboard. The way the messages are constructed from individual words is defined by the language that is being used.

Just as the English language can be either written or spoken, so computer languages can be input to computers by typing or by speaking into a speech recogniser; if advances were made in speech recognition but not in computer programming, the speaker would need to resort to dictating a traditional program listing.

The long-awaited breakthrough

Another popular dream is that there will, some time this century, be a sudden breakthrough which makes speaker-independent recognition of an unlimited vocabulary possible. This is sadly not to happen, for another fundamental reason; whilst much of the variability in speech is susceptible to analysis, a major part is due simply to the fact that one cannot control how people speak! However, there continue to be many major advances each year in both the techniques of recognition and in the technology – the process will be a series of steady improvements coupled with maturing methodologies for using speech input in applications.

FICTION BECOMING FACT

Having identified the areas where fact has already been proven, and where fiction will remain as fiction, the reader is entitled to ask: which of the current fictions will become fact?

The facts presented above show that words, and indeed sentences, can be automatically selected out of a predefined list of such words and sentences. If an appropriate set of rules is also defined in advance, actions can be taken by computers or equipment according to the voice commands received. At present the rule sets used usually describe exact sentence structures that must be recognised before a certain action is taken; a word-string that has not been listed would not be 'understood' by the machine.

However, whereas certain aspects of the word recognition problem are intractable, the problem of deriving sentence structures from a string of words is a soluble (although very difficult) one. Natural language grammars are extremely complex and change with time, but they are nevertheless finite and well defined.

There are, of course, ambiguities in the meaning of many sentences, as with written text and (to a lesser extent) with normal human speech communications. However, we are accustomed to a certain degree of confusion and have evolved methods of resolving it. For example, how often does one hear the question: *Are you asking me or telling me?*

Here, then, is a problem which has only remained unsolved because of the large number of man-years of research required to define an appropriate model, and the cost of the computing power required to run it. Both of these constraints will be removed over time and we can soon expect to be interacting with machines that deduce meaning from our utterances. These machines will use speech recognising *pre-processors* based on the techniques described in this book.

The problem of deducing the *semantic* content (meaning) of speech, known as *speech understanding*, falls within the field of *artificial intelligence*, and is described in Chapter 5 of this book.

1.2 *A short history*

MODELLING THE VOCAL MECHANISM

Man has always been fascinated by his ability to speak. Without this advanced form of communication the establishment of society as we know it would have been impossible; ideas would not be readily communicated and man's superiority over other animals would be diminished.

As early as the eighteenth century, attempts were made to model the human speech mechanism[1]. Without the aid of electricity these were physical analogues of the vocal apparatus – the lungs, vocal cords, vocal tract, tongue, teeth and lips – but were accurate enough to yield sounds recognisable as human utterances.

If such a model of speech production was possible using a purely physical analogue, then clearly modelling with electrical impulses – and later with digital computers – was an easy extrapolation.

In 1939 a device called the 'Voder' (Voice Operation Demonstrator) was produced at the Bell Telephone Labs in New Jersey which could be operated by trained operators to emit speech sounds (see Fig. 1.2). Voder used a set of 10 band-pass filters (one controlled by each finger of the operator) to simulate the variable resonances of the vocal cavity.

Following the Second World War, much more advanced speech synthesisers were produced using developments of the same technique. Algorithms which were suitable for digital implementation were then produced in laboratories and universities around the world as soon as minicomputers became readily available in the 1960s.

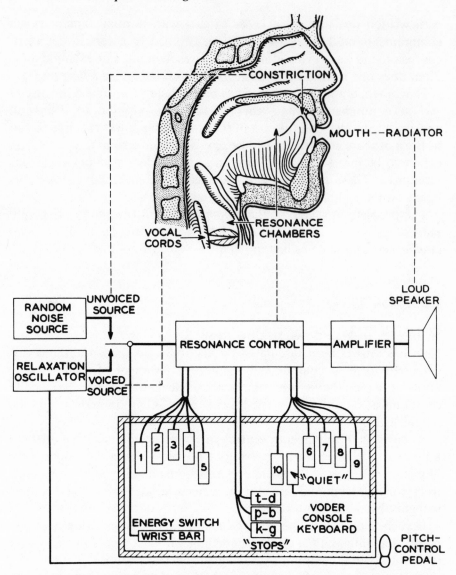

Figure 1.2 Schematic diagram of the Electric Speaking Machine, *Voder* (Reproduced from 'Voices of Men and Machines', chapter by J. Flanagan in *Electronic Speech Synthesis*, Granada, 1984).

RECOGNISING SOUNDS

Speech, synthesis, then, got off to a very early start, although it took two centuries for the technologies to become available that were to render the techniques truly useful. Such early implementations of devices to *listen to*

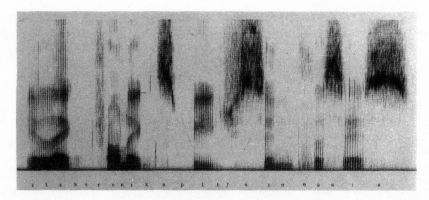

Figure 1.3 Spectrogram of the phrase 'electronic speech synthesis'.

and interpret speech utterances – speech recognisers – were not to be found, however.

Even the simplest attempt at speech recognition requires electronic equipment, in order to capture utterances with a microphone and to analyse them. In 1947 this process was demonstrated by an important device known as the *Spectrogram* (see Fig. 1.3) which produced a graphical representation of the continuous spectrum of the speech[2]. Whilst the Spectrogram is not an automatic recognition device, the analysis that was used formed the foundation of much of the speech recognition work that was to follow over the next two decades.

From 1950 onwards many experiments began in which the parameters extracted from speech utterances by some form of electronic filtering were used to make automatic 'decisions' about the speech itself. In 1950 Dreyfus-Gaf produced a 'Stenosonograph' using 6 band-pass filters, the outputs of which were used to deflect an oscilloscope beam in different directions. This gave a unique position of the spot for each speech sound[3].

In 1952 a team at Bell Labs[4] developed the first device that could be properly called an automatic speech recogniser. The signal was filtered at 900 Hz to yield two signals (one above 900 Hz and one below) and the frequency of energy concentration in each band was measured by counting the number of times the zero axis was crossed (known as the *zero-crossing* technique). The graph of these two parameters against time was then compared with similar profiles that had been previously stored, and the word which had the closest such *template* was chosen.

Since 1952 many techniques have been developed to enhance the performance of speech recognisers beyond the ten-word speaker-dependent capability of the Bell Labs device, including (from about

1960) the use of digital computers. However, the basic principle of stored information representing various options for comparison is always used, together with some form of parameter extraction and pre-processing that takes place before the decision-making process.

THE SILICON REVOLUTION

Any reasonably compact algorithm that has been implemented successfully on a computer can be put onto an integrated circuit on silicon ... if the economics are right. The technology to conduct such *large-scale integration* (LSI) became available in the late 1970s, and at that time the algorithms for good synthetic speech output were already mature enough to 'freeze' onto a silicon chip.

The first LSI synthesis device produced commercially used a technique known as *linear predictive coding* to separate the pitch of the speech sound and to model the resonances of the vocal chamber. This was made available in large volumes in 1979 at a price of less than $10 each (compared with the price of a minicomputer, which was around $50 000 at that time).

Many new applications then became commercially viable; the cost of giving a piece of equipment the ability to speak was actually less than the price of giving it an alphanumeric liquid crystal display, and less than a tenth of the cost of adding a conventional cathode-ray tube!

The absence of any universally applicable algorithms for speech recognition meant that silicon integration could not immediately be used to the same commercial advantage for speech input as it could for voice output. What is more, the amount of processing power that is required for recognition is far greater than for synthesis, since the task of parameter extraction (which is generally of similar complexity to that of synthesis) is only the beginning of the calculations; the remainder of the task involves lengthy calculations to fit the parameters to various models and hypotheses.

Accordingly, the equivalent 'silicon revolution' for speech recognition did not occur until the early 1980s with the advent of *Digital Signal Processors*, LSI devices with vast general-purpose calculation power on a single chip.

The first such example – the *7720* from the Nippon Electric Company – was used widely to implement recognition algorithms, followed quickly by devices from AMI and Texas Instruments. The calculation power of these chips was well suited to the digital parameter extraction and mathematical modelling techniques described in this book, having the capability of multiplying two fixed point numbers (16 bits each) together more than 5 million times a second.

Whilst Digital Signal Processors can make possible application designs costing less than $100, the nature of voice input means that its application spectrum will continue to span a very wide range of capability and associated cost – perhaps from $10 to $10 000. The reasons for this, which will be described in this book, are related to the diverse nature of our communication through speech: if in a given circumstance we only require a simple discrimination of the words *yes* and *no*, the electronics can be extremely simple and cost a few dollars only; if, on the other hand, we require a speaker-independent voice-controlled robot, we will need a powerful computer running some application software, interfaced to a speech recognition pre-processor that contains digital signal processors. In each of these streams of activity, though, the new commercial feasibility is entirely dependent upon good silicon integration of sub-system components.

1.3 *The shape of the problem*

THE INFORMATION CONTENT OF SPEECH
The problem of speech recognition can be stated as follows:

How can information be deduced from a speech wave received at a microphone, such that man can communicate with machine using his voice?

First, what do we mean by *information*? Consider the following sentence:

Waiter, what's this fly doing in my soup?

Several types of information could be deduced by a human being who was listening to this utterance. Examples might be (in order of increasing level within the information hierarchy):

 (1) A noise has happened.
 (2) Someone has spoken.
 (3) The words were spoken more loudly than the preceding sentences.
 (4) The words were spoken quickly.
 (5) The words were spoken in a small, crowded room.
 (6) About 8 words have been spoken.
 (7) The first word was *waiter* (etc.).
 (8) The pitch rises and falls again during the first word.
 (9) The speaker is male/young.
(10) The speaker is from Yorkshire, England.
(11) The speaker is John Smith.
(12) The speaker is warm/drunk/happy.
(13) The speaker is confident in this environment.

(14) The speaker is about to tell a joke.

(15) The joke is from page 25 of *After Dinner Speeches.*

(16) The joke is probably not going to be funny.

Deciding what level of information is required

When human beings speak to one another, each of these levels of information is processed, although items 1 to 7 would not be consciously noted, and items 8 to 13 would only be noted once. Thus the human listener, after first setting clear in his mind certain ideas about the speaker, would divert his attention to the *meaning* of the communication, the semantics; in this example he will probably be mainly interested in the joke itself.

When expecting a machine to listen to and act upon such an utterance, on the other hand, one must be clear exactly what level of information is required to be extracted. A burglar alarm system, for example, may include a sound-activated device to detect intruders, and this would in effect be a speech recogniser working on type 1 information (above). Many 'speech recognition toys' work on this same principle, where a toy dog (for example) may sit up and bark in response to a voice, but where similar noises such as hand-clapping may be found to invoke the same response..

At the other extreme, the popular 'dream' of speech recognition would be typified by a machine which could understand the example utterance above as being a joke, and instruct the associated speech synthesiser to laugh!

CATEGORIES OF SPEECH RECOGNITION PROBLEM

The first requirement in the design of a speech recognition system, then, is to define clearly what particular aspects of speech are to be recognised. Some of the best used categories in this respect, in order of increasing complexity and expense, are:

Recognition of isolated words

Recognisers of this type require that the human speaker utters the words with long pauses between each one. This is adequate for many applications but is far from being a natural way of communicating.

Recognition of discrete words in connected speech

If pauses do not have to be inserted artifically to separate the words to be recognised, the communication becomes much more natural but the technical problem becomes correspondingly more difficult. In a typical sentence of natural speech there are only pauses between a few of the words and the rest of the sounds occur in a continuous string. Thus the task of spotting the beginnings and ends of the words becomes a major one for the recogniser.

Recognition of strings of words in connected speech
An application which involves the recognition of single words only, whether spoken in isolation or in connected speech, is necessarily limited because the number of actions that can be taken as a result of positive recognition is no larger than the size of the vocabulary. Far more scope is available, therefore, if strings of words or complete phrases can be identified.

The allowable structure of words within such a phrase can be defined either by an artificial rule set designed for the application (as in the example of the car, above), or by an attempt to model the grammar of a natural language. In either case, the accuracy of word-recognition can also be increased, because the identification of each word in the phrase can be reviewed retrospectively in the light of the rest of the identified phrase.

Speech understanding
The highest level of complexity is associated with speech understanding, where the ultimate goal is to identify the meaning without constraining the speaker's sentence structure.

Although it has been noted above that human conversation has mechanisms for resolving some degree of confusion at sentence level, most of the ambiguities that occur in written text are normally resolved in speech by the information present in the *intonation contour* (the rhythm, and the contour of the pitch).

For example, the phrase *a glass of water* may have any of the following meanings, each of which could be distinguished by the intonation pattern:

> *Would you like a glass of water?*
> *Could I have a glass of water?*
> *Here is a glass of water.*
> *You call that a glass of water?*

If speech understanding systems are to restrict these ambiguities to the same level as in human conversation they will be required to track the intonation pattern as well as word-level information.

OTHER CATEGORIES OF VOICE INPUT PROBLEM
Speaker identification
Speaker identification uses techniques very closely related to those of

speech recognition. However, whilst speech recognition aims to ignore the differences between speakers and recognise the differences between words, speaker identification aims to highlight the differences between speakers.

Referring again to the example of the waiter and the soup – John Smith did not intentionally put into his speech the information that characterises his voice as his own, but nevertheless his identity can be deduced from his speech waves.

Word spotting

Finally, a further voice input problem one may wish to solve is that of ignoring all speech that is uttered until a keyword is spoken. This technique has been used in the military environment and has obvious applications in the sifting of large amounts of archived audio material for relevant sections of conversation. The systems used are derivatives of speech recognisers, tuned to reject any words that do not have a very high correlation to one of the keywords.

1.4 *The shape of the solution*

THE PRINCIPAL ELEMENTS OF A SPEECH RECOGNITION SYSTEM
As indicated in Section 1.2, the process of speech recognition includes the capture of a speech utterance (*data acquisition*), the analysis of the raw speech into a suitable set of parameters (*feature extraction*), the comparison of these features against some previously stored templates (*reference features*), and a decision-making process (see Fig. 1.4).

DATA ACQUISITION
The acoustic waves that are detected by a microphone do not in themselves constitute 'speech' – speech is a type of information that may

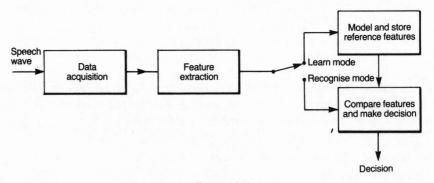

Figure 1.4

be transmitted (along with other types of information) on an acoustic wave. Indeed, speech information may also be transmitted as electrical impulses along nerves, as a set of muscular movements, as bone vibrations, or – if a piece of electronic equipment has been allowed to monitor this process – as an electrical signal.

It is impossible to capture a speech wave with a microphone without also capturing the acoustic effects of the surroundings and (except in professional recording studios) considerable other noise that was not emitted from the speaker's mouth! Nevertheless, most applications of voice input do require that a simple microphone is used as the data acquisition method.

The electrical signal derived from a microphone must also be preconditioned in a number of ways, and then digitised (represented by a continuous stream of binary digits) so that it may be analysed by a digital circuit. This preconditioning consists at minimum of the removal of the high frequencies in the signal which would otherwise cause distortion in the resulting digitial signal.

All these issues, including the design of audio amplifiers and choice of microphones, are covered in Chapter 12 of this book, *Audio and Acoustical Aspects*.

FEATURE EXTRACTION

The data rate required to describe the acoustic speech wave is far higher than that required to convey the information about the words that are being spoken. This is because the human vocal mechanism has modulated the slowly changing speech information onto a higher frequency sound wave.

In order to capture the detail of the actual speech wave it is necessary to sample the waveform more than 10 000 times per second, whereas to capture the movement of the tongue, jaw, lips and other articulators, a sampling rate of 100 times per second will do. For this reason it is essential to extract some meaningful speech features from the speech wave before any decision-making process can be started.

Many feature extraction techniques consist of extracting spectral parameters, either as energy concentrations in each of a number of frequency bands, or as some transform of this information. Still more popular though, partly because of its applicability to digital processing techniques, is linear predictive coding – the same technique that is used extensively in speech synthesis (see Section 1.2). Here the analysis separates out the independent feature of pitch from the other characteristics of the sound.

A detailed analysis of linear predictive coding is given in Chapter 5 of the companion book in this series, *Electronic Speech Synthesis*.

MODELLING REFERENCE FEATURES AND MAKING THE DECISION
The simplest approach to feature modelling and decision-making is to store the list of parameters that have been derived from a given utterance, along with similar lists for other utterances – the templates. When a new utterance is captured and a decision as to its word-identity is required, its corresponding parameter set is derived by the same process and compared against the templates to see which is the closest match. Such a method is suitable for isolated-word recognition where each word is spoken in the same way each time.

The task of storing the templates in the recogniser is usually known as *enrolment* (conducted in *learn mode*) and the subsequent task of comparison of further utterances is known as recognition (in *recognise mode*). In speaker-independent recognisers, the templates are stored at the time of manufacture so that no explicit learn mode is required in the end system. In speaker-dependent recognisers, on the other hand, there will always be some sort of switch available to allow the user to revert to learn mode to *train* the recogniser on a new word or a different voice.

Where it is required to recognise connected speech, however, more sophisticated modelling techniques are required. For example, even if words sound the same to the ear, when they appear in different contexts they rarely last for the same length of time each time; a stretching of the same utterance would fool a simple template matching system.

Further, it is not always possible to split a single utterance into separate words – for example, acoustically the first two words of the phrase *a red bus* will almost certainly appear as one. Accordingly the model must be chosen carefully and must be able to take into account the surrounding context of the sound element being considered. The decision-making mechanism may then output a probability that the utterance belonged to a certain class, rather than give a categorical definition of the word.

These issues are considered in depth in Chapters 3 and 4 of this book, and are responsible for much of the complexity – and efficiency – of the eventual computational algorithm used.

1.5 *References*

1. Flanagan, J. (1972) 'Voices of Men and Machines', *Journal of the Acoustical Society of America*, **51**, 1375–1387.

2. Potter, R.K., Kopp, G.A., and Green, H.C. (1947) *Visible Speech*, New York: D. van Nostrand Co.
3. Dreyfus-Graf, J. (1949) 'Sonograph and sound mechanics', *Journal of the Acoustical Society of America*, **22**, 731–739.
4. Davis, K.H., Biddulph, R., and Balashek, J. (1952) 'Automatic Recognition of Spoken Digits', *Journal of the Acoustical Society of America*, **24**, 637–645.

CHAPTER 2

THE NATURE OF SPEECH

Francis Nolan

In this chapter, the reader is introduced to the physical nature of human speech production and to the fascinating way in which natural languages exploit this communication channel.

2.1 *Images of speech*

Atoms are clusters of tiny, orbiting billiard balls. This is probably how many of us, with only rudimentary familiarity with atomic physics, are accustomed to making sense of them. Imagery can provide useful steps towards understanding a phenomenon; but images can be dangerous, because they portray appropriately only some facets of a phenomenon, and are otherwise misleading.

Our most accessible image of speech is its written form; followed, perhaps, by its acoustic waveform as seen on an oscilloscope. Its written form needs no introduction. Figure 2.1 shows a plot of the acoustic waveform of the utterance *a speech wave.*

But neither of these images *is* speech; they are merely representations of two facets of speech. The oscilloscope waveform is a representation of the physical event by which speech is normally transmitted; writing is a representation of some aspects of the information encoded in that event, and reflects the linguistic structures involved in the encoding.

This chapter will attempt to provide a more complete view of the nature of speech. In doing so, it will be concerned with the acoustic speech signal and the vocal activity which produces it; but equally, it will outline the kinds of linguistic structuring which underlie the act of speaking, and determine the way in which information is encoded in the speech signal.

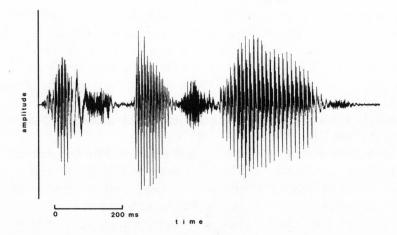

Figure 2.1 Plot of the acoustic waveform of the utterance *a speech wave*.

The final picture will be complicated, as is inevitable with as powerful a communicational system as speech; and it will become apparent why, despite technological advances, automatic speech recognition (ASR) still holds many challenges.

2.2 *Levels of linguistic structure*

Suppose we tried to create a language in which each possible 'message' was associated with a unique, simple sound. *Help!* might be represented by a scream; *I'm tired* by a sigh of specified length; *You bore me* by a 'raspberry' or 'Bronx cheer', and so on. But what about *Some imported wines are suspected of containing antifreeze*? It is clear that, despite the versatility of our vocal tracts, we would quickly run out of adequately distinct noises to convey the potentially infinite variety of messages we need to convey. Not surprisingly, no human language uses this kind of direct mapping of messages onto sounds.

Instead, **all human languages exhibit what might be thought of as a componential approach: they construct larger units of communication out of smaller components;** and the construction process is governed by linguistic rules of various kinds.

Thus at one level we select from a stock of words, and the words are combined into utterances. Areas of our mental experience are mapped, as it were, by a limited number of discrete units – the words in our vocabulary – and then the grammatical rules of the language guide the construction of an unlimited set of utterances, each with well-defined structural properties appropriate to the information to be conveyed.

At another level, any language utilises a comparatively small set (often less than 50) of sound units – called *phonemes* – from which words can be 'built'. In *pin*, *tin*, *kin*, we have three different words composed of the same units – with the exception of the first of the three. And by adding *s* to the beginning of each of these sequences, we get three new words. (*Stin*, in fact, is not an existing word of English, but one which could be adopted if needed.)

The writing system of English, and those of other alphabetically written languages, reflect both levels of componentiality outlined above. We leave spaces between words; and, in ideal cases, we represent each phoneme within a word by a single unique letter, as in *pin*, *tin*, *kin*.

In contrast, traditional Chinese writing, for instance, approximates to a system where there is a separate symbol for each word – but no indication of the sound structure of the word. Native speakers of Chinese, of course, know the pronunciation associated with each symbol, just as we do when we encounter symbols such as $ and @. But whereas any image of speech furnished by English writing would reflect two levels of linguistic representation – words, and phonemes – an image furnished by Chinese writing would reflect only the word level. Notice that there is no crucial difference between the English and Chinese *languages* in this respect; today Chinese is frequently written alphabetically too.

So, writing is not a representation directly of speech, but of selected aspects of the linguistic structuring underlying an (actual or potential) utterance. We shall see later how aspects of this structuring which are clear to us in the written form are obscured in the physical speech event. This is a central problem in speech recognition, where the object is to recover linguistic structure from the physical signal.

Conversely, there is a whole area of linguistic structure – prosodic structure – which is continuously coded in speech but reflected only very sporadically in writing. Prosody is the organisation of, in particular, the pitch, loudness, and timing of speech. Punctuation gives some clue: we can tell that the prosody of

he's getting married.

is different from

he's getting married?

but in neither case do we know whether the utterance is incredulous, matter-of-fact, or sarcastic; hence the need for authors to give explicit information, such as

> *... he asked politely.*

Finally, the speech signal contains a range of information about the characteristics of the speaker (age, sex, size ...) which receives no representation at all in written transcripts, because it is irrelevant to the linguistic structure. But the presence of this information, enmeshed with the linguistic information, poses a serious problem for the processing of the speech signal in ASR.

2.3 *Grammar*

SYNTAX

The rules governing the meaningful arrangement of words in the construction of sentences in a particular language comprise its SYNTAX. The syntactic rules of English allow a sentence of the form

> *The farmer frequently pursues trespassers*

but not

> *Farmer trespassers frequently the pursues;*

further, they specify that

> *The farmer frequently pursues trespassers*

and

> *The farmer pursues trespassers frequently*

are equivalent in meaning, whilst the superficially similar change in word order yielding

> *Trespassers frequently pursue the farmer*

constitutes a very significant alteration.

All words can be assigned to GRAMMATICAL CATEGORIES, such as NOUN (e.g. *trespasser*), VERB (*pursue*), ADVERB (*frequently*). The process of assigning words to grammatical categories is traditionally known as *parsing*. Although, for instance, adverbs often end in *-ly*, it is far from possible always to tell the grammatical category of a word from its form. The well-known ambiguous sentence

Time flies

(either '... do that with your new stopwatch', or '... but it drags if you're lonely') exploits this; the ambiguity is whether the structure underlying the words is [verb]-[noun] or [noun]-[verb].

In fact, it is not quite accurate to think of the structure of a sentence being defined in terms of grammatical categories. For the first reading of the example above we could substitute

Time those horrible black things buzzing round my head

In some sense *those horrible black things buzzing round my head* plays the same part in the structure as the noun *flies*; but it is itself a complex phrase – a noun phrase. Thus the structure of a sentence is described in terms of CONSTITUENTS such as noun phrase, verb phrase, adverb phrase, which may themselves consist of further quite large constituents (such as *buzzing round my head*). In

The farmer pursues trespassers,

the farmer is a noun phrase consisting of a definite article and a noun, and *pursues trespassers* a verb phrase, with constituents verb and noun.

Finally, in this brief introduction to syntax, we need to consider GRAMMATICAL RELATIONS. Subject of, and object of, the sentence describe two such relations. They can be defined in terms of the constituent structure described above, and in the case of subject and object, express the relation of noun phrase constituents to the action of the verb. Thus in

The farmer pursues trespassers,

the farmer is SUBJECT and *trespassers* OBJECT; in

Trespassers pursue the farmer

the relations are reversed.

Clearly, a speech recognition device designed for isolated words scarcely need trouble itself with syntax, whereas at the opposite extreme a system for understanding or interpreting continuous speech will need to incorporate a great deal of syntactic knowledge in order to appreciate the significance of the arrangement of words. Perhaps less obviously, any system which has to deal with continuous speech – for instance, yielding a text transcript without any attempt at interpretation – will benefit from syntactic knowledge. This is because the recognition decision for a particular word will be able to exploit syntactic constraints, such as the expectation that *the* will usually be followed by a noun or adjective.

MORPHOLOGY

So far we have assumed it to be words that are the smallest component in grammatical analysis. But we are already familiar from the layout of dictionaries with the fact that words can be broken down into smaller meaningful units; for instance, if we look up the word *telegraph*, we are likely to find entries under the same heading for *telegraph-ist*, *telegraph-ic*, *telegraph-ese* and so on. **These smallest components of grammatical analysis are known as MORPHEMES.** The independent constructional role of such morphemes is demonstrable by their freedom to combine in other formations, e.g. *telegraph-y*, *arson-ist*, *scen(e)-ic*, *journal-ese*. The formation of related sets of words (like *telegraph-y*, *-ic*, etc.), usually differing in grammatical category (noun, verb, adjective, etc.), is known as DERIVATIONAL morphology.

Notice that the pronunciation of derived forms may not be as similar as implied by their spelling; in *'telegraph*, *te'legraphist*, *tele'graphic*, *telegraph'ese*, the main stress (indicated by the raised dash before the relevant syllable) changes, and there are major changes in the phonetic quality of some of the vowels. This sort of variation would make it harder than might at first be obvious to design an ASR system based on morphemic units.

Morphology also operates to mark grammatical functions in utterances. Here the term INFLEXIONAL morphology is used. English is not as rich in inflexional morphology as, say, Latin (as those who have had to learn Latin noun and verb paradigms will know to their chagrin); but we do know that a verb form with *-ed* on the end (*walked*, *calculated*) relates to the past, that with *-s* (*walks*, *calculates*) relates to an activity in the present, and that the subject of the verb is a third person singular subject (*he/she/it walks*, but *I/you/we/they walk* are the possible forms – in standard English at least). In *He hit her* we know both from the word order and from the form of the pronouns (*he* not *him*, *her* not *she*) who the attacker was; *him hit she*, though stylistically perhaps only acceptable in poetry, would mean the opposite.

Inflexional morphology in English, as in most languages, is far from totally regular; speakers have to know that *sheeps* is not the plural of *sheep*, and that *ringed* is only the past tense of *ring* in the sense of 'put a ring on' – contrast *he rang the bell*. An ASR system which aims to approach speech understanding will have to be sensitive to the cues to linguistic structure provided by morphology; but there may also be applications of single-word recognisers requiring morphological knowledge. It might, for instance, be undesirable to have to store separate dictionary entries for the singular and plural of every noun.

2.4 *Phonology*

The way in which a language organises the sound-producing capability of the vocal apparatus is its phonology. For one thing, a 'mapping' is imposed on the continuum of possible vocal noises to define an inventory of discrete units – the PHONEMES. Secondly, the phonology of the language governs the linear arrangement of the phonemes; just as *The farmer frequently pursues trespassers* is a possible sentence of English, and *Farmer trespassers frequently the pursues* is not, so *strip* is a possible word of English but *rtspi* is not, being ruled out by the PHONOTACTIC constraints of English. Thirdly, the phonology determines various different realisations of a phoneme – its ALLOPHONES – which occur depending on the phonetic environment in which the phoneme lies.

All these are aspects of SEGMENTAL phonology, the segments in question being the 'phoneme-sized' units. In addition, the phonology of a language specifies its PROSODY. Prosody comprises patterns of pitch, loudness, and timing extending over larger domains – up to complete utterances – and conveying information in ways specific to each language and variety.

PHONEMES

PHONEMES are the distinctive elements which a language can combine to form different words. Pairs of words like *pin-tin*, *pin-pen*, and *pin-pit*, are called MINIMAL PAIRS; in each case the two words differ in only one (of their three) segments – that is, they differ minimally. Any two phonemes, by definition, CONTRAST with each other in the sense that we are able to tell them apart (and hence can use them to distinguish words).

Alphabetic writing aims to represent the phonemes of a language. However, particularly with an old spelling system like that of English, where the conventions are a mixture of two traditions (Anglo-Saxon and Norman), and reflect a pronunciation left behind by many centuries of phonetic development, there will be many inconsistencies. *Ceiling* and *sealing* look different, but they sound the same – and are therefore made up of the same phonemes. *Cough* and *bough* end alike visually, but they don't rhyme – and so must contain different phonemes.

To represent phonemes unambiguously, phoneticians use one of a number of established systems of PHONEMIC TRANSCRIPTION. It would be possible to represent each phoneme with a number, or an invented symbol of unique shape; but since our writing system goes a long way towards indicating phonemes, it is more convenient to adopt familiar letter shapes, and add a few more where necessary.

Table 2.1 lists the phonemes of *Standard Southern British* (SSB) English of the kind spoken by many English newsreaders, which is therefore widely familiar. It gives a key word for each phoneme, and then a further set of words showing some other ways in which the phoneme is represented in spelling. Depending on your accent, you may find cases where you disagree that a given phoneme occurs in certain words. Generally this will rarely be a problem with the consonants; but the vowel phonemes vary widely across accents of English. Later on (Section 2.6), a comparison will be made with American pronunciation.

The phonemic transcription in Table 2.1 is a widely used one, devised by Gimson[9]. Other transcriptions may differ superficially – for instance, omitting the colon-like 'length mark' which here explicitly marks LONG (e.g. /iː/) as opposed to SHORT (/ɪ/) vowels; or may reflect alternative phonemic analyses, such as treating DIPHTHONGS (vowels which change in quality) as sequences of short vowel plus approximant: e.g. /ɒ/ + /j/ for /ɔɪ/. (A widely-used convention adopted here is to cite phonemic forms in obliques: /ðʌs/.)

PHONOTACTICS

Any language places restrictions on the combination of phonemes it allows. **Phonotactic rules express which combinations of phonemes are possible and which are prohibited in the language.** /glɪmps/ and /strɪkt/ are possible in English, /dlɪmsp/ and /rtsɪtk/ ruled out. The combination /blaʊn/ is possible even though it doesn't occur (cf. *blou*se and *clown*), whilst /mlaʊŋ/ is not – /ml-/ is not possible initially, and only short vowels (those written with a single character in the transcription of Table 2.1) can occur before /ŋ/.

The appropriate domain for the statement of phonotactic contraints is the SYLLABLE. The definition of the syllable is far from easy, but speakers will usually confirm that there is a unit (the syllable) of which there is one in the word *like*, two in *likely*, and three in *likelihood*. A syllable will consist of one segment of comparatively high acoustic energy (most frequently a vocoid – see below) which forms the syllable PEAK; other segments, optionally, may precede and follow the peak and constitute the MARGINS of the syllable. /aɪ/ (*eye*) is a syllable consisting of just a peak; /streŋθs/ (*strengths*) a syllable with complex initial and final margin clusters.

Table 2.1 The phonemes of Standard Southern British English

Consonants

/p/	PiP	
/b/	BarB	
/t/	TighT	TH (THames), D (typeD)
/d/	DeeD	
/k/	KiCK	C (Code), CH (CHemist), KH (KHaki), /kw/ = QU (QUit)
/g/	GaG	GH (GHost), GU (GUarantee)
/tʃ/	CHurCH	TCH (piTCH), TI (quesTIon), T (naTure)
/dʒ/	JuDGe	G (Gem), DJ (aDJust), DI (solDIer)
/f/	FiFe	PH (PHysics), GH (couGH)
/v/	VerVe	F (oF)
/θ/	THirtieTH	
/ð/	oTHer	
/s/	CeaSe	SC (SCene), /ks/ = X (siX)
/z/	ZooS	/gz/ = X (eXample)
/ʃ/	SHeepiSH	CH (maCHine), SCH (SCHist), S (Sugar), TI (naTIon), SI (penSIon), CI (soCIal), SCI (conSCIence)
/ʒ/	meaSure	G (beiGe), Z (seiZure)
/h/	Hand	
/r/	Rear	WR (Wrong), RH (RHubarb)
/l/	LoyaL	
/m/	MiMe	MB (cliMB), MN (hyMN)
/n/	NoNe	KN (KNee), GN (GNome), PN (PNeumonia)
/ŋ/	riNGiNG	N before /k/ (thiNk, uNcle, aNxious) N before /g/ (aNger)
/j/	Year	I (millIon) /juː/ = U (tUne), EW (nEW), EU (fEUd), EAU (bEAUty)
/w/	Weal	/wʌ/ = O (One), /kw/ = QU (QUit)

SPEECH PRODUCTION

So far we have looked at speech simply as a system of abstract units – a fixed inventory of units with specific possibilities for co-occurrence. We have treated the units merely as symbols on the page and have said nothing about their REALISATION as sounds. Phonology is crucially concerned with this process of realisation; but in order to discuss it, we need first to understand how speech is produced in the vocal tract, and become familiar with some of the terminology used in phonetics.

The VOCAL TRACT runs from the larynx upwards, dividing at the back of the mouth into the ORAL and NASAL tracts. **Acoustic energy is**

Table 2.1 (cont.)

Vowels

/iː/	bEAd	EE (bEEt), E (bE), IE (thIEf), EI (recEIve), E.E (delEtE), EY (kEY), Y (pitY)
/ɪ/	bId	E (dEcidEd), O (wOmen), A (villAge)
/e/	bEd	EA (hEAd), A (Any)
/æ/	bAd	AI (plAId)
/ɑː/	bARd	AL (bALm), A (fAther), AU (AUnt), ER (clERk)
/ɒ/	bOdy	A (wAtch), OU (cOUgh), AU (sAUsage)
/ɔː/	bAWdy	OU (bOUght), AU (sAUce), AL (tALk), AR (wAR), A (wAter) OR (fOR), OUR (fOUR), ORE (ORE), OOR (dOOR)
/ʊ/	bOOk	U (fUll), OUL (shOULd), O (wOman)
/uː/	bOOt	OU (sOUp), U (flUte), O (dO)
/ʌ/	bUd	OU (trOUble), OO (flOOd), O (sOn), OE (dOEs)
/ɜː/	bIRd	ER (hERd), EAR (hEARd), UR (fUR), OR (wORd), OUR (jOURney)
/ə/	bAnanA	E (agelEss), O (Objection), U (campUs), ER (bettER), OU (famOUs), URE (natURE), etc.
/eɪ/	bAY	AI (wAIt), EY (whEY), EI (slEIgh), A.E (hAtE), A.y (lAdy), EA (grEAt)
/əʊ/	bOAt	O (nO), OE (fOE), O.E (nOtE), OU (sOUl), OW (knOW)
/aɪ/	bUY	Y (skY), IGH (sIGH), I.E (tIme), I.y (tIdy)
/aʊ/	bOUgh	OW (hOW)
/ɔɪ/	bOY	OI (grOIn)
/ɪə/	bEEr	EAR (EAR), ERE (hERE), EA (idEA), EIR (wEIRd), IER (tIER)
/ɛə/	bEAr	ARE (cARE), AIR (AIR)
/ʊə/	pOOr	URE (sURE), OUR (tOUR), Ur (allUring)

produced when air flowing in the vocal tract is obstructed; the precise nature of different obstructions, their combination, and the overall shape of the vocal tract determine the variety of acoustic effects which are used in speech. Figure 2.2 shows a cross-section through the vocal organs.

The airflow for all English sounds is produced by the lungs; and except in the rare case of someone speaking on an in-breath, the airflow is outwards. The phonetic term for sounds produced in this way is PULMONIC EGRESSIVE. Acoustically the simplest sounds to describe are VOCOIDS. **In VOCOIDS there is no obstruction in the midline of the oral vocal tract to impede airflow from the lungs** (except at the

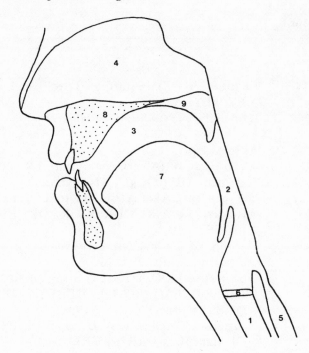

Figure 2.2 Cross-section of the vocal organs. 1 trachea (from lungs); 2 pharynx; 3 oral cavity; 4 nasal cavity; 5 oesophagus; 6 vocal cords; 7 tongue; 8 hard palate; 9 soft palate (velum).

larynx). Sounds which are not vocoids – those in which there *is* such an obstruction – are CONTOIDS.

These classes of sound are often termed VOWEL and CONSONANT; but it is useful to draw a distinction between the physical nature of sounds, according to which we are classifying them as vocoid and contoid, and their patterning in the syllables of a language. Here VOWEL will be used for a vocoid which functions as the centre of a syllable, as with the *oo* in *food*; and CONSONANT for any sound which functions as a syllable margin. This convention is followed in Table 2.1 which lists the phonemes of English under the headings of vowels and consonants. Notice that, for instance, if the /w/ of *wet* is prolonged, it is very similar to the vocoid in the middle of *food*; indeed, in terms of production it *is* a (short) vocoid, but in terms of the phoneme system it is classified as a consonant because it cannot occur as the centre of a syllable.

The production of vocoids
Generally in vocoids the vocal cords – two flaps of tissue projecting into

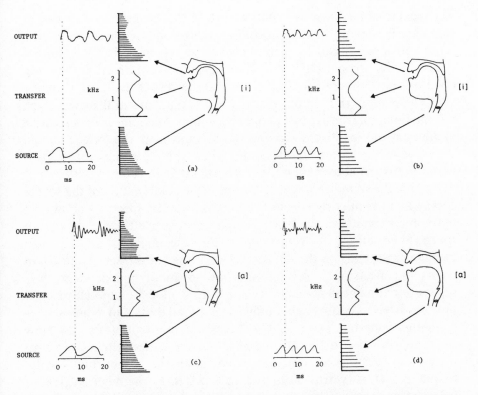

Figure 2.3 Vocoid production seen as the combination of a laryngeal acoustic source and the filtering effect of the vocal tract. At the top, /i/; at the bottom, /a/; at the left 100 Hz, and at the right 200 Hz fundamental frequency.

the trachea within the larynx – vibrate, in what is termed VOICING. Most vocoids, then, are VOICED sounds. The frequency of the vibration may be between around sixty and several hundred Hertz, and determines the FUNDAMENTAL FREQUENCY (and hence the perceived PITCH) of the voice.

In vibrating, the larynx is acting as a quasi-periodic sound SOURCE. The spectrum of this source is rich in harmonics; these decline in amplitude with increasing frequency, but are of significance up to a frequency of several kHz.

Figure 2.3 shows schematically the production of four vocoids. In each case the arrow from the larynx points to the spectrum and larynx waveform associated with the larynx source. Notice that in the diagrams on the left (a,c), the fundamental frequency is 100 Hz (the harmonics are 100 Hz apart), while on the right (b,d) the fundamental is 200 Hz.

The acoustic energy produced at the larynx passes into the vocal tract.

The vocal tract functions as a complex FILTER. The response function of this filter is shown, for each vocoid, in the second of the three spectral representations. It can be seen that in these schema this TRANSFER FUNCTION depends on the shape of the vocal tract; in the top diagrams (a,b) the transfer functions, and the vocal tract shapes, are the same; likewise in the bottom pair (c,d). **It is the shape of the vocal tract, and the resultant transfer function, which mainly determines our perception of different vocoids.** In the top pair of diagrams, with the tongue high in the front of the mouth, the vocoid is [i] as in *beet*; in the bottom pair, with the tongue constricting the pharynx, [ɑ] as in *balm*.

Finally, the sound radiated at the lips is the combination of the source energy and the filtering effect of the vocal tract. Its spectrum shows the harmonic structure of the larynx source (compare left and right output spectra) and reflects its overall slope, whilst the amplitude of individual harmonics depends on the filtering effect of the vocal tract. Although in reality the effects of source and filter are not totally independent, their separate treatment in the SOURCE-FILTER model of speech production has been of considerable utility in both analysis and synthesis.

Summarising the layout of Fig. 2.3: horizontal pairs (a,b; c,d) show the same vocoid at different fundamental frequencies (pitches); vertical pairs (a,c; b,d) show different vocoids at the same fundamental frequency. It is worth noting here that **it is the high degree of independence of the larynx source and the vocal tract filter which underlies our ability to use intonation (involving pitch patterns) to convey information over and above that conveyed by segments**; we can say *three* on a decisive, falling pitch, or on a questioning rising pitch – but the vocoid *ee* ([iː]) and the identity of the word are not affected.

The phonetic description of vocoids

Phoneticians analyse vocoids according to auditory categories learned through rigorous training. It is useful, however, to relate these auditory impressions to the physical nature of vocoids, and it would seem from Fig. 2.3 that either the vocal tract shape or the filter function would provide appropriate descriptive mechanisms. The problem is that both shapes are too complex to be convenient. A computer model of the vocal tract might happily quantify a vocoid in terms of 20 cross-sectional area values along the length of the vocal tract, but that would be a cumbersome way for humans to describe it.

In fact, given that the tongue body has only limited flexibility, it was found as phonetics evolved that **quite useful categorisation of vocoids could be achieved by noting the position of the estimated highest point of the tongue in the mouth.** Figure 2.4 shows how the position of this point

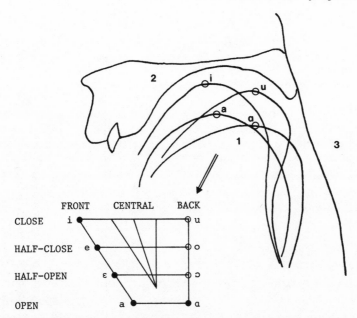

Figure 2.4   The derivation of the vocoid quadrilateral from the highest point of the tongue in extreme vocoids. The eight (primary) 'Cardinal' vocoids are shown on the periphery of the quadrilateral; open circles indicate rounded vowels.

varies for four extreme vocoids – roughly those of *heed* [i], *had* [æ], *hard* [ɑ] and *who'd* [u] – and how the area of possible vocoid articulations can be schematised as a straight-sided figure – the VOCOID QUADRILATERAL. Vocoids can then be described in terms of two dimensions: HEIGHT, using the four-way distinction CLOSE, HALF-CLOSE, HALF-OPEN, and OPEN (or alternatively a three-way distinction, HIGH, MID, and LOW); and BACKNESS, using the three-way distinction FRONT, CENTRAL, and BACK. For a full description it is also necessary to specify whether the vocoid is ROUNDED or UNROUNDED – that is, whether the lips are close together (and protruding) or not.

On the perimeter of the vocoid quadrilateral in Fig. 2.4 are placed eight points corresponding to eight widely used auditory reference vocoids – the so-called CARDINAL vocoids (CVs). As examples of the phonetic description of these CV 1 ([i]) is a close, front, unrounded vocoid; and CV 6 [ɔ] is a half-open, back, rounded vocoid (like the vocoid of *law* for many speakers).

Turning to the acoustic properties of vocoids, the complex shape of the transfer function can be usefully abbreviated in terms of its peaks.

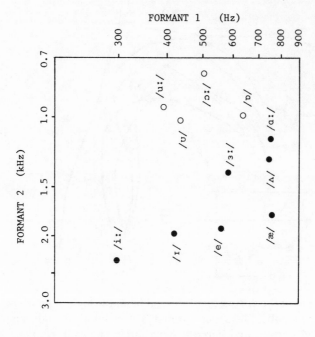

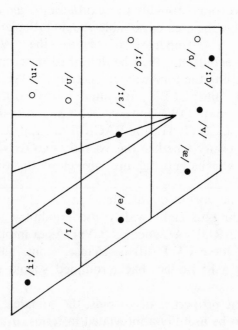

Figure 2.5 The vowels of (SSB) English; (left) placed on the traditional quadrilateral; (right) plotted acoustically by first and second formant frequency, with axes rotated to resemble the vocoid quadrilateral. (Acoustic data taken from Wiik (1965).)

These peaks are referred to as FORMANTS; and the frequency of the first two or three is crucial to our perception of vocoid quality (Fig. 2.3 only shows the first two formants of each vocoid).

If vocoids are plotted on a graph of first formant against second formant, the relationship of the vocoids on the graph resembles that on the traditional vocoid quadrilateral. Figure 2.5 compares the placement of English vowels on the traditional quadrilateral, with that on a two-formant plot. It can therefore be questioned whether the traditional phonetic descriptive dimensions for vocoids (height, and backness) were motivated by articulatory relationships, or acoustic relationships, or indeed loosely by both. However, these unresolved questions do not affect the general utility of the descriptive system.

To summarise, **we can so far describe vocoids in terms of their HEIGHT, BACKNESS, and (lip) ROUNDING. There are two additional dimensions which must be considered: NASALISATION and RHOTICISATION.**

We have assumed so far that acoustic energy has been deliberately excluded from the nasal branch of the vocal tract by keeping the VELUM (the soft, rearward part of the palate) raised. If the velum is allowed to lower, acoustic coupling to the nasal tract will take place, and the spectrum (and therefore the quality) of a given vocoid will change, sometimes considerably. In English this is most likely to happen when a vocoid occurs next to nasal consonants, as in the word *man*. Some languages, such as French, use NASALISED vocoids as phonemes – that is, they have a separate set of vowel phonemes distinguished by being nasalised. Thus the words *beau* /bo/ and *bon* /bõ/ are distinguished by the nasalisation (indicated by the ˜) of the vowel in the second word.

RHOTICISATION is an auditory quality which can, like nasalisation, be superimposed on vocoids; that of *bird*, for example, in many American pronunciations is rhoticised. The effect is produced by bunching up the tongue body (and, in some cases, curling back – retroflexing – the tongue tip), thus making the space in the mouth in front of the tongue larger, together with a narrowing of the lower pharynx; the main acoustic result is a lowering of the third formant.

The production of contoids
In the production of contoids a narrowing or STRICTURE is made which impedes the flow of air in the midline of the vocal tract. In many cases this stricture acts as a sound source. For instance in /f/ the stricture between lower lip and upper teeth causes turbulence in the airstream, heard as a hiss; in /k/, a complete closure between the back of the tongue and the velum allows air pressure to build up behind the stricture; and when the

stricture is released, there is a shock-wave excitation of the vocal tract (together with brief turbulence as the air flows through the still narrow gap).

Contoid strictures complicate the shape of the vocal tract from the acoustic point of view, and, as well as altering the frequency and bandwidth of its resonances, introduce anti-resonances or zeroes into the spectrum. This relative acoustic complexity of contoids is compounded by the fact that they tend to be comparatively brief and rapidly changing events, and to be cued as much by associated changes in neighbouring sounds as by their inherent properties.

As an example, the /ʃ/ of *machine* would be cued partly by its inherent spectral properties, and partly by its effect on the adjacent vocoids. Its inherent spectrum reflects the combination of a noise source in the oral cavity, and the filtering effect of the resonances and anti-resonances of the vocal tract on that noise. The spectra of the adjacent vocoids change as the vocal tract moves towards, and away from, the configuration for /ʃ/.

The phonetic description of contoids

Because of their acoustic complexity the advent of acoustic analysis has not made much impact on the traditional phonetic technique for classifying contoids. **Phonetic classification of contoids focuses on the nature of the obstruction in the vocal tract. Usually this is specified in terms of the PLACE and MANNER OF ARTICULATION of the contoid.**

PLACE OF ARTICULATION refers to where the contoid's PRIMARY (i.e. narrowest) stricture is located. This is done by reference to one of a number of defined regions of the upper surface of the vocal tract, and, where necessary, to the part of the lower side of the vocal tract which moves to make the stricture. Thus /f/ at the beginning of *fin* is a LABIO-DENTAL sound, articulated by the lower lip against the upper teeth. Figure 2.6 shows traditional articulatory labels. In Table 2.2 the consonant phonemes of English are arranged, from left to right, according to place of articulation.

MANNER OF ARTICULATION subsumes a number of facets of the articulation. Firstly, there is the DEGREE OF STRICTURE of the sound. If the vocal tract is completely blocked, the resultant sound is a STOP, e.g. the first and last sound in *pit*. If the vocal tract is not closed, but the stricture is so narrow that air flowing through it is made turbulent, creating an audible noise component in the sound, the sound is a FRICATIVE, e.g. the first and last sound in *thief*. Finally, the stricture can be open enough to allow air to flow through it without creating audible friction. This applies to all vocoids; but there are other

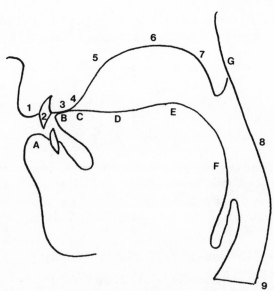

Figure 2.6   Place of articulation. 1 labial; 2 dental; 3 alveolar; 4 postalveolar; 5 palatal; 6 velar; 7 uvular; 8 pharyngeal; 9 glottal. Lower articulators: A lip (labio-); B tongue-tip (apico-); C tongue-blade (lamino-); D tongue-front; E tongue-back; F tongue-root. G indicates a velic closure, sealing off the nasal cavity. The configuration shown is for a non-nasal (apico-) alveolar stop, /t/ or /d/

sounds (such as the lateral /l/ in *law*) which have this degree of stricture, but which for other reasons fail to satisfy the criteria for vocoids (in the case of a lateral, because there is no escape for the airstream in the *midline* of the vocal tract). Such contoids are known as APPROXIMANTS.

Other major aspects of the classification of contoids usually subsumed under manner of articulation include VOICING, NASALITY, LATERALITY, AFFRICATION, and INTERMITTENCY.

VOICING – vibration of the vocal cords – has already been mentioned in relation to vocoids. Languages often have pairs of contoids distinguished by a greater versus smaller amount of voicing. We shall see below in the section on allophones that in English, as in many languages, it is not simply a case of a phoneme being realised always with, or without, voicing; but we can be reasonably sure that in *rabid-rapid* the /b/ versus /p/, and in *lazy-lacey* the /z/ versus /s/, are realised as VOICED versus VOICELESS respectively.

NASALITY refers to the auditory effect of acoustically coupling the nasal tract by lowering the velum. /m/, /n/ and /ŋ/ are the English

Table 2.2 Consonant phonemes of English categorised according to place and manner of articulation. Note that such categorisations of *phonemes* are compromises (see pages 37–8).

		bilabial	labio-dental	dental	alveolar	postalveolar*	palatal	velar	uvular	pharyngeal	glottal
STOPS	voiceless	p			t			k			
	voiced	b			d			g			
NASALS		m			n			ŋ			
AFFRICATES	voiceless					tʃ					
	voiced					dʒ					
FRICATIVES	voiceless		f	θ	s	ʃ					h
	voiced		v	ð	z	ʒ					
APPROXIMANTS	central	w				r	j	(w)			
	lateral				l						

* /tʃ, dʒ, ʃ, ʒ/ are slightly palatalised postalveolars (often known as palatoalveolars), /r/ is usually a rhoticised postalveolar.

NASALS (nasal contoids); their articulation is like that of /b/, /d/, and /g/ respectively except that in these latter the velum is raised, shutting off the nasal tract.

In LATERAL sounds the air passage along the midline of the oral vocal tract is blocked, but air is able to escape around one or both sides of the stricture. This is the case with English /l/, in which the tongue tip makes a central closure against the alveolar ridge.

AFFRICATION is the production of an audible fricative during the release of a stop closure, as in the English /tʃ/ and /dʒ/ phonemes (found in *chew* and *Jew* respectively). This results from a prolongation of the phase of close approximation through which the articulators must pass during the release of a stop, combined with a configuration of the lower articulator appropriate for producing a fricative.

In the trilled variant of /r/, which might be used when trying to communicate the word *three* in very noisy conditions, there is an INTERMITTENT, repeated closure. The airstream passing through the gap between the loosely held tongue tip and the alveolar ridge sets the tip in vibration. Such a sound is called a TRILL. If the vibration is halted after only one closure, the sound is a TAP. (Note that by far the commonest realisation of /r/ is, however, an approximant.)

Notice that in the last two paragraphs we have had to take account of the dynamics of contoid production, rather than describing merely in terms of static postures. **Static descriptions of sounds are possible only through considerable idealisation**; this will become more evident in Section 2.5.

Finally, we need to consider the possibility of further strictures in the vocal tract. Occasionally a contoid may have two equal strictures, which may be termed COORDINATE strictures. This is the case with /w/, which has a stricture of open approximation at both labial and velar places. More often a second stricture will be less narrow, and is termed a SECONDARY stricture. Secondary strictures often arise under the influence of adjacent articulations; for instance, the /θ/ of *thought* is labialised because of the lip rounding of the following vowel, while the /θ/ of *thief* is palatalised in anticipation of the close front vowel following.

ALLOPHONES

It will be apparent from the examples just given that a particular phoneme – such as /θ/ – is not associated with a single configuration of the vocal tract, but rather is realised in different ways according to the phonetic ENVIRONMENT in which it finds itself. **The variants which realise a given phoneme are known as its ALLOPHONES.** Part of the phonology of any language is concerned with specifying which allophones occur in which environments.

It is usual to cite allophone symbols in square brackets, so that we might write of the /θ/ phoneme being realised as [θ̞] (labialised) in *thought* and as [θ] (palatalised) in *thief*, where the diacritics added to the phoneme symbol indicate the phonetic detail of interest. This notational convention serves to underline the conceptual difference between a unit in the abstract phonological pattern of a language, serving as a word-building component (the phoneme), and the combination of phonetic properties which represent the phoneme in a particular environment (one of its allophones).

In many cases there seem to be clear reasons for particular allophones to occur where they do. For instance the [k̟] of *key*, where the realisation of /k/ is 'advanced' to the front of the velum, clearly anticipates the following close front vowel, and in parallel fashion the 'retracted' [k̠] of *caw* is appropriate given the following back vowel. Likewise, the nasalisation of the vowel in [mẽn] makes sense in that it allows the velum, which has to be lowered for the two nasal contoids, to avoid a raising gesture requiring precise timing.

In other cases allophones appear to be simply the arbitrary habits of a given language or variety; in SSB English the realisation of /l/ which occurs at the end of a syllable has a secondary articulation of uvularisation (a bunching of the body of the tongue towards the back of the mouth) giving it a 'dark' quality; this occurs regardless of the quality of the adjacent vowels, thus [liːf] *leaf*, but [fiː ɬ] *feel*.

Allophonic variation means that the labels attached to phonemes can at best be compromises: the distinction between 'voiced' /b/ and 'voiceless' /p/ is the presence versus absence of vocal cord vibration when they occur between other voiced sounds–[ræbɪd]–[ræpɪd]; but they are cued by other phonetic properties when adjacent to voicelessness–for instance, in utterance-initial position both are voiceless but /p/ is realised with an [h]-like burst of fricative noise (aspiration) after it as in [biː]-[pʰiː] (*bee-pea*). Similarly the name 'alveolar' applied to /t/ and /d/ glosses over the fact that they are sometimes dental: [eɪt̪θ] *eighth*, [meɪd̪ðəm] *made them*. And the placement of a dot on the vocoid quadrilateral for a given vowel phoneme disguises considerable allophonic variation; for instance, the realisation of /uː/ after /j/ is a central, as opposed to back, close vowel (/ʉː/ as opposed to /uː/ as in [jʉːθ]).

It is not possible here to give more than a brief glimpse of the allophonic variation of English. A phonetic analysis of even moderate detail will identify several allophones of each phoneme–although many general patterns become apparent so that, for instance, the effect of nasal contoids is similar on all vowels.

The point which emerges strongly in relation to ASR is that it is unrealistic to seek in the acoustic waveform a single invariant complex of cues to each phoneme. Rather, if recognition is to proceed on a segmental basis, the recogniser must incorporate knowledge about at least the more substantial cases of allophonic variation in the language in question.

PROSODY

PROSODY consists in patterns in the preceptual dimensions of pitch, loudness, and timing. Since pitch and loudness depend to a large extent on adjustments of the pulmonic airstream and of the larynx, it is possible for these dimensions of speech to vary largely independently of the vocal tract activity producing the different vocoids and contoids.

In many languages prosodic patterns can function, like segments, to distinguish words. Thus, in Thai, the phonemes /khaa/ make up five quite separate words depending on which of five distinct TONES or pitch patterns they are spoken on.

This word-distinguishing function of prosody hardly exists in English. The exception, arguably, is the use of STRESS to distinguish a few pairs of words such as (*an*) *'incline*/(*to*) *in'cline*, and (*a*) *'digest*/(*to*) *di'gest* (where the raised dash indicates that the following syllable is the stressed one). Instead, **the main prosodic system in English is INTONATION**, which consists in patterns of pitch, timing, and to a lesser extent loudness, which extend over complete utterances.

Intonation is determined jointly by syntax, by the function of an utterance in a discourse, and by the attitudes a speaker wants to convey. As a simple example it is possible to convert the function of an utterance from statement to question by the use of a pitch pattern which rises at the end: *two*, versus /*two?* or \\/*two?*

If we take the longer utterance

> *he's eaten the peaches*

we find it natural to make two syllables in particular prominent – we can indicate these with capitals:

> *he's EATen the PEAches.*

The utterance can then be given different attitudinal force depending on the intonation patterns on which it is spoken. If we are just making a matter-of-fact observation we might use a falling pitch beginning at each of the prominent syllables:

> *he's \\EATen the \\PEAches.*

As an expression of indignation, a rising pattern might be used in place of the first fall:

> *he's /EATen the \\PEAches!*

And on hearing this, another person might, astounded, echo our words with a falling-rising pitch at the end:

> *he's \\EATen the \\/PEAches!?*

The syllables which we perceive as prominent are (often) termed ACCENTED syllables. They are made prominent partly by the pitch contour of an utterance, and partly by timing factors. There is a tendency in English that the more syllables there are intervening between accents, the shorter their duration, so that the time interval between each accented syllable is nearer to being equal than if all syllables had the same duration. We may then perceive the accented syllables as falling on or near a rhythmic 'beat' inherent in the utterance.

The syllable or syllables of a word which can be accented when the word is spoken are termed STRESSED syllables. Thus if we are asked to pronounce the verb (*to*) *di'gest*, we know that the more prominent syllable of the word will be the second: *diGEST*. This will be true regardless of the intonation pattern – compare (*to*) *di/GEST?* and (*to*) *di\GEST*. However, in continuous speech, not all stressed syllables of words will be accented; for instance, whilst we might say, as a one-word response to a request to cite an English preposition, *a\BOUT*, we would be more likely to give the time as *about \FIVE*, where *about* receives no accent.

Any more detailed discussion of prosody would quickly run up against the problem that there are many competing views on how prosody should be analysed. This is so in part because of the very nature of prosodic phenomena: the information they convey is less categorical than in the case of segmental phonology. That *pin* and *tin* are 'different words' is clear-cut; that *are you /READY?* is more polite than *\ARE you \READY?* is much less categorical. Even this brief account, however, allows us to consider the importance of prosody in ASR.

On the one hand, in a simplistic recognition device which attempts to match incoming speech to stored templates, prosody provides an unwelcome source of variation. The intonation with which a word is spoken in isolation, or as part of a connected utterance, will affect its duration and the relative duration of its parts (accented syllables are lengthened relative to those which are not; different intonation patterns have distinct effects on duration; different types of segment, e.g. vocoids and contoids, are affected differently by lengthening/shortening). This variation in the temporal characteristics of a word has to be catered for (most successfully by the technique of 'dynamic time warping' – see Chapters 3 and 4).

On the other hand, prosodic information should assist the process of continuous-speech recognition, rather as it aids in our perception of speech. In the long term, it should be possible to extract some of the cues to syntactic structure and to meaning which intonation provides. In the shorter term, there may be advantages in concentrating recognition effort on those syllables which are rendered prominent by the intonation contour. This is because in these, the phonetic information tends to be more explicit and reliable; and because accented syllables normally carry the greatest information load in an utterance.

2.5 *Components and continuum: the conflict*

Talking about an intonation 'contour' already implies a continuous function running through an utterance. Although, at an abstract level, description may be in terms of discrete components such as a 'fall' or a 'level' or a 'fall-rise' which are then concatenated, our perceptual impression suggests, for instance, that pitch movement in an utterance is continuous. This is essentially a correct impression – the fundamental frequency of the speech signal, except for unavoidable breaks caused by voiceless segments, rises and falls throughout the utterance.

In other respects, however, our image of speech may be so strongly influenced by our knowledge of writing, with its spaces separating words, and its individual letters corresponding (roughly) to phonemes, that we expect these components to maintain their linear discreteness in the physical speech signal. This expectation is to some extent reinforced by traditional phonetic description which, as we have seen, relies heavily on an assumed static 'target' posture in the description of a sound.

Unfortunately, **the physical events of speech show no respect for the componentiality of the linguistic system**. An extreme example can be seen in Fig. 2.7. This presents a spectrogram, which is a visual record of a

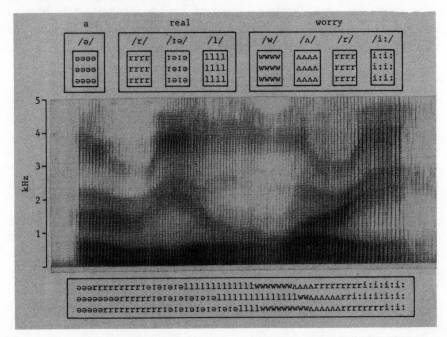

Figure 2.7 Discrete linguistic components coded as an acoustic continuum. A spectrogram (centre) of *a real worry* shows constantly varying energy-frequency patterns through time. At the top linguistic components – words and phonemes – are represented schematically; the representation below the spectrogram shows schematically how cues to a given phoneme are dispersed and overlap those to other phonemes

spectral analysis of speech. Specifically, time runs from left to right; the vertical axis represents frequency; and the darker the display, the greater the energy at that point. The dark bands rising and falling on the pattern reflect the changing formants, the resonances of the vocal tract.

The utterance is *a real worry*; and such it is – for anyone expecting neat word and phoneme divisions. Linguistic components (in this case words and phonemes) are shown discretely above the spectrogram, and below, an attempt is made to show how cues to any one component are dispersed and overlap with those to other components. **The crucial fact is that in speech production the vocal apparatus is in almost constant movement – held postures are the exception not the rule, and boundaries between words are ignored in the continuum of gestures.**

In some cases the acoustic signal does manifest discontinuities corresponding to phoneme boundaries; fricatives, in particular, may appear as discrete entities on a spectrogram. But in yet other cases the acoustic record will provide *more* segments than are implied by the linguistic content.

In short, **the most basic problem of speech recognition is how to reconstruct the discrete linguistic components from the overlapping and interwoven cues in the acoustic signal.**

2.6 *Variation*

When a person speaks, it is possible to detect a considerable amount of information over and above the linguistic content of what is being said. We can infer – with more or less accuracy – where speakers come from, their sex and age, their state of health, their level of stress and fatigue, and so on. From the point of view of speech recognition, information like this in the speech wave constitutes background 'noise', from which the linguistically-determined signal has to be extracted.

Separating out the linguistic content is made difficult because the acoustic dimensions which convey much of the extraneous information about the speaker are the same as those onto which the linguistic content is mapped. Thus, for example, formant frequencies are determined partly by the current shape of a vocal tract (hence, for instance, conveying a particular vowel quality); but also by the overall size of the vocal tract (reflecting, for instance, whether the speaker is a man, woman, or child).

In considering the variation encountered in speech it is useful to separate out kinds of variation which can be described in terms of the linguistic system from those kinds which stem from personal characteristics of the speaker. Under both headings there are aspects which will remain relatively constant for a given speaker, and aspects which will vary across utterances made by the same individual.

LINGUISTIC VARIATION

Varieties of a language which differ principally in terms of their pronunciation can be termed ACCENTS; if they differ also in terms of their syntax, vocabulary, and morphology, they tend to be termed DIALECTS. Speakers of two different varieties may or may not be able to understand each other; whether or not such varieties are called different dialects or different languages is largely a matter of history and politics.

Because of its early codification in written form, a 'standard' dialect of English has attained wide currency throughout the world – even if many of the people who write or speak it also use another dialect. The accent with which this standard dialect is spoken, however, differs widely. It is appropriate, therefore, to look briefly at how differences between accents may be described, comparing *General American* (GA, spoken in the USA with the clear exceptions of New England and the South East) and Standard Southern British (SSB) pronunciation. Both these are really abstractions from a number of closely related varieties, but they will serve for a broad comparison.

Accents may differ in terms of SYSTEM (usually the number of phonemes of equivalent types, e.g. vowels), PHONOTACTICS (the allowed combinations of phonemes), LEXICAL-INCIDENCE (the choice of phonemes in specific words), and REALISATION (the phonetic quality of allophones).

The consonant SYSTEMS of GA and SSB are similar, except that GA may have an additional phoneme /ʍ/ – a voiceless counterpart of /w/ – such that in GA, words like *whet* (/ʍet/) and *wet* (/wet/) are distinguished. Table 2.3, however, shows vowel systems of rather different structure; in particular, GA lacks the phonemes /ɜː/, /ɪə/, /ɛə/, and /ʊə/, which in SSB resulted historically from loss of /r/ after vowels. Also, GA does not contrast three different vowels in *lot*, *taught*, and *palm*.

Table 2.3 thus reveals consequences of a major PHONOTACTIC difference: the fact that SSB allows /r/ to occur only if the sound immediately following is a vowel. In SSB, pairs such as the following rhyme: *shah-car*; *caught-court*; *idea-deer*; *data-later*.

Differences of LEXICAL INCIDENCE are perhaps the most salient of all, the use of /eɪ/ (GA) versus /ɑː/ (SSB) in the second syllable of *tomato* being a famous example.

Finally, the phonetic REALISATION of each of the phonemes differs in greater or smaller degree between the accents. Well remarked are the tendency in GA to voice /t/ between voiced sounds when the following vowel is unstressed, causing e.g. *biting* to rhyme nearly or completely with *biding*; and sometimes to realise /æ/ as a long, front, half-open

Table 2.3 British (SSB) and General American (GA) vowel phonemes with key words. (Adapted from Wells[18]: 117ff.)

	SSB	GA	
kit	ɪ	ɪ	*kit*
dress	ɛ	ɛ	*dress*
trap	æ	æ	*trap, *bath*
*lot, *cloth	ɒ		
strut	ʌ	ʌ	*strut*
foot	ʊ	ʊ	*foot*
a(ttain), (Chin)a	ə	ə	*a(attain), (Chin)a*
fleece	iː	i	*fleece*
palm, *bath, **start	ɑː	ɑ	*palm, *lot*
thought, *force, **north	ɔː	ɔ	*thought, *cloth*
goose	uː	u	*goose*
**nurse	ɜː		
face	eɪ	eɪ	*face*
price	aɪ	aɪ	*price*
choice	ɔɪ	ɔɪ	*choice*
mouth	aʊ	aʊ	*mouth*
goat	əʊ	o	*goat*
**near	ɪə	(ɪ + r	***near*)
**square	ɛə	(ɛ + r	***square*)
**cure	ʊə	(ʊ + r	***cure*)
		(ʌ + r	***nurse*)
		(ɑ + r	***start*)
		(o + r	***force*)
		(ɔ + r	***north*)

* Words which differ between the two varieties by lexical incidence of phonemes
** Words exhibiting differences in phonotactic distribution

vowel [ɛː] or centring diphthong [ɛə] so that e.g. GA *bad* may sound more like SSB *bared*.

So far we have considered varieties of pronunciation as they occur across different (groups of) speakers. All speakers, however, command a range of pronunciations which they will use in different circumstances.

On the one hand, the more formal a speaker perceives a situation to be, the more he will tend to produce pronunciations which he considers to be 'correct' or prestigious. For instance, many accents of English pronounce the -*ing* ending /ɪn/ instead of /ɪŋ/. But many individuals who would use /ɪn/ in casual conversation would, when speaking in a formal setting, use a high percentage of /ɪŋ/. Similarly, in a variety which sometimes uses a glottal stop instead of an alveolar stop to realise /t/ (*be'er* for *better*, etc.), the percentage of glottal stops in appropriate cases will increase as the speech becomes more casual.

Other factors such as a higher speech rate, and high redundancy (as when the speaker knows that the listener can predict most of what is being said), favour PHONETIC REDUCTIONS; here the speaker takes 'short cuts' in articulating the words, for instance saying [neks wiːk] for *next week*, [hæmbæg] for *hand-bag*, and even [mpspəʊz . . .] for *I don't suppose* (*I could trouble you for a minute*).

As yet it is not well understood how far informality, rate, and redundancy interact in their control of such phonetic processes. Ultimately it should be possible to give a rule-based description of these processes; but there are many of them, and the description will be complex. In designing speech recognisers there will be a payoff between the difficulty of incorporating increasingly sophisticated knowledge of these stylistic processes, and the advantage of reducing the constraint on speakers to adhere closely (and perhaps unnaturally) to a single speaking style.

PERSONAL VARIATION

Personal variation in the sense intended here stems not from the use of a particular language variety, but from the make-up of the individual human being producing the speech. The predominant factor is the person's physique, as reflected in the dimensions of their vocal apparatus; but psychological factors may also play a part, as when habitual tension is reflected in the quality of a person's voice.

The physique of the vocal apparatus determines the *range* within which acoustic parameters can vary, rather than fixed values. For instance the smaller size and mass of female vocal cords compared to male determines (other things being equal) a higher fundamental frequency range; but there is usually some overlap between the normal ranges of a man and a woman, and a man can override his natural range by producing falsetto.

Unfortunately (from the point of view of speech recognisers aiming to cope with different speakers) **the relation between the acoustic output of different vocal tracts is not straightforward**. Whilst it is possible to say, for instance, that female formant frequencies are on average about 20% higher than those of male speakers, a mean value such as that disguises considerable non-uniformity in the effects – resulting partly from the fact that vocal tracts differ more in pharynx length than in length of the mouth cavity. A procedure to equate male and female formant frequencies has to be specific to different types of vocoid and to each formant.

Most of the work in this area has concentrated on male–female scaling of vocoids; but similar scaling problems exist between any two speakers even of the same sex, and across the whole range of sounds. Considerable progress needs to be made before an automatic speech recognition system can be achieved which will adapt to any new speaker without a lengthy 'training' phase – that is, one which will replicate what human listeners do without difficulty on encountering a new voice.

In such a recogniser adaptation may well have to be a continuing process, since the personal characteristics of a person's voice change even in the short term. Even assuming a constant linguistic style (see above), some of the properties of a voice will change as the speaker becomes tired, stressed, irritable, louder (perhaps as a result of increased background noise), and so on.

In the longer term, changes correlate with diurnal rhythm, health (such as colds and ailments of the larynx), and (probably of least consequence to speech recognition) the ageing process.

2.7 *Conclusions*

We started off by considering two images of speech which might be generally accessible – writing, and the acoustic waveform. In retrospect, how adequate are these images in relation to natural, continuous speech?

Alphabetic writing is strictly segmented into words and letters, and is inherently well-suited to representing the lexical and phonemic aspects of linguistic structure, which are central to the communication of 'cognitive' or 'factual' information. It does not, however, give explicit information about syntactic structure (as opposed to the mere ordering of words).

It does not provide explicit information about pronunciation, for instance in terms of the allophonic realisations of phonemes. This is fair enough, since writing most often functions as a linguistic medium divorced from speech. It merely hints, by use of a very few punctuation marks, at one aspect of linguistic structure in speech – prosody. Prosody is to some extent a correlate of syntactic structure, but also functions to communicate information, for instance about the speaker's attitude, over and above what is conveyed by the words.

Generally, there are no agreed conventions in writing to represent the kind of linguistic variation which a speaker may employ in different situations – apart from occasional resort to spellings such as *geroff* for *get off* – or to express accent. And personal characteristics of the speaker receive no representation.

But by far and away the most seductively misleading aspect of writing as an image of speech is its segmentation. Speech performance involves continuous movement of the vocal apparatus; static postures are few, and pauses are left (sometimes) between intonation units, not between words and certainly not between allophones. The result is an acoustic signal in almost constant flux, and whose steady-state portions often do not correspond straightforwardly to phonemes.

As an image, the waveform itself is deceptively simple. Its record of air pressure variations represents the physical link between speaker and hearers, and its continuity reflects the continuous activity of the vocal organs.

What is not evident from the waveform, or from its spectral transform, are the number of different strands whose physical mappings are interwoven in it – from highly structured and categorical linguistic content, to adventitious clues to the 'machine' producing the signal.

The task of speech recognition consists largely in teasing out one of these strands – the linguistic content. So far, greatest progress has been made by carefully controlling other strands; most speech recognisers, for instance, require that only one individual (at a time) speak isolated words carefully and unemotionally. In this way, they limit much of the richness of spoken communication and risk undermining claims for its naturalness in man–machine communication.

Much more than on technological advance, progress towards natural communication with machines by speech will depend on an increased and more explicit understanding of human speech communication in its totality.

2.8 *Further reading*

Introductory linguistics textbooks, such as Akmajian *et al.*[1], give a wide-ranging view of the nature of language. For theoretical syntax, see Brown and Miller[3]; and King[12] for computer parsing. Matthews[14] gives an introduction to morphology.

O'Connor[16] and Ladefoged[13] cover a range of topics in general phonetics, while Hawkins[10] provides a grounding in phonology, including specific reference to the phonetic reductions of casual speech. Gimson[9] is a classic manual on British English pronunciation; for American, see Kenyon[11] or Bauer *et al.*[2].

A non-mathematical introduction to speech acoustics is that of Fry[8]; while a classic textbook on the topic is Flanagan[7].

Crystal[4] provides a comprehensive treatment of prosody within a traditional approach. For a range of recent work on modelling prosody, see Cutler and Ladd[5].

An introductory survey of regional and social variation can be found in Trudgill[17], or more recently Downes[6]. Details of English accents world-wide are collected in Wells[18]. The voice characteristics of individuals are discussed, in the context of talker recognition, in Nolan[15].

2.9 *References*

1. Akmajian, A., Demers, R.A., and Harnish, R.M. (1984) *Linguistics: an Introduction to Language and Communication*. Cambridge, Mass.: MIT Press.
2. Bauer, L., Dienhart, J.M., Hartvigson, H.H., and Jakobsen, L.K. (1980) *American English Pronunciation*. Copenhagen: Gyldendal.
3. Brown, K., and Miller, J.E. (1980) *Syntax: a Linguistic Introduction to Sentence Structure*. London: Hutchinson.
4. Crystal, D. (1969) *Prosodic Systems and Intonation in English*. Cambridge: Cambridge University Press.
5. Cutler, A., and Ladd, D.R. (1983) *Prosody: Models and Measurements*. Berlin: Springer-Verlag.
6. Downes, W. (1984) *Language and Society*. London: Fontana.
7. Flanagan, J.L. (1972) *Speech Analysis, Synthesis and Perception*. 2nd edn. Berlin: Springer-Verlag.
8. Fry, D.B. (1979) *The Physics of Speech*. Cambridge: Cambridge University Press.
9. Gimson, A.C. (1980) *An Introduction to the Pronunciation of English*. 3rd edn. London: Edward Arnold.
10. Hawkins, P. (1984) *Introducing Phonology*. London: Hutchinson.
11. Kenyon, J.S. (1958) *American Pronunciation*. 10th edn. Ann Arbor: Wahr.
12. King, M. (ed.) (1983) *Parsing Natural Language*. London: Academic Press.
13. Ladefoged, P. (1982) *A Course in Phonetics*. 2nd edn. New York: Harcourt, Brace, Jovanovich.
14. Matthews, P.H. (1974) *Morphology*. Cambridge: Cambridge University Press.
15. Nolan, F. (1983) *The Phonetic Bases of Speaker Recognition*. Cambridge: Cambridge University Press.
16. O'Connor, J.D. (1973) *Phonetics*. Harmondsworth: Penguin.
17. Trudgill, P. (1974) *Sociolinguistics*. Harmondsworth: Penguin.
18. Wells, J.C. (1982) *Accents of English*. (3 vols.) Cambridge: Cambridge University Press.
19. Wiik, K. (1965) *Finnish and English Vowels*. Turku: Turku University.

CHAPTER 3
THE ELEMENTS OF SPEECH RECOGNITION

Wayne A. Lea

In this chapter the reader is introduced to the principal techniques used in speech recognition.

3.1 *Alternative viewpoints about how to achieve speech recognition*

In this chapter we consider the principal alternative approaches to speech recognition, such as mathematical schemes and linguistic and perceptual modelling. Four general viewpoints about how to design recognisers are described. The traditional template matching methods, which have dominated the research and commercial systems, are introduced, and the leading alternative candidate method based on phonetic analyses is described. Basic 'building blocks' or components for composing complete recognition systems are outlined, and a typical system structure is described. Next, we review what some workers say is seriously wrong with such techniques. Some promising improvements in pattern matching procedures are outlined, for a popular dynamic programming method.

This discussion is purposely not mathematical, to give a suitable overview of concepts without demanding reader proficiency in statistics or signal processing. The author's bias toward phonological models also creates an emphasis more on phonetic, prosodic and linguistic aspects of recognition.

FOUR GENERAL VIEWPOINTS

Speech communication is a process whereby linguistic messages are converted into acoustic waveforms through a complex articulation process, then the acoustic signal is transmitted and picked up by the auditory system for conversion back into a message through the speech

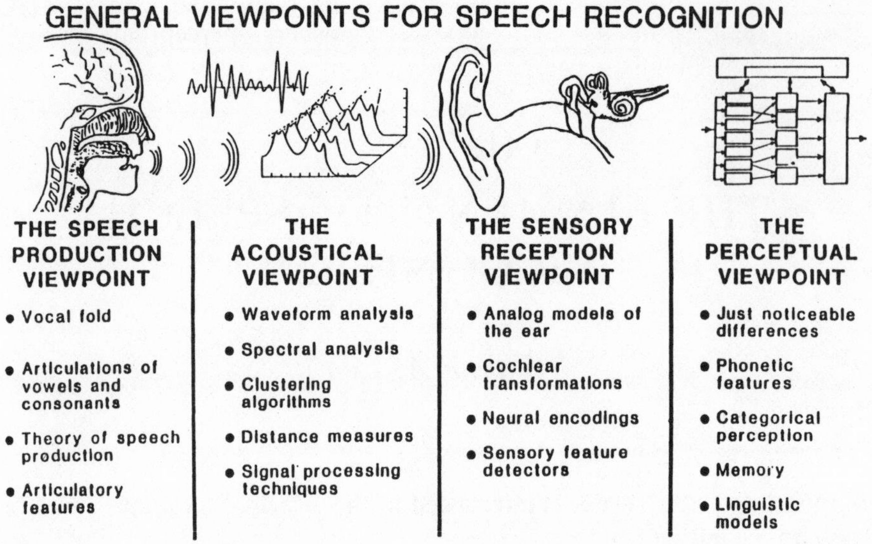

GENERAL VIEWPOINTS FOR SPEECH RECOGNITION

THE SPEECH PRODUCTION VIEWPOINT	THE ACOUSTICAL VIEWPOINT	THE SENSORY RECEPTION VIEWPOINT	THE PERCEPTUAL VIEWPOINT
• Vocal fold	• Waveform analysis	• Analog models of the ear	• Just noticeable differences
• Articulations of vowels and consonants	• Spectral analysis	• Cochlear transformations	• Phonetic features
• Theory of speech production	• Clustering algorithms	• Neural encodings	• Categorical perception
• Articulatory features	• Distance measures	• Sensory feature detectors	• Memory
	• Signal processing techniques		• Linguistic models

Figure 3.1   Based on the stages in communicating a message, we can define four general viewpoints about how to do speech recognition

perception process. As illustrated in Fig. 3.1, four basic viewpoints are thus suggested for how to accomplish speech recognition:

1. The *acoustic signal viewpoint* asserts that since the speech signal is just another waveform (or vector of numbers), we can simply apply general signal analysis techniques (e.g. Fourier frequency spectrum analysis, principal component analysis, statistical decision procedures, and other mathematical schemes) to establish the identity (or representative 'nearest neighbour') of the input.

2. The *speech production viewpoint* suggests we understand the communication 'source' of the speech signal, and capture essential aspects of the way in which speech was produced by the human vocal system (e.g. look for vocal tract resonances, rate of vibration of the vocal cords, manner and place of articulation, coarticulatory movements, etc.).

3. The *sensory reception viewpoint* suggests duplicating the human auditory reception process, by extracting parameters and classifying patterns as is done in the ear, auditory nerves, and sensory feature detectors of the ear-brain system.

4. The *speech perception viewpoint* suggests we extract features and make categorical distinctions that are experimentally established as being important to human perception of speech (e.g. voice onset times

and formant transitions as cues to state of consonant voicing, 'single equivalent formants' as vowel distinguishers, perceptual 'feature detectors', linguistic category detectors, etc.).

Of course, mixtures or combinations of these viewpoints can also be devised, and have been evident in some of the previous work. The four viewpoints reflect different ways in which the linguistic message being communicated is encoded at various stages in the production and reception of speech. The sensory reception and speech perception viewpoints have had much less effect on actual recognition systems than the speech production and acoustic signal viewpoints. Indeed, in part because engineers have dominated the work in this field, the acoustic signal processing viewpoint has been most dominant.

Taking the 'acoustic signal viewpoint', most designers of recognisers focus only (or primarily) on mathematical representations of the recogniser's input-output characteristics, asserting that each input must merely be compared with previously stored *representatives* or *templates* of each equivalence class of inputs, and the *nearest neighbour* or minimally different representative must be selected as the identity (or equivalence class) of the current input signal (or, if no template is near enough, an error message or 'input rejected' message, might be given). The two stages of training a machine, and recognising by similar pattern construction processes, are illustrated in Fig. 3.2. This is the basis of generalised input-output functions (Newell, 1975), linear discriminant analyses, other statistical models, and general pattern recognition and signal processing schemes. Such recognition models could apply as well to signals other than speech, and indeed their technology is highly developed because of such other applications. They do not consider how the signal was produced by the speaker, nor how it is normally perceived by the human listener. They, of course, do not require that the recogniser operate internally in any way similar to the human's perception processes.

The speech production, sensory reception, and speech perception viewpoints may be characterised as what Newell (1975, p. 15) called 'knowledge-source-driven representations', which assume that recognition can be based on available knowledge of how speech is usually encoded or decoded. These three viewpoints assert that knowledge of the acoustic speech signal alone is not enough to determine fully the message (or intended machine response); other sources of knowledge must be brought to bear on the recognition problem. These viewpoints also acknowledge that, while a machine need not operate internally in the same manner as the human, the human speech processing abilities can

Training Concept:

Signal S_i is declared to be in equivalence class M_C

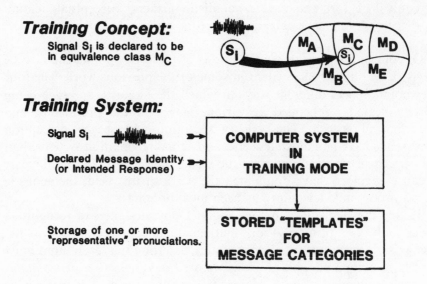

Training System:

Signal S_i

Declared Message Identity (or Intended Response)

COMPUTER SYSTEM IN TRAINING MODE

Storage of one or more "representative" pronunciations.

STORED "TEMPLATES" FOR MESSAGE CATEGORIES

Recognition Concept:

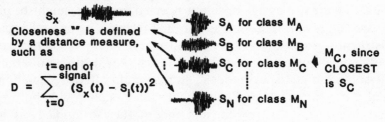

S_x

Closeness "" is defined by a distance measure, such as

$$D = \sum_{t=0}^{t=\text{end of signal}} (S_x(t) - S_i(t))^2$$

S_A for class M_A

S_B for class M_B

S_C for class M_C

S_N for class M_N

M_C, since CLOSEST is S_C

Recognition System:

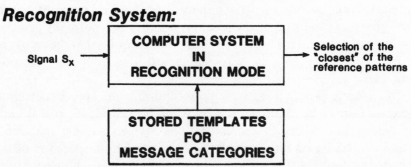

Signal S_x

COMPUTER SYSTEM IN RECOGNITION MODE

Selection of the "closest" of the reference patterns

STORED TEMPLATES FOR MESSAGE CATEGORIES

Figure 3.2 The template matching method involves training the machine in advance, with representative pronunciations, and selecting the 'closest' of stored templates when unknown inputs are later analysed

serve as a successful 'prototype system' for guiding the development of machine algorithms for speech recognition. The conversion from acoustic signal to machine response, without the intervention or help of the human, involves the machine functionally duplicating the overall (input-output) function of a human perceiver. It need not structurally duplicate the human ear-brain system, but the knowledge-source-driven viewpoints would suggest that recognisers may glean guidelines for effective recognition from study of human speech processing techniques.

Computers can currently do some analyses better than humans, and some others less adequately, and so a controversy continues between mathematical (statistical, information-theoretic, signal processing, or pattern classifying) methods and human-oriented (phonetic, linguistic, perceptual or neurological) approaches. This controversy has persisted for decades, and may be expected to continue in future work.

For a full review of alternative methods for speech recognition, the reader is referred to this author's textbook (Lea, 1986a), other chapters in this book, and previous reviews of this technology (e.g. White, 1976; Martin, 1976; Reddy, 1975, 1976; Lea, 1980; Dixon and Martin, 1979). This chapter is devoted to brief overviews of needed components in recognisers and significant insights about specific issues.

DISTANCE MEASURES AND TEMPLATE MATCHING
A critical task in speech recognition is to extract all (and only) those parts that convey the message. No matter how many parts or time slices we divide the speech signal into, to permit minute study of all its timing data, an even finer analysis is always possible. Similarly, no matter how exactly we measure the pressure (or voltage) of a speech wave at an instant, a finer grain analysis is conceivable. Thus, speech is a two-dimensional non-denumerable continuum. It is possible to analyse it without arbitrary or linguistically dictated divisions into time segments and no quantisations into significant changes in signal levels. Point-by-point differences in incoming and stored signals can be calculated, without regard to the possibility that some signal differences are more important than others.

This continuous representation of speech signal comparisons is shown in Fig. 3.3 as the left-most branch of the 'tree' of alternative decoding schemes. To determine the identity of the incoming speech and effect the correct machine response, a recogniser can determine the difference between the incoming signal and the expected signal for each message. 'Expected' signals, or templates, can be actual stored training samples that were previously declared by the human to be associated with each appropriate machine response, or they can be averages or other

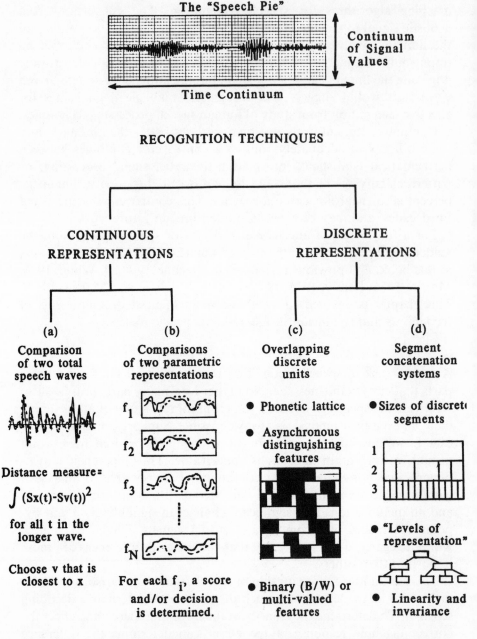

Figure 3.3 Alternative methods for dividing the two-dimensional speech continuum ('the speech pie') into parts can form the basis for speech pattern recognition procedures

composite signals obtained from many such training samples (*cf.* Fig. 3.2). For each equivalence class of utterances (associated with a specific correct response), a template (or perhaps several templates, representing allowable variations within the equivalence class) must be specified, and a distance measure determined such as the calculation of a 'Euclidean distance' formed from the squares of the point-by-point differences in signals. The selection of an appropriate 'distance measure' is thus one of the important concerns in this signal-matching approach to recognition.

This (in its simplest form) is basically an 'ignorance model' of the significant aspects of the incoming signal. Each deviation from previously stored signals is assigned equal significance, and no particular features of the speech are considered more important than others. This ignores or disregards whatever we can learn about the important physiological and linguistic regularities of both the source of the speech, and the intended intelligent receiver of spoken messages. It requires accumulation of representative training signals for each possible message. For large message sets (large vocabularies of isolated words, or large numbers of alternative sentences that might be continuously spoken), obtaining training templates is a time consuming and costly process, and results in extensive storage requirements in the machine. Users are required to invest the time in training the machine to their voices, or speaker-independent templates must be devised by the developers, based on averages or alternative variants of word pronunciations.

In addition, it is difficult to obtain truly 'representative' training signals, that are quite distinct from message to message, and that are likely to be closely approximated by all repetitions by all speakers in all environments. To account for speaker differences, variations from time to time, speaking rates, and variations due to environmental noise and channel distortions, several alternative templates usually have to be stored for each message and each set of conditions. This further increases the storage requirements and makes recognition costly and unwieldly. However, with the rapidly advancing speeds and storage capacities in low cost computers, this storage need is less of a problem than it might have seemed in earlier years. Also, the template approach avoids the danger of inadvertently 'throwing away' important information while focusing on only certain parameters that are expected to be important. While there are several arguments that can be raised against template matching procedures, actual experiments show repeatedly that, for small unchangeable problems, these techniques work well, yielding higher accuracies than the 'more sophisticated' phonetic approaches.

One can attempt to assign higher weights (or levels of significance) to certain aspects of the continuous waveforms, such as focusing on the higher signal levels that are less susceptible to corruption by noise. This can be achieved either by modifying the distance measure calculations from various pieces of the speech, or by the process of extracting parameters, or continuously varying features from the speech signal, and assessing closeness of values of those parameters only (*cf.* Fig. 3.3). One can also warp the incoming signal to match certain features of the stored templates, and assess whether the warpings required for one vocabulary item are more reasonable than those for other words. A common warping that has proved very valuable in recognisers has been to match the duration of an input word to that of each alternative template before they are otherwise compared. This *time normalisation* process, and similar processes of *speaker normalisation* and *channel normalisation*, use certain detected features of the signal to adjust the signal to match more closely the correct stored templates. For example, by detecting the fundamental frequency or 'pitch' of the signal, or by complex processes that determine the speaker's vocal tract length, one can adjust for speaker differences such as male *vs.* female speakers. Similarly, by monitoring the long term average frequency spectrum of the signal, and applying a mathematical process called *blind deconvolution* (Stockham, *et al.*, 1975), one can adjust for some differences in the spectral characteristics of channels. Such extractions focus on relevant aspects of speech and remove or diminish the confusions introduced by irrelevant differences from templates.

This is the beginning of the acknowledgement that no two utterances of the same message are exactly alike, and the communicative ability of speech is due to 'resemblances' between successive utterances. The task of recognition is thus said to be that of determining the 'information carrying features' common to all utterances of the 'same' message, and using those features to classify utterances according to their intended meanings or expected responses. Mathematical procedures exist for automatically 'learning' features that are common to all utterances which the human declares to be equivalent, while assuring that the features are quite different for non-equivalent utterances. Alternatively, features can be selected based on trial-and-error procedures or *heuristics*, which capture some of the regularities in previously processed data.

The variety of template matching procedures is extensive, since a slightly different technique can appear to emerge from each new set of possible parameter patterns to extract, each new method of data alignment, each new distance measure and each decision or word-matching method. *Vector quantisation* (*cf.* Burton and Shore, 1986; Tsao and Gray, 1986) is an example of a template matching process that at the same time may seem very different from, and yet essentially a terminological equivalent of, previous methods. One advantage that some methods like vector quantisation provide is the ability to define automatically the set of alternative spectral templates for categorising portions of speech. For further information on various template matching methods, the reader is referred to other chapters in this book, and to related publications (Lea, 1986b; IEEE Proceedings of annual International Conferences on Acoustics, Speech, and Signal Processing, etc.). Our next consideration is how to *segment* the speech into units that provide a linguistically attractive alternative to template matching.

TRADITIONAL PHONETIC RECOGNITION PROCEDURES
The acoustical theory of speech production, and some models of human perception, suggest the merit of 'dividing and conquering', if one is to represent best the important information in speech. Here we consider the justifications of discrete representation of speech, and the traditional view of segmentation of speech into phonological units of various sizes and kinds.

Discrete representations of speech
The non-denumerable continuum of possible acoustic pressure values at any one time and the continuous variation of sound pressure with time yield a two-dimensional 'speech pie', as shown in Fig. 3.3(a). Selecting and comparing features of the signal and stored templates may be viewed as a process of slicing the speech 'pie' into horizontal slices, with each slice still possibly being a continuous function of time (Fig. 3.3(b)). There is extensive justification for characterising speech by discrete units in time and as a finite set of simultaneous features.

Engineering and information-theoretic considerations suggest discrete representations. Speech must be converted into discrete voltages and switching states in digital computers, so that a discrete representation will be required for speech recognition using practical digital computers. Also, the *sampling theorem* (*cf.* Pierce, 1961, pp. 66f; Rabiner and Gold, 1975, pp. 26–28) asserts that any bandlimited signal (such as speech may be considered to be) can be completely represented by $2Fu$ samples per unit time, where Fu is the upper bound on the frequency content of the signal (which can certainly be taken to be at most 10 kHz for speech). The *fidelity criterion* of communication theory (*cf.* Chomsky and Miller, 1963, p. 273) acknowledges that certain sound changes (e.g. those due to emotion, fatigue, speaker idiosyncrasies, etc.) are irrelevant to the receiver, while others are significant, so that the infinity of possible speech waves of a limited length can be partitioned into a finite set of discrete, mutually exclusive 'equivalence classes', such as we have declared to be basic to speech recognition. Each such class, taken from the finite set of signal equivalence classes, may be represented by a discrete symbol taken from a finite 'alphabet' of distinguishable signs (*cf.* Fig. 3.2).

Speech perception studies also suggest that certain acoustic changes are not perceivable until they reach a minimal change called a 'just noticeable difference' or 'limen' (Flanagan, 1972). Thus, there seem to be 'quantum steps' in perceivable values of speech parameters. Just noticeable differences have been studied for the amplitude or energy in a wave, the duration of the wave, the frequencies contained in the wave, and other parameters. Similar thresholds of major acoustic distinction also exist in articulation of speech. For example, there are definite rates of respiratory airflow below which airflow is laminar and above which flow is turbulent, yielding sharp distinctions between what are called 'sonorant' sounds and 'fricatives'. Also, there are rather abrupt changes in the acoustic features corresponding to opening the velic valve for nasalisation. Not all articulatory changes produce significant acoustic changes, and many acoustic changes that do occur (e.g. whispering, speaking loudly, etc.) are not linguistically significant (i.e. do not usually signal a change in intended response at the receiver). Kenneth Stevens (1969) has indicated that there is a quantum nature in the acoustic changes that accompany articulatory motions, which natural languages tend to exploit, choosing sounds and articulation positions that are most stable, and not sensitive to slight misplacements of articulators. A discrete code results.

Linguist Morris Halle (1954, p. 198) has also noted that 'if a discrete view be adopted, correction of errors can begin upon receipt of each discrete unit (quantum)', so we don't have to wait until the entire continuous signal is completed to correct errors in reception of such named segments. This may prove significant in the real time recognition of spoken sentences. Finally, we may note that most messages for machine input would have identical intended responses if they had been written (or typewritten), rather than spoken, so the fact that the written code is discrete suggests the sufficiency of a discrete representation of speech.

Thus, there are a number of arguments favouring discrete represent- ations of speech. Notice that no representation could be fully discrete unless it breaks up each of the two acoustic continua (continuum of time and continuum of pressure levels) into a countable (in practice, finite) number of discrete parts. A non-denumerable infinity of possible speech waveforms of a fixed length must be identified in the same discretely representable class. Likewise, an infinity of possible lengths must be classified as 'equivalent'. Thus, a discrete representation of the time domain requires a segmentation of the continuous speech waveform into some sort of units or 'segments'. While the segments or units need not be separated with strict 'boundaries' between them, and could actually overlap each other or be spaced apart from each other, the usual method is to segment speech into juxtaposed units of non-zero length, which classify as equivalent any of an infinity of 'insignificantly different' wave shapes spanning about the same stretch of time.

Sequences of such classified segments then determine the important information about the speech. Figure 3.3(c) illustrates discrete representations that do allow overlapping units ('lattices', or incomplete specifications of alternative units which may be in the incoming speech), and ones that involve strict concatenations, or sequences, of non-overlapping, juxtaposed segments. Both forms of representation have been used in speech recognisers, though the predominant approach is to use strict segmentations into non-overlapping units.

Given the many justifications for discrete representations, the primary question is: how should we quantise, or discretely represent speech, and how do we identify which of the finite set of categories each unit of speech belongs to? One of the simplest answers would be to segment speech at fixed time intervals. Commonly, such segments are selected to be short enough to be a small fraction of the length of normally sustained vowels and consonants, but long enough to allow proper feature extractions, such as proper spectral averaging, or detections of periodicities in the waveform. This smallest unit of time (such as a short 10 ms unit) can be sensibly categorised into one of a finite number of sound categories, such as the most similar of a set of stored training templates obtained from previous processing of training data (*cf.* Baker, 1975; Klatt, 1980). Alternatively, the segment may be assigned to a phonetic category based on the spectral content and other distinguishing features of the waveform within that unit.

At the other extreme, the total utterance (which may be a word, for isolated word recognisers, or a sentence, or discourse, for continuous speech recognisers) can be interpreted as an undivided entity which determines the appropriate machine response. This maximal input unit also may be assigned to one of a countable (realistically, finite) set of discrete units (which are the labels of the equivalence classes of desired machine responses). Thus, we have the extremes in simple segmentation of speech as shown in Fig. 3.3(d1) and (d3). Both the total-utterance-classification and the arbitrary classification of each short (10 ms) segment into spectral categories have been used in previous speech recognition systems.

Segmentation of speech into phonological units

The most controversial aspect of segmentation has concerned the relative values of intermediate size units, such as 'phones'; phoneme-to-phoneme transitions or 'diphones'; syllabic subunits like 'syllabic onsets', 'syllabic nuclei', and 'coda'; 'syllables'; 'words'; and 'phrases'. There is a vast literature on the 'psychological reality' and the linguistic utility of segments like phonemes and syllables (*cf.* Sapir, 1938; Bloomfield, 1933; Pike, 1945; Wells, 1947; Trager and Smith, 1951; Chomsky, 1957; Chomsky and Miller, 1963; Chomsky and Halle, 1968; Hockett, 1972). For example, it has long been observed that utterances can resemble or differ from other signals, based on similar or clearly distinctive *portions* of speech. For examples, *pin* begins like *pig, pill* or *pit*, but ends differently; it ends about the same as *fin, sin, tin*; it contains something close to the sound of *in* but adds something at the beginning. Also, *pin* begins like *pat, push* or *peg*, but its resemblance to them is less than that to *pig, pill* or *pit*; it ends somewhat like *man, sun* or *when*, but its resemblence to them is smaller than to *fin, sin, tin* or *in*; its beginning and ending are both similar to those of *pen, pan* or *pun*, but the middle is different. Only the middle part of *pin* is like *dig, fish* or *will*.

Thus, parts of words are similar or different; further experiments with such paired comparisons can (at least in the simplest cases) reveal how many replaceable parts are in a word or utterance, and we can demonstrate that a good representation of the word is that it is divisible into a certain number (for the examples above, exactly three) linguistically contrastive parts. Such minimal units of distinctive contrast are called *phonemes*. Thus, *pin* consists of three phonemes. Despite variations in the written form, the following words also have only three phonemes: *thick, ping, phone, tough*, etc. This motivates a message distinguishing *segmentation* of the message into phonemes.

Of course, segments are not simply interchangeable; if you remove a p from 'pan' and put it in place of the beginning of another word like 'pin', or *vice versa*, it may sound disjointed, 'wrong' or confusing, or even, in some extreme cases, may sound like another phoneme (Yilmaz, 1967). The reason, in part, is that it is difficult to define precisely where one linguistic unit ends and the next one begins; they tend to overlap, and affect each other, so that some anticipation of the next sound may affect the pronunciation of its predecessor, and there are lingering effects from previous sounds. To account for the variations between versions of a particular phoneme that occur in different contexts, linguists refer to each distinguishable subclass as an *allophone* of the phoneme. Some recognisers have detected allophones as the primary small units of recognition. Thus, for example, some versions (allophones) of unvoiced

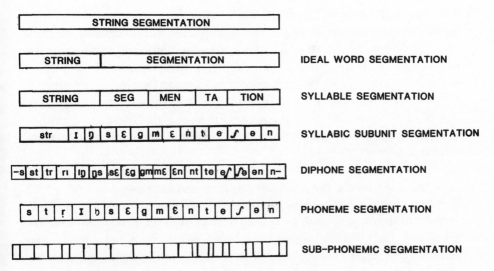

Figure 3.4 Segmentation of speech into phonological units can be done with various size units

stops (/p, t, k/) will be 'aspirated' (such as at the beginnings of words) while others are 'unaspirated' (after /s/ within a word, etc.); some stops will be 'released' while others will be manifested as 'unreleased' allophones.

Figure 3.4 shows a variety of alternative segmentations of speech. Since transitions into and out of phonemes are affected by surrounding sounds, some recognisers use *sub-phonemic* units, such as dividing a stop consonant into a silence, followed by a burst, then aspiration, and then a transition into following vowels or other sounds. Alternatively, one may segment speech at the steady state centres of phonemes, producing transitional sounds called *diphones*. With such segments, the coarticulatory influences of one sound on its predecessor and successor can be directly incorporated into the nature of the two transitional units that meet in the centre of the phoneme. Some workers have advocated the use of syllable parts (onsets, targets and offsets) and whole syllables as unanalysed units, for which detection might be more reliable since the coarticulatory transitions of speech are captured within the larger syllabic unit. If such diphones, syllable parts or total syllables are used, the 'alphabet' of the basic recognition units becomes much larger, but some of the transitional phenomena of flowing speech are represented directly in those minimal units. With smaller units like subphonemic units, allophones, or phonemes, coarticulatory and 'phonological' rules may be needed to account for such transitional effects.

A TYPICAL SPEECH RECOGNITION SYSTEM

So far, we have noted the merits of continuous signal processing, discrete representations, segmentation into some useful units, and procedures for matching incoming patterns to expected pronunciations. We have actually begun to describe basic processes that can be used in building up a speech recognition system. Before we discuss best choices among potential components of a recogniser, it should be useful to consider some abstract concepts of how to process speech signals or sequences of symbolic segments.

Basic building blocks for processing speech and language

Figures 3.5(1) to 3.5(7) show some basic 'building blocks' that perform transformations pertinent to speech recognition. A *waveform modifier* takes an input speech signal, and produces a modified signal. The modification might be a clipping of large values of the signal, a distortion of its duration, a frequency spectrum filtering that alters the shape of the signal or enhances the speech and de-emphasises noise that is present, etc. In a somewhat parallel fashion, a *symbol transducer* can take in one discrete symbol sequence, and yield a modified sequence on its output. If the input were a sequence of words in one language, and the output were an equivalent word sequence in another language, this transducer would be a language translation device. If the input were a sequence of phonemes or other phonological units, and the output were a different phonological sequence, we would have a 'phonological rule', or set of such rules.

We have talked about monitoring specific aspects, or *parameters*, of the speech wave, and yielding continuous (or, possibly, discrete) functions of time, by essentially 'slicing the speech pie' into simultaneous functions of time. The *parameter extractor* does such an operation. In recognisers, it is often called the *pre-processor*. The parameters might be energies in various frequency bands, *vs.* time, or linear prediction coefficients (LPC), or the fundamental frequency of the voice, or counts of the number of zero-crossings of the signal (or band-limited portions of it), *vs.* time, etc. This might be looked upon as a preliminary *data reduction* stage in recognition, whereby attention is focused on some parameters that are expected to preserve important data, while de-emphasising irrelevant data.

A *feature extractor* can receive parameters and produce a more abstract (further data-reduced) set of important 'information carrying' features, such as determining what portions of the speech are voiced, where the brief silences (that cue the presence of stop consonants) may be, whether the sound is loud and resonant like a vowel, whether the

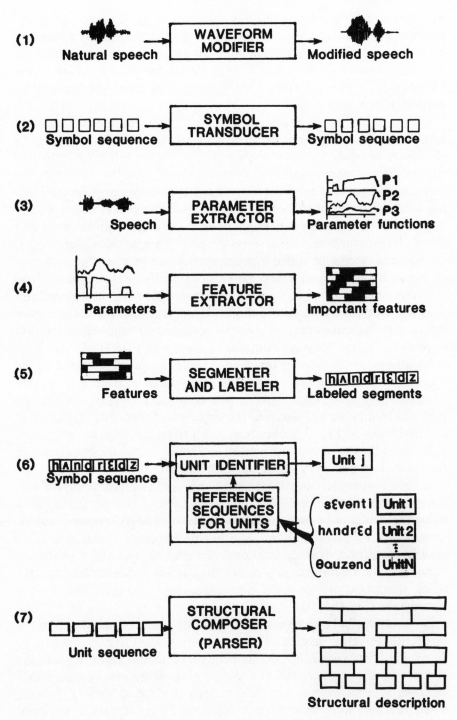

Figure 3.5   Basic building blocks for processing speech and language

speech in a time region is noisy like so-called 'fricatives', etc. Often, the continuous parameters get converted into discrete (especially yes-or-no) decisions that are discretely changing, yielding separate features that are 'on' during parts of the utterance (as shown by the dark bars at the bottom right of Fig. 3.5(4)) and 'off' during other times (the blank white areas in Fig. 3.5(4).

As shown in Fig. 3.5(5) a *segmenter and labeller* can receive the set of asynchronously changing features and produce a linear string of phonemes or other identified segments. The output might be called the 'analysis string' of segments.

Some recognisers combine (specifically, cascade) a *parameter extractor* (perhaps even preceded by a *waveform modifier*) and a *feature extractor* to obtain what they might collectively call a 'feature extractor'. Others might combine a *feature extractor* and a *segmenter and labeller*, to yield what might be called a 'segmentation scheme', a 'segmenter', or an 'acoustic phonetic analyser'. Some workers divide the *segmenter and labeller* into two parts: one that segments based on acoustic changes, and a subsequent part that labels those segments. Since most experience shows that segmentation should not be done without some consideration of intended labels, they are combined together in Fig. 3.5(5).

Common terminology in this field includes frequent reference to the 'front end' of a recogniser, or the 'acoustic-phonetic front end', or the 'phonetic analyser'. These refer to the combination of blocks that go from the input acoustic signal to the sequence of segments. Thus, based on the blocks of Fig. 3.5, the front end involves a possible waveform modifier, followed by a parameter extractor, followed by a feature extractor, followed by a segmenter and labeller.

After a segment string is obtained, an 'analytic phonological rule component' will often be used to modify the actual analysis string into a string that will more closely match expected 'dictionary' pronunciations. Conversely, a 'generative phonological rule component' can be used to modify the expected pronunciations into context dependent pronunciations that should more closely match the analysis string. Either way, the string manipulations of such phonological components are symbol transducers (Fig. 3.5(2)).

An input symbol sequence ('analysis string') may be compared to the expected 'reference sequences' for various units (usually words), to determine what linguistic units appear to be in the input. This is the purpose of the *unit identifier* of Fig. 3.5(6). The most common unit identifier is a 'word matcher', which finds the closest matching word, based on which word's stored pronunciation string is most like the input string. Unit matchers could also be used for smaller units, like phonemes or syllables, or for larger units like phrases or sentences.

Finally, a linear sequence of units or segments can be structurally analysed to determine what grouping of units into larger units seems to have been intended. The *structural composer* does this process of assigning a hierarchy of levels, by which units are grouped together to form larger units, and combinations of those larger units are grouped to form even larger units, etc. A *syntactic parser*, which finds how a word sequence may be analysed into phrases and sentences, is the most common structural composer. However, structural composers can also work at other levels, working with combinations of subunits of words, or working with combinations of sentences into discourses.

It is possible to reverse the arrows on some of these building blocks and have relevant components of *synthesis* systems, or to have 'generative' (top-down) approaches to analysis.

With these building blocks, and the other basic principles discussed earlier in this section, we have the essential prerequisites for discussing the main knowledge sources needed for machine understanding of speech.

A typical system structure

Figure 3.6 illustrates a typical recognition system structure. The speech signals of representative training samples are processed to detect utterance boundaries. A typical procedure for utterance boundary location is shown in Fig. 3.7. Points where energy rises above a threshold level are declared beginnings of words, unless the energy peak is so short in duration that it is clearly not speech, but rather a noise impulse. Endings occur where energy drops below the threshold and stays down for at least some reasonable time. In fact, to distinguish long silences at the ends of words from short stop consonants within words, a silence (or near silence) must last for a duration of at least 100–200 ms to be declared an utterance boundary for most devices. Short noise bursts have to be excluded from the regions called words, by using their short durations and perhaps their spectral character to distinguish them from speech sounds. Breath noise, lip smacks, stop bursts, weak fricatives, and lack of clear gaps between words within connected speech make word boundary location a difficult problem, and a primary reason for errors in recognisers. Changes of sound structure due to the sound structure of adjacent words also create word-boundary-induced problems for connected speech recognisers.

Between utterance boundaries, various features are extracted, in each short time frame, to yield a matrix of $F_i N_i$ numbers, where F_i is the number of features monitored, and N_i is the number of time segments in

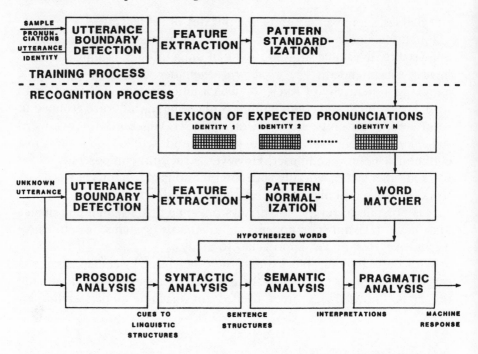

Figure 3.6   A typical speech recognition system involves matching words with stored expectations, and selecting likely word sequences based on prosodic, syntactic, semantic and pragmatic constraints

which such features are extracted. (For simplicity here, we assume that all features are obtained in all time segments, which need not be the case in actual systems.) Each word i that is spoken during training is accompanied by a user-specified (possibly computer-prompted) identification of what that utterance meaning was (i.e. what word sequence was spoken, or what response is expected). A lexicon of expected pronunciations for all the words is thus obtained.

Later, when an unknown utterance is spoken, its matrix of numbers is compared with all the stored matrices, and the one lexical entry that is 'closest' to the input pattern is the selected identity of the word. Hypothesised words may have to be 'warped', or normalised, in time and other parameters, to match the input. Other normalisations may adjust signal amplitudes or other data values to aid proper alignment, comparison and scoring of closeness of fit.

After words have been hypothesised they may be subjected to syntactic, semantic and pragmatic constraints, to select the most likely actual word sequence. Prosodic cues can aid syntactic analyses, by locating phrase boundaries, stresses, regions of phonetic reliability that yield highly reliable word hypotheses, and other structural cues.

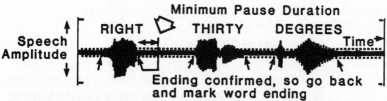

(a) Boundaries between isolated words are detected at ends of silences (low–energy regions) of at least a minimum duration (cf. Martin, 1976).

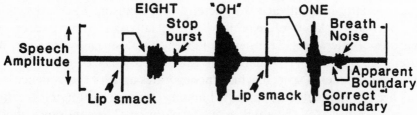

(b) Advanced boundary detection may involve detecting and including stop consonants within words, but excluding lip smacks and breath noise.

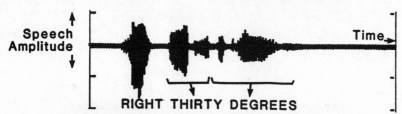

(c) In connected speech, not all energy dips are word boundaries, and most word boundaries will not be exhibited by long silent pauses.

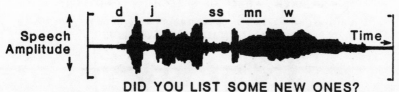

(d) Word boundaries are not evident in continuous speech, and some speech sounds distort or degenerate, and merge with neighboring sounds.

Figure 3.7 The difficulties in finding where words begin and end suggest an error in having word boundaries guide other processes of recognition

As configured in Fig. 3.6, the speech recogniser is a data driven ('bottom-up') extractor of patterns to match to stored patterns. Other system structures are possible.

In Section 3.2 we shall consider recommendations for the best design of each system component, and the best strategies for combining components into systems.

WHAT IS WRONG WITH TRADITIONAL TECHNIQUES?

Ignorance models

Figure 3.8 briefly summarises some limitations that may be noted in the traditional speech recognition algorithms. Most speech recognisers are very dependent upon locating word boundaries, which unfortunately are among the most poorly and inconsistently articulated portions of speech. Locating word boundaries has often proven to be a costly and error-prone critical aspect of most algorithms. Recognisers also give equal attention to all acoustic details. A promising alternative is to consider any 'islands of reliability' or specially consistent portions or features of utterances. Transients and steady states usually receive equal attention. The theory behind such equal focus may be said to be an ignorance model of speech, which incorporates none of the evidence that has been accumulated about how humans focus on certain information carrying aspects of the total acoustic patterns. The ignorance model permits full consideration of any acoustic cues to linguistic contrasts, anywhere in the utterance, but it also can be misled by any acoustic variations not associated with the linguistic meaning.

It can be argued that previous devices for voice input have really been signal matchers, not speech recognisers, since they give no acknowledge-

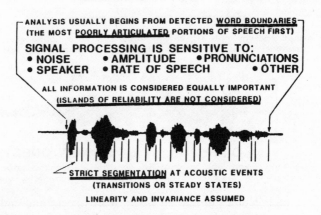

CONCLUSION: Little "speech" knowledge is in current "speech" recognizers.

Such "speech" recognizers could work as well (or as poorly) with sonar signals, seismics, bird whistles, etc.

Figure 3.8 Typical speech recognition procedures appear to be wrong in their failures to acknowledge the special nature of speech, and their improper attention to unreliable data

ment of the distinctive nature of speech, and could work as well with bird whistles, seismic signals, or other non-categorical acoustic contrasts.

At higher levels of linguistic analysis, objections can be raised against the disregard for prosodic features that could provide cues to syntactic structures, and that can provide independent evidence of word identities. A major advantage of prosodic cues is their indication of syntactic structures (such as sentence types, division of sentences into phrases, detection of important words at stressed syllables, cues to subordination and other constructions, etc.). Most recognition techniques, originally designed for isolated words, are thus deficient in seeking or exploiting valuable syntactic bracketing and other acoustic cues to sentence structures. Consequently, recognition techniques often experience combinatorial explosions of alternative word sequences, without the ability to restrict alternative word sequences by prosodic cues. Finite state grammars used in recognition systems have been known for decades to fail to characterise the phrasal groupings of words in continuous sentences, thus leading to wasteful models of allowed word sequences.

Proponents of artificial intelligence can particularly argue the seriousness of the mistake that speech recognition projects have usually ignored the successful human perceiver, and how human perception of speech is accomplished. To AI proponents, it is strange that devices disregard the fact that we do have a working example system that very successfully performs at the speech recognition task, and that system is the human perceiver. Further advances might be expected to come from techniques based on the auditory, phonetic and linguistic categorisation processes that humans do, and the rule-governed variabilities in sound structures that natural English permits. Most recognisers do not even consider phonetic, linguistic, auditory or perceptual methods. No single system currently contains even a major fraction of what is known about speech production, acoustics, hearing and perception within human listeners and linguistic categorisations. General purpose signal processing and pattern matching result in significant sensitivity to irrelevant variabilities due to speaker noise, environmental changes, rate of speaking, microphone movement, etc. Such environmental or acoustic sensitivity is unacceptable in many applications. The knowledge based approaches demand that the development of advanced recognition techniques acknowledge that speech is produced and perceived by humans, and intended to convey linguistic messages.

A common alternative, which is a move towards knowledge based recognition, assumes that recognition should be attempted by detailed phonetic analysis, rather than template matching. That perspective, which has received renewed popularity in the mid 1980s, may be a step in

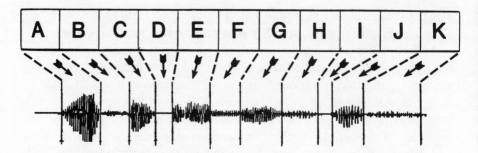

(a) THE LINEARITY ASSUMPTION: IF abstract unit A is before B, THEN there is a segment of speech which is the physical form of A, and it precedes the segment which is the physical form for B. They are like "beads on a string".

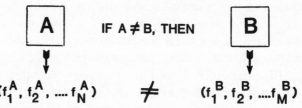

IF A $\neq$ B, THEN

$$(f_1^A, f_2^A, \ldots f_N^A) \quad \neq \quad (f_1^B, f_2^B, \ldots f_M^B)$$

(That is, if A and B are different units, then at least one feature of A and B must be different.)

(b) THE INVARIANCE CONDITION: Every segment A has a defining set of acoustic features, f_1^A, f_2^A, f_3^A, ... f_N^A, for some N, which features all occur for every occurrence of A, and that full set of features NEVER occurs for any other segment B that is distinct from A.

Figure 3.9 Two erroneous assumptions implicitly limiting most recognition procedures are the linearity and invariance conditions

the right direction. However, the traditional phonetic model of speech recognition involves strict assumptions that, by tracking the right 'information carrying' parameters, and using any of several phonemic-segment classification schemes, one can determine the phonemic strings corresponding to those intended by the talker. Then, those phonemic strings may be applied to higher level linguistic analyses to determine words, phrases and utterance meanings. We shall next examine arguments that such a search for a linear sequence of invariant patterns will often fail. Indeed, those assumptions seem to be responsible for the usual experience that limited tasks can be handled more accurately with template matching than with phonemic recognition methods.

Erroneous assumptions of linearity and invariance
Regardless of which specific units are used, recognisers have usually been implicitly based on two reasonable but (in this author's opinion) seriously erroneous assumptions. These assumptions, shown in Fig. 3.9, were characterised by Chomsky and Miller (1963) as the *linearity* and *invariance* conditions. The linearity condition asserts that each segmental unit (phoneme or other size unit) must have associated with it a particular stretch of soundwave, so that if unit A is before unit B in the segmental sequence, the stretch associated with A precedes the stretch associated with B in the acoustic wave. The invariance condition asserts that to each segmental unit A (phoneme or other linguistic unit) there is a specific defining set of physical (acoustic) features, such that each token or variant of A has all those features. Assuming that these two conditions were satisfied for phonemes A, B, ..., a machine could look for the invariant set of features for each phoneme, find all occurrences of each, string these together side by side, and have the basic message distinguishing information needed to establish the wording of an utterance. This is the basis for segmentation and labelling schemes that seek to use the 'information carrying' features of each phoneme (or other unit) to decide what units occur in what sequence in an unknown utterance. Other popular linguistic notions such as 'biuniqueness' and the 'principle of complementary distribution' can be derived from these assumptions. Biuniqueness asserts a one-to-one relationship between abstract linguistic units like phonemes, and physically manifested ('surface') units like phones or allophones, so that each sequence of phones is represented by a unique sequence of phonemes, and each sequence of phonemes represents a sequence of physical phones that is 'unique up to free variation' (i.e. the phonetic sequence is the same in each occurrence, except for irrelevant or non-linguistic variations).

On careful reflection, most phonemicists and most workers in speech recognition would reject the idea that phonemes or other units can always be identified from unique sets of physical features, independent of their context or other factors. Yet, most work in speech recognition has conformed to the linearity and invariance assumptions. They are taken to be at least good approximations to reality, though it is often acknowledged that it is difficult to find the beginning and ending points (boundaries) of phonemes in continuous speech, and phonetic context and other factors will prevent the same features from always occurring for any one unit like the phonemes /t/, /d/, /i/, etc.

What is involved in these usual efforts at labelling segments in speech is some assignment of *associations* between 'levels of representation', involving various size units in the utterance. Thus, sets of 'features' are associated with occurrences of phones, which are in turn assumed to be occurrences of minimal message-distinguishing units or phonemes, which are in turn assumed to pattern into sequences that form words, from which larger units like phrases and sentences are composed.

Linearity and invariance assumptions make for simpler (usually one-to-one) associations, but there are strong reasons to doubt that they are correct. Chomsky and Miller (1963, p. 311) offered examples of words 'writer' and 'rider', which phonemically differ in their fourth segment (/raɪtɚ/ *vs.* /raɪdɚ/), but which are phonetically (i.e. physically) different not in their fourth segments, but rather in their second segments ([rayDr] *vs.* [raːyDr], where the vowel [aː] is longer than the vowel [a]). Thus, vowel length in the second segment is the cue to voicing difference in the consonant in the fourth segment. Linearity and invariance conditions are refuted by these and many other examples of actual distinctions between phonemic and phonetic structures.

These results are by no means isolated exceptions; indeed, the primary reasons for interest in phonological rules for recognition procedures are the context dictated pronunciation variabilities of speech. Phonemes, syllables, and sometimes whole words can be deleted in flowing speech; extra sounds can be inserted as well. The physical shapes of certain phonemes may be quite different in different contexts. For example, Zue and Schwartz (1980) illustrated how the phoneme /t/ may be manifested by unreleased stops, released stops with short bursts, highly aspirated stops, alveolar flaps, etc. In addition to many violations of invariance and linearity that are dictated by the effects of phonetic contexts, other influences such as the grammatical structure of the sentence can alter phonetic manifestations of words (Chomsky and Miller, 1963; Chomsky and Halle, 1968; Lea, 1972).

Engineers and mathematically inclined workers in speech recognition are often inclined to interpret the actual variance and non-linearity associated with linguistic units like phonemes as evidence that those units 'do not exist', 'can't be reliably found', or 'are of little or no use in practical recognisers' (*cf.*, e.g. Grady, *et al.*, 1978). More accurately, these difficulties show the inadequacy of the usual simplistic assumptions involved, and the need for properly characterising the contextual interdependencies and phonological regularities of the language. Detection and identification of linguistic units need not depend on strictly segmenting into linear strings of separate units abutted at strict boundaries, or using features in those segments alone to identify them.

Schemes have been devised for only detecting (but not necessarily establishing the boundaries of) occurrences of various sound categories, using reliable information that is the least variable and most 'robust', including use of contextual cues not coincident with the occurrence of the segment. Experiments have shown that a few general categorisations of speech sounds can be enough to eliminate most words in large vocabularies from being reasonable candidates for identification in the speech (Shipman and Zue, 1982; Huttenlacher and Zue, 1983).

There are some situations where linearity and invariance are more closely approximated than usual. For example (*cf.* Lea, 1980c), stressed syllables are more reliably decoded than unstressed or reduced syllables, and exhibit closer resemblances between surface phonetic form and the underlying phonemic sequence. Also, isolated words and slowly spoken word sequences tend to be more carefully articulated, with less coarticulation and more likelihood of reaching target articulatory positions, so that phoneme-distinguishing features can be more reliably detected. Indeed, it appears (*cf.* Lea, 1975) that rhythm and rate of speech can be used to predict which phonological rules (for fast or slow speech, etc.) apply. Durations, intensities and pitch of vowels can also provide secondary cues to vowel identity, and information about the nature of neighbouring consonants. All this prosodic help to phonemic analysis is in addition to what help prosodics can provide in determining the large-unit (syntactic) structures of phrases and sentences.

Obviously, the fact that prosodic features like stress patterns, rhythm and intonation (which extend over several syllables at once) carry some cues that can be used in the identification of phonemic units provides further proof of the non-linearity and variability of speech. What is more, it would be erroneous to assume that prosodic contrasts themselves are invariably manifested in strict linear sequences. Lea has shown that stressed syllables are sometimes (particularly in phrase-initial positions) manifested by local increases in pitch or voice fundamental frequency, but in other positions other cues are used. Similarly, boundaries between major syntactic phrases can be detected (admittedly, not invariably) from fall-rise 'valleys' in intonation, but those boundaries need not (and, indeed, often do not) occur at the precise time of ending of the wording of one phrase and beginning of the next (Lea, 1973; 1976; 1980c). The boundary cue may be displaced in time from its underlying abstract location at the phrase juncture, thus violating the linearity condition.

Linearity and invariance assumptions are also evident at the level of word matching. The template matching approach to word identification is based on the implicit assumption that, within the tolerance of small 'distances', the word will be manifested by the same pattern. The companion linearity assumption is implicit in the expectation of being able to delimit a region of speech most closely corresponding to each word. The fact that word sequences like *did you* can be pronounced *dija*, and words can merge into each other, suggests the error of assuming invariant pronunciations of each word, which are to be strung in a linear row.

We have seen that stored templates and/or incoming acoustic patterns can be 'warped' in duration (time normalised) or spectral form (e.g. for speaker normalisation or channel normalisation), to provide a closer match for words. The concept is to preserve, and indeed to enhance, invariances, by modifying either the input or the template in systematic ways. In similar fashion, expected pronunciations represented as phonemic strings can be altered by phonological rules, to allow for predictable variations (e.g. *did you* or *dija*) in acceptable pronunciation in various contexts. Such 'phonemic normalisation' or 'controlled sequence warping' can be used to overcome confusions introduced by phonetic changes or errors (insertions, deletions or substitutions). *Generative* phonological rules allow beginning from expected (dictionary) pronunciations of large linguistic units and deriving alternative pronunciations (sequences of small units) which can be directly compared with the acoustic phonetic input. The 'template' is thus warped to match the input. *Analytic* rules work the other way, converting phonetic sequences based on the incoming detailed acoustic data into possible abstract underlying forms that will match lexically stored pronunciations of large units like words or sentences. Most linguistic rules are represented in generative form, and interest in recognition work is either to convert to analytic rules for mapping from inputs to abstract units, or to incorporate a 'hypothesise and test' routine which generates hypothesised messages and tries matching the input with the generatively predicted physical forms for each hypothesised message, until a best match is attained.

ENHANCED TEMPLATE MATCHING SCHEMES
There is some merit in combining ideas from the template matching process with some of the focusing and segmental analyses involved in usual phonetic recognition systems. An example will be illustrated for one of the most popular and successful template matching methods, called *dynamic programming*. Dynamic programming (DP) is a procedure for finding an optimal (least cost) path through a series of states, which, for speech recognition, involves finding a statistically best possible time alignment between an unknown sequence of states (such as

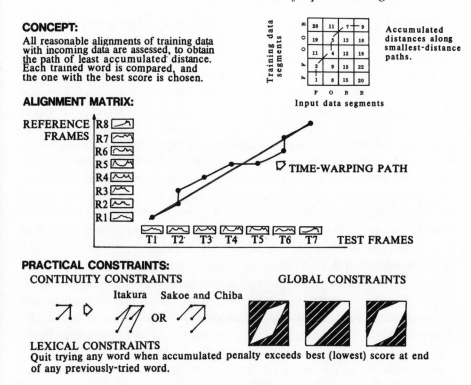

CONCEPT:

All reasonable alignments of training data with incoming data are assessed, to obtain the path of least accumulated distance. Each trained word is compared, and the one with the best score is chosen.

Accumulated distances along smallest-distance paths.

ALIGNMENT MATRIX:

▽ TIME-WARPING PATH

TEST FRAMES

PRACTICAL CONSTRAINTS:

CONTINUITY CONSTRAINTS   GLOBAL CONSTRAINTS

Itakura   Sakoe and Chiba

LEXICAL CONSTRAINTS
Quit trying any word when accumulated penalty exceeds best (lowest) score at end of any previously-tried word.

Figure 3.10 Dynamic programming permits non-linear alignment ('time warping') of input and lexical data, to find the closest matching alignment of data

the short time segments of specific spectral content in a spoken word) and a reference sequence of states. Figure 3.10 illustrates how one can attempt to compare an expected state sequence with an unknown (input) sequence, where, for simplicity of representation here, each spectral template is labelled with a phonetic symbol. (Such segments need not be explicitly labelled or categorised by the dynamic programming system; the notation of phonetic units is illustrated for clarity of presentation, not to imply phonetic analysis in the system.)

Scores, or distance measures, can be defined specifying how far apart the incoming and reference templates are for each alignment of spectral states. Small numbers indicate close similarity, so that reference F is like incoming F (distance = 1), but incoming O is quite different from the reference F (distance = 7). Thus, if we try to align an F with an F, a low penalty will be involved, and such an alignment is locally good. Similarly, aligning an O in another part of the word with an O segment in the reference word will be locally low in penalty.

Practical dynamic programming involves assuming some constraints on reasonable alignments. For example, one typical constraint may state that optimal steps must involve moving vertically up one square (consuming another reference frame, but no more input frames), or right one square (consuming one input frame, but no additional reference frames), or diagonally up and right one square (consuming an equal number of reference and input frames). Other alignment constraints may allow two segments of reference with one segment of input, or *vice versa*. Each such local constraint limits the possible 'global' or whole-word alignment warpings. The minimal accumulation of distances along any path gives the total path score from the beginning of the word to that position along the path. To define the total distance between the reference word and the input, we pick the path with the lowest score that goes from the bottom left corner (word beginnings) to the top right corner (endings of both words). The lowest score path, as shown in Fig. 3.10, collapses the two Fs of the reference into association with the one F on the incoming pattern, and collapses the two reference Os into the one incoming O, while collapsing two incoming Rs into one reference R. Alignment is thus accomplished by choosing the closest of the neighbouring candidate segments.

Such analysis of all allowed alignments of input and reference data is done for each reference word, and the word with the lowest accumulated score on its best path is declared to be the identity of the input word. There are ways of constraining the thorough search of all alignments of all possible vocabulary items, by disallowing alignments that involve more than two segments of input for every segment of reference, or *vice versa* (i.e. that are outside a parallelogram of slopes 2 or 1/2 in the figure), or some such 'reasonableness constraints' on the amount of non-linear warping of alignments. Also, in the midst of computing for any vocabulary reference item, one can rule out that lexical item if its penalties of distances have already accumulated to a score above the lowest score previously obtained for any other whole word in the lexicon. A word could even be ruled out if the accumulated score at some position along its best path suggests that the word will be very likely to yield a whole-word score that is higher than that found for another word.

This algorithm can be enhanced to work with unknown beginning and ending points (Bridle, 1973), and with other refinements. The Viterbi algorithm is a similar algorithm that is also popular (Smith and Sambur, 1980; White and Neely, 1976; Sakoe and Chiba, 1978; Jelinek, 1982).

Although dynamic programming is a major improvement over linear time normalisation or no time normalisation, as earlier systems had, some problems with dynamic programming are: it is very expensive computationally; it depends severely upon locating word or utterance boundaries; it involves *ad hoc* continuity and global constraints on time warping, ignoring speech regularities that might limit allowable warpings; it gives equal attention to all time frames; it gives equal attention to all features or spectral details within any time frame (with usual distance measures); it fails to account for rhythm and rate knowledge, including the tendency for variabilities to occur primarily in unstressed or reduced syllables; it fails to acknowledge that pronunciations change considerably with rate of speaking, so that the coarticulatory undershoot is much greater in more rapid speech; and it is based on strict matching to templates that are determined from simple training samples, thus preserving most of the disadvantages of previous template matching methods.

Figure 3.11 shows several ideas for improving dynamic programming, using knowledge that is domain specific to speech. Several studies have shown the merit of focusing on transient regions in the process of accumulating a distance measure between a reference word and an unknown input. During steady state regions, the spectral data is not changing much, and its redundancy is high, so that segment data are

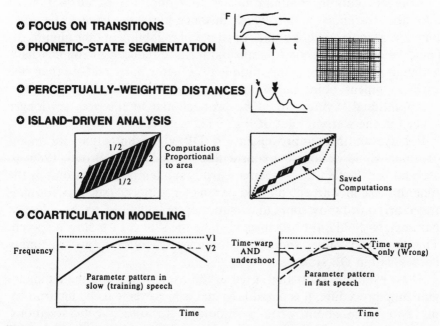

Figure 3.11   Several forms of knowledge about speech can be incorporated as constraints on the dynamic programming process, to increase accuracies and reduce required computations

predictable from previous frames. Transients, on the other hand, provide informative data. By either increasing the frequency of occurrence of data frames in transient regions (i.e. increasing the frame rate) or allowing a higher weighting of the dissimilarity scores where spectral change is rapid, one can focus on important, time-synchronising information.

Segmentation of the feature matrix into sub-phonemic or phonemic units (such as the Harpy system did; Lowerre and Reddy, 1980) can cut computations considerably, since it reduces the number of segments requiring comparisons and distance calculations. If done accurately, such phonetic segmentation could increase word recognition accuracy (*cf.* Silverman and Dixon, 1980).

The distance measure could also be enhanced to focus more significance on perceptually important differences in spectra, rather than attaching equal weight to all spectral differences. For example, a weighting in vowels that was highest on the second formant peak, somewhat lower on the first formant region, even lower on the third formant, and that almost neglected spectral valleys, would be reasonable, based on relative importances of those regions to perception of vowel categories.

A key to cutting computations is to reduce the parallelogram of allowable warpings, within which distance measures have to be computed. If a single 'anchor point', or island of reliability in time alignment, could be obtained, so that parallelograms are reduced to roughly half-length, it could reduce computations by a factor of two. More than one such alignment point could make further reductions possible. The computational savings would be proportional to the area no longer shaded in the warping plot of Fig. 3.11.

Finally, another improvement in DP algorithms that we might consider would be to use a coarticulation model (e.g. Broad, 1986) to account for the fact that, when a word is spoken faster, not only is the time dimension warped, but the parameter patterns (such as formant trajectories) will show more undershoot of target values, so the values of parameters should not be expected to be the same as for slower speech. The parameter values should be non-linearly 'warped', just as timing data is within DP systems.

These examples show that, even in the context of a routine template-matching procedure, it is possible to make improvements by incorporating knowledge about what is important to speech categorisations. Recent work on 'hidden Markov models' ('HMM'; *cf.* Schwartz, 1986; Rabiner and Juang, 1986) can also be viewed as such combinations of statistical template and phonetic approaches.

3.2 *Recommended components in speech recognition systems*

In this section we shall illustrate some of the more promising approaches to various aspects of recognition, and some of the processes that must be accomplished by components of a recognition system. We examine acoustic parameterisation methods, some more reliable ('robust') decisions about major phonetic categories, and detailed phonetic decisions that can determine which phonemes occurred at various regions of the speech. Although such discussions are, for simplicity, described without significant regard for contextual effects, the reader is cautioned to keep in mind the inadequacies of the linearity and invariance assumptions discussed previously. Phonological analyses help adjust sound structures for context and possible variabilities in pronunciation. Word identifications are shown to be facilitated by phonotactic and prosodic constraints, such that even large vocabulary recognition tasks can be handled with a combination of reliable major-category decisions and prosodic patterns coupled with language dictated constraints. The potential contributions from prosodic information are outlined, as are syntactic, semantic and pragmatic constraints. Statistical processes are briefly outlined, and alternative system structures are presented. Rather than attempt to cover every possible type of system, the author has focused here on components suitable for a phonologically based recognition system.

ACOUSTIC PARAMETERISATION AND NORMALISATIONS
Here we consider what parameters might be the most promising to extract, to establish to which equivalence class a speech signal belongs, and how to extract them from the speech signal. As Fig. 3.12 suggests, possible parameters can be divided into *time-domain parameters* and *spectral parameters*.

A glance at a speech waveform such as in Fig. 3.12 suggests that obvious time-domain parameters include peak amplitudes and peak-to-peak measures. One can monitor maxima within the whole utterance, or within moderate size regions like syllables, or within short segments, such as the maximum within each single cycle of the periodic voiced speech regions. Large waveform peaks are produced by the periodic excitations of the human vocal tract by puffs of air from the vocal cords, and the time interval between successive excitation peaks provides the *pitch period*. The pitch period is thus detectable from the time interval between large waveform peaks, or the time interval before the waveform basically repeats itself. A common method for deriving pitch is the *autocorrelation* method (Sondhi, 1968), which assumes that a signal will closely

ACOUSTIC PARAMETERS FOR SPEECH RECOGNITION

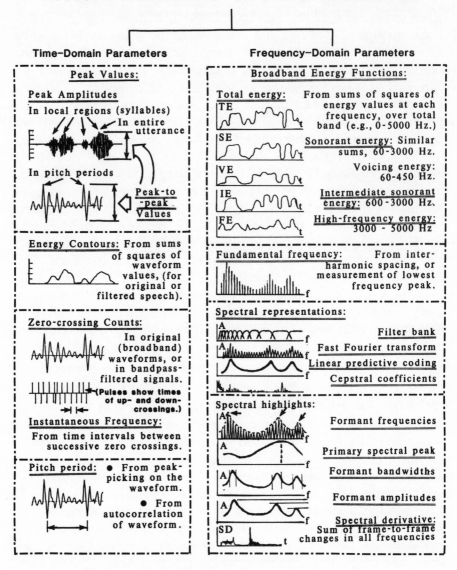

Figure 3.12 A variety of time-domain and frequency-domain parameters can be considered for use in speech recognition systems

correlate with itself at displacements of one (or any integer multiple of one) pitch period. The reciprocal of the pitch period is the *fundamental frequency* of the voice, which is useful in prosodic analysis. Within each pitch period, there are successions of progressively smaller peaks, indicating the resonance characteristics of the human vocal tract as a resonating tube. The number of peaks per pitch period can be a crude indicator of whether the signal is rapidly varying, as in fricatives, or slowly varying, as in vowel-like sounds. For vowel-like sounds, the peak count in each pitch cycle can be a cue to the frequency of the dominant formant or perceptually prominent spectral resonance of the speaker's vocal tract. Crude 'single-equivalent formant' tracking, which estimates the perceptually prominent formant, has been done by simply extracting the duration of the first half-cycle of the waveform after the glottal excitation (Focht, 1967).

Counting the number of times the signal goes through any specific signal level (in either the positive or negative direction, or both) can be a measure of repetitiveness. For example, many research efforts and a few commercial products have explored the use of the number of zero crossings per unit time. The reciprocal of the time interval between two successive zero crossings has been called the *instantaneous frequency* (Baker, 1975). Zero crossing counts and instantaneous frequencies are high for noise-like sounds like fricatives and low for vowel-like periodic sounds.

Another measure of the speech signal, frequently used in recognisers, is the intensity, or energy of the wave, which can be computed as the sum of the squares of the values of the wave at each point in time, within some window of time. Absolute energy is not of interest, since a speech sound like /a/ spoken twice as intensely is usually still intended to be interpreted as the same linguistic unit. Relative energy values in successive time segments is what is of interest. Some speech sounds are inherently more intense than others, given the same vocal effort: an /s/ is more intense than an /f/ or /θ/, so that the word 'sixth' (/sIksθ/) will have less energy in the /θ/ than in the /s/, making it possible to distinguish it from 'six'. A low vowel like /a/ is more intense than a high vowel like /i/ or /u/. All such energy judgements are relative, and some systems thus use an *amplitude-normalisation* procedure, to reference all energy values to a simple maximum number, like 100, and to measure decibels down from that maximum.

Most speech analysis has been done in the frequency domain, with techniques such as *filter banks*, *Fourier analysis* (especially the Fast Fourier transform, or FFT), *linear predictive coefficient* (*LPC*) *analysis*, and *cepstrum analysis*. Decomposing complex speech signals into periodically recurrent sinusoidal components is the central activity of signal processing work, and is justified by (1) sinusoids being 'natural signals' of linear physical (electronic) systems; (2) resonances being prominent cues to articulation configurations; (3) voiced sounds being composed out of harmonics of the voice fundamental frequency; and (4) the ear appearing to do a form of spectral analysis. Also, sinusoids (and some other exponential signals) can be added ('superimposed') in linear systems without interfering with each other; thus the sinusoidal parts that we decompose the signal input into for frequency analysis act as independent, 'orthogonal' signals. In the frequency domain, the periodic glottal puffs that excite the speaker's vocal tract can be represented by a frequency spectrum of harmonics that decrease in relative amplitude at about 12 dB per octave. Resonances of the vocal tract as an acoustic tube are represented in the frequency domain as bands of energy peaked at the resonant frequency. Combinations, or superpositions, of these resonances can represent the overall effect (or *transfer function*) of the complex vocal tract. Radiation out of the mouth or nose can be represented by a frequency spectrum that rises at about 6 dB/octave. Thus, the spectrum of the speech wave is then a product $S(f) = G(f) \cdot H(f) \cdot R(f)$ of the glottal spectrum, the transfer characteristic of the vocal tract, and the radiation factor. The task in speech recognition is usually to establish the transfer function aspects, which indicate the intended speech sound.

Similarly, in the ear of the usual perceiver of speech, the acoustic tube of the outer ear shows a broad resonance at about 2–4 kHz, and the inner ear shows peak responses to high frequencies near the beginning of the cochlea, while low frequencies peak near the far end. Nerves thus pick up different frequencies at different positions along the cochlea, and the auditory nerve seems to accent such spectral cues. The sensory reception view thus suggests the merit of a spectral analysis, though the best models of the ear operations involve portions of transmission lines, rather than parallel bandpass filters.

A resulting advantage for spectral analysis in recognisers is that specific speech sounds tend to produce consistent, recognisable frequency patterns, whereas the time-based acoustic waveforms are difficult to find consistent patterns in. Trained people can successfully 'read' spectrograms to identify phonemes and words, and we might expect machines to reliably use such spectral information to identify correctly unknown inputs. Some recognition systems (Bakis, *et al.*, 1978; Klatt, 1980c, 1986) have been based on using the full short-time frequency spectrum as a local template for matching with spectral data in reference patterns.

Within the spectrum, several parameters have been observed to be particularly useful, while others are observed to be of less value. Again, as with time-based analyses, energies (derived from summing the squares of energy values within frequency regions, rather than summing squares of waveform values) are quite useful. A primary cue to the manner of articulation is the relative energy level; vowels are high energy, while sonorant consonants have less energy, sibilants have lower energies, weak fricatives have quite low total energies, and stops (plosives) may have little or no radiated energy during vocal tract closures. We will consider how to obtain various linguistic categories from various spectral parameters.

In the frequency domain, voice fundamental frequency can be found from the spacing between harmonics, or from cepstral analysis, which separates the harmonic activity from the more gradual changes in spectra due to vocal tract resonances. Alternatively, pitch is derived from the prominent periodicity of the linear predictive residual function, after the poles of the vocal tract resonances are removed from the signal spectrum. Fundamental frequency, or pitch, is particularly useful in prosodic analysis, but is usually not used in phonetic or template-matching schemes.

Among the other possible spectral parameters, bandlimited energy contours, such as the 'sonorant energy' in the frequencies from 60 to 3000 Hz, or the 'voicing energy' in the low frequencies from 60 to 450 Hz, or the high frequency 'sibilant' energy from 3000 to 5000 Hz, can be useful. Tracking natural resonances of the vocal tract, or formants, is difficult to do reliably from the complex FFT spectrum or the output levels from a bank of narrowband filters distributed across the spectrum. However, the smoothed frequency spectrum that results from LPC analysis permits formant tracking to be done with some reliability, using simple peak picking on the LPC spectrum, or pole tracking on the actual LPC model. It is generally acknowledged that if one can derive accurate formant frequency tracks *vs.* time, they can be valuable for determining the phonetic content of speech.

A few studies (e.g. Davis and Mermelstein, 1978) suggest that 'mel-scale cepstral coefficients' can be at least as effective as LPC coefficients or other spectral parameters in determining the phonetic content of speech. Experiments have shown fairly comparable performance in word matching with either LPC coefficients, filter bank outputs, or FFT outputs (*cf.* White and Neely, 1976; Wohlford, Smith, and Sambur, 1980; Dautrich *et al.*, 1983). Less effective were zero crossings counts, formant amplitudes and formant bandwidths. A survey of experts with an average of ten years experience in speech recognition (Lea and Shoup, 1979, 1980) indicated that among the most preferred acoustic parameters were the formants (derived from LPC spectra, for example), fundamental frequency, LPC coefficients, energy measures, and poles of the LPC spectrum. This author favours LPC-derived formants, fundamental frequency (usually derived from autocorrelation analysis), sonorant (60–3000 Hz) energy contour, very low frequency (60–450 Hz) energy, high frequency (3000–5000 Hz) energy, a two-pole (primary spectral peak) analyser, a spectral derivative (monitoring how much the spectrum changes from one 10 ms frame to the next), detection of wideband nasal resonances, and mel-scale cepstral coefficients.

One way to answer the question regarding which acoustic parameters to use in a speech recognition system is to try out all conceivable parameters, and mathematically determine which parameters account for the largest portions of the variance in large samples of speech. Several studies of *principal component analysis*, or *eigenvector analysis*, have demonstrated that the energy in the signal, the balance of energy between high *vs.* low frequencies, and the energies and resonances in the second, first, and third formant regions, are among the consistently important parameters. Speech scientists might argue that they could have told the engineers those parameters, based on the importance recognised in linguistics and speech circles for energy as a manner of articulation cue, the knowledge that high frequency energy is indicative of fricatives while low frequency energy cues voicing and vowel-like character, and the formants are known to be important to articulatory modelling and perceptual models. However, the mathematically oriented proponents of principal component analyses can argue that the rigorous, 'unbiased' derivation of such features from ignorance models of mathematics thus verifies such theoretical or experimental claims, and is more in keeping with machine models.

Developers of new recognition systems will need good microphones, tape recorders, audio cables, earphones, speakers, audio amplifiers, and other acoustics, signal processing and computer equipment. An excellent way to get started quickly on parameter extractions is to purchase standard data acquisition equipment (such as the Digital Sound Corporation A/D conversion system or the Data Translation or Analog Devices A/D boards), and standard software packages, such as the Interactive Laboratory System (ILS) from Signal Technology Incorporated, which includes previously programmed procedures for deriving many of the parameters noted above, and which also permits principal component analyses, and easy experimental comparisons of alternative parameters for specific tasks. Even some basic methods for dynamic programming or word matching are immediately possible with such facilities. For easy research and development, abilities to listen to the speech, display the waveform or its portions, move cursors, alter amplitudes, 'zoom in and out' on the local details of the signal, and slide analysis frames along the waveform, are all desired and possible with standard commercial software. Such software can aid in implementing peak-picking algorithms, zero-crossing counters, energy calculations, fundamental frequency estimation, autocorrelation analysis, design and application of digital filters, FFT analysis, LPC analysis, formant tracking, and other parameterisations.

We shall next consider the use of various parameter sets in deriving various linguistic contrasts, or categorical features.

ROBUST CATEGORICAL FEATURES

Figure 3.13 illustrates how various parameters may be used to derive useful categorical decisions. For example, voicing can be detected either by (1) observing that the very low frequency energy exceeds a threshold; (2) noting a high value of the ratio LF/HF between the low frequency (60–900 Hz) energy and the high frequency (3000–5000 Hz) energy; (3) detecting small numbers of zero crossings per unit time; or (4) noting whether an F_0 value is detected for the local region. These alternatives are listed in order of decreasing merit, in this author's judgement.

Syllabic nuclei are detectable from peaks in the sonorant energy function, bounded by significant dips (such as 4 or 5 dB dips) (Lea, 1974, 1976, 1980, 1986d). The boundaries of each nucleus may be fairly reliably taken to be at the points where energy drops down to half of the total amount of dip at that syllable boundary. A slight refinement could involve replacing the sonorant energy function by a 'perceived loudness function', which is spectrally weighted to be large in vowels and other parts of the syllabic nucleus. It is also conceivable to adjust sonorant energy contours, and durations of nuclei, based on vowel height as determined from the value of formant F_1. This could help equalise the chances of all syllables being detected as substantial high energy 'chunks' surrounded by energy dips.

Algorithms exist for accurate detection of syllabic nuclei (Lea, 1974; Mermelstein, 1975), and their performances indicate that this is one of the most reliable decisions that can be made in recognition. When syllables are bounded by sonorant consonants, not obstruents, the energy dips are not sufficient to be always reliably detected, but Lea (1976) still obtained over 90% correct syllable nucleus detection in the difficult case of all-sonorant sentences.

Sibilant detection is possible with either the high frequency (3000–5000 Hz) energy function, or, preferably, the ratio of the low frequency (60–900 Hz) to the high frequency (3000–5000 Hz) energy (see Fig. 3.13(c)). If this ratio is below a threshold value, the spectrum is dominated by high frequencies, so that a noisy, intense fricative (specifically, a *sibilant*) is present. (Many axis crossings per unit time is also a cue to sibilants.) Another testing factor is that the sound should

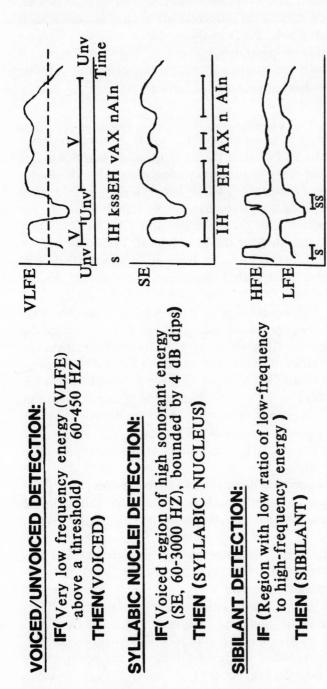

VOICED/UNVOICED DETECTION:

IF(Very low frequency energy (VLFE)
   above a threshold)   60-450 HZ

THEN(VOICED)

SYLLABIC NUCLEI DETECTION:

IF(Voiced region of high sonorant energy
   (SE, 60-3000 HZ), bounded by 4 dB dips)

THEN (SYLLABIC NUCLEUS)

SIBILANT DETECTION:

IF (Region with low ratio of low-frequency
   to high-frequency energy)

THEN (SIBILANT)

PHONETIC LATTICE:

Incomplete segment identifications, with
possible overlaps and multiple categorizations.

Figure 3.13   Rules for detection of robust phonetic features

have moderate to high energy, to contrast it with weak fricatives like /f, θ/. The duration of the sibilant noise must be longer than 40 ms or so, to ensure that the sound is not simply a short noisy stop burst.

Sibilants are another one of the most reliably detected categories of speech sounds, with well over 90% usually correctly detected (*cf.* Medress, 1980).

Retroflexive detection is another reliable analysis procedure. Retroflexives (/r/ and /ɝ/) are detectable from a low value of the third formant F_3 (below a threshold of about 1750 Hz, and possibly as low as 1600 Hz), plus a pattern of F_2 and F_3 being very close (i.e. $F_3 - F_2$ is small). Such prominent F_3 movements down into a retroflexive and out again are evident in Fig. 3.14(a). Retroflexives also have no energy 'valley' in mid frequencies, so they look somewhat like back vowels.

One problem with retroflexive detection is that F_2 and F_3 also come very close together in velar consonant transitions (such as around /g/ or /k/), but those are usually at a distinctively higher frequency than for retroflexives, and they usually show the low energy of obstruents, in contrast to that of a sonorant retroflexive.

Nasal stops, as shown in Fig. 3.14(b), are associated with broad formant bandwidths, very low (250 Hz) formant F_1 and dominant very low frequency energy, and abrupt spectral changes in formant patterns, as new formant positions occur due to the nasal tract resonances. Nasals are weaker than vowels, and they show antiresonances, or spectral dips. F_2 is weak or absent. The low energy around 800 Hz (due to an antiresonance) and weaker high frequencies help distinguish nasals from /l/s.

Vowel detection is also quite reliably accomplished, based on the high (sonorant) energy region of each syllabic nucleus and the presence of voicing, and procedures for stripping away the non-vowel parts of the nucleus. The nucleus includes at least one vowel, plus possible sonorant consonants (nasal, retroflexives, laterals, or glides). Beginning with the delimited high energy region of the nucleus, one can strip off the retroflexives and nasals that are already detected, to leave the vowel and any yet undetected sonorants (including laterals and/or glides). Other primary cues to vowels are the prominent formant structures and the major energy concentration at low frequencies. While it is usually true that the vowel is the highest energy region in the syllable, this is not invariably true; in a word like 'peel', the vowel will have lower energy than the /l/.

If the formants change rapidly or in major amounts, and especially if the vowel seems long in duration, there is a possibility of two steady state regions due to two or more vowels in the region, or a diphthong, or a vowel plus yet unidentified sonorants.

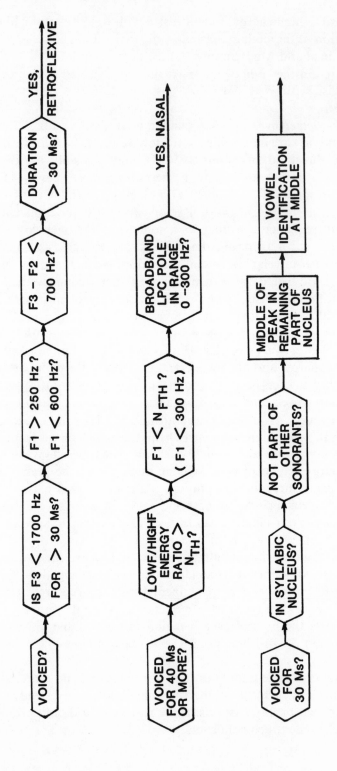

Figure 3.14   Procedures for detecting major classes of sonorant sounds

This general procedure for vowel detection and handling of complex vocalic nuclei has proven quite successful in phonetic analysis routines (Medress *et al.*, 1978; Medress, 1980).

Alternatively, algorithms can be designed to search directly for a match to the specific vowel sound patterns, such as the formant structures for /i/, /a/, /u/, etc. Throughout the history of speech recognition, vowel identification has been generally successful, particularly for simple syllable structures.

Stop consonants are another general class of sounds which have often been included in preliminary classification procedures, with considerable success. Stops are evidenced by: gaps, or clear steady states of low energy (either silences or low energy voicing bars); large values of the spectral derivative, or extensive frequency spectrum change from one time frame to the next, at the opening of the closure; bursts of noisy, broadband energy of short duration; and aspiration, or frictional sound following the gap and burst, of moderate duration ($\sim$ 50 ms), for unvoiced stops. Durations of the gap, burst, etc., need to be within expected limits. Problems with stop detection include these:

- Unreleased utterance-final stops are hard to detect, except by sudden changes and energy drops at the consonant closure.
- Voiced stops don't always show clear gaps, and have less distinctive cues (no burst, no aspiration, lower spectral derivative).
- Alveolar flaps are very short, and voiced regardless of intended phonemic state of voicing, thus being difficult to detect reliably.
- Glottal stops (such as at vowel–vowel boundaries) can be confused with oral stops.

These general categorical decisions leave one or more 'left over categories' to account for weak fricatives /f, θ, v, ð), laterals /l/, glides /w, y/, and possible flaps, latter parts of diphthongs, transitional areas, and other areas that can't be readily classified as sibilants, retroflexives, nasals, vowels or stops. At this point most of the reliably detected manner classes have been isolated. Several recognisers have depended on such preliminary manner-of-articulation decisions as the first stage of speech segmentation and labelling. It will be shown that such manner-class information can aid word identifications in large vocabulary applications.

DETAILED PHONETIC DECISIONS
Given preliminary decisions, a recogniser can attempt to narrow down the alternatives by attempting vowel identification, specific determination of diphthongs, detection of laterals, glides, affricates, weak

fricatives, stop identification, and nasal identification. Effects of context can be taken into account, and phonological rules applied to compile a pronunciation that can be matched to expected pronunciations of words in the vocabulary.

Vowel identification is a rather well developed aspect of recognition. Given the high energy regions of syllabic nuclei with formant structures that do not robustly classify as non-vowel sonorants, but which have major energy concentrations at low frequencies, we can identify vowels by formant values or other acoustic features.

Vowels can be identified by their formant positions. A simple identifier could match incoming formant values to stored expectations about formant values for various vowels, where the stored templates were obtained from standard published values, such as the Peterson–Barney (1952) studies obtained, or from previous spoken versions of those vowels by the current speaker, etc. Figure 3.15 shows two ways of summarising the formant values for various English vowels. These displays suggest distinctive formant patterns for each vowel, and also illustrate the tie back to articulatory positions that determine those formant frequencies.

The regularities summarised in Fig. 3.15 help one remember the formant frequencies and other spectral relationships for various vowels. If F_1 is low, the vowel is high; if F_1 is high, the vowel is low. If F_2 is low, it is a back vowel; if F_2 is high, it is a front vowel. The vowel /ɝ/ has a low F_3, and F_3 and F_2 close. We thus have five general vowel categories: high front, low front, high back, low back, and ɝ-like.

A few other parameters help establish vowel identities. The 'spectral balance' is a general shape variable, indicating whether more energy is at low frequencies (under 1000 Hz), which is true for back vowels, or if higher frequencies (above 1200 Hz or more, as for front vowels) have a higher energy than for neutral vowels. 'Roundedness' of vowels (as for /u, o, ɔ/) is characterised by lower than usual values of the sum $F_1 + F_2 + F_3$ (overall effect is lower frequency concentration).

The 'prosodic' features of vowel energy and duration (and even fundamental frequency, F_0) also provide confirming cues to vowel identity. High vowels have low energy, short durations and high F_0; low vowels are the opposite. Another vowel distinction, occasionally referred to as *tense vs. lax* levels, distinguishes the longer /æ, a, u/ *vs.* shorter but articulatorily similar /ɛ, ʌ, ʊ/, respectively.

When two formants (like F_2 and F_3 for front vowels, and F_1 and F_2 for back vowels) are closely spaced and look like one peak, the bandwidth and the increased (combined) amplitudes can be used to detect that there really are two formants there, and thereby establish all three formant frequencies.

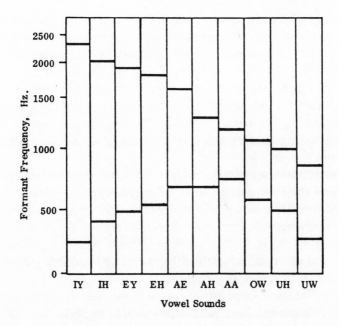

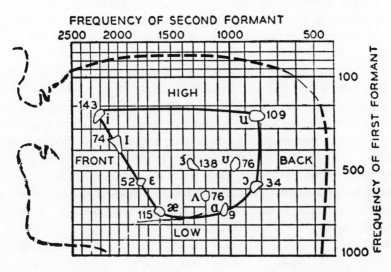

Figure 3.15   Alternative illustrations of the formant values of various vowels. The F1–F2 vowel diagram shows an association with articulatory positions.

Durations of vowels are basically a result of the time it takes to move from a consonantal obstruction to the position for the vowel, and back to another obstruction, so that low vowels are longer than high vowels because the distance travelled is greater. Also, it is easy to recall that wide open tubes ('horns'), like the /æ/ and /a/ involve, produce higher energy sounds, while sound is 'closed off' more by the high tongue articulations of /u/ and /i/. Equivalently, it is easier to remember that the amplitudes of the formants are determined by the frequencies of the lower formants (especially F_1) by recalling that the lower formants 'ride on' the high amplitude 'skirts' of higher resonances. Nearby resonances boost a formant's amplitude. Thus, vowel amplitude is determined largely by the F_1 frequency, since its level is always greater than the amplitudes of higher frequency resonances, and low frequencies also mask higher frequencies.

Since a formant amplitude is thus determined considerably by the frequency of the formant, formant amplitudes are not usually expected to provide much useful additional information in recognition. Amplitudes primarily help confirm what detected formant frequencies suggest. If a spectral peak is higher amplitude than what might have been expected (and of broader bandwidth), it can be hypothesised to contain two very close, unresolved formants.

We have discussed formant information without saying where in the duration of the vowel these parameters should be measured. Generally, such 'cross-sectional' information is obtained from the region of the highest energy in the vowel, or from a point which is about one-third of the way from the apparent beginning to the apparent ending of the vowel.

Other cues to vowel identity can be extracted from how the formants or other parameters move during the vowel. More movement will be evident for diphthonal vowels. Also, in connected speech, the ideal values of formants may never be actually reached, as articulation moves quickly from a consonant into the vowel, and before ideal positions are attained, movement begins to reach the following consonant configuration. Some initial attempts have been made to extrapolate formant 'trajectories' to intersect at 'intended target' values of the formants, and to associate that target set of values with the intended vowel identity (*cf.* Broad, 1986).

Diphthong detection represents another refined categorical decision that might be attempted. Diphthongs are characterised by long durations, and may be confused with vowel plus glide, or vowel plus liquid, combinations. A prominent characteristic is the smooth changing formant pattern, which is strictly dictated by the diphthong identity: /OI/ moves from a low frequency pattern similar to /ɔ/ to an /I/-like, or /i/-like, pattern; aI moves from an /ɑ/-like pattern to an /I/- or /i/-like pattern; /aʊ/ shows movement from /a/-like to an /ʊ/-like formant pattern. During such transitions, the spectral balance changes prominently, as higher formants are masked by the two close (and hence intense) lower formants during the /ɑ/-like and /ʊ/-like portions, but those higher resonances become evident as articulation movement causes the low formants to separate. Notice that F_1 drops for all three diphthongs, and F_2 rises prominently for /ɔI/ and /aI/, and drops and almost disappears for /aʊ/. To find diphthongs, look for long vowel-like areas with these characteristic formant patterns.

Several remaining refined categorical decisions still need to be discussed, including detection of lateral, glide, affricate and fricative manners of articulation, plus place of consonant articulations to identify.

Laterals are fairly difficult to detect. They have F_1 and F_2 low (F_1 lower than for vowels, usually) and are /o/-like in spectrographic appearance, but they are weaker than /o/ usually, and they appear on the edges of detected syllabic nuclei. Laterals have less energy in F_2, F_3, or F_4 due to a zero in the spectrum. They have an extra formant at high frequencies, and they show discontinuity with neighbouring vowels.

Glides are also difficult to detect. The glide /y/ is /i/-like, but shows more rapid transitons. A little dip in F_3 often is evident in F_3 contours during /y/s. The glide /w/ is characterised by a low F_2, and major transitions into or out of low F_2 condition. These glides show constantly changing patterns. Low frequencies rise in amplitude before the higher frequencies do, when /w/ is released.

In general, for /w, y, r, l/, F_1 is low in the first 50–100 ms, and each of these sounds have lower amplitudes at low frequencies than vowels do. The low frequency peak is wider for /r/ and /l/ than for /y/. The second formant in /w/ is lower (about 700 Hz). While /r/ and /w/ have essentially no energy about 1800 Hz, /l/ and /y/ have high frequency peaks. Transitions from identified vowels help identify these sounds.

Affricates are combinations of stop characteristics followed by fricative characteristics. They can be confused either with stop plus fricative combinations or with aspirated stops. They can sometimes be distinguished from aspirated stops by duration and intensity. Some systems simply categorise affricates as stop-fricative sequences.

Fricatives, in general, have a broadband spectrum, for which the high frequency energy is as much as or more than the low frequency energy. They are noisy, and can be detected from many zero crossings, also. *Weak fricatives* (f, θ, in contrast to sibilants) are weak throughout their durations, and sometimes difficult to distinguish from silences. Weak fricatives are usually longer than stops in duration, however. Voiced fricatives are shorter but higher in amplitude due to the presence of vocal cord vibration. Recognisers can tell /s/ from /ʃ/ by whether the prominent spectral peak is at higher (4000 Hz or higher) or a lower

(2500 Hz) frequency region. A flat noise spectrum characterises an /f/. In general, it is the overall spectrum of the noise for a fricative that suggests its identity. Also, it is valuable to determine its state of voicing, to distinguish /s/ from /z/, /f/ from /v/, etc. This, as we have already seen, can usually be determined reliably. However, in connected speech, or medial portions of isolated words, phonemically voiced sounds may be devoiced, and phonemically unvoiced sounds may be at least partially voiced in actual physical form.

Stop identification involves voicing detection and a decision about place of articulation. Voicing tells us whether we have the class /p, t, k/ or the class /b, d, g/; place of articulation tells us which one of the three in the appropriate class is actually present. In addition to usual energy-based voicing decisions throughout the stop, other stop voicing cues include whether there is aspiration, and whether there is a delay after opening of the consonant closure before the formant structure becomes apparent (*voice onset time*).

Place of articulation has in the past been determined primarily from the features of the release period of the stop (i.e. the burst). The frequency of concentration in the burst is low for [p] and [b], medium for [k] and [g] but quite variable for these velar/palatal sounds, and high (like an /s/ spectrum) for [t] and [d]. A prepalatal position of the tongue (as in /t/) is characterised by $F_2 - F_1$ being large, and F_2 and F_3 being maximally high. A bilabial closure has a low frequency energy concentration as do other labial articulations (recall /u/ and /w/). A useful mnemonic is to recall that as you look at the human vocal system, the closed lip of /p/ is 'lowest', the alveolar [t] is highest, at the roof of the mouth, and the velar [k] is somewhere in between; this is the lowest-highest-medial pattern of burst concentration for p-t-k, respectively.

Thus, the F_2 energy concentration rises in the transitions after labial stops, and one can characterise transitions as moving away from 'locus' positions or 'hubs' for the stops, which hubs can be estimated by extrapolating formant trajectories further into the stop.

Some spectral balance changes also indicate the stop identity, as indicated here:

ba: low frequencies rise in amplitude before higher frequencies; same for wa;

pa: no pronounced high intensity spectral peaks are evident while the vocal tract is closed, and a stable spectrum is evident after release (there is, after all, no resonating tube in front of the /p/ articulation);

da: higher frequencies rise in amplitude first (same for ya);

ta: /t/ exhibits a higher frequency spectral peak (it has a short tube in front of the closure position);

ga: the earliest energy onset is at mid frequencies;

ka: the burst has a mid-frequency spectral peak (it has a longer tube in front of the closure).

The alveolar flap [r] is like a [t] or [d], but reduced in intensity, short in duration and without aspiration.

Nasals [m], [n], and [ŋ] are distinguishable by their spectral peaks during closure, with [m]'s peak at about 1300 Hz, while the peak for [n] is at about 1800 Hz, and that for [ŋ] about 2000 Hz. Transitions into and out of nasals also show the spectral characteristics of the corresponding labial, alveolar, and velar oral stops.

PHONOLOGICAL ANALYSES

The various acoustic parameter extractors and phonetic category detectors provide the information needed to specify the sound structures of utterances, but procedures are needed for combining all these decisions into a specification of the phonetic sequence of the utterance. We can detect and identify vowels, diphthongs, nasals, laterals, retroflex-ives, glides, sibilants, weak fricatives, stops and affricates. However, we then need a strategy for combining all that information so it is suitable for comparing with expected pronunciations, to decide what message was said. Several somewhat distinctive strategies for phonologic se-quence matching have been considered, including:

Centisecond labelling. Phonetically classify each 10 ms time frame of the speech, based on its own internal features and how they match those expected for each phoneme, as they have been outlined previously, then use that long sequence of classifications to match to expected pronunciations.

Separate segmentation and labelling. Segment at major acoustic bound-aries, defined by major variations in robust important features, and then select the best phonetic label for each of those acoustic segments.

Phonetic detection without boundaries. Detect presence of phonetic categories and specific phone identities based on the previously discussed manner and place characteristics, and thus specify *central positions* of those apparent occurrences as detected phonetic units, but do not specify segment boundaries (and then attempt to match the order of detected units with the expected order of phonetic units for various words).

Phonetic lattice. Detect, and find the beginning and ending (boundaries) of, phonetic units, based on the manner and place characteristics, and allow alternative choices as to the identity of various regions as well as alternatives as to where units begin and end, to yield a phonetic 'lattice' of overlapping alternative sound sequences which can be matched to expected sequences.

Strict phonetic segmentation and labelling. Find (i.e. detect, and specify boundaries of) a strict sequence of phonetic units (either sub-phonemic segments, or phonemes, or transemes, etc.) that completely cover the utterance without overlapping.

The usual goal sought in recognition has been either strict phonetic segmentation and labelling or else separate acoustic segmentation and subsequent first-choice phonetic labelling. Studies, as in the ARPA SUR project, have allowed several alternative choices for labelling each segment, where labels have been based on the most likely or 'closest' phonetic categories. Thus, probability vectors or preference lists are composed for each segment, indicating the first choice label for the segment, the second choice label, the third, etc. Order of choices is based on the closeness to the acoustic characteristics of the analysed segment. Some systems, like the BBN HWIM system, have allowed alternatives on segmentation, so any region might be divided into one, two or more labelled portions.

Since there is some variability in the phonetic sequence that might be found for repetitions of the same word, there are several issues involved in word matching from phonetic sequences. They include: how to deal with phonetic analysis errors; how to score, or rate, alternative phonetic sequences and their matches to stored sequences; how to use phonological rules to best match the analysis and stored sequences, and account for acceptable variability; how to handle word boundary effects; and how prosodic features interact with phonetic analyses.

Any actual context-independent phonetic analysis will introduce errors, like misidentification of a vowel or consonant, failure to locate a segment that actually was in the word and is useful to know in determining the word identity, and insertion of apparent segments that were 'not there' or not expected to be found in the word. The word matching process, including any phonological rules, must be able to recover from such errors.

Segmentation and labelling must include scoring procedures, for assessing how sure the analysis is about the various claimed segments and their identities. A measure of likelihood of correctness or error might be used for scoring. Then, another task for the word matcher will be how to combine those local assessments to obtain a score for how close the whole phonetic sequence is to that of each stored word.

Recognisers must consider whether to retain knowledge of only the best scoring phonetic unit for each portion of speech, or whether to retain a vector of scores of various phonetic labels, and thus to give a priority list of most likely labels for each of the segments. The same issue arises at the word level; shall we choose only the most likely (highest scoring) word, or retain a list of possible words and their relative scores, for each region of the incoming speech. These are typical problems in the search mechanisms of AI systems, regarding the merit of 'best-first' analysis, *vs.* 'breadth-first' analysis, *vs.* a compromise like the 'best-few-first' analysis used in several speech recognisers (Reddy and Lowerre, 1980; Wolf and Woods, 1980).

Alternative acceptable pronunciations of words can be represented in any of several ways: (1) *generative rules* that explicitly expand a dictionary pronunciation into alternative realistic strings such as might be derived from acoustic phonetic detectors; (2) *analytic rules* that alter the detected phonetic string to match more closely expected pronunciations; or (3) implicit *enumeration* of alternative word pronunciations, as in phonetic networks that expand the full set of dictionary sequences and physical sequences that might be expected. The rules are procedural methods for transducing one sequence into another, while the enumeration is a structured listing of choices without any explanation of how one pronunciation might be derived from another.

Alternative word pronunciations can be specified by a *pronunciation network* that acts like an implicit set of phonological rules (*cf.* the branches in a pronunciation network indicate acceptable alternative pronunciations, such as for the word 'Lafayette'. The first syllable can be pronounced with an /ɑ/ vowel or an /æ/ vowel; the latter half of the word can have an /i/, or an /ɑɪ/ diphthong, or an /ə/ followed by a glide /y/.) This network permits efficient specification of six alternative pronunciations.

Phonological rules can perform pronunciation modifications, such as changing the values of features (+ voiced $\gg$ − voiced, etc.), deleting segments (/potæsiəm/ $\gg$ /ptæsim/), and adding segments (/pritɛns/ $\gg$ /pritɛnts/). Sample rules in Fig. 3.16(b) show how alveolar flapping (/t/ $\gg$ /d/), palatisation (/didju/ $\gg$ /dijə/), homoorganic stop insertion (/ns/ $\gg$ /nts/) or deletion (/nts/ $\gg$ /ns/), and other pronunciation changes can be represented by rules. See Oshika *et al.* (1975) and Cohen and Mercer (1975) for other phonological rules.

One other type of phonological information might help in identifying words in speech. That is the so-called 'phonotactic information' or language dictated constraints on allowable sound sequences of the language. For simple examples, it is known that no English words have /ŋ/ or /ʒ/ initially in the word, while /h/ does not appear word-finally.

FEATURE-CHANGING RULES:

(a) ALVEOLAR FLAPPING

$$\left\{\begin{matrix} t \\ d \end{matrix}\right\} \rightarrow [\text{ɾ}] \Bigg/ \left[\begin{matrix} V \\ \alpha\,\text{stress} \end{matrix}\right] \left(\begin{matrix} r \\ n \end{matrix}\right) \underline{\quad} \left[\begin{matrix} V \\ \beta\,\text{stress} \end{matrix}\right]$$

$\alpha > \beta$ or both reduced,
or both primary–stressed

(b) PALATALIZATION

$$\left[\begin{matrix} +\,\text{alveolar} \\ +\,\text{obstruent} \end{matrix}\right] \rightarrow [+\,\text{palatal}] \Bigg/ \underline{\quad} (\text{\#})[+\text{palatal}]$$

DELETION RULES:

(c) SCHWA DELETION

$$[\text{ə}] \rightarrow \phi \Bigg/ \left[\begin{matrix} C \\ +\,\text{stop} \\ -\,\text{voice} \end{matrix}\right] \underline{\quad} \left[\begin{matrix} C \\ +\,\text{stop} \\ -\,\text{voice} \end{matrix}\right]$$

(d) HOMORGANIC STOP DELETION

$$\left[\begin{matrix} C \\ +\,\text{stop} \\ \alpha\,\text{place} \end{matrix}\right] \rightarrow \phi \Bigg/ \left[\begin{matrix} C \\ +\,\text{nasal} \\ \alpha\,\text{place} \end{matrix}\right] \underline{\quad} (\text{\#})\;C$$

(e) GEMINATE REDUCTION

$$C_1 \rightarrow \phi \underline{\quad} \text{\#}C_2 \text{, where } C_1 \equiv C_2$$

INSERTION RULES:

(f) HOMORGANIC STOP INSERTION

$$\phi \rightarrow \left[\begin{matrix} C \\ +\,\text{stop} \\ \alpha\,\text{place} \end{matrix}\right] \Bigg/ \left[\begin{matrix} C \\ +\,\text{nasal} \\ \alpha\,\text{place} \end{matrix}\right] \underline{\quad} \left[\begin{matrix} C \\ +\,\text{fricative} \end{matrix}\right]$$

Figure 3.16 Phonological rules are illustrated which can change features, and delete or insert segments. Rule 'A arrow B/C' is read 'A is rewritten as B in the context C'. Square brackets enclose phonetic features of segments, while parentheses enclose optional elements. Symbols α and β are numeric variables, # means a word boundary, V is a vowel and C a consonant, and ϕ is the 'null' segment (so that A arrow ϕ deletes unit A, and ϕ arrow A inserts an A)

Some consonants /v, ð, z, č, ǰ/ can only occur alone (as the only consonant, with no clustering with other consonants) in the beginnings of English words. Others can be alone or only as the first one in a cluster: /b, d, g, s, š, θ/. Others must be the last member if such a cluster occurs: /y, w, r, l, m, n/. Some consonants /p, t, k, f/ can be the first, last, or middle consonant in such clusters. If a word begins with a fricative followed by a consonant followed by another consonant, and then at last the vowel comes, the initial fricative must be an /s/, the next consonant must be an unvoiced stop, and the third initial consonant may be a liquid or glide. Other consonant cluster constraints are known, including ones for *word-final* consonant clusters.

LEXICAL CONSTRAINTS

Figure 3.17 illustrates the results from studies by Zue and his colleagues at Massachusetts Institute of Technology (MIT; Shipman and Zue, 1982; Huttenlocher and Zue, 1983), which vividly show the merits of exploiting phonotactic constraints of the English language. We have already seen that the general manner and voicing classes illustrated in Fig. 3.17(a) can be fairly reliably detected in speech. The phonemes are grouped in Fig. 3.17(a) according to the degree of vocal tract constriction they involve. Obviously, knowledge of the general classes illustrated will reduce a phonemic recognition problem down from 40 or so alternative phonemes to a selection among a few remaining candidates within the detected class. Zue and his colleagues showed that recognition with a large (20 000 word) vocabulary can be reduced to a selection among just a few confusable words, once the major phonetic categories are established.

Each word in the 20 000 word dictionary was represented in two ways: as a sequence of consonant (C) or vowel (V) labels, or as a sequence of cover symbols (for illustration purposes, this author used T for stops, S for sibilants, F for weak fricatives, N for nasals, R for retroflexives and V for vowels), each one representing one of the six classes. If all that is known is the sequence of Cs and Vs making up a word, it is still the case that the number of words having that sequence is a small fraction of the large vocabulary; 300 words were uniquely specified, and the average number of candidate words with that sequence of Cs and Vs is 25. In the worst case (CVC words), 1500 words, or only 7.5% of the vocabulary, are confusable with the word after C–V distinctions. If all six major categories can be reliably determined, throughout the word, then one-third of the vocabulary is uniquely identified, the average number of words with the same pattern is only 2, and the worst case is only 200

BASED ON DEGEE OF VOCAL-TRACT CONSTRICTION (MANNER OF ARTICULATION)

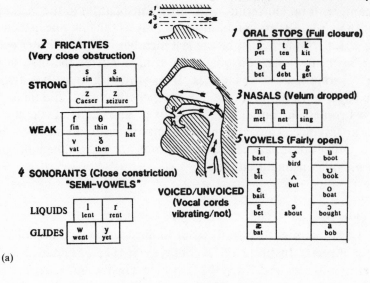

2 FRICATIVES
(Very close obstruction)

STRONG	s sin	s shin
	z Caeser	z seizure

WEAK	f fin	θ thin	h hat
	v vat	ð then	

4 SONORANTS (Close constriction)
"SEMI-VOWELS"

LIQUIDS	l lent	r rent
GLIDES	w went	y yet

VOICED/UNVOICED
(Vocal cords
vibrating/not)

1 ORAL STOPS (Full closure)

p pet	t ten	k kit
b bet	d debt	g get

3 NASALS (Velum dropped)

m met	n net	n sing

5 VOWELS (Fairly open)

i beet	ɜ bird	u boot
I bit	ʌ but	ʊ book
e bait		o boat
ɛ bet	ə about	ɔ bought
æ bat		a bob

(a)

FREQUENCY IN KHz			

TIME, MS → 0   100

ɔ ɔ s p ɛ ktr ə m ɒ v s p i tʃ ɪ ə t ɑ ɪ n
C V C C V CCCVC VC CC V CC VC C V V   C
F V S T V TRV VF ST V TS VN T V V   N

MIT EXPERIMENTS

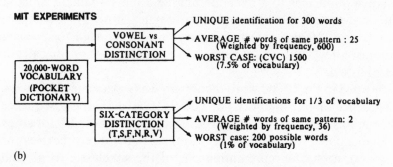

20,000-WORD VOCABULARY (POCKET DICTIONARY)	VOWEL vs CONSONANT DISTINCTION	UNIQUE identification for 300 words
		AVERAGE # words of same pattern : 25 (Weighted by frequency, 600)
		WORST CASE: (CVC) 1500 (7.5% of vocabulary)
	SIX-CATEGORY DISTINCTION (T,S,F,N,R,V)	UNIQUE identifications for 1/3 of vocabulary
		AVERAGE # words of same pattern: 2 (Weighted by frequency, 36)
		WORST case: 200 possible words (1% of vocabulary)

(b)

Figure 3.17   Major phonetic categories, based on manner of articulation, can be sufficient to reduce a large vocabulary recognition problem down to a selection among a very small number of words with the detected sequence of categories (*cf.* Shipman and Zue, 1982; Huttenlocher and Zue, 1983)
(a) Reliably detected phonetic categories can be based on the manner of articulation
(b) Using either a simple vowel-consonant discrimination or the reliable 6-category manner classification can reduce a large vocabulary problem down to a selection among a small set of similar words

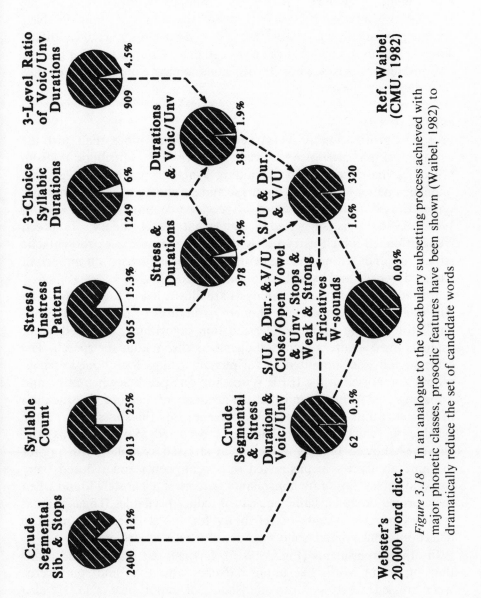

Figure 3.18 In an analogue to the vocabulary subsetting process achieved with major phonetic classes, prosodic features have been shown (Waibel, 1982) to dramatically reduce the set of candidate words

remaining candidates, or only 1% of the vocabulary.

Figure 3.18 illustrates results from a similar study (Waibel, 1982), at Carnegie-Mellon University, which showed that prosodic features could also drastically reduce the set of candidate words from a large vocabulary. The stress pattern of the word, the durations of the syllables, and the portion of each syllable that is voiced can cut the set of candidate words down to about 1.6% of the vocabulary. Coupling such prosodic information with crude phonetic decisions can leave only a few words as candidates, on the average.

PROSODIC AIDS

Prosodic information provides acoustic cues to more than just the wording of an utterance. Indeed, the primary contributions from prosodics may prove to be in aiding syntactic parsing and guiding phonetic analyses. Based on linguistic and psychological arguments that syntax is used in the early stages of speech perception, Lea (1973, 1974, 1980c, 1986d) has suggested a somewhat novel theory of speech recognition, in which early use is made of prosodic cues to syntactic structures, and, within that structure, analysis is focused on important (stressed) words and 'islands of phonetic reliability'.

Justifications for prosodic analysis are illustrated in Fig. 3.19(a). Lea had listeners mark perceived phonetic structures to provide the 'standard' for judging phonetic classification algorithms, and had other listeners provide stress pattern judgements throughout the speech. The same speech was submitted to various algorithms for phonetic recognition, as reported at the IEEE Workshop on Speech Segmentation and Labelling (1974). Lea found that the accuracy of machine classification of phonetic units was significantly influenced by the stress level on the syllable in which the phonetic units occurred. Vowels, stops and fricatives showed highest reliability in stressed syllables, with poorer machine accuracies in unstressed (less prominent) and reduced (very weak) syllables. Sonorant consonants were most accurately found when they formed the full syllabic nucleus of reduced syllables. Thus, stressed syllables provide islands of reliability for vowel, fricative, and stop detections, and syllabic sonorants are also reliably detected.

In other experiments (Fig. 3.19(b)), Lea showed the expected result that important words like nouns, adverbs, adjectives and some verbs were stressed, so stresses provide islands of importance, also. He also found that boundaries between major syntactic phrases could be detected from fall-rise 'valleys' in intonation (i.e. fundamental frequency contours; Lea, 1972, 1973, 1980c). Experimenting with problem cases for the HWIM speech understanding system, he showed that intonationally

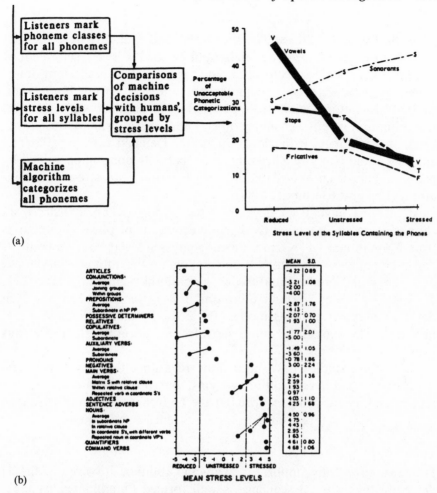

(a)

(b)

Figure 3.19 The prosodic feature 'stress' has been shown to provide cues to regions of phonetic reliability and structural importance.

(a) Experiments show that machine algorithms for recognition of phonetic units work most accurately in stressed syllables, for most types of phonemes, so that stress patterns provide information about 'islands of phonetic reliability' in the speech.

(b) Listeners' perceptions verify the expected tendency for important words to be stressed, so that locating stressed syllables helps locate islands of important information in the utterance.

detected phrase boundaries could drastically cut combinatorial explosions and increase sentence understanding accuracy, by ruling out word sequences that did not agree with detected prosodic patterns (Lea, 1976, 1980c).

An extensive series of experiments showed other benefits offered by prosodic features. Lea showed that interstress intervals were the best indicator of rate of speaking, and could be used to select suitable (e.g. fast speech *vs.* slow speech) phonological rules. Unusually long interstress intervals were cues to major phonological phrase boundaries. Intonation contours and stress patterns could indicate sentence type, subordination of phrases under others, and special grammatical structures like conjuncts with word repetition. Detailed acoustic phonetic analyses could be more efficiently and accurately done when guided by prosodic cues such as syllabic nucleus locations and stress determinations (Lea and Clermont, 1984).

Algorithms have been developed for finding syllabic nuclei from chunks of energy bounded by dips, detecting major phrase boundaries from intonational valleys, and locating stressed syllables from context-dependent analyses that involve position within the intonational phrase, and energy and fundamental frequency patterns near the syllable (Lea, 1973, 1976, 1980c; Lea and Clermont, 1984). Recently, Lea has been developing expert systems models for prosodic aids to speech recognition, which should be more flexible and accurate than previous prosodics algorithms.

Few actual studies have been done regarding the use of prosodic features in speech recognition systems, but prosodic aids to speech understanding are being explored at the University of Nancy (France), several groups in Japan, and at Speech Science Publications.

SYNTACTIC CONSTRAINTS
Humans have four important syntactic abilities, involved with (1) detecting that a word sequence is well formed ('grammaticality'); (2) dividing a sentence or discourse into a hierarchy of structural units ('phrasal bracketing'); (3) determining the syntactic categories associated with various units ('labelling phrases'); and (4) establishing the semantic and referential functions of words or phrases, such as who is the agent in a sentence, and what is the action done and the object of the action, etc. ('determining grammatical relations'). Unfortunately, most recognition systems have focused entirely on using the grammaticality constraints to 'weed out' alternative word sequences, without offering any abilities in phrasal grouping, labelling and definition of grammatical relations. This filtering of word sequences to establish which ones satisfy grammatical rules can be a major factor in assuring correct sentence understanding and reducing computations for alternative word sequences.

Generative models of language define a grammar as a vocabulary of symbols for representing utterances and their parts, coupled with rules for combining the symbols to produce acceptable and interpretable utterances. A generative derivation of an acceptable sentence is then a series of steps by which a sentence is divided into phrases such as a noun-phrase 'subject', followed by a verb-phrase 'predicate', then the composition of those phrases is specified in a step-by-step fashion, until each word is specified and positioned in the final string of words. There are many types of grammars, of varying powers to generate complex languages (Lea, 1966; Chomsky and Miller, 1963) but perhaps the most important to speech recognition are *finite state, context free, context sensitive*, and *augmented transition network* grammars.

Finite state grammars are at the forefront of current capabilities in highly reliable speech recognition. Harpy (Reddy and Lowerre, 1980), the IBM systems (Jelinek, 1982), all commercial recognisers, and dynamic programming systems have endeavoured to recognise with this restrictive form of grammar, and systems like the BBN HWIM system (Wolf and Woods, 1980) that have tried to go beyond the limitations of finite state grammars have had comparatively limited successes. A finite state grammar is equivalent to a 'finite state automaton' or 'Markov model', in which generation (or recognition) of the next word in a sentence is determined by a fixed memory of the previous n words (where n is frequently only one, so the immediately previous word restricts the allowable next word).

A common representation of the allowable word sequences is a state diagram composed of nodes representing states of machine memory, and transitions between the nodes which are labelled with words that are generated (or recognised) with that state change. Probabilities of taking transition can also be assigned to each transition.

Linguists (e.g. Chomsky, 1957) have shown that finite state grammars cannot properly characterise major subsets of English sentences if no fixed limit is placed on the complexity of sentences. Thus, finite state grammars cannot generate (or recognise) all such English sentences and only the acceptable sentences. Context free grammars have been devised to permit more generative power, in which sentences need not be generated a single word at a time, but large units can be divided into phrasal sub-units, which in turn get expanded until the smallest units are represented by words of the acceptable vocabulary.

However, even such context free grammars cannot capture some of the contextual constraints that seem to be involved in aspects of the English language, again assuming no fixed limit on sentence complexity. Transformational grammars (*cf.* Chomsky, 1957, 1965) were devised to account systematically for complex contextual effects and total derivational histories of sentence types (such as passive *vs.* active sentences, etc.).

However, transformational grammars have proven difficult to use in recognition procedures, so the 'augmented transition network' (or ATN) grammar has been devised as a practical substitute, of equally general power. The ATN grammar operates like a finite state grammar with special transitions that are associated not with the generation of a single word, but rather with instructions to insert a whole phrasal unit at the next point in the structure, to 'push' down into a subprocedure to fully expand those sub-units, then to 'pop' back to process the next node and transition in the network. Transitions are thus allowed to call for local subroutine-like expansions of phrases, and also to build total structural descriptions for the sentence and its phrases, and to assign relevant interpretations or 'meanings'. The HWIM system (Wolf and Woods, 1980) and the SRI work (Walker, 1980) were based on the powerful ATN grammars.

Thus, there is a hierarchy of ever more powerful grammars, ranging from finite-state grammars up to ATN grammars. The more powerful the grammar, the more versatile the language that can be characterised. More importantly, however, for the current uses of syntax in recognition, the more restrictive the grammar the better it is for strictly limiting the acceptable word sequences.

Finite-state grammars such as Harpy used may be argued to be limited in utility to only small sentence understanding tasks, but they definitely constrain alternative word sequences, so that incorrect word hypotheses can be eliminated. Powerful grammars such as the ATN grammar in HWIM may offer more versatile, natural communications (i.e. closer to 'habitable' languages; Watt, 1968), but their lack of constraints makes the recognition very difficult (perhaps to a degree just beyond the limits of then current capabilities). Most current efforts in recognition involve limited languages that can be effectively handled with finite-state grammars, despite the ultimate desirability of more versatile language structures.

As noted previously, one problem with currently popular finite-state grammars is that they cannot efficiently distinguish well formed from ill formed sequences, in a manner that agrees with the restricted English utterances that are likely to occur in various complex human–machine dialogues. What's more, finite-state grammars assign highly restricted (typically, 'right branching') structures that do not adequately characterise the phrasal groupings, syntactic categories, and grammatical relations in subsets of English sentences, which can be adequately characterised by more powerful grammars like ATN grammars.

Recognition of spoken utterances need not involve the usual generative processes used in grammar description, but rather involves parsing of sentences (i.e. to determine well-formedness, to represent the structural phrases and categories, and, ultimately, to establish the intended meanings). Traditional parsing procedures with typewritten input will simply reject any inputs as soon as any error in spelling or format is detected, and they typically operate in strict 'left-to-right' fashion, starting with the first (leftmost) word and checking successive acceptability conditions in the order in which the words come. However, parsing of spoken utterances involves several complications, including (1) uncertainty and conflicting alternatives about the identity (and beginning and ending points) of each word; (2) possible errors in word identifications (due to acoustic or phonetic errors, etc.); and (3) the need to consider starting the analysis from reliable words in the middle of the utterance, and working both directions from initially reliable 'islands'. The structural analysis must be able to overcome occasional losses of whole words due to sloppy articulation or poor acoustic analysis.

An important issue in syntactic analysis for speech recognition concerns the assessment of the complexity of a language for speech interaction with machines. Goodman (1976) developed the idea of an average 'branching factor', which indicates the average number of words that can appear next in a sentence of the voice input language. The higher the branching factor, the more difficult the recognition task, though this is hardly a fully adequate measure. Other measures have been developed that also consider the confusability of words in the vocabulary and the statistical likelihoods of various word sequences occurring (Reddy, 1976, pp. 524–525; Sondhi and Levinson, 1977, 1978; Jelinek *et al.*, 1977).

SEMANTIC AND PRAGMATIC CONSTRAINTS

'Semantics' means different things to different people. While some work has been done on the use of 'truth conditions' for testing the meaningfulness of word sequences in speech recognisers (*cf.* Wherry, 1976), most work on semantic constraints in speech recognition has been concerned with determining the meaningfulness or anomalous character of word sequences, based on either (a) semantic networks or (b) semantic conditions embedded in the syntactic rules of the grammar. Semantic models for speech recognition do not try to capture all that is involved in a human's ability to attach meanings to utterances or to associate signs with referents; rather, they focus on relations between words or phrases, which can help verify the meaningfulness of sentences in which certain combinations of words are hypothesised. Theoretical linguistic models suggest semantic features that show commonality among meanings of words, such as 'bull', 'man', 'uncle', 'rooster' all being masculine. Tests for common features ('semantic selectional restrictions', Woods, 1975) can be used to verify the semantic well-formedness or 'meaningfulness' of two or more words occurring in specific places in utterances.

Semantic networks can be used to show semantic relations between words, such as the inclusion of 'uncle' as a special case of 'males' and 'humans', and the inclusion of all those in larger categories such as 'animate' and 'concrete object', etc. Objects that can be 'contained in' other objects may be connected in a semantic network, like 'calcium' being contained in 'rock sample A', etc. Thus, a sentence with the phrase 'calcium in rock sample A' is meaningful, while 'rock sample A in calcium' may not be. In early works on speech understanding systems, semantic networks were expected to play an important independent role in determining the correct word sequences to hypothesise in a system, and which hypothesisable word sequence should be ruled out due to their semantic anomalies (Nash-Webber, 1975).

Pragmatic information may be used in speech recognisers to verify or rule out hypothesised word combinations by establishing their agreement with prior discourse or their applicability to the task being undertaken during the human–machine interaction. Knowledge of previous discourse can help and can permit the full expansion of elliptical (truncated) utterances that follow similar utterances.

There is a substantial gap between linguistic and semiotic theories of semantics and pragmatics, on the one hand, and the effective application of semantic and pragmatic information in speech recognisers, on the other hand.

ROLES FOR STATISTICAL PROCESSING

Given the variability of speech signals due to conditions beyond the explicit control of the recogniser (e.g. speaker variability, emotion, rate of speech, noise, etc.), the process of determining the intended linguistic message is necessarily a non-deterministic one of decision making under uncertainty. The signal will not exactly match the stored templates for alternative messages, and probabilities and statistics can predict which message was intended. This is true at each level of decision making in the machine, whether it be deciding whether a sound is voiced or unvoiced, or is an /s/ or an /f/, or if the word is 'nine' or 'five', or if the structure was declarative or a command. Statistics permit one to use summary characteristics of past experience to choose the hypothesis that is most likely to be correct, and to assign scores about level of certainty based on likelihoods of errors. When one reflects that recognition is a process of functionally duplicating the usual receiver of a transmitted message, the techniques of statistical information theory come immediately to mind.

This has been the basis of major efforts in speech recognition, such as that at IBM (Jelinek, 1976).

Even predominantly linguistically based recognisers use probabilities and statistics. Maximum likelihood ratios are used in rating hypotheses, and Bayes' theorem is frequently used to predict the likely message intended, given the acoustic signal and the prior statistics of likely acoustic encoding of messages. Probably the most dangerous aspect of statistics to use in recognition is the relative frequency of occurrence of a message or part of a message. Unless extensive statistics are obtained, such as IBM does with hours of training speech (Jelinek, 1976; Bahl *et al.*, 1978), some messages (or words or phrases) may appear to have essentially no likelihood of occurring. Then, if hypotheses are selected in priority on the basis of their likelihood of occurrence, some unlikely but correct words will be ruled out (or delayed in being tested), forcing expensive analysis of more likely but wrong word sequences (*cf.* Woods *et al.*, 1976, Vol. I, p. 14). Since information content in a message increases with the unlikelihood of what was said, the most informative parts of messages might thus be least properly handled. For these reasons, HARPY, HWIM and other recognisers have not considered the *a priori* probabilities of alternative hypotheses in their decisions about which hypotheses to pursue.

One link between statistics and system structures comes in *scoring procedures*. Typically, each component of a complex speech understanding system selects hypotheses on probabilistic grounds, and assigns a 'score' or relative confidence to its selection, based on information gathered in that component of the system. Different components may give conflicting hypotheses about the wording of an utterance. How does the system as a whole then select what hypotheses to pursue, or which component(s) to 'listen to'? This depends in part on a general scoring philosophy and upon the system structure and control procedures.

In Wolf and Woods (1980), and Woods *et al.* (1976, Volume I) the BBN researchers outline systematic procedures for finding optimum or near-optimum selection processes, based on 'uniform scoring procedures'. Other systems make heuristic judgements about which components should direct the system to the 'best' next hypothesis to pursue, and those judgements may vary from time to time or from one set of conditions to another. The goals are to reduce the likelihoods of going down very expensive futile 'paths' (sequences of tentatively selected hypotheses), and to maximise the likelihood of selecting sequences of hypotheses that efficiently find the correct solutions. Some systems attempt to pursue the most promising ('best') path, by selecting the highest scoring hypothesis for a word (or other sub-unit), then extending that hypothesis with words that give the best score when combined with that word, and so forth. Such a best-first strategy gets the system ever more deeply committed to the consequences of the initially most promising hypothesis, giving a 'depth first' search strategy. Other strategies acknowledge the possibility of promising alternatives, and conduct a 'breadth first' search of alternatives, and only after all alternatives for one aspect of the analysis are exhausted and comparatively rated or ruled out do they go on to pursue extensions of those hypotheses to cover other parts of the utterance. In addition to such depth-first and breadth-first strategies, there are also 'optimal strategies' which exhaustively search all alternatives (e.g. the Dragon system, Baker, 1975), and hybrid or compromise strategies ('best few' or 'beam' search strategies; *cf.* Reddy and Lowerre, 1980).

Developers of the HEARSAY II system (*cf.* Goodman and Reddy, 1980) offered several principles for control and search:

(1) *The competition principle*. Explore the best of several alternatives first.
(2) *The validity principle*. Give priority, and permit more processing for, knowledge sources that are operating on more valid data.
(3) *The significance principle*. Permit more processing, and give priority, to knowledge sources whose expected results are more significant.
(4) *The efficiency principle*. Give priority, and more processing time, to knowledge sources that perform more reliably and inexpensively.
(5) *The goal satisfaction principle*. Give priority, and more processing time, to knowledge sources whose responses are more likely to satisfy processing goals.

These principles suggest a balance between best-first and breadth-first search, primarily using the most reliable, robust information that has the most impact on the goal of total sentence understanding.

ALTERNATIVE SYSTEM STRUCTURES
Several knowledge sources have been discussed that provide guidelines for how to determine the intended machine response, but each of those knowledge sources is necessarily incomplete and currently somewhat inaccurate. Error, uncertainty and potential ambiguity remain, and we have the task of completing the decisions, eliminating errors and selecting appropriate responses. How do we get all these knowledge sources to cooperate, and how do we decide which one to listen to when they offer conflicting hypotheses? The answer is by way of a total system structure with well defined scoring procedures and control strategies.

Figures 3.20 to 3.22 offer several alternative structures for interactions

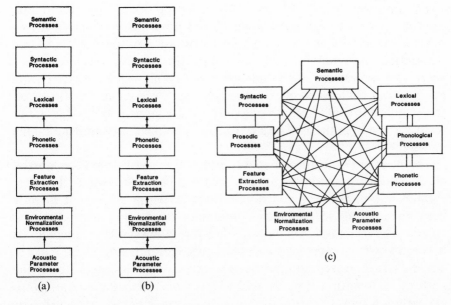

Figure 3.20 Alternative system structures for a complex speech recognition system.

(a) The data-driven, or 'bottom-up' speech recognition system provides a hierarchy of components working in cascade.

(b) The goal directed, or 'top-down' speech recognition system hypothesises acceptable and relevant sentences, and then seeks to verify such hypotheses through a cascade of processes that is essentially the reverse of the bottom-up system. Some top-down systems do allow bottom-up 'feedback' between successive processes.

(c) The 'heterarchical' system structure permits any module to talk to any other module in the system, so that data flow and feedback is not restricted to neighbouring modules as with the top-down or bottom-up systems. Controlling interactions is difficult with such a complex system, however.

among various knowledge sources in speech recognisers. The *hierarchical model*, or 'bottom-up system' of Fig. 3.20(a) is a straight forward pass from acoustics to parameters, to phonetic features, to segments and prosodic patterns, to words, to phrases and sentences, to meanings, and finally to machine response. Control is simple, but errors in early stages of the 'front end' (or 'bottom end') will propagate to successively higher levels, so that errors multiply (or at least add), unless upper levels can correct errors detected in the output of lower levels. No knowledge source can ask for further information from another knowledge source or demand a re-analysis to remove propagated errors. Feedback is not possible.

The opposite model is a *goal-directed* ('top-down') one as in Fig. 3.20(b), in which high level linguistic information predicts words or other units, and the lower components must attempt to verify the actual presence of such units in the data. Since the top end specifies all the acceptable utterances, this avoids some impossible sequences from being pursued, but the top end offers all possible and acceptable hypotheses, so the 'search space' of alternatives to test is quite large, and it is difficult to recover from hypothesised and erroneously verified units misleading the system.

The problem with these two systems is the 'daisy chain' or 'gossip' effect. No early component can check ahead for what the later components might say, and no feedback is permitted except directly between adjacent levels. Such communications might help eliminate errors. The *heterarchical model*, however, allows direct interactions between any (or almost any) pair of knowledge sources (*cf.* Fig. 3.20(c)). The cost is increased complexity and extensive alternatives about the path of information flow around the system. Each path requires an agreed-upon representation of mutually interesting information so that the representations of the speech dramatically expand in number and complexity. Also, how are all these 'free-for-all' communications to be controlled? Which components should really listen to which other ones, and which ones should control interactions?

The blackboard model of Fig. 3.21 seems to be a reasonable compromise between unlimited communication and over-structured paths of successive communications. A central database with a well defined form of representation (a 'blackboard') acts as the 'meta-language' or common framework through which components can communicate. Each knowledge source can evaluate hypotheses placed on the blackboard by other knowledge sources, and use such inform-ation (perhaps simultaneously use information from several other knowledge sources) to make further hypotheses, correct apparent errors, etc. Control still remains a problem with this rather complex interaction of modules.

The *Locus model* of Fig. 3.22 has syntactic, lexical and front end (phonetic and phonological) knowledge precompiled into an 'integrated network' which represents the complete pronunciation of every possible sentence. The input signal is converted to a symbol sequence, which was a string of spectral templates in the Harpy system. That symbol sequence is matched against alternative paths through the integrated pronun-ciation network, using a 'beam search procedure' that preserves only the most promising few alternative paths at each point through the network. Control is simple because of only one conglomerate representation of all

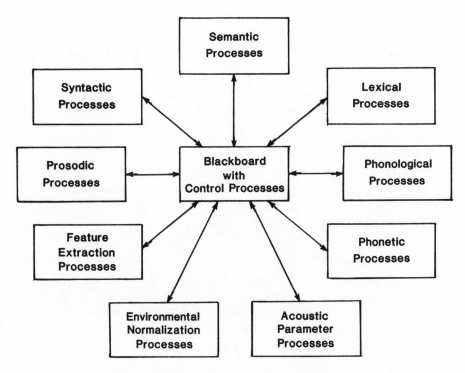

Figure 3.21 The 'Blackboard' system structure permits modules to interact through a database with control strategy, permitting the modules to operate independently while avoiding propagation of errors that occurs with hierarchical structures

the knowledge sources. However, modifying the Locus system is very difficult because all information is pre-compiled into the complex network.

Recent trends in artificial intelligence system designs, the CMU control and search principles, and past experience in speech recognition, all suggest that an ultimately promising strategy would be one such as the prosodically guided speech understanding strategy outlined by Lea *et al.* (1975), but with more of the versatile, flexible structure and component interactions of a blackboard system. Prosodic information and the most reliably encoded segmental information provide the needed emphasis on best-first, valid, significant, inexpensive, reliable and ultimately-goal-seeking aspects of speech structure. For more on prosodically guided strategies, see Lea *et al.* (1975), Lea and Shoup (1979), and Lea (1980a).

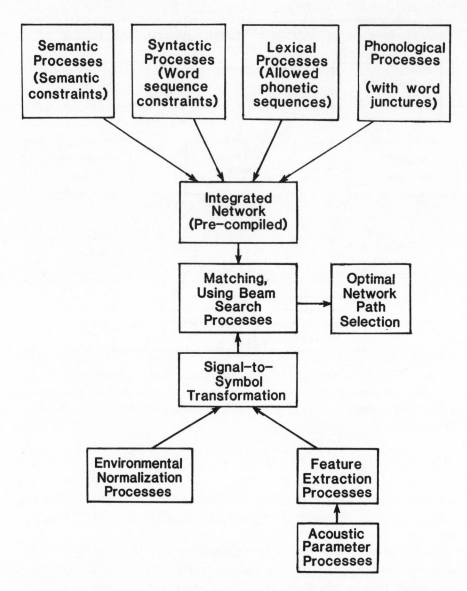

Figure 3.22 The 'Locus' model, such as used in the Harpy speech recognition system (Lowerre and Reddy, 1980), precompiles semantic, syntactic, lexical, and phonological information into an integrated network that specifies all possible sound sequences. Incoming data is processed for sound sequences that are then matched to the best matching paths through the integrated network, with allowance of several candidate paths provided by a 'beam search' of nearly best matches, until the best total path for the sentence is selected.

3.3 *Current needs and future trends*

Each component in speech recognition systems, and their control structures, are in need of further enhancements. Similarly, the conditions for effective use of speech recognisers need improvement. Here we briefly outline needed work in voice input technology, the types of projects that should be undertaken, and the short range and long range trends to expect.

GAPS IN CURRENT TECHNOLOGY

After over 35 years of research, and about 15 years of commercial ventures, speech recognition technology has had some success and technical advances, but there is very much yet to be done to achieve the exponential market growth and user-friendly breakthroughs that have often been projected for it. Figure 3.23 illustrates the priorities that this author assigns to various topics or issues in this field. These judgements are very similar to those given during a survey of experts (Lea and Shoup, 1979) and subsequent projects which this author directed, to guide various governmental and industrial funding programmes. There is plenty of room for new ideas and new advances from projects that might be undertaken by readers of this book.

Several topics associated with the external factors influencing recognisers are of top priority, as shown by their bars reaching the first-priority line on the right in Fig. 3.23. Procedures need to be improved for systematically assessing the utility and feasibility of voice input for various human–machine interaction tasks. The actual benefits of continuous speech need to be established, and general guidelines need to be defined for when to use isolated word recognition, when connected speech is best, and when more elaborate continuous speech processing is required. Measures of the confusability of vocabularies could be very beneficial in guiding the user to word selections that ease the demands on the machine, and assure high accuracy. Effects of noise seem to be not as catastrophic as had been expected in earlier years, but further work on handling noise and minimising its impact on recognition performance seems warranted.

Other topics of high priority include the determination of field requirements, handling of stress and fatigue (and other 'adverse environments'), ways of assessing user acceptance of recognisers, databases and testing procedures for assessing voice input facilities, systematic comparisons of alternative speech recognisers, and methods for correcting errors and reducing their costs to the user. Projects should be devised to 'fill the gaps' in ruggedisation, handling of human factors

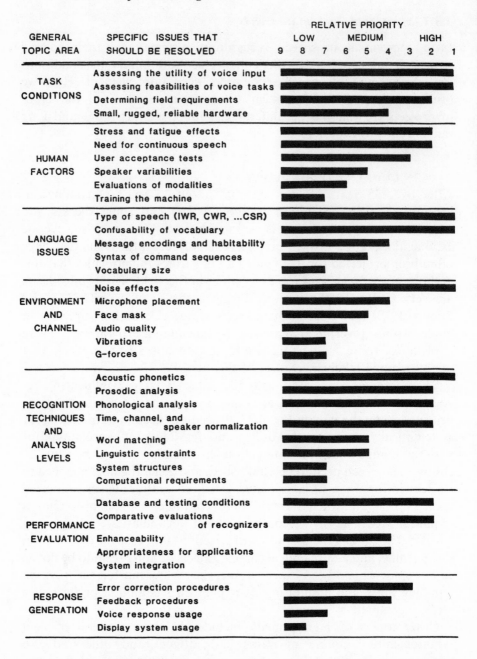

Figure 3.23 Relative priorities of various topics in speech recognition technology are indicated by the lengths of bars, with highest priorities reaching the rightmost level '1'. These topic areas show needed work throughout the entire process of designing advanced recognition algorithms, configuring an accurate system, and applying it in practical applications.

(like speaker variabilities, alternative modality choices, and training procedures), improved language design, dealing with unusual field conditions (like face masks, audio quality changes, vibrations, *g*-forces, etc.), and improving performances with task-specific enhancements, tools for guiding users about the appropriateness of voice and how to integrate voice within full systems, and improved feedback procedures (including proper use of voice response from the machine, and graphical displays).

Within the recogniser itself, all components and procedures could use improvement. However, it has repeatedly been noted (*cf*. Lea and Shoup, 1979; Lea, 1979, 1981; Flanagan, 1984; and Lea, 1986) that acoustic phonetics is a primary area needing further work. Close to that in importance are prosodic analysis, phonological procedures and normalisation methods. Some improvements in word matching and linguistically constraining recognition problems can be expected. System structures and computational constraints do not seem to have significantly handicapped this field, but further work is warranted on such topics, also.

At the 1983 Conference on *Towards Robustness in Speech Recognition*, participants argued that only a small fraction of what we do know about speech has been incorporated into recognition systems, and that we probably only know a small fraction of what knowledge could be exploited about speech communication processes. While considerable basic research may be warranted, it must be accompanied by extensive efforts to *apply* such knowledge to improve voice input facilities.

An important need is to adopt an interdisciplinary view of voice input technology, since it requires much more than just good engineering. Speech scientists, linguists, experimenal psychologists, computer scientists, human factors experts, and others of related disciplines will need to work together on the many challenging problems in this field. Hopefully, the future will not be dominated so severely by signal processing and pattern matching techniques as the past has been.

A PROGRAMME OF NEEDED PROJECTS

Throughout the world, extensive projects are being devised to address voice interactions with machines, as a part of the international thrust towards fifth generation machines, or supercomputers that 'think' or exhibit 'artificial intelligence'. Large programmes include the DARPA strategic computing effort in the USA, the MITI projects in Japan, Alvey in the UK, and ESPRIT in Europe. Industrial efforts in artificial intelligence, which became very popular in the mid 1980s, will also devote considerable attention to speech recognition. This author has offered several lists of needed projects (Lea, 1980d, 1981, 1986d), and the United States National Research Council committee on speech recognition also offered suggestions (Flanagan, 1984). Suitable coordination of such efforts, and interchange of results, will hopefully help advance this field quickly.

One danger in such times of large commitments is for government agencies and companies to delay their smaller, more immediate projects, while they wait for the outcomes from such overwhelmingly larger programmes. That mistake was made in the USA during the ARPA SUR project in the early 1970s, so that the needed ties between ambitious advances and practical needs of the immediate future were unnecessarily lost. There is still full justification for undertaking limited projects on limited topics while such long range efforts continue.

LONG RANGE TRENDS
At the request of EDN magazine, this author speculated about what trends might occur in this field in the next twenty five years (Lea, 1981b). Stages of change were outlined for each decade. After five years, the initial trends seem to be holding good, and the new commitments to this field may even accelerate the projections offered there. We can expect the new century to find voice interactions with computers and other machines to be commonplace, with speaker independence, continuous speech, and success in dealing with many difficult environments. Talking to machines with reasonably powerful languages will be possible, and a major industry will have emerged from the integration of voice input with other automation capabilities. Widespread use of voice-controlled machines will raise legal issues ranging from how to account for errors in voice-controlled transactions to how the legal system's tradition of viewing spoken actions as hearsay will have to evolve. Although we will not have attained the full capabilities of science fiction stories, versatile voice interaction with machines will be so common that the remaining constraints of machines will occasionally be forgotten.

In moving towards those long term goals, short term trends will include lower costs for speech recognisers, and a growing choice of hardware and software implementations, including licensed software for recognition. Robustness will be partially attained through focus on reliable, important information, phonetic processing, and advanced signal processing that includes prosodic components and other previously untapped knowledge sources. Speaker independence and enhanced connected speech recognition will be provided to users who will be increasingly able to assess when voice is really needed for their work. A large variety of companies, including most of the corporate giants, will be exploring speech recognition products. Considerable gain in both the internal workings of recognisers and the design of cost effective systems will be possible with the use of expert systems methodology and other aspects of artificial intelligence.

In short, the coming era should be one of improved capabilities and increased public visibility, with human-based methodologies. Voice input promises to be a fascinating and productive thrust in the future of office automation, military and governmental systems and consumer products. Challenges remain in the development of better devices, and the provision of tools that will help the user in selecting, designing and using speech recognisers. Monitoring the performances of recognisers under realistic field conditions, and defining standard testing procedures, are needed. While waiting for the limitations of current technology to be relaxed, developers and users must be ready to accommodate the application conditions to the restricted capabilities of current (or soon-forthcoming) devices. The benefits from this natural, versatile human communication modality will thus be increasingly evident.

3.4 *References*

Armstrong, J.W., and Poock, G.K. (1981a) *Effect of Operator Mental Loading on Voice Recognition System Performance*, Naval Post-graduate School Report NPS55-81-016, NTIC Access A107442, Monterey, Ca, USA.

AVIOS (1982–1985), *Proc. of Ann. Voice Data Entry Systems Applic. Conf.*, c/o Leon Lerman, Lockheed Missiles and Space Co., Box 504, Sunnyvale, Ca, USA.

Baker, J.K. (1975) 'The DRAGON System – An Overview', *IEEE Trans. ASSP*, **23**, 24–29. Also, 'Stochastic Modeling for Automatic Speech Understanding', in *Speech Recognition* (D.R. Reddy, Ed.), New York: Academic Press, 1975, 521–542.

Baker, J.M. (1975) *A New Time-Domain Analysis of Human Speech and Other Complex Waveforms*, Technical Report CMUCSD, PhD Dissertation, Carnegie-Mellon University, Pittsburgh, Pa, USA.

Baker, J.M. (1982) 'How to Measure Up: Testing Speech Recognizers', *Proc. of the Workshop on Standardization for Speech I/O Technology* (D. Pallett, Ed.), Gainesville, Md, USA.

Baker, J.M., and Baker, J.K. (1983) 'Aspects of Stochastic Modeling for Speech Recognition', *Speech Tech.*, **1**, 4, 94–97.

Bakis, R. (1976) 'Continuous Speech Recognition via Centisecond Acoustic States', *JASA*, **59**, S1, 597(A).

Barnett, J.A., Bernstein, M.I., Goodman, R.A., and Kameny, I.M. (1980) 'The SDC Speech Understanding System', *Trends in Speech Rec.* (Lea, 1980a), 272–293.

Baudrey, M. and Dupeyrat, B. (1978) 'Utilisation de Methodes Syntaxiques et de Filtrage Logique en Reconnaissance de la Parole', *Congres AFCET/IRIA, Reconnaissance des Formes et Traitment des Images*, Paris, February 21–23, 1978.

Bloomfield, B. (1933) *Language*. New York, Holt.

Bridle, J.S. (1973) 'An Efficient Elastic Method for Detecting Given Words in Running Speech', *Proc. Brit. Acoust. Soc. Meeting*, paper 73SHC3.

Broad, D.J. (1986) 'Vowels in Context: Dynamics, Statistics, and Recognition', *Towards Robustness in Speech Recognition*, (W.A. Lea, Ed). Apple Valley, Mn, Speech Science Publications.

Burton, D.K., and Shore, J.E. (1986) 'Applications of Vector Quantization to Speech Recognition', in *Towards Robustness in Speech Recognition* (W.A. Lea, Ed). Apple Valley, Mn, Speech Science Publications.

Chapanis, A. (1975) 'Interactive Human Communication', *Sc. Amer.*, **232**, 36–42.

Chomsky, N. (1957) *Syntactic Structures*, The Hague, Mouton.

Chomsky, N. (1965) *Aspects of the Theory of Syntax*, Cambridge, Ma, MIT Press.

Chomsky, N. and Halle, M. (1968) *The Sound Pattern of English*, New York, Harper.

Chomsky, N. and Miller, G.A. (1963) 'Introduction to the Formal Analysis of Languages', *Handbook of Mathematical Psychology*, (R.D. Luce, R.R. Bush, and E. Galanter, Eds.), vol. II, New York, Wiley, 269–321.

Cohen, P.S., and Mercer, R.L. (1975) 'The Phonological Component of an Automatic Speech Recognition System', *Speech Recognition: Invited Papers of the IEEE Symposium*, New York, Academic Press, 275–320.

Dautrich, B.A., Rabiner, L.R., and Martin, T.B. (1983) 'On the Use of Filter Bank Features for Isolated Word Recognition', *Proc. 1983 IEEE Intern. Conf. on Acoustics, Speech, and Signal Proc.*, 1061–1064.

Davis, S.B., and Mermelstein, P. (1980) 'Comparison of Parametric Representations for Monosyllabic Word Recognition in Continuously Spoken Sentence', *IEEE Trans. Acoust. Sp. and Signal Proc.*, **ASSP-28**, 4, 357–366.

Dixon, N.R. and Martin, T.B. (1979) Editors, *Automatic Speech and Speaker Recognition*, New York, IEEE Press.

Drennen, T.G. (1980) 'Voice Technology in Attack/Fighter Aircraft', *Proc. Symp. on Voice Interactive Systems: Applications and Payoffs* (S. Harris, Ed.), Dallas, TX. 199–211.

Fant, G. (1970) *Acoustic Theory of Speech Production*, The Hague, Mouton.

Feuge, R.L., and Geer, C.W. (1978) *Integrated Applications of Automated Speech Technology, Final Report and Program Plan on ONR Contract N00014-77-C-0401*, Boeing Aerospace Co. (with Logicon Inc.), Seattle, Wa, USA.

Flanagan, J.L. (1972) *Speech Analysis, Synthesis, and Perception*, 2nd Ed., New York, Springer-Verlag.

Flanagan, J.L. (1984) chairman, 'Automatic Speech Recognition in Severe Environments'. *Final Rep. of the Comm. on Computerized Speech Rec.*, National Research Council, Washington, DC, USA.

Focht, L.R. (1963) 'The Single Equivalent Formant', *IEEE Intern. Commun. Conf. Digest*, Philadelphia, Pa, USA, 108–115.

Grady, M.W., Hicklin, M.B., and Porter, J.E. (1978) 'Practical Applications of Interactive Voice Technologies – Some Accomplishments and Prospects', *Proc. 1977 Workshop on Voice Tech.*, 217–233.

Halle, M. (1954) 'The Strategy of Phonemics', *Word*, **10**, 197–209.

Haton, J.P. (1979) 'Speech Recognition Work in Western Europe', *Trends in Speech Rec.*, (W.A. Lea, Ed.), Englewood Cliffs, NJ, Prentice-Hall, 512–526.

Haton, J.P. (1986) 'Present Issues in Continuous Speech Recognition and Understanding', in *Towards Robustness in Speech Recognition* (W.A. Lea, Ed), Apple Valley, Mn, Speech Science Publications.

Hockett, C.F. (1972) 'Language, Mathematics, and Linguistics', in *Current Trends in Linguistics*, **3**, (T. Sebeok, Ed.), The Hague, Mouton, 155–304.

Huttenlocher, D.P., and Zue, V. W. (1983) 'Phonotactic and Lexical Constraints in Speech Recognition', *Proc. Amer. Assoc. for Art. Intell. Conf.*, 172–176.

IEEE Int. Conf. on Acoustics, Speech, and Sig. Proc., Proceedings available from IEEE Headquarters:

1976, Philadelphia, Pa, IEEE Cat. No. 76CH1067-8 ASSP;
1977, Hartford, Ct, IEEE Cat. No. 77CH1197-3 ASSP;
1978, Tulsa, Ok, IEEE Cat. No. 78CH1285-6 ASSP;
1979, Washington, DC, IEEE Cat. No. 79CH1379-7 ASSP;
1980, Denver, Co, IEEE Cat. No. 80CH1559-4 ASSP;
1981, Atlanta, Ga, IEEE Cat. No. 81CH1610-5 ASSP;
1982, Paris, France, IEEE Cat. No. 82CH1746-7 ASSP;
1983, Boston, Ma, IEEE Cat. No. 83CH1841-6 ASSP.

Itakura, F. (1975) 'Minimum Prediction Residual Principle Applied to Speech Recognition', *IEEE Trans. ASSP*, **ASSP-23**, 67–72.

Jelinek, F. (1976) 'Continuous Speech Recognition by Statistical Methods', *Proc. of IEEE*, **64**, 532–556.

Jelinek, F. (1982) 'Self-organized Continuous Speech Recognition', in *Automatic Speech Anal. and Rec.*, (J.-P. Haton, Ed.), London, D. Reidel Publ., 231–238.

Jelinek, F., Mercer, R.L., Bahl, L.R., and Baker, J.K. (1977) 'Perplexity – A Measure of Difficulty of Speech Recognition Tasks', **ASSP-23**, 38–49.

Jelinek, F., Mercer, R.L., Bahl, L.R., and Baker, J.K. (1977) Perplexity – A Measure of Difficulty of Speech Recognition Tasks', *JASA*, **60**, S1, Fall, 1977, (A).

Klatt, D.H. (1975) 'Word Verification in a Speech Understanding System', *Speech Recognition: Invited Papers of the IEEE Sym.*, (D.R. Reddy, Ed.), New York, Academic Press, 321–341.

Klatt, D.H. (1980b) 'Scriber and LAFS: Two New Approaches to Speech Analysis', *Trends in Speech Rec.*, (W.A. Lea, Ed.), Englewood Cliffs, NJ, Prentice-Hall, 529–555.

Klatt, D.H. (1986) 'Understanding and Characterizing Acoustic and Phonetic Variability: The Key to Improved Performance in Speech Recognition', In *Towards Robustness in Speech Recognition* (W.A. Lea, Ed.), Apple Valley, Mn, Speech Science Publications.

Klatt, D.H., and Stevens, K.N. (1973) 'On the Automatic Recognition of Continuous Speech: Implications from a Spectrogram-Reading Experiment', *IEEE Trans. Audio and Electroacoustics*, **AU-21**, 210–217.

Klein, W., Plomp, R., and Pols, L.C.W. (1970) 'Vowel Spectra, Vowel Spaces, and Vowel Identification', *JASA*, **48**, 999–1009.

Kuhn, G.M. (1975) 'On the Front Cavity Resonance and its Possible Role in Speech Perception', *JASA*, **58**, 578–585.

Lea, W.A. (1968) 'Establishing the Value of Voice Communication with Computers', *IEEE Trans. Audio and Electroacoustics*, **AU-16**, 184–197.

Lea, W.A. (1970) 'Towards Versatile Speech Communication with Computers', *Intern. J. Man–Machine Studies*, **2**, 107–155.

Lea, W.A. (1972) *Intonational Cues to the Constituent Structure and Phonemics of Spoken English*, PhD Dissertation, School of Electrical Engineering, Purdue U., Lafayette, In, USA.

Lea, W.A. (1973a) 'An Approach to Syntactic Recognition without Phonemics', *IEEE Trans. Audio and Electroacoustics*, **AU-21**, 249–258.

Lea, W.A. (1973b) 'Evidence that Stressed Syllables are the Most Readily Decoded Portions of Continuous Speech', *JASA*, **55**, 410(A).

Lea, W.A. (1974) 'Prosodic Aids to Speech Recognition: IV. A General Strategy for Prosodically-Guided Speech Understanding', *Univac Report No. PX10791*, Sperry Univac DSD, St. Paul, Mn, USA.

Lea, W.A. (1975) 'Isochrony and Disjuncture as Aids to Syntactic and Phonological Analysis', *JASA*, **57**, S1, 533(A).

Lea, W.A. (1976) 'Prosodic Aids to Speech Recognition: IX. Acoustic-Prosodic Patterns in Selected English Phrase Structures', *Univac Report No. PX11963*, Sperry Univac DSD, St. Paul, Mn, USA.

Lea, W.A. (1979) 'Critical Issues in Airborne Applications of Speech Recognizers', *SCRL Final Report to Naval Air Development Center*, NADC Contract N62269-78-M-3770.

Lea, W.A. (1980) Editor, *Trends in Speech Recognition*, Englewood Cliffs, NJ, Prentice-Hall.

Lea, W.A. (1980a) 'The Value of Speech Recognition Systems', Chap. 1 in (Lea, 1980), 3–18.

Lea, W.A. (1980b) 'Speech Recognition: Past, Present, and Future', Chap. 4 in (Lea, 1980), 39–98.

Lea, W.A. (1980c) 'Prosodic Aids to Speech Recognition', Chap. 8 in (Lea, 1980), 166–205.

Lea, W.A. (1980d) 'Speech Recognition: What is Needed Now?' Chap. 27 in (Lea, 1980), 562–569.

Lea, W.A. (1980e) 'Issues in the Selection and Practical Use of Speech Recognizers', *Proc. Symp. Voice Interactive Systems* (S. Harris, Ed.), 357–372.

Lea, W.A. (1980f) 'Future Directions in Speech Recognition: A Researcher's Perspective', *Proc. Symp. on Voice Interactive Systems* (S. Harris, Ed.), 483–494.

Lea, W.A. (1981a) 'Speech Recognition: The Next 25 Years', *EDN*, October 14, 1981 (25th Anniversary Issue).

Lea, W.A. (1981b) *Assessing the Feasibilities of Airborne Speech Recognition Tasks*, Report CR-5 to Honeywell Systems and Research Center, St. Paul, Mn, from Speech Science Publications. SSP Report CR-5. Also: *A Research Program for Advancing Airborne Uses of Voice I/O*, Report CR-8 to Honeywell Systems and Research Center, SSP Report CR-8.

Lea, W.A. (1982a) 'What Causes Speech Recognizers to Make Mistakes?', *Proc. 1982 ICASSP*, 2030–2033.

Lea, W.A. (1982b) 'Problems in Predicting the Performances of Speech Recognizers', *Proc. Workshop on Standardization for Speech Tech.*,

(D. Pallett, Ed.), National Bureau of Standards, Gaithersburg, Md, USA.

Lea, W.A. (1983) 'Selecting the Best Recognizer for the Job', *Speech Tech.*, **2**, Jan–Feb, 1983.

Lea, W.A. (1984) 'Voice Recognition Systems: A Review of the Current Status and Outlook', *SSP Report SS7*, Apple Valley, Mn, Speech Science Publications.

Lea, W.A. (1986a) editor, *Trends in Speech Recognition* (SSP edition), Apple Valley, Mn, Speech Science Publications.

Lea, W.A. (1986b) editor, *Towards Robustness in Speech Recognition*, Apple Valley, Mn, Speech Science Publications.

Lea, W.A. (1986c) *Computer Recognition of Speech*, Apple Valley, Mn, Speech Science Publications.

Lea, W.A. (1986d) *Selecting, Designing, and Using Speech Recognizers*, Apple Valley, Mn, Speech Science Publications.

Lea, W.A. and Clermont, F. (1984) 'Algorithms for Acoustic Prosodic Analysis', *Proc. IEEE 1984 Intern. Conf. on Acoustics, Speech and Sig. Proc.*, **42**, 7, 1–4.

Lea, W.A., and Kloker, D.R. (1975) 'Prosodic Aids to Speech Recognition: VI. Timing Cues to Linguistic Structures', *Univac Report No. PX11534*, Sperry Univac DSD, St. Paul, Mn, USA.

Lea, W.A., Medress, M.F., and Skinner, T.E. (1975) 'A Prosodically-Guided Speech Understanding Strategy', *IEEE Trans. ASSP*, **ASSP-23**, 30–38.

Lea, W.A., and Shoup, J.E. (1979) *Review of the ARPA SUR Project and Survey of Current Technology in Speech Understanding*, Final Report, Contract N00014-77-C-0570, from Speech Communications Research Laboratory to Office of Naval Research, Arlington, Va, USA.

Lea, W.A., and Shoup, J.E. (1980) 'Specific Contributions of the ARPA SUR Project', *Trends in Speech Rec.* (W.A. Lea, Ed.), Englewood Cliffs, NJ, Prentice-Hall, 382–421.

Lea, W.A., and Woodard, J. (1983) 'New Procedures for Comprehensive Assessment of Voice Entry Systems', *Proc. 1983 Voice Data Entry Systems Applications Conf.*

Leonard, R.G., and Doddington, G.R. (1986) 'A Speaker-Independent Connected-Digit Database', in *Towards Robustness in Speech Rec.*, (W.A. Lea, Ed.) Apple Valley, Mn, Speech Science Publications.

Levinson, S. (1986) 'Statistical Methods for Speaker Independence', in *Towards Robustness in Speech Rec.*, (W.A. Lea, Ed.), Apple Valley, Mn, Speech Science Publications.

Lim, J.S. (1983) *Speech Enhancement*, Englewood Cliffs, NJ, Prentice-Hall.

Lowerre, B.T. (1976) *The Harpy Speech Recognition System*, Technical Report CMUCSD, PhD Dissertation, Carnegie-Mellon U., Pittsburgh, Pa, USA.

Lowerre, B.T., and Reddy, D.R. (1980) 'The Harpy Speech Understanding System', *Trends in Speech Rec.*, (W.A. Lea, Ed.), Englewood Cliffs, NJ, Prentice-Hall, 340–360.

Martin, T.B. (1976) 'Practical Applications of Voice Input to Machines', *Proc. IEEE*, **64**, 4, 487–501.

Martin, T.B., and Grunza, E.F. (1974) 'Voice Control Demonstration System', *Techn. Report AFAL-TR-74-174*, Wright-Patterson AFB, Oh, USA.

Martin, T.B., and Welch, J. (1980) 'Practical Speech Recognizers and Some Performance Evaluation Parameters', *Trends in Speech Rec.*, (W.A. Lea, Ed.), Englewood Cliffs, NJ, Prentice-Hall, 24–38.

Medress, M.F. (1980) 'The Sperry Univac System for Continuous Speech Recognition', *Trends in Speech Rec.*, (W.A. Lea, Ed.), Englewood Cliffs, NJ, Prentice-Hall, 445–460.

Medress, M.F., Diller, T.C., Kloker, D.R., Lutton, L.L., Oredson, H.N., and Skinner, T.E. (1978) 'An Automatic Word Spotting System for Conversational Speech', *Proc. 1978 ICASSP*, 468–473.

Medress, M.F., Skinner, T.E., Kloker, D.R., Diller, T.C., and Lea, W.A. (1977) 'A System for the Recognition of Spoken Connected Word Sequences', *Proc. 1977 ICASSP*, Hartford, Ct, 468–473.

Mercier, G. (1986) 'Rules and Strategies for Syllabic Segmentation, Phoneme Identification, and Tuning in Continuous Speech Recognition', in *Towards Robustness in Speech Rec.*, (W.A. Lea, Ed.), Apple Valley, Mn, Speech Science Publications.

Mermelstein, P. (1975b) 'Automatic Segmentation of Speech into Syllabic Units', *JASA*, **58**, 880–883.

Miller, G.A. (1962) 'Decision Units in the Perception of Speech', *IRE Trans. Inform. Theory*, **IT-8**, 81–83.

Miller, G.A., and Nicely, P.E. (1955) 'An Analysis of Perceptual Confusions Among Some English Consonants', *JASA*, **27**, 338–352.

Moore, R.K. (1977) 'Evaluating Speech Recognizers', *IEEE Trans. on Acoustics, Speech and Sig. Proc.*, **ASSP-25**, 178–183.

Nash-Webber, B. (1975) 'The Role of Semantics in Automatic Speech Understanding', *Representation and Understanding* (D. Bobrow and A. Collins, Eds.), New York, Academic Press.

Newell, A. (1975) 'A Tutorial on Speech Understanding Systems', *Speech Rec.: Invited Papers Presented at the 1974 IEEE Sym.*, (D.R. Reddy, Ed.), New York, Academic Press, 3–54.

North, R.A., and Adsit, D.J. (1983) *Applications of Interactive Voice*

Technology for the Advanced Attack Helicopter, Final Report 83SRC36 to Hughes Helicopters, from Honeywell Systems Research Center, Minneapolis, Mn, USA.

North, R.A., and Lea, W.A. (1982) *Application of Advanced Speech Technology in Manned Penetration Bombers*, Honeywell Systems and Research Center Report AFWAL-TR-82-3004 to Flight Dynamics Lab., Wright-Patterson AFB, Oh, USA.

Oshika, B.T., Zue, V.W., Weeks, R.V., Nue, H., and Aurbach, J. (1975) 'The Role of Phonological Rules in Speech Understanding Research', *IEEE Trans. ASSP*, **ASSP-23**, 104–112.

Pallett, D. (1982) Editor, *Proc. of the Workshop on Standardization for Speech I/O Tech.*, (D. Pallett, Ed.), Gainesville, Md, USA.

Peterson, G.E., and Barney, H.L. (1952) Control Methods Used in a Study of the Vowels', *JASA*, **24**, 175–184.

Pierce, J.R. (1961) *Symbols, Signals, and Noise*, New York, Wiley.

Pike, K.L. (1945) *The Intonation of American English*, Ann Arbor, U. Mich. Press, USA.

Pols, L.C.W. (1982) 'How Humans Perform on a Connected-Digits Data Base', *Proc. 1982 IEEE Intern. Conf. on Acoustics, Speech, and Signal Proc.*, 867–870.

Poock, G.K. (1980a) *Experiments with Voice Input for Command and Control: Using Voice Input to Operate a Distributed Computer Network*, Naval Postgraduate School Report NPS55-80-016, NTIS Access A106138, Monterey, Ca, USA.

Poock, G.K., Martin, B.J., and Roland, E.F. (1983) *The Effect of Feedback to Users of Voice Recognition Equipment*, Naval Postgraduate School Report NPS55-83-003, Monterey, Ca, USA.

Rabiner, L.R., and Gold, B. (1975) *Theory and Applications of Digital Signal Processing*, Englewood Cliffs, NJ, Prentice-Hall.

Rabiner, L.R., and Juang, B.H. (1986) 'An Introduction to Hidden Markov Models', *IEEE ASSP Magazine*, **3**, 1, 4–16.

Rabiner, L.R., Rosenberg, A.E., and Levinson, S.E. (1978) 'Considerations in Dynamic Time Warping Algorithms for Discrete Word Recognition', *IEEE Trans. Acoust. Sp. Signal Proc.*, **ASSP-26**, 6, 575–582.

Rabiner, L.R., and Sambur, M.R. (1975) 'An Algorithm for Determining the Endpoints of Isolated Utterances', *Bell Syst. Techn. J.*, **54**, 297–315.

Rabiner, L.R., and Schafer, R. (1978) *Digital Processing of Speech Signals*, Englewood Cliffs, NJ, Prentice-Hall.

Reddy, D.R. (1975) *Speech Recognition: Invited Papers Presented at the 1974 IEEE Symposium*, New York, Academic Press.

Reddy, D.R. (1976) 'Speech Recognition by Machine: A Review', *Proc. of IEEE*, **64**, 501–531.

Sakoe, H., and Chiba, S. (1978) 'Dynamic Programming Optimization for Spoken Word Recognition', *IEEE Trans. Acoust. Sp. and Signal Proc.*, **ASSP-26**, 1, 67–72.

Sapir, E. (1938) 'La Realité Pyschologie des Phonèmes', *J. Psych.*, **30**, 247–265.

Schwartz, R.M. (1986) 'Probabilistic Methods for Modeling Acoustic Variability in Speech Recognition', in *Towards Robustness in Speech Rec.*, (W.A. Lea, Ed.), Apple Valley, Mn, Speech Science Publications.

Scott, P.B. (1975) *Voice Input Code Identifier*, Final Techn. Report, Rome Air Development Center, NY, USA.

Shannon, C.E., and Weaver, W. (1949) *The Mathematical Theory of Communication*, reprinted 1962, Urbana, U. Illinois Press.

Shipman, D.W., and Zue, V. W. (1982) 'Properties of Large Lexicons: Implications for Advanced Isolated Word Recognition Systems', *Proc. 1982 ICASSP*, 546–549.

Silverman, H.F., and Dixon, N.R. (1980) 'State Constrained Dynamic Programming (SCDP) for Discrete Utterance Recognition', *Proc. 1980 ICASSP*, 169–172.

Smith, A.R., and Sambur, M.R. (1980) 'Hypothesizing and Verifying Words for Speech Recognition', *Trends in Speech Rec.*, (W.A. Lea, Ed.), Englewood Cliffs, NJ, Prentice-Hall, 139–165.

Sondhi, M.M. (1968) 'New Methods of Pitch Extraction', *IEEE Trans. Audio and Electroacoustics*, **AU-16**, 262–266.

Sondhi, M.M., and Levinson, S.E. (1977) 'Relative Difficulty and Robustness of Speech Recognition Tasks that Use Grammatical Constraints', *JASA*, **63**, S1, 64 (A).

Sondhi, M.M., and Levinson, S.E. (1978) 'Computing Relative Redundancy to Measure Grammatical Constraint in Speech Recognition Tasks' *Proc. 1978 ICASSP*, 409–412.

Stevens, K.N. (1972) 'The Quantal Nature of Speech: Evidence from Articulatory-Acoustic Data', *Human Communication: A Unified View* (E.E. David and P.B. Denes, Eds.), New York, McGraw-Hill.

Taggart, J.L., Jr. and Wolfe, C.D. (1981) *Voice Recognition as an Input Modality for the Tacco Preflight Data Insertion Task in the P-3C Aircraft*, Naval Postgraduate School Masters Thesis, NTIC Access A105568, Monterey, Ca, USA.

Trager, G.L., and Smith, H.L., Jr. (1951) *An Outline of English Structure*, Studies in Linguistics: Occasional Papers, Norman, Ok, Battenburg Press.

Tsao, C., and Gray, R.M. (1986) 'An Approach to Speaker-Dependent Vowel Recognition Using Vector Quantization', in *Towards Robustness in Speech Rec.*, (W.A. Lea, Ed.), Apple Valley, Mn, Speech Science Publications.

Tsuruta, S. (1978) 'DP100 Voice Recognition System Achieves High Efficiency', *JEE* (Japanese Magazine), DEMPA Publ., Japan, July 1978, 50–54.

Vickroy, C.A., Silverman, H.F., and Dixon, N.R. (1982) 'Study of Human and Machine Discrete Utterance Recognition (DUR)', *Proc. 1982 IEEE Intern. Conf. on Acoustics, Speech, and Signal Proc.*, 2022–2025.

Viterbi, A.J. (1967) 'Error Bounds for Convolutional Codes and an Asymptotically Optimal Decoding Algorithm', *IEEE Trans. Info. Theory*, **It-13**, 260–269.

Waibel, A. (1982) *Towards Very Large Vocabulary Word Recognition*, Report CMU-CS-82-144, Dept. of Computer Sci., Carnegie-Mellon Univ., Pittsburgh, Pa, USA.

Wakita, H., and Matsumoto, H. (1986) 'Vowel Normalization by Spectral Warping', in *Towards Robustness in Speech Rec.*, (W.A. Lea, Ed.), Apple Valley, Mn, Speech Science Publications.

Walker, D.E. (1980) 'SRI Research on Speech Understanding', *Trends in Speech Rec.*, (W.A. Lea, Ed.), Englewood Cliffs, NJ, Prentice-Hall, 294–315.

Watt, W.C. (1968) 'Habitability', *American Documentation*, **19**, 338–351.

Wells, R.S. (1947) 'Immediate Constituents', *Language*, **23**, 81–117.

Wherry, CDR R. (1976) *The VRAS Voice Recognition and Synthesis System*, Naval Air Development Center, Warminster, Pa, USA.

White, G.M. (1978) 'Continuous Speech Recognition, Dynamic Programming, Knowledge Nets and Harpy', *Proc. Wescon*, Los Angeles, Ca, 28 February.

White, G.M., and Neely, R.B. (1975) 'Speech Recognition Experiments with Linear Prediction, Bandpass Filtering, and Dynamic Programming', *IEEE Trans. ASSP*, **ASSP-24**, 183–188.

Wilpon, J.G. (1986) 'A Study of the Effects of Telephone Transmission Noise on Speaker Independent Recognition', in *Towards Robustness in Speech Rec.*, (W.A. Lea, Ed.), Apple Valley, Mn, Speech Science Publications.

Wohlford, R.E., Smith, A.R., and Sambur, M.R. (1980) 'The Enhancement of Wordspotting Techniques', *Proc. IEEE 1980 Intern. Conf. on Acoustics, Speech, and Signal Proc.*, 209–212.

Wolf, J.J., and Woods, W.A. (1980) 'The HWIM Speech Understanding System', *Trends in Speech Rec.*, (W.A. Lea, Ed.), Englewood Cliffs, NJ, Prentice-Hall, 316–339.

Woodard, J.P., and Lea, W.A. (1984) 'New Measures of Performance for Speech Recognition Systems', *Proc. 1984 IEEE Intern. Conf. on Acoustics, Speech, and Signal Proc.*, **9**, 4, 1–4.

Woodard, J.P., and Nelson, J.T. (1982) 'An Information Theoretic Measure of Speech Recognition Performance', in Pallett, D. (1982), Editor *Proc. of the Workshop on Standardization for Speech I/O Tech.*, (D. Pallett, Ed.), Gainesville, Md, 35–41.

Woods, W.A. (1975) 'Syntax, Semantics, and Speech', *Speech Rec.: Invited Papers of the IEEE Sym.*, (D.R. Reddy, Ed.), New York, Academic Press, 345–400.

Woods, W.A. *et al.* (1976) *Speech Understanding Systems*, BBN Report No. 34–38 (5 Volumes), Final Report on ONR Contract No. N00014-75-C-0533, Bolt Beranek and Newman, Cambridge, Ma, USA.

Yellen, H.W. (1983) *A Preliminary Analysis of Human Factors Affecting the Recognition Accuracy of a Discrete Word Recognizer for C3 Systems*, Master's Thesis, Naval Postgraduate School, Monterey, Ca, USA.

Yilmaz, H. (1967) 'A Theory of Speech Perception', *Bulletin of Math. Biophysics*, **29**.

Zue, V.W., and Schwartz, R.M. (1980) 'Acoustic Processing and Phonetic Analysis', *Trends in Speech Rec.*, (W.A. Lea, Ed.), Englewood Cliffs, NJ, Prentice-Hall, 101–124.

CHAPTER 4

COMPUTATIONAL TECHNIQUES

Roger Moore

In this chapter, the reader is invited to review a wide range of established computational techniques for automatic speech recognition within one unified framework – that of 'speech pattern matching'. The review includes the simple as well as the complex, and lower-level sub-word processes as well as higher-level grammatical processes.

4.1 *The principles of speech pattern matching*

It is widely acknowledged that it may be many years before the techniques of automatic speech recognition (ASR) are able to challenge the accuracy and reliability of normal human speech perception; the development of a machine with the ability to transcribe accurately any spoken message from a wide range of talkers under less than optimal environmental conditions is still a long way off (see Chapter 16). However, since the early 1970s an approach to ASR has been evolving which, although rather superficial in appearance, is nevertheless achieving a modest amount of success, both from a scientific and from a commercial point of view[1]. This approach has become known as *speech pattern matching* (SPM).

Like most other approaches to automatic speech recognition, SPM is based on the premise that for a machine to be able to recognise speech, it must have access to *knowledge* about speech and about how words and sounds manifest themselves in acoustic signals. It also requires that this knowledge should be structured and manipulated in appropriate ways. However, SPM differs from other approaches in that it attempts to minimise the amount of heuristic a priori information about these structures and manipulations by capitalising on the fact that a prime

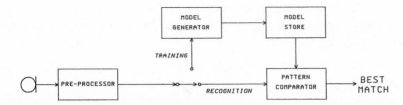

Figure 4.1 Pattern matching approach to automatic speech recognition

source of potentially reliable speech knowledge is the information contained in actual speech patterns.

The basic principle underlying SPM is illustrated in Fig. 4.1. First, a speech signal undergoes some kind of pre-processing which transforms the acoustic waveform into a sequence of analysis vectors. Then, during an initial *training* phase, example patterns are used to generate suitable *models* which are subsequently stored in the model store. The complexity of these models varies; in the simplest case a model might just be an example of a particular word, on the other hand more advanced schemes use relatively sophisticated statistical models. Finally, in the recognition phase, an unknown utterance is compared with the models in the model store and is assigned to the class of the model with which it is (in some sense) most similar.

This chapter is thus intended to provide an overview of how SPM techniques may be used to build appropriate computational models of speech patterns, and also, how these models may be used for the automatic recognition of unknown speech signals. It starts in Section 4.2 with a brief description of the most common signal-processing methods that are used to provide the initial representation of speech pattern data. Section 4.3 then introduces a range of techniques for modelling speech patterns and brings into one framework apparently different approaches such as *templates* and *hidden Markov models*.

Section 4.4 shows how unknown speech patterns may be recognised by matching them against stored models, and presents a detailed description of several isolated-word and connected-word recognition techniques including *dynamic time warping* (DTW).

Section 4.5 then presents a range of techniques for setting up the appropriate speech pattern models and also techniques for optimising the information contained within the models. It is shown how most of these advanced training procedures require the ability to compare speech patterns with the models (and with each other), thus drawing on the algorithms discussed in Section 4.4.

Finally, Section 4.6 describes how the processing requirements for the speech pattern matching algorithms may be reduced in order to achieve real-time practical operation.

4.2 *Pre-processing*

There are two main reasons why it is necessary to pre-process speech signals in advance of the pattern matching stages. First, it is desirable to transform the audio waveform into a domain where the patterning of speech is more explicit. Second, the data-rate in the transformed signal may be too high for the subsequent stages. Hence a large range of signal processing techniques are applicable to speech signals, both for achieving a suitable signal representation and for reducing the data-rate[2, 3].

SIGNAL REPRESENTATION
Fourier analysis
The most common and perhaps most informative way to analyse a speech signal is to estimate its short-time power spectrum using the *Fourier transform*. With a suitable choice of analysis window, the harmonic structure of the excitation function (voice pitch) may be ignored, and the resulting wide-band envelope spectrum contains information which derives mainly from the shape of the vocal tract.

This process may be effected digitally using the *discrete Fourier transform* (DFT) or, more easily, using a bank of analogue band-pass filters. The latter has the advantage that the distribution of frequency bands (channels) may be readily modelled on the critical bands of the human ear.

The UK channel vocoder analyser[4] employs such a filter-bank, and its particular arrangement of filter frequencies has been used in commercially available automatic speech recognition equipment. Figure 4.2 illustrates a *spectrogram* of the phrase *Sue will knock on the door at noon* obtained using this analyser. The design criteria for this particular analyser were concerned with minimising the digital output data-rate,

Figure 4.2   Speech spectrogram of the phrase 'Sue will knock on the door at noon'

and hence it derives an estimate of the spectrum (one frame) every 20 ms and it has only nineteen channels. In general, to preserve some of the faster transitional components of speech signals it is often desirable to have a much higher frame-rate. Also, unless a very large number of channels is used, it is difficult to obtain a good estimate of the spectrum shape around spectral peaks.

Cepstral analysis

Direct Fourier analysis requires a short data window in order to ignore the harmonic structure of speech signals. However, an alternative approach which is able to use a wider time window is homomorphic or *cepstral* processing. Essentially, a narrow-band spectrum (which contains the harmonic structure) is further transformed, using Fourier analysis, into the cepstral domain (the spectrum of the spectrum) where the components due to the pitch of the voice may be filtered out, and then transformed back to obtain a smooth envelope spectrum.

In practice, the first few terms (excluding the zero'th) of a cosine transform of the short-time log power spectrum may be used as an approximation to the cepstrum.

Linear predictive analysis

Linear predictive coding (LPC)[5] is a speech analysis technique which is particularly attractive from the computational point of view. In this scheme the autocorrelation characteristics of the speech waveform are exploited by estimating the value of the current sample using a linear combination of the previous *n* samples. The result is an analysis which is based on an all-pole model of the vocal tract. This means that LPC is particularly good at estimating the positions of spectral peaks during vowel sounds. However, during speech sounds which do not conform to an all-pole model (nasals and many consonants), LPC tends to over-estimate the bandwidths of the peaks.

DATA REDUCTION

The result of the initial transformation of a speech waveform is thus typically a regular sequence of analysis vectors, where each vector describes the distribution of energy at different frequencies (or the configuration of the vocal tract) at different times during an utterance. Further processing is then able to reduce the data-rate by capitalising on the *redundancy* in the transformed signal[6].

Vector quantisation

Since speech sounds do not fully occupy the space of all possible sounds implied by the dimensionality of the initial analysis vectors, it is possible to reduce the data-rate of a speech signal by *vector quantisation* (VQ). VQ is a technique whereby each frame of spectral data is coded by comparing it with a pre-stored set of reference frames, each of which is associated with a different output symbol. This means that a speech signal may be transformed into a sequence of symbols with a data-rate of **b** bits per frame if there are 2^b reference frames.

The set of reference frames (or *codebook*) is normally generated by a clustering procedure which minimises the average distortion resulting from coding a suitably long sequence of vectors. However, care is necessary in the use of VQ in automatic speech recognition, since the set of reference frames must be large enough to preserve the smallest distinctions required by the subsequent pattern matching algorithms.

Data-adaptive coding

Whereas VQ reduces the amount of information associated with a single frame of speech data, *variable rate coding* techniques may be used to exploit sequential properties. Such schemes are based on the observation that the changing pattern of sound in a speech signal gives rise to analysis vectors (e.g. spectra) which are often fairly similar over several frames. In these circumstances it is possible to re-sample the analysis vectors at a rate dictated by the amount of change in the signal, thereby reducing the overall frame-rate.

For a continuous signal, the simplest scheme is to set a threshold such that an analysis vector is produced only if the similarity between it and the previous vector exceeds the threshold; the higher the threshold, the fewer samples will be taken in the more stationary regions of the signal. In the special case where the first and last frames of data are known, it is possible to set the threshold such that a fixed number of frames are retained; this particular method is known as *trace segmentation*.

4.3 *Modelling speech patterns*

The underlying principle of speech pattern matching is that *a priori* knowledge (i.e. insight and assumptions) about the structure of speech (e.g. words) is supplemented with *analytical* knowledge (examples of actual speech patterns) in order to construct models against which unknown patterns may be compared for recognition. Therefore, having established some techniques for producing an appropriate and efficient representation of speech data, the next stage in SPM is the collection and storage of reference speech patterns in a form that is amenable to the subsequent pattern comparison processes.

The quality of both *a priori* and analytical knowledge is obviously of paramount importance; assumptions about suitable model structures must not be too far from reality, and the example speech patterns must be reasonably representative. The key to successful model building is to maximise the use of the actual measured data by sharing information (*pooling*) where possible, whilst at the same time minimising the loss of information by inappropriate pooling.

However, by far the most important concept is that, no matter how well the derived data structures model the example patterns, it must be possible to generalise that information in appropriate ways in order to accommodate the inherent variability of speech and to be able to correctly recognise speech patterns that have not been observed previously. This means that the models can be regarded as having the capability of *generating* (synthesising) a range of patterns conditioned by the structure of the model and by the examples that have actually been observed.

SIMPLE WHOLE-WORD MODELS

Perhaps the simplest possible model for a particular word is an actual example of that word. Such an example could then be used as a reference pattern or *template* in the subsequent recognition process. In this case the SPM process is known as *whole-word pattern matching* (WWPM).

However, the inherent variability of speech patterns means that no two words are ever exactly the same, even when spoken carefully by one talker. Hence to be useful, a model must incorporate some *stochastic* (statistical) knowledge, either measured or assumed, which may be used as a first-order method for generalising from a particular example.

STOCHASTIC MODELS

The manner in which words and their speech patterns vary is obviously highly structured and is in some way related to the performance of a talker's speech production mechanism. However, from a speech pattern modelling point of view, it may be sufficient to characterise the variability within the explicit dimensions prescribed by the patterns themselves. Thus, taking a word as a pattern of acoustic energy in time and frequency, it should be profitable to consider the variability in each of these dimensions.

This means that even a single example of a word may be treated as a model and may be generalised by assuming, for example, that the actual values in the analysis vectors in fact represent the means of some multivariate distribution of values. Further, it would be reasonable (in lieu of any other information) to assume that these distributions are normal with unit variance and zero covariance. The consequences of these assumptions will be made clear in Section 4.4.

The above discussion indicates how the information in the analysis vectors may be generalised; the time evolution of the pattern remains unaffected. However, a major source of observed variability is that a talker is not able to produce patterns which are consistently the same length. Hence this behaviour must also be modelled.

Markov models

A suitable framework for dealing with the time structure of speech patterns can be found in *Markov modelling*. Each analysis vector in a speech pattern may be regarded as the output of a Markov process, where each vector is associated with a *state* in a *Markov chain*; transitions between the states describe the time evolution of the pattern.

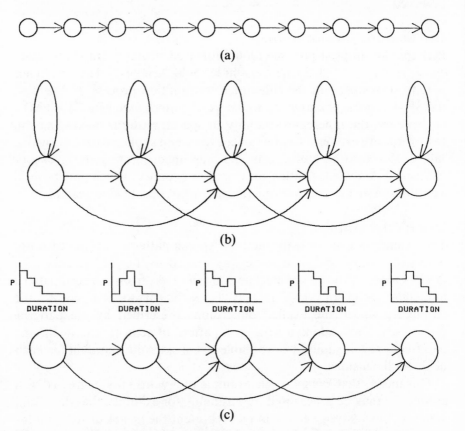

Figure 4.3 Three forms of Markov model: (a) simple Markov chain; (b) Markov model with alternative transitions; (c) semi-Markov model

For a single whole-word model such as a template, transitions simply step from one state to the next (see Fig. 4.3(a)). However, a suitable generalising assumption might be that the variability in the observed sequence of analysis vectors could be described by the possibility of repeating the same frame several times, or missing out a frame completely. Such a Markov model is thus able to generalise from a single example of a speech pattern by the expedient of adding extra transitions to the model (see Fig. 4.3(b)).

Hidden Markov models
A Markov model with its various transitions from state to state may, of course, be made stochastic by assigning probabilities to each transition. It can also employ a stochastic generalisation for the analysis vectors, in which case it is known as a *hidden Markov model* (HMM), 'hidden' because there is no longer a unique association between a state and a particular analysis vector[7].

If **H** is a hidden Markov model with **S** states, then such a model is completely specified by:

$$\mathbf{H} = (\boldsymbol{\pi}, \mathbf{A}, \mathbf{B}) \tag{4.1}$$

where $\boldsymbol{\pi}$ is an initial state probability vector $(\mathbf{S} \times 1)$, **A** is a transition probability matrix $(\mathbf{S} \times \mathbf{S})$, and **B** is a state output probability matrix which may contain continuous multivariate probability density functions or discrete probability density functions over a finite set of symbols (due to vector quantisation).

The importance of HMMs is that the number of states in the model does not have to be the same as the number of frames in an example pattern. In fact it is an advantage if the number of states is significantly lower than the number of frames because this means that more than one frame is associated with each state in the model. Thus more data is available at each state for modelling the analysis vector probability density functions (information is pooled).

A state in a hidden Markov model is thus able to model a *segment* of a speech pattern over which the analysed data is observed to be relatively stable. A sequence of such states is therefore a structural description of a speech pattern which can generalise to a wide range of potential speech patterns by reflecting the stochastic variability that is present in the different dimensions of the original pattern.

Semi-Markov models
The way in which a stochastic Markov process models the length of a segment of a speech pattern is through the probability associated with

the transition which connects a state back to itself: the *loop transition probability*. This mechanism means that (within a state) the probability of a sequence of vectors of length **n** is $\mathbf{p}^{n-1}$, where **p** is the loop transition probability. Obviously as **n** increases, $\mathbf{p}^{n-1}$ decreases, hence the model contains an in-built assumption that the most likely segment duration is only one frame.

Intuitively, the loop transition probability appears to be a rather weak model of segment durations in speech patterns. It is perhaps more likely that such regions would have a most probable duration of several frames and a lower probability of being either longer or shorter.

A Markov model which incorporates this assumption is termed a *semi-Markov model*, and it is achieved by eliminating the loop transition probability and substituting instead a suitable statistical distribution of the amount of time spent in a state (see Fig. 4.3(c))[8].

SUB-WORD MODELS
Phonetic segments
The foregoing discussion has talked in general terms about speech patterns, but was mainly concerned with modelling whole words. Of course, whole-word modelling eventually reaches a limit of usefulness, since the total number of models required (for languages like English) would be prohibitively high.

It might seem desirable, therefore, to employ the same principles at the sub-word level in order to exploit the phonetic structure which is common to all the words in a given language. However, this is somewhat more difficult since the boundaries between phonetic segments (if they exist at all) are rather unclear. Nevertheless, such an approach has been demonstrated to be reasonably successful, particularly for modelling data from a range of talkers.

For example, Fig. 4.4 shows a Markov model for a phonetic network which characterises some of the alternative ways of pronouncing the word *apprentice*[9].

Discriminative networks
An alternative to explicitly modelling phonetic segments is to combine whole-word models in a way which capitalises on the sounds that are shared between different words. For example, the whole-word models for the utterances *stalagmite* and *stalactite* might contain only limited information about the common *stala-* and *-ite* sounds. If, however, that common information were to be pooled, then both words would enjoy a far better model for these regions. The stochastic generalisation processes would then become common to both words and would

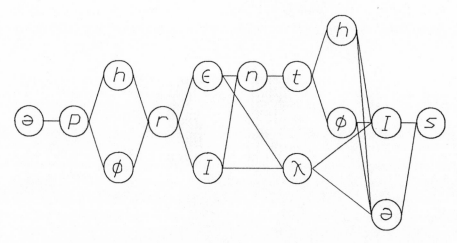

Figure 4.4 Phonetic network for the word 'apprentice'

therefore not interfere differentially with the recognition process for the *discriminative* parts of the patterns[10].

This process is equivalent to deriving a network-type data structure for speech patterns by combining word-models in appropriate ways. The combined model is thus able to *focus* the recognition process onto the regions of the patterns which are most relevant to the distinctions between them. Figure 4.5 illustrates the discriminative spectrogram network for *stalagmite* and *stalactite*, together with the equivalent Markov model.

4.4 *Recognition: matching speech against the models*

Having established a range of techniques for modelling speech patterns, this section addresses the central theme of SPM: how to recognise an unknown pattern.

In statistical pattern recognition terms it is possbile to obtain the best classification of an observation vector $\mathbf{O}$ with respect to a set of classes $\mathbf{C}$ by finding for which $\mathbf{j}$ the probability of the $\mathbf{j}$th class given the data is a maximum[11]:

$\mathbf{O}$ is from class $\mathbf{C}_i$ if

$$\mathbf{P}(\mathbf{C}_i|\mathbf{O}) = \max_{\mathbf{j}} \mathbf{P}(\mathbf{C}_j|\mathbf{O}) \qquad (4.2)$$

(where $\mathbf{P}(\mathbf{C}_i|\mathbf{O})$ is defined as the conditional probability of $\mathbf{C}_i$ assuming $\mathbf{O}$).

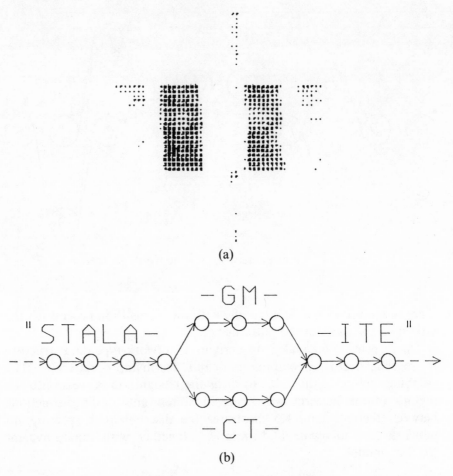

Figure 4.5 Discriminative network for the words 'stalagmite' and 'stalactite'; (a) spectrogram network; (b) equivalent Markov model

It is difficult to measure $P(C|O)$ directly; however, using Bayes' theorem:

$$P(C_j|O) = \frac{P(O|C_j).P(C_j)}{P(O)} \qquad (4.3)$$

Thus by substituting, and by ignoring the *a priori* frequencies of occurrence of the classes, a *maximum likelihood classifier* is obtained:

O is from C_i if

$$P(O|C_i) = \max_j P(O|C_j) \qquad (4.4)$$

The advantage of equation (4.4) is that $P(O|C_j)$ is more easily measurable for each class. Hence for an observation vector which is a speech pattern $O(N, T)$ (where N is the size of the analysis vector and T is the number of frames in the pattern) it would be possible to construct the optimal statistical classifier.

In practice, such a high dimensionality problem ($N \times T$ parameters) requires an inordinate amount of training data and is therefore unfeasible. Thus to make recognition tractable it is necessary to introduce some assumptions:

1. Assume multivariate normal probability density functions – this means that it is only necessary to measure class means and covariance matrices;
2. Assume that each analysis vector and each element of each analysis vector are independent – this means that the covariance matrices are diagonal;
3. Assume that all variances are equal, and equal to 1.

These assumptions lead to the following consequences:

$$P(O|C_j) = \prod_{n,t} P(O(n, t)|C_j) \qquad (4.5)$$

where $\prod$ denotes the product of the values of the following expression for all n and t, and $O(n, t)$ is the scalar value of the unknown speech pattern at element n of the analysis vector at time t.

Also, from the one-dimensional form of the normal distribution:

$$P(O(n, t)|C_j) = \frac{e^{-[O(n,t) - \mu(n,t)^\circ C_j]^2/2}}{\sqrt{2\pi}} \qquad (4.6)$$

where $\mu(n, t)|C_j$ is the mean value of element n of the analysis vector at time t for the class j speech pattern.

If, for convenience, logarithms are taken and constant terms are ignored then:

$$\log P(O(n, t)^\circ C_j) \propto -[O(n, t) - \mu(n, t)^\circ C_j]^2 \qquad (4.7)$$

and the product of terms in equation (4.5) becomes a sum:

$$\log P(^\circ C_j) \propto -\sum_{n,t} (O(n, t) - \mu(n, t)|C_j)^2 \qquad (4.8)$$

which is simply the *squared Euclidean distance* between two speech patterns. Hence, by applying the assumptions stated above, the maximum likelihood classifier may be replaced by the more familiar *nearest neighbour classifier*, which determines the best match by finding the class for which the distance between the unknown pattern and a set of stored patterns (templates) is the minimum:

O is from **C**$_i$ if

$$\log P(O|C_j) = -\min_j \sum_{n,t} (O(n, t) - \mu(n, t)|C_j)^2 \qquad (4.9)$$

DIRECT PATTERN MATCHING

The preceding argument indicates how isolated-word recognition may be performed very simply using example whole-word patterns as templates, and then recognising an unknown input by finding which template is the smallest distance from the unknown. However, the arguments only hold if **N** and **T** are fixed; the patterns which are to be compared must be of equal sizes. It is unlikely that the size of the analysis vector will vary, but it has already been mentioned in an earlier section that the length of a word may vary a great deal. Thus in order to construct a practical recogniser it is necessary to fix **T**.

One way of doing this is simply to align the beginnings of the patterns which are to be compared and then to 'chop off' the parts of the longer pattern which do not overlap the shorter. Such a technique can be thought of as an *absolute pattern match* and, although rather simple-minded, it requires the minimum of computation and has been shown to exhibit some useful performance.

LINEAR TIME-ALIGNMENT

A better solution to the problem of variability in the lengths of speech patterns is to *time-normalise* words in order to make all patterns have the same length **T**. In its simplest form, such a normalisation may be applied uniformly along the length of a pattern. Such a process is termed *linear time-normalisation*.

Figure 4.6 illustrates the process on a pair of utterances of the word *helicopter.* The two original patterns are shown at right angles so that the time-scales may be compared. It is clear that the vertical utterance is much longer than the horizontal version. The rectangle to the right is prescribed by the lengths of the two original words, and the diagonal line is therefore the linear time-alignment between the patterns.

If the horizontal pattern is regarded as a Markov model for the word *helicopter*, then the linear time-alignment between it and the vertical pattern can be seen as a generalisation of the horizontal utterance by the duplication of every other analysis vector throughout the word. The synthetic pattern generated by this process can be seen alongside the original vertical pattern. It can be seen that the two vertical patterns are fairly similar (more similar than the originals), hence the calculated distances will reflect this similarity reasonably well.

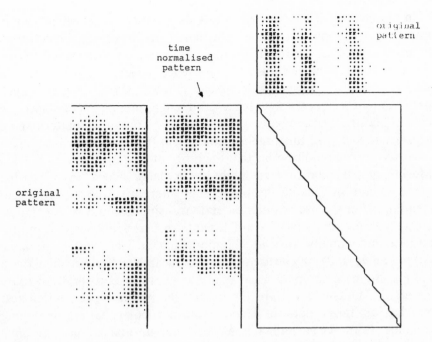

Figure 4.6 Example of linear time-normalisation of the word 'helicopter'

Linear time-alignment requires only a small amount of computation and the recognition accuracy for a small vocabulary is sufficient for this technique to have formed the basis of many of the earliest commercial isolated-word recognisers in the 1960s and 70s.

NON-LINEAR TIME-ALIGNMENT

The recognition accuracy of linear time-normalisation begins to drop significantly when the number of patterns to be distinguished (the vocabulary) grows beyond about 30 to 100 words. The reason for this is that linear time-scale distortion is ultimately not an adequate model of what actually takes place when talkers produce words which are shorter or longer. Also, linear time-normalisation is susceptible to *endpoint detection* errors, since correct normalisation depends on the first and last frames in one pattern being correctly aligned with the first and last frames of the other pattern. This can be seen in Fig. 4.6, where the end of the horizontal pattern has been missed and extra silence has been included; it is clear that a better match would have resulted if the end of the horizontal pattern had been determined more accurately (unfortunately this may not always be possible due to the presence of background noise).

In practice, what happens when talkers produce words which vary in length is that some sounds are shortened (or lengthened) more than others. Hence a better model of time-scale distortion is one which allows different parts of the patterns to be shortened (or lengthened) more than others, and this behaviour is precisely what Markov-based speech pattern models can capture. Hence, for recognition, it is necessary to be able to find the best time-alignment between an unknown pattern and a Markov model, and this time-alignment will be *non-linear*.

However, it should be clear that the range of possible patterns which a Markov model could generate might be very large indeed – even if such a model is not stochastic, the number of alternative output sequences resulting from the use of different state transitions could be enormous. Hence computationally it is not feasible to assess all possible output patterns individually. Instead, the mathematical technique of *dynamic programming* (DP) may be used[12]. DP is a search technique which (with the minimum of computational effort) is guaranteed to find the route through a Markov model which generates the synthetic pattern that best matches an input pattern. Hence, this particular pattern matching technique is known as optimal non-linear time-normalisation or *dynamic time warping* (DTW)[13, 14].

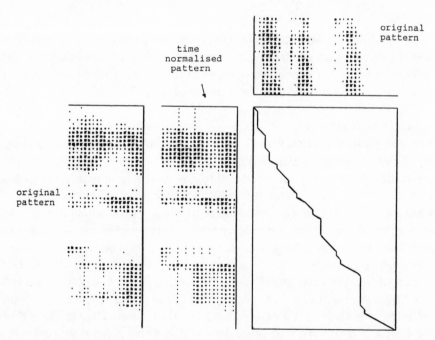

Figure 4.7 Example of optimal non-linear time normalisation of the word 'helicopter'

Dynamic time warping

Figure 4.7 shows the result of using DP to find the best time alignment between the two examples of *helicopter* discussed earlier. The example clearly shows how similar the original vertical utterance is to the non-linearly time-normalised version of the horizontal utterance. It also shows how this process is able to overcome the end-detection error.

In this example, the second vertical utterance is generated according to the Markov model for the horizontal utterance that is shown in Fig. 4.3(b): one state per frame, loop transitions which allow frames to be repeated, and state skipping transitions which allow frames to be deleted. Also, since the model is in fact only one example of the word, squared Euclidean distances were used, and all transitions were equiprobable (therefore accruing no extra distances). DP is thus able to find the *time registration path* which minimises the sum of squared Euclidean frame to frame distances along its length.

Hence, if

$$d(i, j) = \sum_n (O(n, t_i) - \mu(n, t_j))^2 \qquad (4.10)$$

is the distance between frame i $(1 \leqslant i \leqslant I)$ in an unknown pattern and frame j $(1 \leqslant j \leqslant J)$ in the model pattern, then the formulation for the dynamic programming calculation is the following recursive expression:

$$D(i, j) = d(i, j) + \min [D(i - 1, j), D(i - 1, j - 1), D(i - 1, j - 2)] \qquad (4.11)$$

where $D(i, j)$ is the *accumulated distance* between the two patterns up to frames i and j, with the initial condition $D(0, 0) = 0$. Hence the resulting distance between the complete patterns is $D(I, J)$. This is termed the *cumulative distance*.

The three terms within the minimisation in equation (4.11) specify the allowable transitions in the underlying Markov model; $D(i - 1, j)$ corresponds to staying in the same state (the loop transition for state j), $D(i - 1, j - 1)$ corresponds to moving from one state to the next (state $j - 1$ to state j), and $D(i - 1, j - 2)$ corresponds to moving on two states by missing one out (state $j - 2$ to j).

To illustrate how these techniques are used in practice, Fig. 4.8 shows an example of isolated-word recognition using DTW. In the example there are three reference patterns, the digits *one*, *two* and *three* shown vertically. The horizontal pattern is the word to be recognised, in this case a *one*. The unknown word has been compared with each of the three reference patterns using DTW, and the resulting non-linear time-alignments are shown. Also shown are the cumulative distances for each

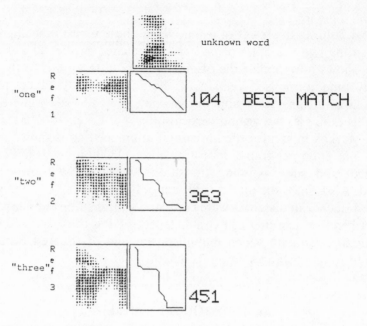

Figure 4.8   Isolated word recognition using dynamic time warping

match, and the best match is determined by the smallest. Hence the unknown word has been correctly recognised as *one*.

DTW is computationally much more expensive than linear time-normalisation, but since the late 1970s it has been within the capabilities of modern electronic circuitry and several DTW-based recognisers are available commercially.

Viterbi classification

The DTW technique is particularly interesting since, by ignoring state transition probabilities and by operating in the log-probability domain (distances), the resultant computations are intuitively rather simple and can function using only one example pattern for each word. However, exactly the same DP technique may be used to match an unknown pattern with the more sophisticated Markov modelling techniques which operate in the probability domain and which include the transition probabilities.

For example, to compare a speech pattern **O** with a hidden Markov model **H**, the required recursive expression is:

$$\hat{\alpha}(t, i) = \max_{j = 1, i} \hat{\alpha}(t - 1, j) \cdot a_{ji} \cdot b_{it} \qquad (4.12)$$

where $\hat{\alpha}(T, S)$ is the probability of the most probable state sequence finishing in state **S** at time **T**.

Recognition conducted on this basis is commonly termed *Viterbi* classification.

Maximum likelihood
As has just been demonstrated, Viterbi classification determines the most probable match between a speech pattern and a model. However, from equation (4.4) it might be considered more appropriate to calculate the likelihood of the observations given each model: $P(O|H_j)$, and to do this it is necessary to sum the probabilities of *all* state sequences of length T. This may also be achieved using dynamic programming by means of the following recursive expression:

$$\alpha(t, i) = \sum_{j=1,i} \alpha(t - 1, j) . a_{ji} . b_{it} \qquad (4.13)$$

hence

$$P(O|H) = \alpha(T, S) \qquad (4.14)$$

and recognition based on this measure of similarity is called maximum likelihood or *Baum-Welch* recognition.

CONNECTED MODELS
The use of time-alignment techniques is obviously very important for achieving practical recognition performance for isolated-word recognition. However, it turns out that it is possible to extend the techniques from single patterns (*isolated-mode*) to sequences of patterns (*connected-mode*) using relatively simple modifications to the algorithms.

The basic notion is that, in order to recognise a speech pattern which contains a sequence of sub-patterns (for example, a sentence containing a sequence of words), it is necessary to find a time *registration path* between the unknown pattern and the best sequence of reference patterns or models. Obviously there will be a very large number of possible sequences which must be compared in order to find the best, but this also turns out to be soluble using DP.

Two-level algorithm
The first practical attempt to extend SPM beyond isolated words explicitly employed two levels of DP: one at the word level to find the optimal reference patterns to match parts of the unknown pattern, and one at the phrase level to find the optimal way of connecting together the partial matches resulting from the first level[15].

At the first level, DTW is used to find the minimum cumulative distance between each reference pattern **R** and all possible start frames **O(s)** and all possible end frames **O(e)** in the unknown pattern **D(R, s, e)**. At the second level, DP is used to find the path through **D(R, s, e)** which minimises the total cumulative distance starting with **s = 1** and ending with **e = T**.

$$D'(m, e) = \min_{s} \left[\min_{R} (D(R, s, e)) + D'(m - 1, s - 1) \right] \quad (4.15)$$

where **D'(m, e)** is the cumulative distance obtained by matching the best concatenation of **m** reference patterns to the portion of the unknown pattern between frame 1 and frame **e**, and the minimum of **D(R, s, e)** over **R** is the distance resulting from the best reference pattern match between frames **s** and **e** of the unknown pattern.

The computation may be stopped once **m** is considered to be large enough to cover the maximum number of words expected in a phrase. The result can then be found by selecting the maximum value of **D'(m, T)** over **m** and then backtracking through **D(R, s, e)** to find the best sequence of **m** words.

One-pass algorithm

An alternative algorithm which achieves precisely the same result may be obtained by combining the two levels of DP into a single DP optimisation[16]. This results in a considerable saving in computation, and also makes the process somewhat easier to understand.

The technique simply introduces transitions from the end states of each reference model to the beginning states of all models (including back to the same model). This means that a time registration path is allowed to jump from one reference pattern to another, and the DP technique is effectively matching the unknown phrase against a 'super' reference pattern consisting of the best sequence of individual patterns.

Figure 4.9 illustrates the scheme for DTW. The reference patterns are the same as in Fig. 4.8, but this time the unknown pattern consists of the sequence of words *one one two one three*. The best time registration path is shown, and it can be seen jumping around from reference to reference. The trajectory of the path reveals that the phrase is correctly recognised.

Either the two-level algorithm or the one-pass algorithm may be used for the recognition of connected sub-word models. However, unless the precise pronunciation of the words is required as an output from the process, it would be appropriate to use Baum-Welch recognition below the word level, and Viterbi recognition above the word level[17].

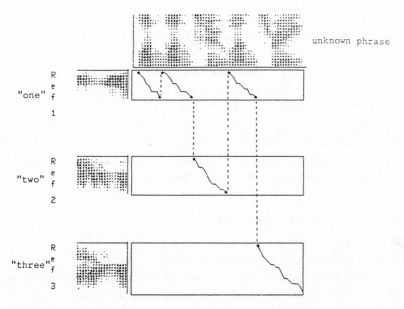

Figure 4.9 Connected word recognition using dynamic time warping

4.5 *Training: constructing the models*

The previous sections have identified different types of whole-word and sub-word models and have also outlined the various ways in which such models may be compared with unknown speech patterns in order to achieve recognition. This section discusses the procedures that are necessary for establishing the models in the first place; having decided the type of model to be used, the relevant speech data has to be loaded into it. This is referred to as the *training* process and is primarily concerned with estimating the parameters of the speech pattern models.

The training process may be viewed as having three major components: first, the overall structure of the model must be determined (what type of model, how many states, etc.); second, some initial estimates must be made for the parameters of the model (the output probabilities, for example); third, iterative techniques may be applied to improve the parameter estimates. The goal of the whole process is to maximise the accuracy of the modelling (which, if done appropriately, should improve the performance of the resulting recogniser).

CHOOSING THE TYPE OF MODEL
The type of model that is preferred will depend to a great extent on the amount of processing power available for training, the processing power

available for recognition, and the recognition accuracy required. In general, stochastic models are more accurate than simpler models, but they inevitably require more training. The processing required for recognition is lower for reduced-state models than for one-frame-per-state models, but the training algorithms are much more sophisticated and the processing requirement is higher again.

The number of states required in a reduced-state model is not easy to determine. However, since these models assume that speech patterns consist of a sequence of quasi-stable spectral regions, it has been found that about five states are appropriate for English words[18].

GENERATING THE INITIAL MODEL

Whole-word models

Following on from the arguments in previous sections which showed that a single word-pattern may be treated as a stochastic model with suitable simplifying assumptions, it is often only necessary to have one example of each pattern in order to generate the initial models. This means that the easiest training procedure for most of the recognition techniques discussed in Section 4.4 (including DTW and connected-word recognition) is simply to obtain from each talker one example of each word in the vocabulary; these patterns constitute *one-frame-per-state* Markov models and no extra processing is involved.

If more examples of each pattern are available, then storing them all can be helpful in capturing a degree of variability. However, it is also possible to reject examples which contain unwanted artefacts, or to select good reference patterns, by comparing training patterns with each other using a recognition procedure[19].

Reduced-state models

If advantage wants to be taken of the increased recognition performance offered by the information sharing properties of reduced-state models (e.g. hidden Markov models), then a certain amount of processing of the training examples is required. For a given number of states in the reduced-state model, it is necessary to divide an example pattern into that number of segments. The resulting groups of analysis vectors are assigned to the relevant states.

One way of achieving this segmentation is to exploit the properties of a data-adaptive coding technique such as trace segmentation (Section 4.2). Alternatively, DP may be used to find the segmentation which minimises some objective cost function associated with minimum distortion of the original pattern[20].

Sub-word models

The phonetic-segment based models are perhaps the most difficult and time-consuming to produce. Various approaches have been attempted, but the most successful involves carefully segmenting the speech patterns by hand; a process which can only sensibly be undertaken by a person with the appropriate phonetic training.

On the other hand, the discriminative network approach to sub-word modelling employs an automatic technique for establishing the network structure. In the simplest case only one example pattern of each word is required and DTW is used to compare the different word patterns. This determines the parts of the patterns which are similar and the parts which are dissimilar. An iterative technique is then used to find the level of similarity required to decide whether the corresponding parts of the different words should be combined or not. The value found is the value which maximises the recognition accuracy on a small test set of patterns. This value then defines the structure of the appropriate discriminative network.

ESTIMATING THE PARAMETERS

State output probabilities

The relevant state output distributions may be estimated from the collection of analysis vectors at each state. The simplest method for collecting such vectors is to use more than one example of each word pattern. The resulting state output distributions would thus represent the average of the examples. Such a technique is applicable to all types of model, although it is sensible to use time-aligned patterns otherwise the pooling process is likely to blur the distributions and give rise to a loss of information.

For a reduced-state model, each state will also have a collection of vectors produced by the initial model generation process. Only one example pattern is required to make a crude estimate of the state output probabilities but again, more examples will give more reliable estimates.

State transition probabilities

As well as the state output probability distributions, it will also be usual with reduced-state models to obtain estimates of the state transition probabilities. This is obviously essential for semi-Markov models (whether reduced-state or not).

One technique for measuring the transition probabilities is known as *time-scale variability analysis* (TVA)[21] and requires at least five examples of each word pattern. The principle of TVA is quite straightforward: an initial model is time-aligned with each training pattern in turn, and the relative frequencies of use of the allowable transitions in the model are calculated. The resulting probabilities are then attached to the appropriate transitions. The importance of TVA is that it may be applied to one-state-per-frame models and hence to DTW-based recognition. In this case the pattern matching process is known as *locally constrained dynamic time warping* (LCDTW)[22] and is equivalent to Viterbi classification but in the log-probability (distance) domain.

IMPROVING THE ESTIMATES

The training steps outlined earlier in this section are all that are required to estimate the parameters of any of the speech pattern models presented in Section 4.3 (even one as sophisticated as a hidden semi-Markov model). However, it should be clear that the better parameter estimation techniques employed time-alignment in order to match extra training examples against the initial model. This means that the quality of the parameter estimation depends on the quality of the initial model because of its effect on the accuracy of the time-alignment. Consequently a bad initial model may not be improved with more training.

On the other hand, if a model is improved by the parameter estimation process, then the resulting model may be used as a new initial model and the parameter estimation procedures may be applied once more. It is thus possible to derive iterative procedures which gradually refine the parameters of a model until the best estimates are obtained for a given training set.

Such an iterative procedure which is of particular interest is the *Baum-Welch re-estimation* algorithm[23, 24]. This algorithm has been used for hidden Markov and hidden semi-Markov models[25], and is founded on a theorem which guarantees that, given a set of training patterns **U(1)**, ..., **U(S)** and a model **M**, a new model **M*** will be produced where:

$$P(U(1), ..., U(S)|M^*) > P(U(1), ..., U(S)|M) \qquad (4.16)$$

Thus the Baum-Welch re-estimation formulae may be applied repeatedly until the change in the value of **P(U(1), ..., U(S)|M)** between successive models **M** falls below some threshold. However, it must be noted that the Baum-Welch algorithm is simply a *hill climbing* technique; the process is only guaranteed to find a model **M** for which **P(U(1), ..., U(S)|M)** is locally maximal: again, the initial model is very important.

4.6 Real-time operation

It should be clear from the previous sections that all of the better techniques for SPM make significant use of the properties of dynamic programming. The guaranteed optimality of this particular search process ensures that the information contained in a speech pattern is used to good advantage in either training or recognition, and that locally bad matches need not affect the final solution.

However, the price that must be paid for this optimality is that, despite being much more efficient than more heuristic search techniques, DP is nevertheless computationally expensive; in a match between a speech pattern and a model, all frames in the pattern must be compared with all states in the model. This means that reducing the amount of computation will almost invariably result in a loss of optimality in the pattern matching process and perhaps lead to a consequential reduction in recognition accuracy.

Nevertheless, for practical reasons associated with the need to achieve real-time operation it is often necessary to sacrifice the optimality of DP, but in a way that is least detrimental to the pattern matching process. Indeed, in some cases it is possible to increase recognition accuracy by not giving DP the freedom it requires.

REDUCING THE SEARCH SPACE
Syntax
The technique for accommodating connected models outlined in Section 4.4 are capable of recognising *any* sequence of words (or sub-word segments) by matching against the complete inventory of available models. The result will be the best sequence of models which matches the unknown speech pattern. However, in a practical situation it is probable that many sequences have no meaning, for example at the word level there are rules which govern the order in which words may be spoken. Similarly, at the sub-word level there may be rules which specify which sound patterns may follow others. In general, there will be a grammar or *syntax* which specifies these sequential properties (see Chapter 2).

This means that it is not necessary for the search process to spend time considering matches which are not allowed by the syntax. Hence, a significant reduction in computation may be obtained and, in this case, an increase in recognition performance would follow (because an unknown pattern cannot be misrecognised as an illegal sequence of models).

A syntax may itself be specified as a Markov model (see Fig. 4.10). Thus the rules of word order may be conveniently integrated into the complete Markov modelling framework; the transition probabilities from one model to another are specified by the transition probabilities in the syntax model. This also means that models may be updated (trained)

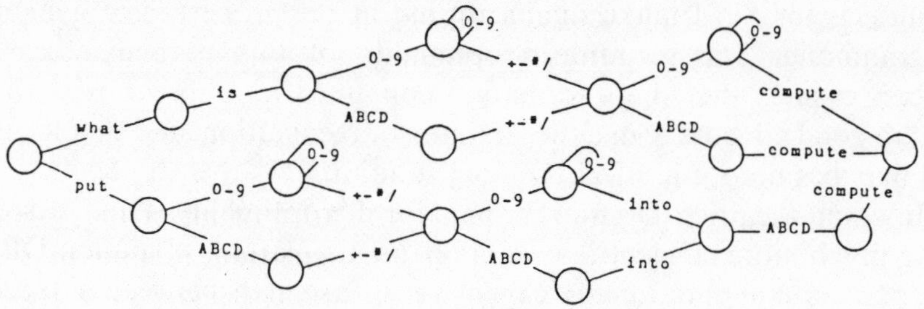

Figure 4.10   Syntax for a voice controlled calculator

even though the input might consist of several patterns in sequence. At the word level this process is known as *embedded training* (in practice it is precisely equivalent to the training techniques already discussed in Section 4.5).

The price to be paid for exploiting syntactic rules is that a talker has to remember the allowable sequences. If a word (or sound) is said in the wrong context, then the pattern matching process will be obliged to misrecognise it.

Beam-search

One reason why DP is optimal is that the search process extends into regions which, although representing possible matches, are in practice highly unlikely. Hence, it is possible to achieve a reasonable reduction in computation, with only a small risk of reaching a non-optimal result, by restricting the search in some way.

A good way of achieving this effect is to use the *beam-search* technique which exploits the fact that part way through DP calculations it is possible to measure the value of the best solution (minimum distance or maximum probability) up to that point. This means that on the next iteration of the process, the search can be limited to solutions which lie within a given range of the current best solution.

The advantage of this technique is that when there is ambiguity in the matching process there will be a range of solutions, all of which are fairly close to each other, and the beam will be wide (heavy computational load). When there is little ambiguity, there will be few competing solutions and the beam will be narrow (light computational load). Thus the scheme ensures that most of the computation takes place when it is most needed in order to resolve pattern ambiguities.

The danger with the beam-search technique is that if the range of alternatives is too restricted (beam too narrow) then the optimal solution might be lost if there is a momentary bad match in the data. However, in practice it has been found that a factor of four reduction in computation can be achieved without affecting recognition performance[26].

CONTINUOUS OPERATION

Another technique which exploits the intermediate properties of DP is based on the concept that by tracing the history of all of the partial matches available at each mid-point in the calculation, it is possible to determine a point in the past where all current matches agree on a partial solution. This means that the result of the matching process is completely determined up to that earlier point, even though the full match is not complete, and it is possible to output that part of the final result.

This technique is known as *partial traceback*[27] and it is particularly useful since it enables a recogniser to run continuously; the pattern matching process can take in new data and apply the DP optimisation at the same time as the results for older data are being output. The process does not sacrifice the optimality properties of DP; the only consequence of the technique is that the delay between input and output is proportional to the amount of ambiguity in the pattern matching. Partial traceback has been found to be particularly useful for continuous connected-word recognition.

If partial traceback is combined with beam-search, then it is even possible to output the identity of a recognised word before it has been completely uttered! This will occur when competing words are sufficiently different that the beam falls totally within only one of them. Partial traceback will detect this resolution of ambiguity at the word level and would output the word. This is a property that may or may not be required; however, if the beam is too narrow in this situation, then it is possible for a recogniser to discriminate between two similar words before the deciding sounds have been uttered and will thus begin to misrecognise badly.

4.7 *References*

1. Moore, R.K. (1985) 'Systems for isolated and connected-word recognition' in *New Systems and Architectures for Automatic Speech Recognition and Synthesis*, DeMori, R., and Suen, C. (Eds.). New York: Springer-Verlag.
2. Flanagan, J.L. (1972) *Speech Analysis, Synthesis and Perception.* New York: Springer-Verlag.
3. Schafer, R.W., and Rabiner, L.R. (1975) 'Digital representations of speech signals'. *Proc. IEEE*, **63**, 662–677.

4. Holmes, J.N. (1980) 'The JSRU channel vocoder'. *IEEE Proc. Communications, Radar and Signal Processing*, **127**, Pt. F, 53–60.
5. Makhoul, J. (1975) 'Linear prediction: A tutorial review'. *Proc. IEEE*, **63**, 561–580.
6. Pieraccini, R., and Billi, R. (1983) 'Experimental comparison among data compression techniques in isolated-word recognition'. *Proc. IEEE Int. Conf. Acoustics, Speech and Signal Processing*, 1025–1028.
7. Levinson, S.E., Rabiner, L.R., and Sondhi, M.M. (1983) 'An introduction to the application of the theory of probabilistic functions of a Markov process to automatic speech recognition'. *Bell Syst. Tech. J.*, **62**, 1035–1074.
8. Ross, S.M. (1970) *Applied Probability Models with Optimisation Applications*. Holden-Day.
9. Jelinek, F. (1976) 'Continuous speech recognition by statistical methods'. *Proc. IEEE*, **64**, 532–555.
10. Moore, R.K., and Russell, M.J., and Tomlinson, M.J. (1983) 'The discriminative network: a mechanism for focusing recognition in whole-word pattern matching'. *Proc. IEEE Int. Conf. Acoustics, Speech and Signal Processing*, 1041–1044.
11. Duda, R.O., and Hart, P. (1973) *Pattern Classification and Scene Analysis*. New York: Wiley.
12. Bellman, R. (1957) *Dynamic Programming*. Princeton Univ. Press.
13. Vintsyuk, K. (1968) 'Speech discrimination by dynamic programming'. *Kibernetica (Cybernetics)* **4**(1), 81–88.
14. Sakoe, H. and Chiba, S. (1978) 'Dynamic programming algorithm optimisation for spoken word recognition'. *IEEE Trans. Acoustics, Speech and Signal Processing*, **26**, 43–49.
15. Sakoe, H. (1979) 'Two-level DP-matching – a dynamic programming based pattern matching algorithm for connected-word recognition'. *IEEE Trans. Acoustics, Speech and Signal Processing*, **27**, 288–295.
16. Bridle, J.S., Brown, M.D., and Chamberlain, R.M. (1983) 'Continuous connected word recognition using whole-word templates'. *The Radio and Electronic Engineer* **53**, 167–175.
17. Jelinek, F., Mercer, R.L., and Bahl, L.R. (1982) 'Continuous speech recognition: Statistical methods' in *Handbook of Statistics 2*, Krishnaiah and Kanal (Eds.), North-Holland, 549–573.
18. Levinson, S.E., Rabiner, L.R., and Sondhi, M.M. (1983) 'Speaker-independent isolated digit recognition using hidden Markov models'. *Proc. IEEE Int. Conf. Acoustics, Speech and Signal Processing*, 1049–1052.

19. Russell, M.J., Deacon, J.C.A., and Moore, R.K. (1984) 'Some implications of the effect of template choice on the performance of an automatic speech recogniser'. *Proc. Inst. Acoustics Autumn Conf.*, 287–292.
20. Bridle, J.S., and Sedgewick, N.C. (1977) 'A method for segmenting acoustic patterns, with applications to automatic speech recognition'. *Proc. IEEE Int. Conf. Acoustics, Speech and Signal Processing*, 656–659.
21. Russell, M.J., Moore, R.K., and Tomlinson, M.J. (1983) 'Some techniques for incorporating local timescale variability information into a dynamic time-warping algorithm for automatic speech recognition'. *Proc. IEEE Int. Conf. Acoustics, Speech and Signal Processing*, 1037–1040.
22. Moore, R.K., Russell, M.J., and Tomlinson, M.J. (1982) 'Locally constrained dynamic programming in automatic speech recognition'. *Proc. IEEE Int. Conf. Acoustics, Speech and Signal Processing*, 1270–1273.
23. Baum, L.E. (1972) 'An inequality and associated maximisation technique in statistical estimation for probabilistic functions of a Markov process'. *Inequalities* **3**, 1–8.
24. Liporace, L.A. (1982) 'Maximum likelihood estimation for multivariate observations of a Markov source'. *IEEE Trans. Information Theory*, **28**, 729–734.
25. Russell, M.J., and Moore, R.K. (1985) 'Explicit modelling of state occupancy in hidden Markov models for automatic speech recognition'. *Proc. IEEE Int. Conf. Acoustics, Speech and Signal Processing*, 26–29.
26. Moore, R.K. (1981) 'Dynamic programming variations in automatic speech recognition'. *Proc. Inst. Acoustics Spring Conf.*, 269–272.
27. Spohrer, J.C., Brown, P.F., Hochschild, P.H., and Baker, J.K. (1980) 'Partial traceback in continuous speech recognition'. *Proc. IEEE Int. Conf. Cybernetics and Society*, 36–42.

CHAPTER 5

SPEECH UNDERSTANDING AND ARTIFICIAL INTELLIGENCE

Steve Young

In this chapter we examine the challenging task of reading meaning into utterances that are fed into machines.

5.1 *What is 'speech understanding'?*

INTRODUCTION

It is the inherent variability of naturally spoken speech, coupled with the lack of segment or word boundary information, which makes automatic speech recognition so difficult. So difficult, in fact, that many research workers in the field take the view that the task is only possible if the utterances to be recognised are spoken in a well-defined context so that high-level knowledge such as syntax and semantics can be applied to support the basic recognition processes. An important consequence of this approach is that speech must be understood in order for it to be recognised and for this reason systems which incorporate high-level knowledge are called speech understanding (*SU*) systems.

SU systems attempt to integrate traditional speech recognition techniques with novel artificial intelligence (*AI*) techniques to give the extra power needed to deal with natural continuous speech. It should be emphasised, however, that their reliance on *understanding* speech currently limits their application to specific well-defined task domains. Thus, they have considerable potential for applications such as conversational database inquiry systems since the domain of a database is sufficiently well-defined to allow the knowledge necessary for understanding to be explicitly coded. They are not, in contrast, currently applicable to more general-purpose systems such as automatic voice-to-text.

The purpose of this chapter is to explain the general principles of SU systems and to show how AI techniques can be applied in speech recognition. SU systems are generally large and complex and are still at the research stage. However, some of the basic ideas of SU can be used to improve the performance of commercially available speech recognisers. For those with an interest in practical applications, therefore, the chapter closes with a brief description of a simple SU system based around a commercially available connected-word recogniser.

THE STRUCTURE OF A SPEECH UNDERSTANDING SYSTEM

Every SU system contains a knowledge base which represents, in some symbolic form, knowledge about the task domain and knowledge about the state of the dialogue with the user. The function of the SU system is to map each input utterance into an abstract representation of its meaning which can then be used to update the knowledge base. Note here that the knowledge base is not normally just a passive receiver of information. For example, in a database inquiry application, the knowledge base will be attempting to construct a user query through a series of questions and answers. The current dialogue context, especially the question just asked, allows the general form of the reply to be predicted, thus simplifying the recognition process. Furthermore, the knowledge base allows nonsensical interpretations of the input to be rejected.

The actual mapping of an input utterance into a representation of its meaning takes place through a series of intermediate representations or levels. The translation from one level to the next higher level is accomplished by applying knowledge from one or more sources (*KSs*). As an example, Fig. 5.1 shows one of the simplest arrangements for an SU system, the so-called hierarchical structure. In this system, the input speech is first analysed by a front-end acoustic processor which segments and labels the speech. Because this is an inexact process, the output from the acoustic processor is not a simple phoneme string but a lattice of alternatives. This *phoneme lattice* is the first and lowest level of representation. The next higher level of representation is a network of *word hypotheses* deduced by the Lexicon KS. These word hypotheses are grouped into syntactically legal *phrase structures* to form the 3rd level of representation by the Syntax KS. Finally, the highest level of representation is the actual *meaning*, derived by the Semantics KS.

In practice, the system may operate either bottom-up, top-down or a mixture of both. In bottom-up mode each level is derived directly from the level below it. In top-down mode, each lower level is extended only when it is needed in order to extend the higher level above. Bottom-up is

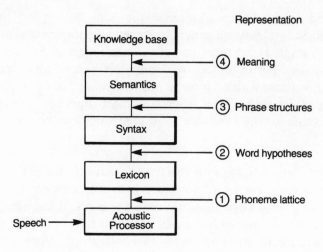

Figure 5.1   Hierarchical SU structure

effectively just another name for straightforward data-driven processing, whereas top-down represents a *hypothesise and test* paradigm.

The above brief description of the structure of a simple SU system overlooks the major problems which make speech understanding so difficult. Firstly, a hierarchical structure is simple to implement because interactions between KSs are limited to those which are adjacent in the hierarchy. In practice, this limitation may be unacceptable since more flexible interactions between KSs will often be needed. For this reason, more general architectures such as the *Blackboard* structure shown in Fig. 5.2 are often employed, where all data is kept in a common memory area (the blackboard) which can be accessed by any KS[1]. However, whilst more general architectures such as these are certainly more flexible, they are also much more difficult to control.

Secondly, and more importantly, SU systems in common with other large AI systems suffer from combinatorial explosion. For example, the Lexicon KS will be capable of hypothesising the existence of hundreds of words from the phoneme lattice, most of which will be wrong. These words may in turn lead to even more possible phrase structures, and so on. This is just another example of search problem in which an exhaustive examination of all solutions is unlikely to be computationally tractable. Hence, heuristic strategies must be used which limit the number of possibilities to just those which are likely to lead to a solution.

Thirdly, an SU system must be able to cope with errors. The acoustic processor cannot segment and label the speech with 100% accuracy and it is for this reason that its output is a lattice of alternatives rather than a

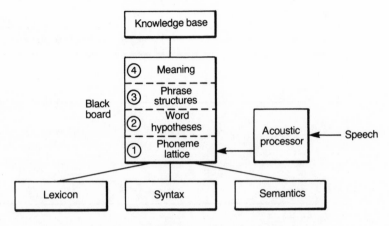

Figure 5.2 'Blackboard' SU structure

single unique phoneme string. However, it must be stressed that even allowing for multiple alternatives, it is still easily possible for the acoustic processor to miss phonemes altogether. Thus, KSs must, in general, be capable of postulating the existence of representational units which have not been found. This exacerbates the combinatorial explosion problem and accounts for the need for flexibility in KS interactions mentioned earlier.

Having said all this, SU systems have been built with sufficient performance to justify continued development of the approach and as a general rule, the attempt to apply higher-level knowledge to the speech recognition problem appears to be worthwhile. The examples above have concentrated on just three KSs: Lexicon, Syntax and Semantics. Whilst others are possible, these are the major ones found in most SU systems. Hence, the next three sections will explain their operation in more detail. Following this, search and control strategies are discussed. The chapter then ends, as mentioned earlier, with a brief description of a practical SU system using a commercial speech recogniser.

5.2 *The Lexicon knowledge source*

The built-in knowledge of the Lexicon KS consists of a pronouncing dictionary giving a phonetic transcription for each word in the system's vocabulary. Since there are often several different ways of pronouncing any given word, a single word entry may actually need to include several alternative transcriptions. This can make the dictionary quite large and difficult to update and since many variations of pronunciation are predictable, often only a *base* form of pronunciation is stored. In this

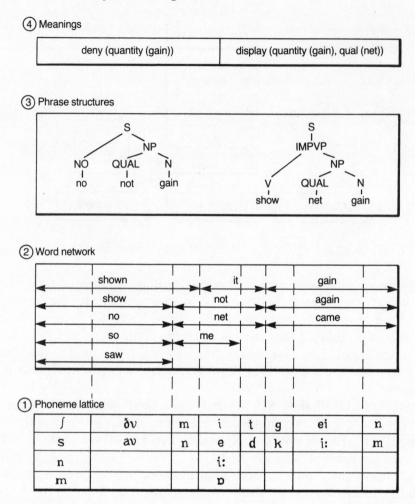

Figure 5.3   Levels of representation for the example 'show net gain'

case, the lexicon also contains a set of phonological rules which are applied to the dictionary to generate sets of alternative pronunciations at run-time.

The operation of the Lexicon KS is illustrated by the example shown in Fig. 5.3. This example shows the phoneme lattice which might be generated for the input utterance *Show net gain*. Above this lattice is the word network generated by the Lexicon KS. Note, however, that not all possible words are shown and, furthermore, the phoneme lattice itself is unrepresentatively simple in order to clarify the presentation.

The simplest and most accurate method of identifying words is to exhaustively match every word in the dictionary against all segments of

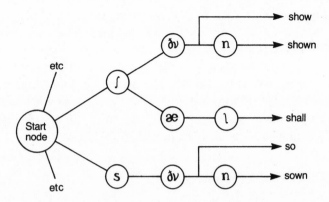

Figure 5.4   Fragment of lexical-decision network

the phoneme lattice. For medium-sized vocabularies, this can be made computationally tractable by compiling the dictionary pronunciations into a single decision network as illustrated by Fig. 5.4. The word-matching algorithm consists of traversing this network, comparing the nodes at each branch with the phonemes in the lattice. Each exit point of the network is labelled with the word which corresponds to that route through the network. Thus, reaching an exit point corresponds to hypothesising a word. Every phoneme in the lattice has an attached score denoting the likelihood of its occurrence. These scores can be accumulated as the network is traversed to yield a total score for each word found, and can also be used to prune the search when partial scores fall below a threshold. Practical word-matching algorithms of this sort must also deal with errors in the phoneme lattice. This can be done by allowing nodes in the network to be skipped or branches followed even when there is no corresponding match in the lattice. Penalties can be associated with these operations to prevent them being applied indiscriminately. An example of this applying in practice is shown in Fig. 5.3, where the word *again* has been hypothesised in the word network even though there is no corresponding initial schwa ('neutral' vowel) in the phoneme lattice.

One of the attractions of the word-matching procedure described above is that it can be formulated as an optimisation problem and solved by dynamic programming. This is not only a computationally efficient procedure but it also guarantees that the best matching words will be found. However, for large vocabularies, the computation involved may still be too high. When this is the case, it is necessary to find a way of reducing the number of words which need to be matched against the phoneme lattice. One way of doing this is to group phonemes into a very few broad classes such as *liquid, nasal, stop,* etc. This allows the phoneme lattice to be simplified and, by including this very broad transcription in the dictionary, allows a subset of dictionary words to be extracted quickly. The final set of word hypotheses can then be determined from this subset using the matching procedure described above. Alternatively, if top-down processing strategies are being used then the higher-level KSs may be able to predict subsets of the vocabulary which are worth searching first.

5.3 *The Syntax knowledge source*

The built-in knowledge of the Syntax KS consists of a formal representation of a grammar describing the input language. The function of the Syntax KS is to extract grammatical word sequences from the word network generated by the Lexicon KS. In Fig. 5.3, two examples of legal word sequences and their corresponding phrase structures are shown: *No, not gain* and *Show net gain.* Thus, the Syntax KS serves two essential purposes. Firstly, it filters the many possible word sequences found by the Lexicon KS to just those which are grammatical, and secondly, it assigns a phrase structure to them to facilitate subsequent understanding.

One of the commonest representations for the grammar in an SU system is the well-known context-free rewriting rule system. Starting with an initial symbol **S** for sentence, rules are given which show how an **S** may be legally expanded into the terminal strings of the language. For example, typical rules might be:

$$\textbf{S} \rightarrow \textbf{NP VP|IMPVP|NO NP}$$

$$\textbf{VP} \rightarrow \textbf{V NP}$$

$$\textbf{IMPVP} \rightarrow \textbf{V NP}$$

$$\textbf{NP} \rightarrow \textbf{[DET]\{QUAL\} N}$$

etc

where the vertical bar denotes alternatives, brackets denote options and braces denote repetitions.

The process of deducing a phrase structure for a given sequence of words is called *parsing*, and for simple context-free grammars of the form shown above, many parsing algorithms have been devised[2]. The difference between parsing in SU and parsing in most other applications is, of course, that there is not just one input string to parse but many. Furthermore, there may also be errors in the word network. Thus, parsing in SU systems involves searching a large space of potential solutions and once again, a combinatorial explosion of possibilities is the ever-present danger.

Context-free parsers in SU systems commonly work bottom-up. The word network is searched for subsequences of words called *handles* which match the right-hand side of one of the grammar rules. Each subsequence so found is then replaced by the non-terminal symbol on the left-hand side. This operation is called a *reduction*. Where a sequence matches several right-hand sides then the alternatives can be tried in parallel, or just one can be chosen, and if this turns out to be the wrong choice, the parser can backtrack and try another. This process is repeated until a word sequence has been reduced to a single non-terminal symbol, in which case a solution has been found.

The main advantage of this method of parsing is that it is not necessary for a phrase structure to span the entire utterance. For example, in Fig. 5.3 if the word *show* was omitted from the word network, the parser would still find the noun phrase *net gain*. Given a suitable dialogue context, it may then still be possible to interpret the user's input correctly. Alternatively, the parser could make a request to the lexicon to search the initial portion of the phoneme lattice again to find a suitable verb.

Bottom-up parsing, however, involves testing a great many potential handles, and to keep this computationally tractable it is necessary to use individual word scores to focus the search. Thus, the search for handles also involves selecting word sequences with high scores. The simplest parsing algorithms require this search to proceed through the word network from left to right but this may cause difficulties if all the initial words have poor scores. Removing the left-to-right constraint greatly complicates the parser but does allow it to start with the highest scoring words and then work outward. This latter variant is called *island driven parsing*[3].

Returning now to the grammar itself. The limitations of context-free grammars with respect to describing natural languages were identified by linguists many years ago. The lack of context makes it very difficult to, for example, enforce such things as subject-verb agreement and makes it impossible to capture common aspects of the language such as the similarity between active and passive forms. These problems led to the development of transformational grammars (TGs) by linguists. TGs have, however, proved to be computationally intractable and for this reason an alternative representation known as the *Augmented Transition Network* (ATN) has been developed which has the same formal power as a TG[4]. Briefly, an ATN is a recursive transition network augmented by registers into which partially built phrase structures can be stored, tested and retrieved later in the analysis. This means that contexts can be saved and phrase structures arbitrarily modified. Overall, ATNs provide a convenient computational framework for developing powerful parsers and have been used successfully in SU systems.

More recently, an alternative approach to parsing has been developed based around the concept of a *chart*. In the description of bottom-up parsing given earlier, it was noted that a bottom-up parser often needs to either pursue alternatives in parallel or be capable of backtracking. In practice, the latter is invariably chosen because it is computationally simpler. Backtracking, however, can be very inefficient because it may be a long time after a decision point before it is realised that the decision was wrong. In the meantime, much useful work may have been done and this is all thrown away on backtracking. The use of a chart parser avoids this problem by providing a formal way of pursuing alternatives in parallel. The basis of a chart parser is the chart data structure on which it operates. Essentially, a chart is a network similar to the word network shown in Fig. 5.3 on which phrase structures are built explicitly. When a handle is identified and reduced, an arc is added to the network spanning the word sequence labelled with the corresponding non-terminal. If there are several possible reductions for the same handle, then multiple arcs are generated. The goal of the chart parser is then to generate arcs which span the entire word network. No backtracking is involved because arcs which do not lead to solutions are simply ignored. Of course, the same problems of combinatorial explosion are still possible and arcs must be scored in order to guide the parser as to which part of the chart should be expanded first. However, the approach appears to have considerable potential and is currently being used in at least one major speech recognition project.

5.4 *The Semantics knowledge source*

The function of the Semantics KS is to convert phrase structures generated by the Syntax KS into a representation of their meaning which can be interpreted by the knowledge base. At the same time, the Semantics KS must filter out non-meaningful phrase structures. Semantics is primarily concerned with word sense. Thus, knowing the senses of the words in *Show net gain* it can establish that *net* is an appropriate qualifier for *gain* but would reject, for example, *Show green gain*. Knowledge of word sense also allows the Semantics KS to interpret *show* as a request to display information and therefore generate the appropriate meaning representation.

Unlike syntax, there is little in the way of formal representations for semantics. Thus, the structures generated by the Semantics KS tend to be *ad hoc* and system specific. They depend mainly on the way that the knowledge base itself is implemented and this is often just a large program written in an AI language such as LISP or PROLOG. In such cases, the structures generated by the Semantics KS are just LISP functions or PROLOG functors as shown in Fig. 5.3. Within the knowledge base, one of the standard representational techniques is used, e.g. semantic networks, frames, first order logic, etc.[6] and the meaning representations generated by the Semantics KS either update the knowledge base, cause some action to be taken or are rejected as being uninterpretable. Thus, in Fig. 5.3, if the knowledge base was unaware of any previous user reference to *gain*, it would be unable to interpret a request to deny it, whereas it may be able to interpret a request to display net gains.

In practice, semantic operations are usually implemented by attaching procedures to the various grammatical rules of the parser. Thus, for example, when a noun phrase is parsed, a semantic routine is called to check the consistency of the noun phrase and generate the appropriate meaning representation. This approach has the advantage of being simple to implement and it also increases efficiency since it enables legal but meaningless phrase structures to be eliminated sooner rather than later.

5.5 *Implementing speech understanding systems*

SEARCH AND CONTROL ASPECTS

The preceding sections have outlined some of the techniques which can be used to map an input utterance into its corresponding meaning through a series of levels. As noted repeatedly, the major problem in all of this is preventing a combinatorial explosion of possibilities. Overall, an SU system can be regarded as searching for solutions in a very large space and the basic principles of searching apply (see, for example, Nilsson[7]).

There are two basic search methods: *depth first* and *breadth first*. In depth first mode, possible word sequences are generated one by one, each is parsed and interpreted in turn and the best interpretation is saved. When all possible word sequences have been tested the process halts. In breadth first mode, all possible word sequences are generated first, these are then all parsed to find all possible phrase structures which are in turn all processed to find the best interpretation. Both of these search strategies will find the best interpretation but in practice, depth first will often take too much time and breadth first will consume too much memory.

Variations on these two basic search modes can be made to work, however. In depth first, the word sequences may be generated in score order and the process stopped as soon as an acceptable interpretation is found. This is called *best first*. In best first mode, a set of the best scoring word sequences is generated and these are then processed in breadth first fashion. This is called *best few* or *beam searching*. Both of these methods are practical but are sub-optimal in the sense that they will not always find the best interpretation.

In addition to these formal approaches to searching, SU systems often include a variety of heuristic methods for attempting to focus the search on the most promising partial interpretations of the utterance. Space does not allow a detailed discussion of these here, but it is interesting to note that of the SU systems built in the *US DARPA* Speech Understanding Project in the mid 1970s, the Harpy system, which had a simple well-defined global beam search, outperformed the much more complicated *HEARSAY II* system, which had a complex, heuristically-controlled search strategy[8].

A PRACTICAL SPEECH UNDERSTANDING SYSTEM

Perhaps the major lesson to be drawn from the above is that whilst high-level knowledge sources can be used to make continuous speech recognition feasible, the complexity which results and the lack of any (as yet) agreed design strategy makes SU systems of limited use for immediate commercial exploitation. As frequently noted, the main source of this complexity is the potential for combinatorial explosion and this potential originates in the phoneme lattice. Clearly, an SU system could be greatly simplified if the need for this lattice could be avoided.

A recent development in speech recognition technology has been the emergence of commercially available connected-speech recognisers. These devices operate by storing representative examples (templates) of each vocabulary word and matching them directly against the incoming speech. The details of how these work are given elsewhere in this book but the key features of relevance here are that, firstly, they guarantee to find the sequence of templates which best matches the input; secondly, the sequences tried can be constrained by a finite state grammar; and thirdly, they operate in real time. Hence, although vocabulary is limited and recognition accuracy modest, these devices could be used to eliminate the phonemic and lexical levels of a conventional SU system. They should therefore be useful for building real-time SU systems of

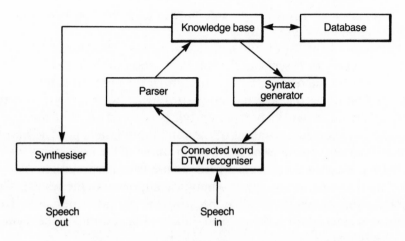

Figure 5.5 A simple practical SU system

manageable complexity suitable for immediate commercial exploitation. To test this hypothesis, an SU system for implementing a voice-operated railway timetable inquiry system has been built by the author. This system is presented in detail elsewhere[9]; here just the main features will be described.

A block diagram of the system is shown in Fig. 5.5. The core of the system is the knowledge base which contains static knowledge about the task domain and dynamic knowledge about the user dialogue as it evolves. The knowledge base is implemented in a language called UFL, using frames[10]. Each frame represents a particular concept (e.g. a time, or a place) and consists of slots which hold data values, nested frames and procedures. The goal of the system is to instantiate a frame structure which contains all the information necessary to make an inquiry to the timetable database. For example, in a simple case, this would be the departure and arrival places and the approximate desired departure or arrival time.

The system operates as follows. Suppose that the 'arrival place' frame is required to be instantiated. To do this, the knowledge base outputs a question to the synthesiser such as *Where do you want to go to?*, and at the same time sends a list of syntax rule names to the syntax generator. These rule names describe a subset of the total input language defined by a set of context-free rewriting rules. In this case, the rule names passed to the syntax generator would allow replies which refer to places (e.g. *I want to go to London*) and might also allow other related topics to be mentioned (e.g. *to London by six p.m.*), but would not allow replies on unrelated topics (e.g. *What is the fare?*). In this way, the search space of the recogniser is focused on the most likely user inputs, thereby improving recognition accuracy.

On receipt of the list of rule names, the syntax generator constructs a finite state network describing the specified subset of the input language, and passes it to the recogniser. The recogniser then processes the spoken input and produces the best matching word string, which it returns to the parser. The parser works bottom-up but is fast and efficient because it only needs to consider a subset of the total input language. The output from the parser is a frame encoding the meaning of the user's reply which is finally passed back to the knowledge base for interpretation.

Notice that there is no explicit semantic component in the system. This simplification is made possible because the syntax rules are given semantic rather than grammatical labels. For example, the syntax includes the rule

$$\textbf{TOPLACE} \rightarrow \textbf{TO PLACE}$$

rather than

$$\textbf{PP} \rightarrow \textbf{PREP NOUN}$$

Hence, the phrase *to London* is parsed into a phrase structure which can be converted immediately into the frame

$$\textbf{TOPLACE(PLACE(}\textit{London}\textbf{))}$$

In practice, the system works very well, its main limitation being that it is currently speaker-dependent. The use of an intelligent knowledge base allows very natural and flexible dialogues to be implemented and the syntactic constraint mechanism enables adequate recognition performance to be obtained from a relatively crude pattern matching device.

5.6 *Conclusions*

This chapter has explained the general principles of speech understanding systems and has described the organisation of the major high-level knowledge sources: Lexicon, Syntax and Semantics. In addition, a simple practical SU system has been described which uses a commercial connected-word recogniser as its front-end.

The major conclusions to be drawn are that speech understanding and the use of AI techniques offer a potential solution to the long-term goal of speaker-independent continuous speech recognition, but that real success is still some way off. In the meantime, the selected use of AI techniques in conjunction with proven speech technology can lead to immediate and practical benefits.

5.7 *References*

1. Erman, L.D., and Lesser, V.R. (1980) 'The Hearsay II speech understanding system', in *Trends in Speech Recognition*, Ed. W. Lea. New York: Prentice-Hall.
2. Aho, A.V., and Ullman, J.D. (1972) *The Theory of Parsing, Translation and Compiling: Vol 1, Parsing*. New York: Prentice-Hall.
3. Bates, M. (1975) 'The use of syntax in a speech understanding system'. *IEEE Trans ASSP* **23** 1 p. 112.
4. Woods, W.A. (1970) 'Transition network grammars for natural language analysis'. *Comm ACM* **13** 10 p. 591.
5. Thompson, H., and Ritchie, G. (1984) 'Implementing natural language parsers' in *AI: Tools, Techniques and Applications*, Eds. O'Shea, T., and Eisenstadt, M. Harper Row.
6. Barr, A., and Feigenbaum, E.A. (1981) *Handbook of AI: Volume 1*, Chapter 3. William Kaufmann.
7. Nilsson, N.J. (1981) *Principles of AI*. Berlin, New York: Springer-Verlag.
8. Klatt, D.H. (1977) 'Review of the ARPA speech understanding project'. *J. Acoust. Soc. Am.* **62** 6 p. 1345.
9. Young, S.J. (1985) 'Designing a conversational speech interface' in submission, *IEE Computers and Digital Techniques*.
10. Young, S.J., and Proctor, C.E. 'UFL: An experimental frame language based on abstract data types'. To appear, *Computer Journal*, April, 1986.

CHAPTER 6

HUMAN FACTORS IN SPEECH RECOGNITION

Jeremy Peckham

In this chapter we discuss the psychology of voice communication with machines, to determine when speech recognition is best applied and what special issues must be borne in mind in the design.

6.1 *Speech – for men or machines?*

Speech is one of the prime means of human-to-human communication and as such is often argued as being the ultimate medium for human–computer interaction. Spoken language has, however, developed to communicate all the complexities of man's thoughts and intentions and includes many kinds of social and artistic uses – to impress, persuade and convey emotion. Despite the evidence of the classic experiments of Chapanis (reviewed below) which indicated that language was a faster means of communication than manual methods in certain tasks, the advantages of current speech recognition technology over manual methods of interaction remain a matter of debate and experiment. This is so largely because current technology, and indeed that for many years to come, is far from capable of emulating human language understanding. Even if it were, there is still a question over the degree to which speech universally provides a better means of human–computer interaction than manual methods. This chapter reviews the characteristics of speech versus manual alternatives in a human–computer interface and provides a framework for assessing the potential benefits of speech technology versus technology capabilities in differing applications. It also focuses on a number of aspects of the design of a human–computer interface incorporating speech technology.

6.2 Verbal versus manual computer interaction

In the mid 'seventies a number of interactive human-to-human communications experiments were carried out at the Johns Hopkins University (Baltimore, USA) by Prof. Chapanis and his colleagues. The experiments were designed to provide insight into the effectiveness and efficiency of a number of methods of communication used in isolation, or in various combinations (see Table 6.1).

Table 6.1 Combinations of communication methods

	handwriting	voice	video
typewriting	*	*	*
handwriting		*	*
voice			*

The experiments demonstrated that in a cooperative problem-solving situation the time taken for a team of two to reach a solution was dependent on the communication medium used, the most significant factor being the availability or not of the voice channel. The time to solution was found to be significantly faster for communication channels involving voice, a result which proved robust both for different problems and tasks.

At the IBM Research Centre, experiments have been carried out to compare writing, dictating and speaking performance in letter generation[1, 2, 3]. Performance was measured in terms of letter quality and generation time. The results indicate that speaking and dictating had significantly faster composition and generation times than writing (Table 6.2).

Such results clearly demonstrate that in certain circumstances speech is a faster means of communication than other methods. It is however important to note the context within which these results occur – that of unrestricted natural language generation (Fig. 6.1). Many have been tempted to extrapolate these results to justify the advantages of speech recognition devices in human–computer interaction, and in so doing have grossly overstated the case. Current technology allows for only very restricted and constrained language and requires a cooperative speaker. It is therefore unwise to assume that speech recognition will always provide a more effective method of interaction than alternative manual methods such as the keyboard, mouse and touch screen. How then does a more restricted form of speech interaction compare with these alternative devices and when should its use be considered?

Table 6.2 Results per letter from 8 executives[1] and from 8 novice dictators[2] each of whom composed 8 routine business letters

	Writing	Method of composing Invisible writing	Dictating	Speaking
Composition time (min)	7.1 (6.4)	7.0 (6.8)	4.6 (5.7)	3.5 (3.6)
Generation time (min)	5.2 (4.9)	5.1 (4.9)	2.9 (2.7)	2.0 (1.7)
Pause time (min)	1.8 (1.5)	1.9 (1.7)	1.4 (2.1)	1.3 (1.7)
Review time (min)	–	–	0.3 (0.8)	0.3 (0.2)
No. generation periods	4.8 (5.8)	4.7 (4.8)	4.8 (6.7)	3.7 (3.6)
No pauses	4.8 (5.9)	4.7 (4.6)	3.8 (5.5)	3.1 (3.2)
No. reviews	–	–	1.9 (2.6)	1.7 (0.4)
No. words	80.6 (87.5)	82.8 (83.8)	91.6 (95.6)	95.1 (95.1)
Words/min	12.1 (14.1)	12.0 (13.0)	20.9 (17.4)	29.3 (29.2)
Words/min generation	16.2 (18.6)	16.3 (17.3)	33.9 (36.5)	49.9 (61.6)
Quality ratings	On average, all acceptable or above			

So: *Well, it's, it's a clip now, right?*
Sk: *Yeah, it's a clip.*
So: *How how wide is the clip?*
Sk: *It's ah, a little wider than than the socket.*
So: *How does it fit now, does it fit ... Is it go on the bottom of it or it's it's definitely parallel to it?*
Sk: *Right.*
So: *It's definitely parallel.*
So: *to it?*
Sk: *It's*
⎰Sk: *parallel so that when you clip it ...*
⎱So: *Okay I got you, but it's wider than it right?*
Sk: *Yeah, a little bit wider.*
So: *A little bit wider ... Okay wait a second. Uh how wide is the socket is it, you know the socket itself.*
So: *Is it/*
Sk: *Okay.*
So: *wide or thin 'cause I have uh two two just about like that, what you described.*
Sk: *Okay now, uh there's a socket and then there's a clip ...*
So: *I have the clip on and everything I've got that.*
Sk: *Right. Okay now perpendicular to the socket there are two flanges ...*

Figure 6.1   Start of the interchanges between two persons who communicated by voice to solve an object identification problem. **So** refers to the source; **Sk** to the seeker. Brackets on the left identify instances in which both source and seeker were talking at the same time. A solidus (/) means that the speaker was interrupted at this point.

We begin with a general comparison of the characteristics of various manual input methods, and contrast them with verbal alternatives, including that of a restricted nature.

Function keys are often seen as a solution to some of the problems of 'QWERTY' keyboard entry: they do not involve typing skills, are quicker to operate, and can be labelled to remind the operator of the possibilities available. In applications where only a small number of commands are needed, function keys may provide a satisfactory means of input. However, as the number of commands grows, so must the size of the keyboard, with a resulting increase in search time, particularly for inexperienced users. In addition, the demands on space must be considered in applications such as cockpits, where space allocated to a large keyboard may mean that other devices must be omitted.

Although multi-function keyboards can be used to reduce the amount of space needed by discrete function keys, they impose a hierarchical structure on the commands. Commands are divided up into 'modes' such as 'edit mode', whereby a key has a different function for each mode. To carry out a command that is not in the current mode the operator needs to exit from the current mode, enter the new mode, carry out the command, exit from that mode, enter the old mode and continue. As speech allows a larger range of commands, the commands need not be organised hierarchically, so that every command can be given at any time. With restricted speech recognition the operator may be limited by the size of vocabulary, requiring him to learn the word appropriate to each command. The use of words easily associated with the command function helps to alleviate the learning problem. The availability of less restricted speech for interaction, whilst freeing the user from remembering the precise commands, does pose a potential problem of ambiguity which may be difficult to resolve and require further interaction with the user.

Where space is available the potential advantages of spatial displays and controls in certain situations should not be overlooked. Process control provides one illustration of this point. Traditional controls and status displays are usually discrete and grouped according to function. Experienced operators are generally able to quickly locate controls and scan displays and status indicators. The use of computer-based display technology may reduce the control panels to a few CRTs and limit the instantaneous information available, but it could prove sub-optimum for the operator. Information search and abnormal status detection time is likely to be increased.

Touch screens, light pens and mice are featured on some newer machines as methods of input. Their use lies mainly in selecting an option from a menu, so their efficiency is tightly bound to that of the menu approach. Menus are similar in many ways to multi-function keyboards in that they can be fast, but they may use multiple levels to impose a structure on the commands, with the resulting inflexibility in going from one set of options to another. Choosing an option by pointing has the same time-advantage as speech over other methods of keyboard selection, where an extra level of encoding is needed to transfer from a command to the relevant position on the keyboard.

Pointing devices are much better suited than verbal commands to inputting information on spatial location. This advantage may be combined with speech to good effect where there is a mixture of spatial location and selection tasks. An example in automated electronic circuit drawing is selection of standard circuit symbols from a library (using speech commands) and their placement in forming a circuit diagram by mouse.

One particular disadvantage of speech input over keyboards or pointing devices is the variability of speech production and the resulting speech signal. Keyboards have a standardising effect on the input; as long as the appropriate command is used and there are no spelling mistakes, the system will know what the user's intention is. Any spelling or syntax errors are user-initiated and so can often be detected by the system. Speech is more like handwriting in that each person's is different and some people's is unintelligible, even to the originator. Current speech recognition technology is limited in its ability to deal with variability, and its performance under field conditions must be a matter of concern to system designers, particularly in respect to its impact on error rates.

Where no input data verification is used, the penalty in transaction time is related to the time taken to recover from the incorrect action taken by the system. In applications where the extra time is taken to verify each input, the transaction time for keyboard versus speech input will relate directly to the keyboard skills and talking rate of the operator and to the performance of the recogniser.

Chapter 13 deals with the problem of assessing the performance of speech recognition devices.

Apart from the advantages and disadvantages inherent in speech as a method of input, there are certain types of application where speech can be justified by other criteria. They include situations where the user's hands or eyes are busy, where he needs to be mobile while using the system, or where he is remote from the system.

Unlike keyboards, where the correct key must be located and then pushed, voice input does not involve the use of the hands or eyes, so the operator does not need to stop what he is doing while entering data or commands to a computer. This facility is most useful in applications where the user has objects, plans or drawings to inspect and handle or where he needs to control equipment. Many successful applications of speech recognition have been found in parts inspection in quality control. At the Department of the Hydrographer in the UK, entering of cartographic data in the process of digitising hand-drawn charts or maps has also proved beneficial. Prior to introducing speech recognition in the early 1970s, operators at the digitising table needed to take their eyes and hands away from the equipment in order to enter data at a keyboard. The ability to operate the digitising table and input data simultaneously was felt to be so much less frustrating that operators were tolerant even of the fairly high error rates of the early recogniser used.

Even in hands- or eyes-busy applications, the high price of speech recognition equipment relative to keyboards and pointing devices means that a considerable reduction in transaction time is needed to justify the cost. Welch[4] describes a data entry application where the system operator was required to position an object in a measuring device and then enter the measurement by pushing the relevant button on the keyboard. Although the use of speech recognition dramatically reduced the time spent entering the measurement, the time spent on this part of the task was such a small fraction of the total that the overall reduction in transaction time was not statistically significant.

The motivation for using speech to improve operator mobility is similar to that for hands- or eyes-busy operations. By using a head-mounted microphone or radio the operator does not need to stop his principal task, for example inspecting a car for quality control, to find a terminal where he can enter data. Whether or not the transaction time is significantly reduced again depends on how much time the operator spends locating the terminal and entering data.

Speech recognition also opens up a whole field of applications where the user is remote from the host computer and does not have a terminal available. People rely on the telephone for a large number of enquiry services, and these must be easy to use as the majority of enquirers are untrained and will simply look elsewhere for the information if they are not satisfied. Trying to obtain information using a small number of digit keys would be a laborious task, whereas speech allows a faster and more natural interaction. Voice input would also be useful for the military or police in situations where they wish to communicate with a central computer by means of a radio link.

So far we have given general consideration to the inherent advantages of speech as a communication medium in human–computer interaction, and compared restricted forms of speech with manual interaction devices. To summarise, the major benefits which speech may potentially bring in human–computer interaction are:

(a) reduced mental encoding,
(b) faster interaction/text generation as the information bandwidth increases,
(c) possibility for more effective multiple task execution by combining verbal and manual tasks.

On the negative side, speech is particularly poor for conveying instructions about spatial location, when compared to pointing devices.

6.3 *Determining a role for speech input*

Aside from the potential advantages of speech in human–computer interaction, consideration should be given to the following factors when assessing the role of speech in any given application:

(a) the *tasks* to be performed
(b) the *users* of the system
(c) the *environment* in which the task(s) is carried out
(d) interface technology *capabilities*.

TASK ANALYSIS
Assessing the potential benefits of speech as an input medium should first proceed from an analysis of the proposed or existing tasks. The analysis may proceed from the highest level, providing a specification of the system's objectives and functions, down to a detailed description of the smallest task. The analysis will identify competing tasks and their relative priority and the complexity of each interaction. It will identify the type and nature of each interaction.

Figure 6.2 illustrates this process for a simple package sorting application using a single operator and a keyboard. In the case of an existing task or set of tasks this process can help in identifying possible improvements in task scheduling or where tasks may be removed by the use of alternative interface technology. In Fig. 6.3 the potential saving in the number of tasks involved using speech instead of a keyboard is shown. For this particular application (a sorting depot in the USA), use of speech recognition improved the package throughput by 30% and reduced errors from 4–5% to less than 0.05%.

Task loading
Task analysis may reveal potential for speech input to either reduce

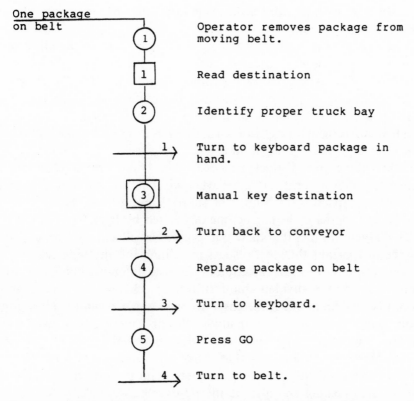

Figure 6.2 Flowchart – package handling, original method

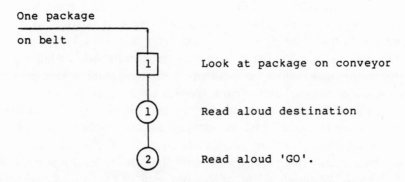

Figure 6.3 Flowchart – package handling, revised method

tasks, as in the package sorting application, or to allow tasks to be carried out concurrently. One of the main motivations for using speech to date has in fact been in applications where the user's hands or eyes are already busy with another task. Parts inspection in the quality control function is an example.

The temptation to use speech as a method of input to allow task concurrency or reduce operator workload must, however, be carefully evaluated. The experience of psychologists investigating the effects of dual tasking may prove useful in determining the requirements of systems used in this kind of high workload environment.

There are four main psychological theories attempting to explain how the brain's processing capabilities are organised[5]. The debate is over whether there are distinct processors for the various channels of attention (motor, oral, etc.), or whether there is one single pool of processing capacity which must be shared amongst the tasks.

The first model is the classic one developed by Broadbent in the late 1950s, which assumes that there is a single pool; allocating some capacity to one task means that there is less remaining for anything else.

The second model is a variation of this, the difference being that total pool of capacity is divided amongst different channels in fixed proportion. Like the first model, there is a decrease in performance when going from single to dual task, but unlike the first model, two tasks using different channels do not interfere with each other.

The third model assumes that different channels are controlled by entirely independent processors, so there is no performance decrement due to dual tasking and also no interference between the tasks.

The final model has independent processors controlled by a higher level executive, which performs functions such as ensuring that two tasks do not interact. This means that, as in the second model, there will be an overall drop in performance when another task is introduced, but as there are independent processors no interference will take place.

McLeod carried out experiments with simultaneous tracking and identification tasks and a more difficult arithmetic and tracking problem. He compared manual and vocal responses to the identification task and two levels of difficulty in the arithmetic task. Both sets of experiments showed a single to dual task performance decrement and also that the two manual tasks interfered with each other, but the vocal and manual combination did not. McLeod claims that these results support the fourth model of independent processors with an executive controller.

The findings of Laycock and Peckham[6] do not seem to follow the same pattern. In an experiment comparing vocal and manual data input during a manual tracking task, they found that the rate of degradation of the tracking task was the same for both manual and vocal input. The overall performance of the tracking task during voice input was superior only because of the reduced period of divided attention produced by faster entry times. However, the accuracy of the data entered was far superior with direct voice input than with keyboard input. This suggests that some advantage could be gained by pilots in a single-seater fighter required to enter or access information from an on-board computer. His primary task in a high speed, low-level flight profile is controlling the aircraft. An interface technology which minimises his transaction time on interacting with the on-board computer, although interfering with his primary task, may degrade his overall performance less.

The relevance of this work lies not only in comparing the efficiency of manual and vocal input but also in showing that simultaneous tasking degrades the performance of both tasks.

USER POPULATION

The type of person using a system – frequent or casual, skilled or unskilled – is also an important factor to be evaluated in the design of an interface and its technology. This will be considered further under dialogue design. In using speech recognition devices, the accessibility of the user population for training the recogniser determines the viability of speaker-dependent systems. The user's level of motivation also plays an important role in achieving adequate accuracy with current technology.

THE ENVIRONMENT

The environment in which the user is expected to operate can have an important impact on the choice and performance of the interface. A few examples illustrate the point: a user who is required to wear protective clothing and gloves will find keyboards difficult to use; speech input may provide a solution. A noisy environment, however, may be detrimental to the accuracy of a speech recogniser, both from the point of view of added noise to the speech signal, and changes in speech production (e.g. increased vocal effort).

TECHNOLOGY CAPABILITIES

When assessing the potential of speech input, consideration must be given to the capabilities and limitations of available recognition technology. Isolated utterance recognition will require slower input than connected, and may require careful prompting to avoid utterances being joined together. Even connected-word recognition technology does not completely solve the problem since some users may speak too rapidly for the technology capability. Various chapters in this book should give the reader a clear understanding of current technology capabilities.

6.4 *Optimising system design*

Figure 6.4 shows a simple model of a human–computer interface using speech and the interaction of various factors, and provides a focus for considering the optimisation of system design.

TRANSACTION TIME

In many human–computer interfaces, particularly where there is no concurrent task, the primary goal in interface design is to minimise the time taken to accomplish the user's goal. Achieving this requires more than just optimising the processor power to minimise host response time. We define transaction time here as the time taken from the receipt of a stimulus to carry out a task or sub-task, to the point at which the user is satisfied that the task is complete. This takes into account a number of factors in the transaction design, such as the optimality of error correction strategies, dialogue design and feedback.

The choice of a suitable dialogue plays an important role in minimising transaction time. Whether menus, commands or question-answering is used depends largely on the type of user involved, and also to a certain extent upon any simultaneous tasks and the input mode (speech or manual), as discussed in the previous sections. Once the user has provided input for the computer, the system will respond in some way. The system may use primary feedback which means that it carries out the task immediately, or it may give the user a chance to verify that the input is correct by offering secondary feedback.

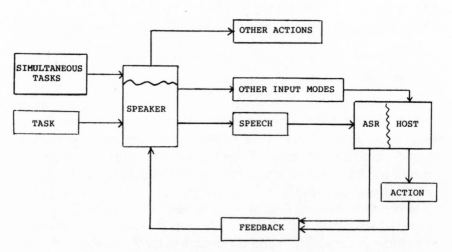

Figure 6.4   A generic model for speech input applications assessment

DIALOGUE DESIGN

A dialogue which will minimise the transaction time must allow for the type of person who will be using the system and for any constraints imposed upon the user by the task environment. We now discuss the different devices used in dialogues, feedback and error correction and the situations in which one is more appropriate than another.

Dialogue acts

Bunt *et al.*[7] talk of man–machine interactions in terms of *dialogue acts* and draw a distinction between *goal-oriented acts*, which directly involve the communication of information needed to carry out a command, and *dialogue control acts*, which are more concerned with preventing and correcting errors in the dialogue.

The goal-oriented act is one in which the computer asks or is told what the user wants it to do. The style chosen to convey this information should be the one which will result in the quickest and most error-free transaction, as a slightly longer but more robust dialogue can save a great deal of time in correcting errors. For example, a naive or infrequent user will probably need a longer transaction time than a more experienced user, as it will be quicker in the long run to give the naive user as much information as is needed for him to provide correct input first time. The experienced user, on the other hand, will want to bypass most help facilities and take the initiative for the dialogue to obtain as quick a transaction as possible.

There are several established ways of conducting a transaction, including command languages, menus and question-answering, or combinations of these. Experienced computer users usually prefer to use command languages; as they are familiar with the system they do not need to wait to be told what the options are. Machine prompts such as menus and question-answering are slower but easier to use and so are more suitable for inexperienced users who will otherwise not know what information or commands to provide.

Where speech is used as the input mode, prompts can help to improve the accuracy of a recogniser since accuracy is partly dependent upon the *branching factor* of the input – that is, the number of choices at any particular point. The branching factor is likely to be lower where questions or menus are used than when a whole range of commands are possible, with a resulting increase in accuracy. Consequently, in tasks where error costs are high or where recogniser performance is likely to be poor due to a large variety of speakers or a low quality communication channel, the speed of a command language will need to be sacrificed in favour of a system using prompts.

If the application dictates that any prompts must be aural rather than visual, further points must be considered. Firstly, menus of more than a few commands will be too much for the user to remember. Also, if the user is carrying out another task simultaneously, his ability to concentrate on entering information is likely to vary according to the demands of the other task; he may therefore prefer to take the initiative by using commands rather than having to respond to prompts. Finally, the constraints of a human's short-term memory are such that if data is to be retained in his working memory, it needs to be rehearsed constantly. Any aural prompts would interfere with this rehearsal, whereas manual interaction would not. (No disadvantage has been found in using non-complementary feedback, that is, in using visual feedback with spoken input or voice feedback with manual input.) In tasks where the oral/aural channel is the only one possible, some kind of 'scratchpad' may be necessary for temporary data storage.

Just as goal-oriented acts can provide a naive user with details of the type of information needed, a dialogue control facility can help to describe how to use a system, the correct form of each command, or the way in which the user should speak for optimum performance.

Some applications may also need the user to confirm that the input has been correctly interpreted. This follows the pattern of human-to-human conversation, where information is repeated back if the channel quality is poor (for example, over a telephone) or if the message is very important. Whether or not there is an opportunity for confirmation depends upon the type of feedback provided by the system.

Feedback
A system is described as having *primary* or *secondary* feedback, according to whether there is a confirmation phase in the dialogue.

Primary feedback occurs if a system responds directly to the user's command. Situations where the action is invisible to the user, such as a database update, may involve the system telling the user what action has been performed, but this is not the same as letting the user check the input before anything happens.

Primary feedback is used in situations where errors are not critical, or where the time saved outweighs the cost of possible errors. In VDU control, for example, it is just as easy to correct a wrong display by repeating the command as it is to confirm an input before action is taken. Primary feedback also tends to be used in applications such as package sorting, where the small percentage of errors made does not warrant slowing down the whole process by introducing a verification phase.

Experiments by Schurick *et al.*[8] on feedback for voice input show that even in applications best suited to primary feedback it is worth having a 'word confirmation dialogue' for cases where the recogniser cannot distinguish between two words. As the majority of inputs do not need this dialogue, there is no significant effect on the time taken to enter data, yet overall accuracy can be increased by about 5%.

With secondary feedback, the user has the opportunity to correct any errors before an action is performed, which can vastly improve accuracy. Applications which might need this facility include those which have permanent data capture (quality control, entry of co-ordinates in cockpits), or those where the cost of errors is high (industrial robot control).

The best way of providing secondary feedback depends on the user's environment and the type of data involved. Comparing visual and aural feedback of words and fields (groups of words), Schurich *et al.* found that visual, word-by-word feedback with a history of the transaction proved optimal in terms of both time and accuracy. Where a large visual display is not available to show the history, for example in a cockpit, visual word or field feedback gives the best results. Some recognisers are used in an eyes-busy environment so that visual displays cannot be used at all; in this case, auditory word feedback is recommended as auditory field feedback takes much longer and is more likely to cause confusion.

Error correction
The type of error correction which should be provided depends on the type of feedback used – word or field, aural or visual. Experiments to investigate the use of error correction commands in data entry were carried out by Schurick *et al.* for various feedback conditions, and by Spine *et al.*[9] for auditory word feedback.

In Schurick's experiments the data was divided up into fields and placed the words recognised in an input buffer until a field was completed. The error correction commands available were 'erase', which deleted the last word in the input buffer so that a misrecognised word could be replaced; 'cancel', which cleared the entire input buffer so that all data could be re-entered; and 'verify' plus a field name, which allowed subjects to access and edit a previously entered field of data.

In visual field and word feedback and in auditory word feedback, subjects used the command 'erase' much more frequently than 'cancel'. With auditory field feedback, 'cancel' became the more popular command, which seems to show that auditory field feedback is more confusing, causing subjects to cancel the whole input rather than try to edit it.

The verification command tended to be used as an editor for words in the input buffer and to help a subject determine where he was in the field. It is not surprising that 'verify' was used more in field feedback than in word feedback.

As with goal-oriented acts, the initiative for error correction can be taken either by the system or by the user. The experiments by Spine *et al.* investigated both automatic and user-directed error correction techniques for auditory word feedback.

Subjects again had the option of 'erase' or 'cancel' and they could also request 'runner-insertion', where the recogniser's second choice for a particular word is inserted in place of its first choice.

The erase command was again the most popular, closely followed by the runner-insertion. The cancel command was used very infrequently, as subjects felt that it would 'waste too much time'. The use of error correction commands increased the number of messages correctly recognised from 63.52% to 89.29%.

The time taken to enter data also increased when error correction was used, but the experiment shows that this time can be kept to a minimum by using smaller message lengths. The experimenters also stress the notion that it is the total transaction time which is important: 'time spent in correcting errors before transmission would be less than the time spent in trying to regain control of the system had the errors been passed through to the host'.

The utterances used were a set of simulated air traffic control messages, which had the advantage of conforming to a strict syntax and so allowing the use of a parser to correct errors automatically. Three approaches to automatic error correction were tried in the Spine experiments. The first method was to determine whether or not substitution of the second-choice word of the recogniser would result in a correctly parsed string. The second method determined whether or not there was only one possible word or class of words dictated by the syntax, regardless of what was recognised. The final method used truncating or deleting when extra words appeared in the message.

When automatic error correction alone was used, the percentage of correct messages improved from 63.52% to 82.91%. This shows that a significant proportion of error-ridden messages can be corrected automatically so that much of the burden of error detection and correction can be removed from the human operator.

6.5 *Further reading*

In a single chapter we have only been able to give a brief coverage of aspects of system design using speech recognition. We have concentrated on underlying principles rather than the nuts and bolts of interfacing a recogniser to a computer, in the hope that readers will have an appreciation of the issues involved at the human interface. For those who wish to delve further into engineering psychology and human performance, a useful bibliography will be found in Knight and Peckham, 1984[10], and many practical applications described in the proceedings of the annual conference of the American Voice Input Output Society and Speech Technology (Media Dimensions Inc.).

6.6 *References*

1. Gould, J.D. (1977) 'How experts dictate'. *IBM Research Report.*
2. Gould, J.D. and Boies, S.J. (1977) 'Writing, dictating and speaking letters'. *IBM Research Report.*
3. Gould, J.D. and Boies, S.J. (1978) 'How authors think about their writing, dictating and speaking'. *Human Factors,* **20** (4), p. 495–505.
4. Welch, J.R. (May 1980) 'Automatic Speech Recognition – Putting it to work in Industry'. *Proc. IEEE.*
5. Chapanis, A., Parrish, R.N., Ochsman, R.B. and Weeks, G.D. (1977) 'Studies in interactive communication: II. The effects of four communications modes on the linguistic performance of teams during cooperative problem solving'. *Human Factors,* **19** (2).
6. Laycock, J. and Peckham, J.B. (1980) 'Improved pivoting performance whilst using direct voice input'. *Royal Aircraft Establishment Technical report,* **80019**.
7. Bunt, H.C., Leopold, F.F., Muller, H.F. and van Katwijk, A.F.V. (1978) 'In search of pragmatic principles in man–machine dialogues'. *IPO Annual Progress Report,* **13**, p. 94–98.
8. Schurick, J.M., Williges, B.H. and Maynard, J.F. (In press) *User Feedback Requirements with Automatic Speech Recognition.* Virginia: Virginia Polytechnic Institute.
9. Spine, T.M., Maynard, J.F. and Williges, B.H. (Sept 1983) 'Error correction strategies for voice recognition'. *Proc. Voice Data Entry Conference,* Chicago.
10. Knight, J.A. and Peckham, J.B. (1984) 'Generic models for the assessment of speech input applications'. *Logica Report.*

PART 2
TECHNOLOGY

CHAPTER 7

TOWARDS THE SILICON BREAKTHROUGH

Larry Brantingham

The commercial viability of speech recognition is dependent upon the level of integration in silicon that is achieved. In this chapter, the reader is introduced to some of the issues involved in the evolution to large-scale integration of voice input/output circuits.

7.1 *The techniques and the technology*

The implementation of speech recognition functions in silicon has only just begun, and only sporadically at that. Though there exist a number of custom circuits and small systems employing general purpose digital signal processors, the high volume general application recognition device has yet to be developed. The lack of such a circuit is due to the complex interplay of a number of factors, including the level of performance of available recognition algorithms, the cost of circuit development, the market risk of specific recognition applications and, though to a lesser extent, the manufacturing technology for integrated circuits.

This state of affairs is in direct contrast to the situation which existed just prior to the advent of integrated circuit voice synthesis devices some ten years ago. In that case, the level of performance available in the laboratory for linear predictive coding algorithms was deemed adequate for a wide range of potential products. What had been lacking was the integrated circuit manufacturing technology and device architectures to allow the transporting of these algorithms to silicon. Even then, the relatively high costs of design were not risked on a purely speculative venture; a well-defined educational product produced the impetus to develop the devices which later became standard semiconductor products.

Recognition presents a far more daunting prospect. The sort of recognition and level of performance generally felt necessary for widespread application simply does not yet exist. What does exist – low performance, speaker-independent, isolated-word recognition and high performance, speaker-dependent, connected-word recognition – deals only with the fringes of the potential available market. These capabilities can be useful, but require very careful matching of the intended product application and the attainable performance. The resultant narrowing of the application base for a hypothetical custom-integrated circuit generally makes its high development cost, of the order of $1 m, too great a risk to take. In addition, there is always the prospect that some breakthrough will occur during the 18-month to two-year design cycle which will render the custom device obsolete.

Finally, the reader should also note that unit cost of the hypothetical device is not an issue; at the time of writing (Dec. 85), virtually any of the available algorithms can be implemented at reasonable cost in silicon. With the rapid advance of integrated circuit manufacturing technology, the situation will only improve. The real barrier is development costs, and the solutions to this problem are already on the horizon.

7.2 *Approaches to silicon implementation*

Generally, the algorithms most favoured for high performance speaker-independent recognition involve significant amounts of digital signal processing for the feature extraction part of the task, followed by a pattern matching process usually involving dynamic time warping to align the candidate word with the stored templates. The digital signal processing itself implies low-pass filtering for anti-aliasing and a conversion from the analogue to the digital domains. The conversion ideally would have enough dynamic range to cover the 72 dB range of the human voice plus a sufficient margin to accommodate variations in signal strength due to, for example, the distance of the speaker from the microphone.

Figure 7.1 illustrates the general case. There are also recognition approaches which dispense with the digital pre-processing by extracting features directly from the input waveform (see Fig. 7.2). Though these techniques range from simple counting of the signal zero level crossings to much more complex analyses, they are usually less demanding of computational resources than the frequency domain methods. Figure 7.2 illustrates the major functional blocks of such a system.

The ideal integrated circuit recognition system would combine all of these functions (and very probably voice synthesis as well) in a single

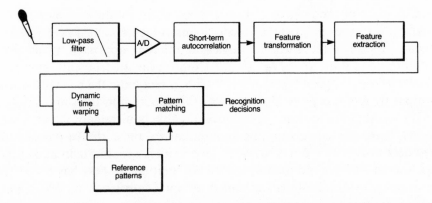

Figure 7.1 Typical frequency-domain based recognition system

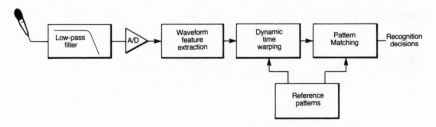

Figure 7.2 Typical time-domain based recognition system

circuit operating at low voltage and power dissipation levels. No such device yet exists, but some interesting partially integrated solutions, and some utilising standard components, have been devised. In both cases, the motivation was to reduce system cost while moderating development costs and preserving some flexibility for future algorithm enhancements.

A number of waveform-based techniques (e.g. those of Voice Control Systems, Watek, Interstate) have been implemented with standard microprocessors augmented by external analogue filtering and conversion circuitry and pattern storage memories. System costs are still high for the level of performance obtained with low-cost microprocessors, but the ratio is better in systems employing higher performance processors. In the frequency domain area, the level of integration has been higher. However, systems have been developed using standard programmable digital signal processors (e.g. the *TMS320* from Texas Instruments and the *7720* from NEC) combined with external memory and analogue filtering and conversion, in a way directly analogous to the time domain systems noted earlier. Unit costs are even higher, due to the substantially higher cost of a signal processor over a standard microprocessor.

Circuits more indicative of future recognition solutions are exemplified by a trio from Toshiba, General Instruments, and Texas Instruments. Each of the three embodies a different approach to system partitioning. Both the *TMS50C40* from Texas Instruments and the *SP1000* from General Instruments explicitly recognise the need for voice output by incorporating all or part of this function in the same device. With recognition accuracy at the level it is likely to remain at for some years, some sort of prompting is essential to allow the recogniser to 'guide' the dialogue in the paths suitable to its internal lexicon hierarchy as well as to alert the user when the recognition process has failed to produce a result. Toshiba's circuit does not incorporate synthesis, but goes considerably further in implementing the entire recognition system in a single circuit. Figures 7.3–7.5 show each of these devices in simple block form to illustrate the partitioning chosen, and Table 7.1 provides a tabular comparison.

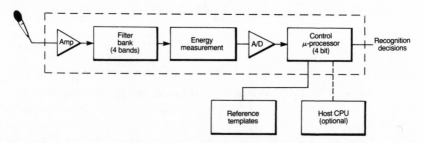

Figure 7.3   Toshiba recognition system

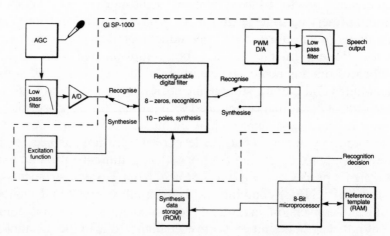

Figure 7.4   General Instruments recognition/synthesis system

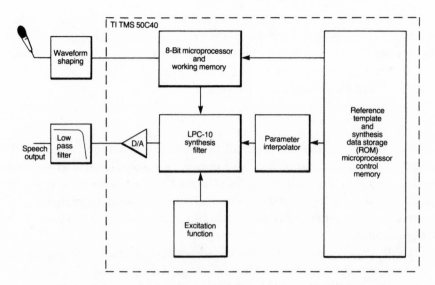

Figure 7.5   Texas Instruments recognition/synthesis system

Table 7.1 Comparison of three approaches to integrated synthesis/recognition devices

	Toshiba	GI SP1000	TI TMS50C40
Recognition type	SD	SD	SI
Vocabulary size	10–40	10	3
Recognition accuracy	90%	98%	85%
Manufacturing process	CMOS	NMOS	CMOS
Minimal system (voice input/output and system control)	device + 4–16 kbit RAM microcomputer synthesiser vocabulary ROM	device + RAM microcomputer filters A/D converter	device + filters

It can be seen that direct comparison is not especially meaningful without the context of a specific application to provide value weighting. For example, the TI device provides the lowest system cost in the minimum configuration, but only if the user can tolerate a minimal vocabulary and the necessary close development with the manufacturer. For larger vocabulary needs, the other two types of systems would be required.

7.3 *Trends in silicon implementation*

It was noted in the introduction to this chapter that development costs for custom integrated circuits, combined with the lack of a guaranteed successful end product, were the major impediments to the design of new circuits for these functions. Several factors in the design of custom circuits are in transition at the moment, and the changes are likely to greatly reduce the high costs of trying.

DEVICE FEATURE SIZE REDUCTION

Device *feature size* (the actual size of the circuit on the silicon chip, which in turn governs the complexity and performance availability at a given cost) does not in itself directly affect the cost of design. However, it can effectively do so by allowing the use of otherwise inefficient programmable or general-purpose structures in place of new, custom designed ones.

Present digital signal processors (described in detail in the next chapter) are a good example. The present generation of such devices are too large and costly to be the basis for a high volume recognition circuit, even if one ignores the necessary addition of analogue processing and digital memory functions. In making these circuits general-purpose, the designers were forced to accept a three-to-one reduction in effective operating speed and a similar increase in circuit size. With the next reduction in feature size, from about 2.5 microns to 1 micron, this disadvantage will be more than eliminated. It is inevitable that customer expectations will rise during the same period, but the overall result should still be that programmable core structures become viable solutions.

Reduction in feature sizes also usually leads to higher speed operation of the device's logic circuits. One effect of higher speed will be to allow the conversion of the filtering step from an analogue function to a digital one. Substituting high precision multiplications and additions for operational amplifiers and passive components may not at first seem an attractive trade, but doing so solves two problems inherent in integrating a conventional design.

First, it eliminates the need for both complex analogue and complex digital circuitry using the same manufacturing process. A high-speed analogue to digital converter and simple anti-aliasing filtering are still necessary, but the requirements are much simpler than for an all-analogue design. Secondly, the conversion of the filtering process to digital eliminates all manufacturing process-dependent variations from the circuit's performance. Testing is simplified and the proportion of good cricuits is increased.

STANDARD CELL DESIGN

Traditionally, integrated circuits have been designed one transistor at a time. Each transistor had to be designed to switch states in the required time, taking into account the specific circuit that device was expected to drive. As computer simulation programs have advanced, it has become common practice to simulate all devices in an integrated circuit and not just those which the designer judged to be marginal. Though this practice has undoubtedly increased the quality of the parts obtained, it has helped raise the development costs for today's 50 000 transistor circuits to a very high level. One-transistor-at-a-time design has just about reached its limit of effectiveness.

Just as design with discrete transistors evolved into design with small-scale integrated circuits, integrated circuit design itself is evolving into design from pre-specified and pre-simulated circuit blocks called *standard cells*. Designing circuits in this fashion results in slightly less efficient use of circuit area, but also provides a much reduced development time and cost. As standard cell design techniques evolve, larger, more complex cells will become available which will further ease the design task.

Parallel to the evolution of standard cell design techniques, the development of design software will eliminate the need for manually defined interconnection routing between cells. The most advanced of these design packages, usually called *silicon compilers*, permit the user to simply specify the functions and their connections as one would a computer program. The design, its simulation, the fabrication tools, and test programs, are all then generated automatically.

The implications of all these trends are dramatic for the area of integrated circuit speech recognition devices. Development cost and time, and thus risk, are reduced by a factor of five without imposing a significant increase in system cost. This alone makes many potential applications of available recognition technology worth pursuing. Additionally, and perhaps more importantly, by hiding the technical detail of integrated circuit design behind powerful software tools, integrated circuit manufacturers will make design accessible to the researchers and engineers skilled in speech rather than just to the much smaller group of dual-role individuals or less-efficient committees.

7.4 Recognition circuits of the future

Taking into account trends in both recognition techniques and integrated circuit technology, one can speculate on the form of a successful

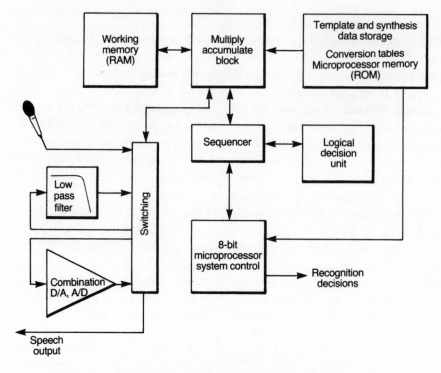

Figure 7.6   Hypothetical single-chip recognition/synthesis system

recognition chip. Figure 7.6 illustrates the salient points of such a device and Table 7.2 shows expected performance.

Table 7.2 Expected performance of an advanced circuit of the type shown in Fig. 7.6

Recognition type	Speaker independent, connected speech
Vocabulary size	25–50 words, minimal restriction
Recognition accuracy	95%
Manufacturing process	Low power dissipation CMOS
Minimal system	This device

The circuit is both a recogniser and synthesiser employing much of the same circuitry for both functions. A single *multiply-accumulate* block performs input and output low-pass filtering, recognition auto-correlation, coefficient conversion and dynamic time warping, and the synthesis lattice filter and coefficient smoothing. A common read-only memory, whose contents are definable after device manufacture, stores synthesis data, recognition templates, input windowing functions and synthesis excitation functions as well as any necessary conversion or reference tables.

Control for these basic blocks comes from a *reconfigurable state sequencer*, which may have been programmed using a higher level language to simplify design, but which operates without the overhead cycles necessary in a conventional digital signal processor. A basic multiply-accumulate cycle of 0.5 microsecond is well within even today's limits, but affords ample time to perform all necessary functions.

Analogue input and output is still present, but is greatly simplified by sampling the data at a rate ten or more times higher than the frequency band of interest. With the digital signal processing available to condition the input and output information, very precise tolerances on filter characteristics can be set and maintained without recourse to complex analogue circuit design. The still necessary anti-aliasing function need no longer be particularly precise, since the frequencies of interest lie a factor of ten below the nominal band cut-off frequency.

Assuming a one-micron *CMOS* (complementary symmetry, metal-oxide semiconductor) manufacturing process, the hypothetical recogniser and synthesiser need not cost more than present day synthesisers alone. With the extensive use of reconfigurable (though not strictly programmable) circuit blocks, advances in recognition and synthesis technology can be incorporated at minimal cost as they occur. In fact, the structure described would also be suitable for voice coding functions, further reducing the market risk of developing the circuit.

The state of the art, or more accurately, the rates of change of the two distinct arts which make up a recognition circuit, preclude making any firm statements about specific device characteristics for future circuits. These same factors mean that the integrated circuits on offer today represent only an instantaneous view of a rapidly changing field and therefore provide only a vague idea of what is feasible. Nonetheless, taken together, present devices and obvious trends make it clear that very effective, low cost recognition devices are not far away.

CHAPTER 8

SILICON DEVICES FOR SPEECH RECOGNITION

David Quarmby

In this chapter, we survey the silicon devices that are available to the electronic engineer who requires to design his own customised circuits for speech input.

8.1 *Current status*

As discussed earlier in this book, speech technology has yet to make a major impact on the general public, mainly because machines which can talk but which cannot listen have only limited uses.

If we look back to the first significant product incorporating speech synthesis, (as opposed to a replay of a recording) most people would point to the Texas Instruments educational toy, 'Speak 'n' Spell'. It had its limitations, but the public paid up and made it a successful product. The success was due mainly to the fact that a good speech synthesiser had been built on *a single chip*, and was being produced in quantity *at a low price*. Many major manufacturers now produce speech synthesis chips. None has yet produced a recognition chip in the required quantity and at a low price. When they succeed in this, we can look forward to a real explosion in the use of speech technology.

The objective of this chapter is to present a review of the devices currently available which offer the possibility of a small, cheap, speech recogniser. A few recognition algorithms have gained fairly wide acceptance, but no one would yet claim to have devised the ideal scheme – even if he had access to unlimited computing resources. The same is true of the speech synthesis algorithms, and in both fields this has lead to the use of general-purpose programmable devices being tailored to the task.

8.2 *Digital signal processors (DSPs)*

There is a particular type of general-purpose programmable device which is aimed towards speech processing as one of its major application areas. The devices are usually called *signal processors*, and are among the most sophisticated of the microprocessor chips yet made[1]. They are applied in areas where previously a computer would have been either too big or too slow. These areas have been dominated by analogue electronic systems, or occasionally by special-purpose, multiple-chip, digital designs.

Looking at an example of a typical speech analysis task is the best way to appreciate the role of the DSP. Let us consider one of many forms of spectral analysis which play a major part in most recognition schemes. In analogue electronics, a bank of filters would be used to separate a signal into a number of frequency bands. The same approach could be taken with digital electronics using digital sampled-data filters. The digital electronics used might be special-purpose hardware, but it is usually neater to use a computer-based system. Until recently it has required a rather specialised large computer to do these operations in real time on a speech signal. The main shortcoming of the older single-chip microprocessors, and even the current mainstream microprocessors, is the comparatively slow multiplication operation. Figure 8.1 illustrates the number of multiplications required with a block diagram of a simple digital filter which is commonly used, the *Biquad filter*. This filter could be used to isolate a selected spectral band. It requires the storage of two delayed signal values, but most importantly it needs five multiply operations for every signal sample which it processes. For most purposes, including recognition, spectral analysis of speech would use a bank of around 20 such filters, needing a total of 100 multiplications per signal sample. Speech signals occupy a bandwidth of up to, say, 4 kHz and so are often sampled at 10 kHz or 100 μs intervals. The multiply time we need is therefore around 1 μs. This is an order of magnitude faster than that provided by even the latest 16/32-bit microprocessors.

Alternative forms of spectral analysis, such as discrete Fourier transform (by fast Fourier transform) analysis, or linear predictive coding (LPC), are similarly intensive in the use of the multiply operation.

Hardware multiplier chips of quite adequate speed have existed for some time. It has, however, needed a moderately large electronic system around them to organise the data manipulation needed.

Signal processor chips are designed to meet the complete requirement, incorporating hardware multipliers which operate in around 200 ns – amply fast enough for the above example. Naturally, they have shortcomings in other functions which the mainstream microprocessors

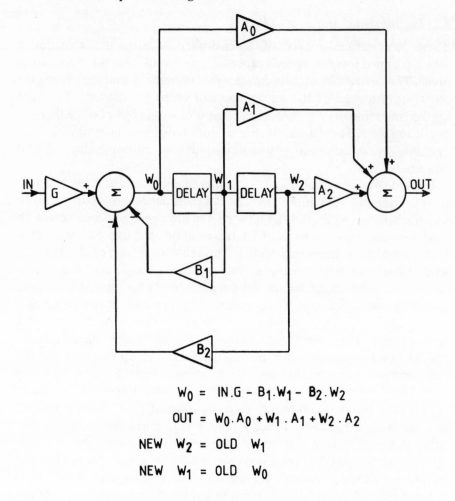

$$W_0 = IN.G - B_1.W_1 - B_2.W_2$$

$$OUT = W_0.A_0 + W_1.A_1 + W_2.A_2$$

$$NEW\ \ W_2 = OLD\ \ W_1$$

$$NEW\ \ W_1 = OLD\ \ W_0$$

Figure 8.1   Biquad filter

carry out more efficiently; for instance, they are much weaker at addressing large amounts of memory, and it is more difficult to implement high-level languages on them.

8.3 *The Texas Instruments DSPs*

THE TMS 32010

The best known of the signal processors, and one which has been applied to speech recognition, is the Texas Instruments TMS 32010. Figure 8.2 shows a simplified block diagram of this signal processor. In a signal processor it is usual to separate off the memory used to store instructions

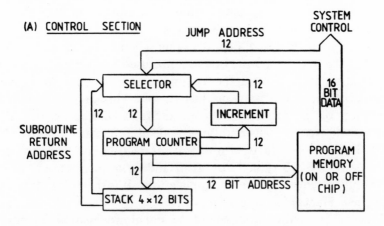

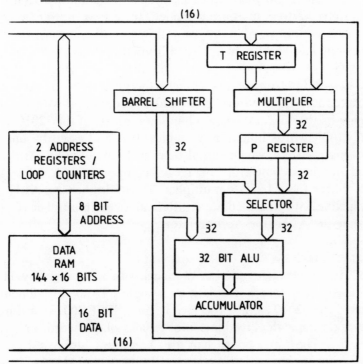

Figure 8.2 TMS 32010 simplified schematic

from the memory used for data storage. When this is done the processor is said to employ *Harvard architecture*. In the conventional processor this is a less common scheme, although in many microprocessor-based instruments it is normal to use read-only memory for the program, and RAM for data, effecting a similar split. The advantage of the Harvard architecture is that separate buses can be used for the program and data information, thus allowing the fetching of an instruction to overlap with the execution of the previous instruction. This doubles the speed of operation of the processor. An incidental advantage is that the bad practice of writing self-modifying code is physically impossible! The TMS 32010 does in fact permit some interaction between program and data areas, by two rather slow read and write instructions, which are used only infrequently in most applications. It is therefore said to have a 'modified' Harvard architecture.

Figure 8.2(a) shows that part of the signal processor which deals with the program and controls the rest of the processor. The program is held in memory either off the chip or in a mask-programmed ROM on the chip. Twelve address lines are provided, for a maximum of 4 kbytes of 16-bit instruction words. Program flow is either sequential, or the instructions can specify Jumps (conditional and unconditional), Calls (jump with current address stored on the 4-deep stack) or Returns. These deviations from sequence incur the penalty of an extra cycle in their execution, taking 2 cycles (of 200 ns), compared with the usual 1.

Figure 8.2(b) outlines the data handling section of the 32010. A RAM of 144 16-bit words holds the variables. It is addressed by one of two addressing registers, which can also act as loop counters. Arithmetic is carried out by a powerful barrage of components; a 32-bit ALU, a barrel-shifter and a 16×16 multiplier. The multiplier and ALU operate in a pipeline with intermediate registers after the multiplier (P register) and after the ALU (the Accumulator).

THE TMS 32010 AS A SPEECH RECOGNISER

The 32010 is a powerful number-cruncher with a tiny memory. How can it be used in a speech recognition system? Texas Instruments programmed the 32010 as the processor in their SBSP 3001 board intended as a speaker-dependent recogniser for either isolated words or connected speech[2, 3]. The same board can also compress, store and play back speech using linear predictive coding (LPC) working at 2.4 kbit/sec. The board is in fact a general-purpose one, with its program held in high-speed RAM (4 kbyte $\times$ 16-bit). In addition to this memory it holds a 16 kbyte $\times$ 16-bit RAM, accessed as a peripheral to the 32010, and shared by a suitable host computer. A/D and D/A converters and low-pass filters complete the major components of the board.

When programmed for speech recognition the 32010 can be regarded as performing two main tasks, in both of which its high speed is important. The first task is to extract the basic 'features' of the signal by performing spectral analysis, and the second is to compare these with the stored 'templates' which represent the stored words. We will examine these two steps separately.

In common with many Texas Instruments speech products the spectral analysis method used is that of linear predictive coding (LPC). The speech waveform is sampled at 8 kHz and is stored in 'frames' of 30 ms. These frames of data are extracted every 20 ms and thus overlap each other by 10 ms. The frame has to be big enough to give a reliable estimate of the spectrum in the form of LPC coefficients, and sampled often enough to give a good time resolution. A Hamming Window is applied to the frame, requiring one multiplication per sample. The LPC analysis method used is the Autocorrelation method. This requires the estimation of the first 10 autocorrelation coefficients – a process requiring 10 multiplications for each sample of the speech signal. This is in fact the most computationally demanding part of the Autocorrelation method, and is clearly well within the capabilities of the 32010's speed. Having derived blocks of autocorrelation coefficients, these are converted to the LPC filter coefficients using an efficient iteration devised by Leroux and Geuguen. This method is especially suitable for fixed-point arithmetic as used in the 32010, because the variables used are all bounded to the same range. In terms of the number of multiplications, the *Leroux-Geuguen* iteration is not too demanding, but the process requires a subroutine of moderate complexity, more complex than the estimation of autocorrelation coefficients.

The classification algorithm, also programmed for the 32010, is the dynamic programming or *time warping* method. This method allows for different speaking rates. A distance is measured between frames of stored 'template' patterns and the spectral features. The dynamic programming looks after the correct alignment of the unknown frames and the template frames. A simplification to halve both the computation load and the memory size needed for the templates is to store and compare every second frame only.

The Texas Instruments board is intended to work at 98% accuracy, when it is trained (or, to use their terminology, *enrolled*) for the particular speaker. This process will require, typically, 5 utterances of each word to be added to the templates. During this training process the words must be spoken in isolation to allow accurate start and stop time determination. This is not such an important factor in subsequent use, as the dynamic programming comparison does not need start and stop times to be marked on its unknown pattern.

THE TMS 32020

The TMS 32010 now has a big brother, the TMS 32020. This new processor extends the power of the signal processor in three major directions, all of which will benefit the speech recognition application. Indeed, looking at the new device one might guess that it was designed specifically with speech recognition in mind. The three major improvements lie in arithmetic speed, access to larger memory space and better program control (see Table 8.1).

Table 8.1 Comparison between TMS 32010 and TMS 32020

Function	TMS 32010	TMS 32020
External memory	Up to 4K words	Up to 128K words
Internal memory (RAM)	144 words	544 words
Instruction cycle	200 ns	200 ns
Internal timer	–	16-bit
Interrupts	1	3
Address registers/ loop counters	2	5

The major arithmetic elements of the 32010 remain. The same 16×16 multiplier is incorporated, running at the same speed. Another 32-bit barrel shifter is included at the multiplier output, feeding into a similar 32-bit ALU. However, significantly better use is made of these components by the control of pipelining. It is now possible to perform the operation of multiply, accumulate, and access new data all in a single instruction. Moreover, this instruction (and others) can be repeated for a specified number of times, controlled by a separate counter which automatically steps on each time the instruction is obeyed. Thus, for instance, the implementation of high order filters (order N) can be accomplished in N clock cycles of 200 ns. The improvement is less useful for lower order filters such as the Biquad filter of Fig. 8.1. In general terms, any operation involving the calculation of the inner product of two vectors is performed by the 32020 in half the time taken by the 32010.

The ability to conveniently use a larger memory space is the main advantage of the 32020 over the 32010. The new device has 68 pins (the 32010 has 40), and some of these have been used to extend the external address to 16 bits. The same external 16-bit buses can be used for either program or data access, the two being distinguished only by a pair of control lines. Thus, 64K words of data and 64K words of program can be accessed, a total of 256 kbytes of memory. The memory arrangement implies a further modification of the principles of Harvard architecture.

A user can very easily configure his hardware to totally ignore the program/data distinction, reverting to the more conventional *von Neumann architecture*. If the distinction is retained, there is a fast block move instruction between the two spaces to further erode their separation. On-chip data RAM is expanded to 544 words. Memory addressing is made easier by the use of five address registers instead of two, with an indexed mode of addressing added. As far as speech recognition is concerned, overall system complexity can be reduced, and its speed increased, since a large memory can now be directly accessed by the signal processor instead of the special peripheral hardware used on the SBSP 3001 board.

Finally, changes to the program memory arrangements result in much neater systems. The large external program memory can fully accommodate the complex recognition algorithms. On-chip RAM (256 words) can be used as program space. This leads the way to systems based on relatively slow but very convenient EPROM memories. In such a scheme, those parts of a program which must operate at full speed could be loaded into the internal RAM for execution, with a wait state (now easily incorporated) added to the timing of externally held instructions.

8.4 *The Nippon Electric Company DSPs*

THE μPD7720

The other major company with significant speech recognition products is the Nippon Electric Company (NEC). As with Texas Instruments, they have based their effort on a signal processor chip using Harvard architecture. Their original device is the μPD7720, which pre-dates the TMS 32010.

The 7720 is a 'peripheral' processor, intended to perform fixed operations at a high speed under the control of a general-purpose processor. It makes good use of parallel operations to achieve its speed. The general-purpose processors widely available at the time of its design were the 8-bit ones, and its parallel interface therefore is via an 8-bit port. This narrow interface symbolises the design philosophy, that the 7720 should normally perform self-contained tasks (such as spectral analysis) with a minimum of interaction with its host computer. This philosophy leads to extremely small, neat, systems.

The 7720 contains 3 on-chip memories: an instruction ROM of 512 23-bit words; a data ROM of 512 13-bit words; and a data RAM of 128 16-bit words. There is no access to external memory, and no question of

Table 8.2 µPD 7720 instruction formats

1. The OP instructions

Field		Return?	ALU source function and accumulator			Data RAM pointer		ROM pointer	Data move source and destination	
	Hardware controlled —	RET	P Select	ALU	ASL	DPL	DPH	RP Dec	SRC	DST
	0	1	2	3	1	2	3	1	4	4
No. of bits										

2. The branch instructions

Field	1 0	Branch type and condition	Next address	Not used
No. of bits	2	8	9	4

3. The load data instructions

Field	1 1	Immediate data	Not used	Destination
No. of bits	2	16	1	4

modification to the Harvard architecture. A great convenience for the system developer is a version of the chip using EPROM memories instead of the mask-programmed ROMs used for production quantities once an algorithm has been programmed and tested.

A 23-bit instruction in the 7720 is obeyed every 250 ns. The instruction format closely reflects the hardware which it controls, indicating simple instruction decoding logic. Table 8.2 shows the instruction formats. It is the first of the three types of format which is the most commonly used, and which illustrates how parallelism in a processor can produce very high speed. The instruction controls different functions, examined from the right of the instruction format:

(1) A move of data from internal registers or memroy, with 16 sources and 16 destinations specified
(2) A possible post-decrement of the data ROM pointer
(3) A possible change to the data RAM pointer, on a restricted, but well-organised basis
(4) One of 16 arithmetic operations performed using a 16-bit general-purpose ALU (32-bit operations can be done, but are difficult)
(5) An optional subroutine return after instruction execution

A 16×16 multiplier is present in the 7720, its output feeding into the general-purpose ALU in a pipelined arrangement similar to the TMS 320 devices.

THE SPEECH RECOGNITION CHIP SET
Programming the 7720 is difficult due to the parallelism, requiring great attention to detail to obtain the very high throughput possible. Many complicated algorithms have been programmed, including LPC analysis and synthesis[4] and a very complex speech synthesiser[5]. One of the most significant applications is the speech recognition algorithm programmed by NEC. The mask-programmed 7720 is sold as one component of a three-chip speech recognition chip-set. It is the µPD7761.

The two companion devices to the 7761 are the MC-4760, the input device, and the µPD7762 – a controlling microprocessor with a large addressing range.

Figure 8.3 shows how the three chips fit together to make a complete recognition system. Overall control is provided by the 7762, though in its turn it acts as a peripheral to some host system. It addresses a separate memory of up to 64 kbyte (which would hold the templates for up to 512 spoken words). The total number of templates which are available to the recognition logic at any one time is restricted to 128, which could be held in a 16 kbyte memory.

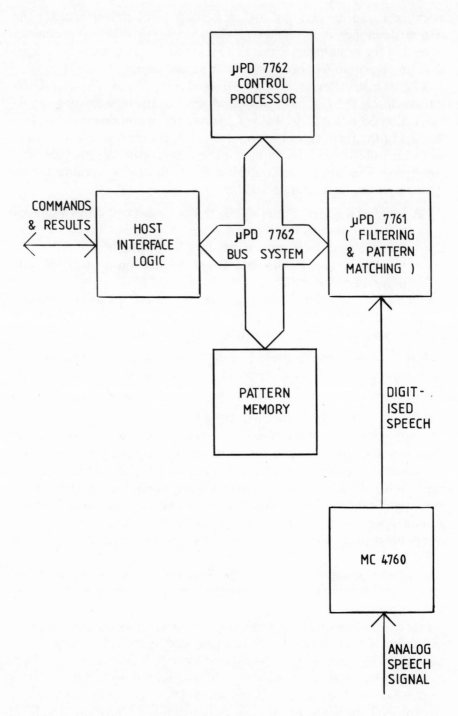

Figure 8.3   The NEC 3 chip speech recognition set

The 7761 is mask-programmed to perform the dynamic programming recognition algorithm, together with the spectral analysis. NEC provide little detail of how this is done, other than to state that the features used are derived from a bank of 8 band-pass filters.

The speech signal is provided in digitised form, over a serial line, by the MC4760 which contains amplifiers to link directly to tape recorder or microphone, an anti-aliasing filter, and an 8-bit A/D converter sampling at 10 kHz.

The three chips, plus memory, are to be assembled in a standard manner, and the user then controls the whole system via ports to the 7762. Through these controls he can adjust the gain levels in the band-pass filters, 'train' the system, resulting in templates being set up in the memory, and perform recognition. The recognition logic can provide first and second choice classes, together with a distance value between the unknown and the template. It is possible when requesting recognition operation to restrict the templates over which comparison is performed. This can be extremely useful if the context of the word is known to exclude certain possibilities, as it increases both speed and recognition accuracy. NEC claim a speed of 0.5 s and a recognition accuracy of 98%, with a selectable rejection rate for close decisions. It is difficult to interpret what this may mean, as performance will vary from speaker to speaker. A better way to specify performance would be to present an average error/reject curve, to show the possible trade-offs. It will be a bold chip manufacturer who first presents his users with such useful information!

THE μPD7764

The most recent speech recognition device to be announced by NEC is the μPD7764. This is a most unusual device in that it has been very specifically designed for speech recognition processing, yet in fact comprises two general-purpose processors, both of which hold their programs in RAM. So, on the one hand, NEC describe it in terms of its speech recognition performance (which implies the incorporation of appropriate algorithms in the two processors) and on the other hand offer the user complete freedom to program the device as he wishes.

The two processors are labelled the *D-processor* and the *G-processor*, and they work independently, in a pipelined structure. The D-processor comes first in the sequence, and is a distance measuring processor, used to calculate a distance between two feature vectors. The actual derivation of the feature vectors is not a function of the 7764, and this operation would typically be a spectral analysis function performed by a 7720 or similar processor. Arithmetic with the D-processor is performed by two 8-bit subtractors able to feed into two adders in pipeline. The subtractors are able to provide the absolute value of their result, and so the processor is good at performing the operation:

$$\text{distance} = \sum_{i=1}^{n} (x_i - a_i)$$

A buffer memory for the vectors, such as those in the above equation, having a 416×8-bit capacity, forms part of the D-processor. It is loaded by DMA (Direct Memory Access) logic, on the chip, from external sources. These sources would be the feature extraction processing, for unknown patterns, and the template store. Figure 8.4 shows a typical system arrangement based on the 7764. Programming the D-processor is clearly not a lengthy matter, as NEC provide space for just 32 instructions to control its operation.

The G-processor is intended to perform the dynamic programming algorithm. It is a more conventional processor, using a 16-bit general-purpose ALU. Its work space RAM has just an 88-word capacity. The program space for this processor is 128 words of RAM, together with a built-in utility ROM of 128 words. The latter has a variety of input/output control routines, together with multiply and divide subroutines.

Using this processor, in an appropriate system, and with appropriate software, NEC claim some very high performance levels in speech recognition. Two examples are quoted, both giving word accuracy rates of 99% and both operating in 0.3 seconds. One works using a vocabulary of 40 words, which can occur in connected speech. The other is for isolated words, and can deal with a 340-word vocabulary. The features used are described as being 8-bit measurements from 16 band-pass channels, using a frame period of 16 ms.

This processor seems to offer the knowledgeable user a chance to vary his features, distance metric and classification algorithm without too great an overhead in programming effort, but with a restricted hardware framework. A typical minimum system might comprise an analogue input device such as the MC4760, a 7720 programmed for spectral analysis, a 7764 and 64 kbytes of memory. When interface logic to a host is added, this would be a small board of possibly single Eurocard size.

8.5 *The way ahead*

OTHER HIGH-SPEED PROCESSORS
Many other manufacturers are announcing devices which have similar potential for speech recognition, but as yet are too new to have been used

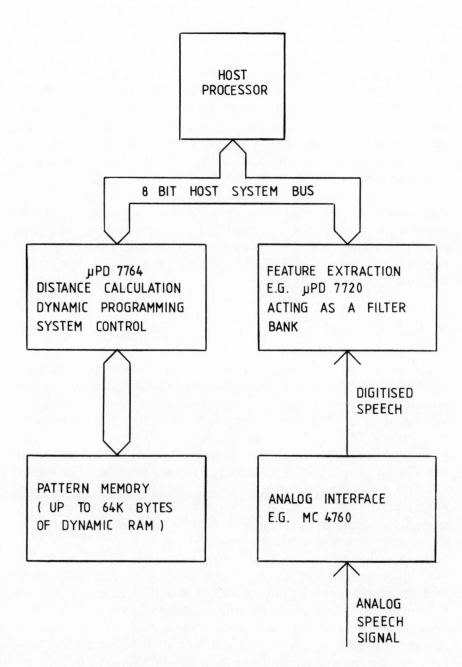

Figure 8.4 Typical use of μPD 7764

in such an ambitious application. There are signal processor devices from ITT and Fujitsu which both offer a 10-MHz basic instruction rate, and processors which are specifically intended for parallel systems, such as the *Transputer* from INMOS.

The ITT and Fujitsu processors have a similar look to them, with an arithmetic section using a 16 × 16 multiplier and higher precision ALU, rather like the TMS 320 arrangement. Each has a small internal RAM, and a 1 kbyte instruction internal program ROM. The general-purpose signal processor is becoming well established as a breed of microprocessor, and factors such as manufacturer support are probably as important now as raw speed capability.

The Transputer represents another quite different way to produce very high throughput. This chip has a 32-bit ALU and substantial memory, together with very well constructed links to other similar chips. The potential of highly parallel structures in recognition systems is very great, but my own feeling is that image, rather than speech, recognition will be the target of these systems.

LIKELY DEVELOPMENTS IN THIS DECADE

To conclude this chapter we should look ahead to the likely developments within the next five years.

The use of the digital signal processor devices is at present fairly restricted. They are new devices, still very expensive, and only a few attempts have so far been made to implement speech recognition algorithms on them. We can expect to see substantial changes here. As with any radically new semi-conductors, as newer devices come along, and the yields on the older devices improve, the price per chip decreases very sharply. The oldest of the signal processors mentioned here is the 7720. It is now available (as the 7720A) in a plastic package, with mask-programmed chips costing little over $10 in quantity. Any user with enough confidence in his algorithm to order 1000 chips can have the cheap, small powerful hardware today.

It seems that theoretical, rather than technological, limitations will hold up the widespread use of speech recognition. The widely used dynamic programming algorithm deals reasonably well with variations in speaking rates, and can handle connected speech to some extent. The right sort of feature extraction to be able to deal with a variety of speakers is still eluding researchers. Recent work demonstrated by IBM has extended recognition vocabularies to several thousand words, and uses simplified training methods. Perhaps when work of this kind is implemented on small signal processors such as the TMS 32020 we may see the sort of breakthrough which has been promised for so long.

8.6 *References*

1. Quarmby, D. (ed.), (1984) *Signal Processor Chips*. London: Granada Technical Books.
2. Schalk, T., and McMahan, M. (1982) 'Firmware-programmable μC aids speech recognition'. *Electronic Design* July 22.
3. Dusek, L., Schalk, T., and McMahan, M. (1983) 'Voice recognition joins speech on programmable board'. *Electronics* April 21.
4. Feldman, Hofstetter, and Malpass (1983) 'A compact, flexible LPC Vocoder based on a commercial signal processing microcomputer'. *Trans ASSP-31* **1**, 252–257.
5. Quarmby, D., and Holmes, J. (1984) 'Implementation of a parallel-formant speech synthesiser using a single-chip programmable signal processor', *IEE Proceedings* Vol. **131** Pt. F **6**, 563–569, October.

CHAPTER 9
COMMERCIAL SPEECH RECOGNISERS

Tom Ivall

In this chapter the techniques discussed earlier in this book are related to the actual recognition products that are available on the open market.

9.1 *Types of recogniser commercially available*

As soon as a body of technology is translated into commercial products it begins to be shaped by the iron laws of economics. Basically this means that there is competition between manufacturers to produce the most useful and attractive products at the lowest possible prices. In practice this general objective applies constraints from two different directions.

The first constraint is the actual, specialised requirements of customers in their industrial, commercial or other activities. In the case of a very new kind of product like the automatic speech recogniser (ASR), the potential customer may not even be aware that he can benefit from the use of it. The ASR manufacturer then has to persuade the customer that a speech recogniser would have a definite advantage over existing methods of information input for improving the productivity of his business. This may well make it necessary for the ASR manufacturer to study the customer's activities very closely and probably modify his ASR standard product to exploit any opportunity for using it shown up by the study.

The second constraint on the available technology is that the ASR product design must try to forestall price and delivery competition from other ASR manufacturers. In turn this means that, on price, the product must be manufactured at the lowest possible cost, and, on delivery, that it must be constructed from readily available standard components – whether hardware or software – from reliable sources of supply.

In the case of commercial speech recognisers currently being sold, these constraints imposed by competition have shaped the design of the products by a process which goes on in many other fields. The limitations of the technology are matched to the often restricted range of tasks, or low level of performance, required by the user in specialised applications. Automatic speech recognition is fundamentally difficult to achieve, so why struggle to provide a better performance or range of facilities than is necessary for the job to be done?

For example, recognising words spoken in a continuous stream is technically more difficult to achieve – and more costly to the customer – than recognising single words spoken in isolation. Some ASR applications only require the recognition of isolated words, so there is clearly no need to provide the higher grade performance of connected-word recognition for these applications. Similarly, techniques for cancelling background noise are wasted in environments where there is little or no such noise.

Any manufacturer, of course, is only too delighted to sell his most expensive, top-performing model, if he can, even to customers who really do not need it. But ASR manufacturing has not yet reached this happy state of a luxury trade. It is still struggling to establish itself in the market place and must operate on the level of strict utility.

VOICE DATA ENTRY

What has emerged from the matching of technology limitations to restricted application tasks is that the major opportunity for speech recognisers is in voice data entry. The main characteristics of this task which make it a restricted one are:

(a) the smallest units of spoken information likely to be needed for voice data entry are whole words
(b) only short groups of words have to be recognised, say half-a-dozen at a time
(c) isolated words are often acceptable
(d) only a small vocabulary is needed, typically less than 50 words

These characteristics distinguish voice data entry from, say, the much more difficult task of speech-to-text recognition. Here the requirement is to provide a commercial machine to replace the human stenographer or shorthand-typist. Essentially, the speech-to-text ASR product must handle relatively long groups of words spoken continuously, namely sentences in natural language; it must have a relatively large vocabulary, running into thousands of words; and to achieve the necessary flexibility for this task it will probably have to operate on phonemes, rather than whole words, as the smallest units of acoustic information.

Because of these technical problems, speech-to-text recognisers are still largely in the laboratory. Four of the companies now developing them are Fujitsu, IBM, Kurzweil and Speech Systems Inc. At the time of writing (1985) no such machines are available on the open market.

Speech recognisers for voice data entry can therefore be considered as acoustic pattern recognisers, and this is what the majority of products on the market essentially are. The acoustic patterns they recognise are usually the spoken words of natural languages, but they need not be. Other sounds such as whistles, musical extracts, machine noises, or animal grunts, howls or barks could be recognised equally well by the same technology.

In responding to spoken words, these data entry devices can be used in two principal ways. One is to generate command signals for controlling machinery, such as robots, computers, machine-tools, mechanical toys or domestic appliances (e.g. for physically disabled people). When a particular command word is uttered, like *start*, it is the equivalent of selecting and pressing a particular button on a control panel. The word is automatically identified and used to generate an associated, previously chosen binary-coded output, which in turn is decoded to produce an electrical power switching signal in a particular circuit.

In the second group of applications, each spoken word is identified and this process is used to generate the written or text form in letters and numerals. The real-time output of the ASR is a sequence of binary encoded alphanumeric characters in some standard data code, corresponding to the spoken form of the word. These alphanumeric characters are subsequently displayed, perhaps on a VDU (see Fig. 9.1), printed out, or transferred into a computer system memory for further processing.

Thus in this mode of use the voice data entry ASR can function as a computer peripheral. Indeed, it is often used as an adjunct to a conventional computer terminal with keyboard and display screen, and the ASR output data code characters are handled by the computer terminal as if they originated from manual operation of the keyboard.

As a voice data entry terminal the ASR device can be used with general-purpose personal, mini- and main-frame computers, and also with dedicated computing systems performing specialised tasks such as programmed control of industrial processes. In such applications the computer acts as a 'host' to the ASR in the sense that it initiates and co-ordinates the voice terminal's operation as an input to an application program run on the computer. This is equivalent to the computer's

Figure 9.1   Speech recognition is used in this voice controlled computer workstation made by Cascade for handicapped people

control of the input/output operations of conventional computer terminals. Special software packages are needed for this voice terminal control, and these are normally supplied by the ASR product manufacturers to be run on particular makes of host computers (see Chapter 10 for more details).

9.2 *The hardware and the software*

CONSTRUCTION OF TYPICAL PRODUCTS
The physical and electrical construction of voice data entry ASRs varies considerably. They can be roughly divided into two categories: stand-alone units (e.g. desk-top, floor-standing, rack-mounted), and plug-in printed-circuit board modules. The PC board modules are designed either for plugging into spare slots inside well-known makes of personal computers or for building into other electronic equipment.

Examples of stand-alone speech recognisers are the Interstate *SYS-300*, Logica *Logos 1*, Marconi *SR-128*, NEC *DP-200* and Votan *VTR6000*. Rack-mounted types include the Scott *VET-232* and a version of the Marconi *SR-128*. In some cases the product comprises more than one unit, as in the NEC DP-200 which has an ASR terminal plus a

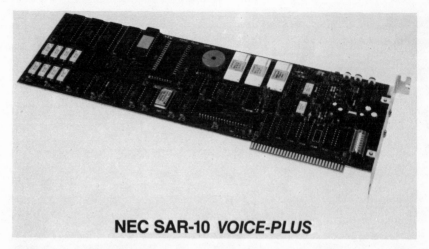

NEC SAR-10 *VOICE-PLUS*

Figure 9.2 Plug-in speech recogniser module, SAR-10, made by NEC for the IBM PC personal computer

remote control terminal incorporating an alphanumeric display. Board modules for plugging into well-known personal computers like the IBM PC and Apple II are made by several manufacturers, including CGD International, Interstate, Microsignal, NEC, Vecsys and Votan (two examples of these are shown in Figs. 9.2 and 9.3). Dragon Systems offer an evaluation board.

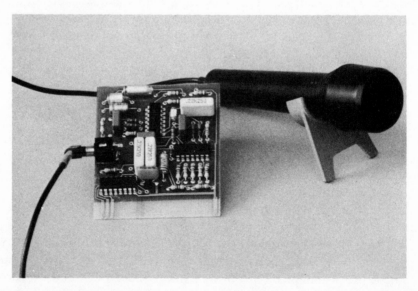

Figure 9.3 Plug-in speech recogniser module, SR-32, made by Microsignal for the Apple II personal computer

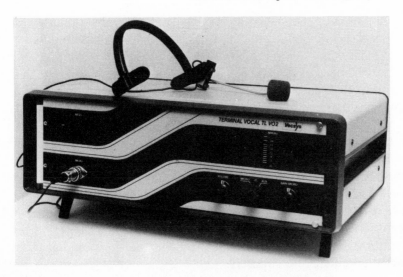

Figure 9.4 Desk-top voice data entry terminal TL VQ2 made by Vecsys, with microphone headset

Microphones are often supplied with these products, certainly with the stand-alone units (see, for example, Fig. 9.4). Here a choice can be made between table-top, hand-held and headset models, also between standard and noise-cancelling types, and between cable and wireless (radio microphone) methods of signal transmission.

The physical construction of the ASR unit does, however, depend on the relative contributions of fixed hardware, firmware and software in determining the functions performed in ASR signal processing. The fixed hardware can be analogue or digital, but the well-known advantages of digital systems – accuracy, stability and repeatability – have all but driven analogue components and circuitry out of commercial speech recognisers. There is an irreducible minimum of analogue hardware in the microphone, its pre-amplifier and gain control, and in the analogue side of an analogue-to-digital (A/D) converter. In addition some manufacturers find the simplicity of analogue filters an advantage for spectral analysis of voice signals (see below).

But the most important advantage of digital hardware is that it allows the extreme operational flexibility given by software programming. Now that 32-bit single-chip microcomputers with 200-ns instruction cycle times are readily available, the possibilities for real-time digital signal processing of acoustic information under software control are extremely wide.

DISTRIBUTION OF SOFTWARE BETWEEN COMPUTER AND RECOGNISER

Apart from this advantage of flexibility there is another highly significant aspect of software programming for ASR product design. Algorithms for speech processing can be translated into program instructions that can be run on the digital hardware of standard, general-purpose computers. Almost the whole of the processing required for speech recognition can be specified in software form. Thus the software need not be restricted to dedicated digital hardware or to special-purpose ASR computers. It does, however, have to be written for specific makes of general-purpose computers.

As a result of these developments there is now a complete gamut in the distribution of software between the totally dedicated digital hardware of certain ASR products and the entirely general-purpose hardware of standard commercial computers.

At one extreme is the completely self-contained speech recogniser, like the Logica Logos 1 or the Marconi SR-128, which has an alphanumeric display built in and needs only a microphone and mains supply. At the other extreme is the ASR software package. One example is the Logica *Logos 2* package, designed to run on the Intel 8086 microprocessor. Another is the Dragon Systems *Mark II* package, which can be run on certain standard personal computers including the ACT Apricot Portable, the Apple II and the IBM PC. The Dragon system requires only a minimum of additional hardware to be fitted in the personal computer by its manufacturer: a microphone pre-amplifier, an 8-bit A/D converter, 16 kbyte of ROM and 8 kbyte of RAM.

Between these two extremes, other ASR products use the software and hardware facilities provided by standard computers in various ways. A common arrangement is to utilise the memory capacity of the host computer and its peripheral memory units (e.g. magnetic disk file) for long-term storage of acoustic reference pattern data and the related text vocabulary data (see Chapter 10). Through a computer program this information can be downloaded to a RAM short-term working memory in the ASR unit. Equally, the contents of the RAM can be uploaded to the host computer.

9.3 *Performance of commercial recognisers*

Apart from these physical and electrical differences, ASR products also differ from each other in performance. A major division in terms of performance is between isolated-word recognisers and connected-word recognisers. The first are simpler and cheaper products because they off-load the task of segmenting an utterance into separate words onto the human speaker. In a spoken sequence of words he is required to utter each word separately, with a short pause on either side of it. The duration of the minimum pause required between words varies from product to product but is generally in the range 50 ms to 500 ms.

Although such pauses are extremely short in terms of human articulation, the effort required of the user to ensure that they are made is an inconvenience at the very least, as such discontinuous speech is unnatural. Hence the development of connected-word recognisers. However, for some applications isolated-word recognition is not a serious drawback. Some ASR products offer both modes of operation.

The permitted duration of an utterance, whether a single, isolated word or a connected stream of words, is another performance parameter. This is commonly a minimum of 0.2 s and a maximum of 2 s, but the NEC DP-200, for example, allows up to 4 s. With connected-word recognisers this means that the length of a complete phrase or sentence can be up to about five words. This is probably adequate, for example, for describing an object by its type code (a string of letters and/or numerals) in a sorting or inspection procedure.

Although data entry speech recognisers are described as real-time devices they do, of course, introduce a slight delay between the utterance and the resulting output data. But this response time, as it is specified, is insignificant for most applications, ranging from about 50 ms to about 300 ms depending on the product. With isolated-word recognisers the response time is the minimum necessary pause between words plus the processing time.

The total number of different words that a data-entry ASR can recognise at any one time (called the vocabulary) is typically up to 50. But this varies from product to product, for example from 32 words in the (isolated-word) Microsignal *SR-32* (Fig. 9.2) to 250 words in Voice Systems International's (connected-word) *Datavox Auditor*. These figures apply to what is called the *active vocabulary* – the data for this being normally held in an on-board RAM. This active vocabulary can be exchanged for a different set of words, of the same maximum size, by the process of uploading/downloading with a much larger, long-term vocabulary filed in a host computer, as already mentioned.

SPEAKER-DEPENDENT AND -INDEPENDENT

A particularly important division in ASR products, as an aspect of performance, is between speaker-dependent and speaker-independent recognisers. A speaker-dependent device is one that will only recognise correctly the utterances of one individual at a time. This is the person who has 'trained' it, by previously supplying it with acoustic reference patterns in his/her own voice. However, because voice data entry ASRs are essentially acoustic pattern recognisers, the speaker-dependent product places no restriction on the type or character of the individual voice using it at a given time. The voice can be male or female, using any language, in any regional accent, with any peculiarities of enunciation, timbre, projection and so on.

Speaker-independent products do not require training in the above sense. They have already been trained by the manufacturer, with data representing a composite reference voice derived from a number of different voices – designed by a committee, so to speak. Because the composite reference voice thus built into the recogniser can be only an approximation to any individual user's voice, there is a strong possibility of errors occurring in the recognition process.

To limit such errors the active vocabulary in some products is deliberately restricted to a few words in a given natural language, which have been selected because they have markedly different acoustic patterns whoever speaks them (e.g. *yes* and *no*). For example, the NEC speaker-independent *SR-2500* Voice Processor will handle up to 16 words in one version and 20 words in another. The makers claim that it will function with voice signals coming via the public telephone network.

Other products offer speaker-independence as an optional extra to standard speaker-dependent operation. The Scott *VET-232SD* voice entry terminal, for example, has a limited speaker-independent option of twelve standard words – *yes*, *no* and the ten decimal digits *zero* to *nine* – or a custom-designed vocabulary of similar size. In contrast, this terminal's normal, speaker-dependent vocabulary is much larger, at 200 words.

RECOGNITION ACCURACY

A very critical aspect of performance for the user is, of course, the accuracy of recognition. When this is quoted in product specifications it appears as a percentage, usually somewhere between 95% and 99%. This means the percentage of correct acoustic pattern recognitions achieved in a test conducted with a specified vocabulary. (Sometimes, percentage error rates are given.) Unfortunately, specifications seldom give much information on the details of the tests, and there are no internationally agreed standards or guidelines for testing, against which the manufacturers' figures could be independently checked. (Standards have been proposed, however – see Chapter 13.)

Thus the accuracy figure in specifications should be treated as a claim and taken with some caution and perhaps scepticism. One manufacturer,

Microsignal, states frankly that recognition accuracy 'depends on speaker experience and choice of vocabulary'.

Other performance parameters include: the maximum number of alphanumeric characters obtainable from the output at any one time; the memory capacity of the on-board RAM mentioned above; the maximum permitted duration of a pause within a spoken word (e.g. *eigh.....t*); the maximum permitted level of background noise; and the audio level and bandwidth. Further aspects of performance can be discussed after we outline briefly the techniques currently employed in speech recognisers (see Chapters 3 and 4 for full details).

9.4 *Techniques in common use*

All commercial products known at the time of writing (1985) are based on the principle of acoustic pattern matching. The input acoustic patterns are compared with reference acoustic patterns previously stored in the ASR (by the user, with speaker-dependent products, and by the manufacturer, with speaker-independent products), as shown in Fig. 9.5.

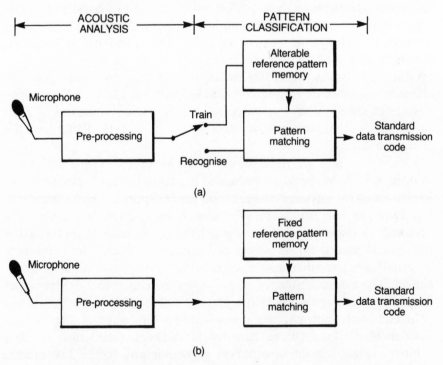

Figure 9.5 Principle of speech recognition by pattern matching: (a) speaker-dependent system with provision for 'training'; (b) speaker-independent system using permanent reference patterns

When an input pattern is found to match a stored reference pattern to a sufficient, pre-determined level of accuracy, the input pattern is thereby 'recognised' and accepted. This event causes the ASR to issue a sequence of binary-encoded characters corresponding to the acoustic pattern which has been matched in this way. The output characters can be used as a command to control machinery or as a text version of the input utterance. The accuracy of pattern matching is measured numerically as a 'score' and this score must exceed a threshold value pre-set by the user to be accepted as valid and generate an output code.

To achieve these functions the commercial recogniser contains a pre-processing or acoustic analysis section followed by a pattern classification or matching section. The pre-processing extracts 'features' of the acoustic information conveyed by the microphone signal and these are used to form input and reference patterns, as sets of digital data, for the matching process.

PRE-PROCESSING

In the majority of ASR products the pre-processing consists of frequency spectrum analysis performed by a bank of band-pass filters. First the microphone signal is band-limited (typically from about 300 Hz to about 3 kHz). The number of filters used, and hence frequency channels identified in the spectral analysis, varies from product to product. The Vecsys *RM150A* isolated-word recogniser uses as few as eight, while Logica's Logos 1 and Marconi's SR-128 (similar designs) have 19 channels. Verbex (now ceased trading) had as many as 32 in an early model. At least three products (CGD, Interstate, NEC) have 16-channel analysis.

Some filters used are analogue and some are digital. The digital filters, in turn, are divided between dedicated digital hardware types and those implemented by software programs on general-purpose host computers. For example, the Interstate *SRB* speech recognition board for IBM personal computers uses 16 analogue, band-pass, active filters formed by integrated operational amplifiers and capacitors. Each filter is followed by a half-wave rectifier and a second-order low-pass filter with 25-Hz cut-off. The centre frequency of each filter is related to a 1-MHz clock frequency used for timing purposes.

In complete contrast, the pre-processing hardware of the Dragon Systems Mark II is no more than an 8-bit A/D converter, thus providing a binary-coded stream of numbers corresponding to the microphone signal amplitude as a function of time. All spectral analysis in this software-based system is performed by digital processing within the personal computer for which this voice data entry is available.

As an example of dedicated digital hardware under software control, the current Votan speech recognisers use an A/D converter followed by a digital transform algorithm for spectral analysis. The digital transform is similar to the *fast Fourier transform* (FFT). An FFT is a convenient way of implementing a *discrete Fourier transform* (DFT) by digital computation. (See Chapter 4 for details of computational techniques.) The digital transform performed here is done by the Texas Instruments single-chip signal processor TMS320 (see Chapter 8) and results in a spectral analysis equivalent to that given by 128 separate 30-Hz bandpass filters.

Cepstrum analysis, a sensitive technique for detecting the fundamental pitch of voiced sounds, is used in the NEC SR-2500. The cepstrum is defined as the inverse Fourier transform of the logarithm of the power spectrum, and the NEC implementation of these processes is shown in Fig. 9.6. This system calculates mel cepstra from the input audio waveform at intervals of 16 ms. First the analogue input signal is band-limited to 0.3–3.4 kHz, then pre-emphasis by a filter increases the amplitude of the high frequency end of the audio band to improve signal:noise ratio. Spectra are calculated by an FFT algorithm and mapped onto the mel scale. Next the logarithms of these values are computed and finally the inverse Fourier transform is computed to give a succession of mel cepstra at 16-ms intervals.

PATTERN MATCHING

The features obtained from the microphone signal in these various ways are essentially short-term spectral analyses, and a time-varying input acoustic pattern, such as that of a single word, is analysed into a whole succession of these *frames*, as they are often called. In many ASR products the reference patterns are formed from these frames. Matching between the input patterns and the reference patterns, sometimes known as *templates*, is achieved by use of a dynamic programming algorithm. This provides *dynamic time warping* (DTW) of the time-scales of the two patterns to compensate for an inevitably non-linear time relationship between them due to different speeds of enunciating the same words even by the same speaker. A digitised reference pattern held in RAM might

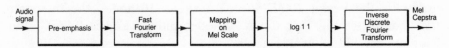

Figure 9.6 Cepstrum analysis technique used for acoustic feature extraction in NEC SR-2500 speech recogniser

typically contain 400 to 900 bits of data. Processing rates are typically in the region of 500 templates per second.

In another group of ASR products the reference patterns are not sets of these frames, but statistical models. This technique, pioneered by Dragon Systems in commercial form, is based on the broad principle that statistical models are often very suitable for time-varying natural processes which contain a good deal of randomness (e.g. Brownian motion). They have the practical advantage that they require a much smaller amount of computation than other methods to achieve a similar level of pattern matching accuracy, though more computation is needed in the formation of reference patterns by training. The Dragon Systems Mark II software is based on a stochastic series called a *hidden Markov model* (seee Chapter 4).

SYNTAX CONTROL

Whatever method of pattern matching is used, recognition accuracy can be greatly improved, particularly in connected-word ASR products, by applying the control or constraint of a permitted order of words. This is described as 'syntax' in specifications, but it does not usually mean anything as advanced as the rules governing the grammatical arrangement of words in natural language. It could equally well be used to lay down a permitted order of unrelated animal or machine noises.

Recognition accuracy is improved in products using syntax control by eliminating those spurious word orders, resulting from inadequate matching, which do not make sense in the application concerned. A perhaps more important commercial advantage of this control method is that it reduces the number of word choices that have to be made at any point in classifying a sequence of words. This in turn reduces the amount of computation required, by restricting the calculation of pattern matching scores to only those word sequences which are allowed by the syntax.

Earlier chapters have explained the tree or branching method by which the prescribed word order is defined and subsequently implemented through a computer algorithm. In product specifications the branching points are often called *nodes*. The more nodes there are available, the greater the possible size and complexity of a branching pattern, and hence the greater the flexibility of the syntax control. As examples, the Vecsys *RME186* board allows 10 nodes, the Interstate SRB board (see Fig. 9.8) allows 20 nodes and the Logica Logos 1 and Marconi SR-128 allow 255 nodes.

In the Logos 1, nodes in the branching pattern may be functionally looped together to allow the word, or a group of words, between them to

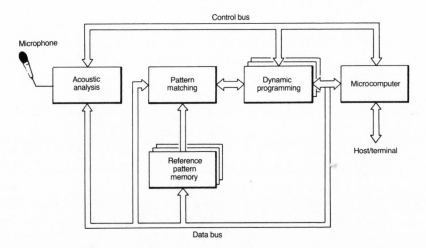

Figure 9.7 Functional diagram of Logica's Logos 1 continuous-speech recogniser

be recognised any number of times. For example, the group of ten numerals *zero* to *nine* could be permitted between two nodes and this would allow the user to speak, at that point in the branching pattern, a string of decimal digits of any length.

Two block diagrams illustrate the use of some of the above techniques in particular commercial products. Figure 9.7 is a simplified, purely functional diagram of the Logica Logos 1, a stand-alone, continuous-speech recogniser designed primarily as a tool for R & D work. Figure 9.8 shows the specific hardware of the Interstate SRB, a plug-in, single-board, isolated-word module designed specifically for the IBM PC and XT as host computers. Although very different in size, purpose, facilities and performance, both of these microprocessor-based systems use analogue filter banks for acoustic analysis, template matching, dynamic programming for time normalisation and syntax control of recognition.

THRESHOLD AND TRAINING

Many ASR products allow the user to pre-set a critical threshold that determines either acceptance or rejection of each input word undergoing the recognition process. This threshold is a value above which the pattern matching 'score' of the candidate words is accepted as valid and below which it is rejected as invalid. In the CGD Voice Input Module for the Apple II personal computer, for example, the user selects a threshold value as a number on a scale between 0 and 128. Here, 0 means no rejection at all and 128 means total rejection of all utterances. Thus the higher the number selected the better the rejection of extra-vocabulary

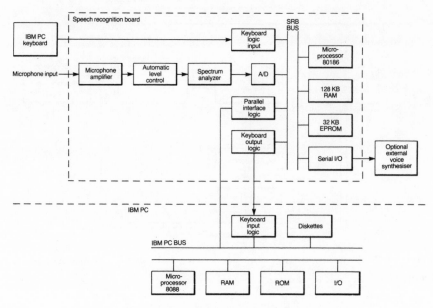

Figure 9.8   Hardware block diagram of Interstate SRB isolated-word re-cogniser module for plugging into IBM personal computer

acoustic patterns – and the better the rejection of background noise and voices of non-permitted users. But these desirable results are achieved at the expense of a greater rejection frequency of valid acoustic patterns.

This threshold number is selected and applied to the system by software programming (see Chapter 10). The CGD module, like most ASR products, is a digital system controlled and coordinated by a programmed, single-chip or single-board microcomputer. It has its own instruction set and this is used in conjunction with the high-level programming language employed in the host computer for applications programs.

To provide reference patterns for a speaker-dependent, whole-word recogniser, the user must 'train' the product to work with his particular voice and individual characteristics of enunciation. This is done by putting the recogniser into a training mode of operation and speaking once or several times each vocabulary word that is to be recognised. Many products specify a single utterance of each word, but some require multiple utterances, or 'passes', to achieve adequate reference patterns. The NEC DP-200 recogniser specifies two passes for each spoken decimal digit. In the self-contained Marconi SR-128 the reference patterns are first recorded on magnetic tape in a miniature cassette recorder, then subsequently loaded into the recogniser's template memory. Products depending on host computers utilise the mass storage devices (e.g. disk drives) that these provide.

Like all other operational functions, the training mode is programmed by software. As far as the user is concerned this means that each vocabulary word is spoken in response to a visual prompt, either on the host computer's or terminal's display screen or on an alphanumeric display. Software also allows updating or editing of the vocabulary (see Chapter 10) and the organisation of the syntax rules.

Nowadays the speech recogniser tends to be seen as one part of a comprehensive, integrated speech-input/speech-output system for industrial and commercial applications. For this reason many products include some means of controlling or generating synthesised speech. In some applications this may be only to reconstitute what has been recognised, for checking purposes. In general the facility is known as *speech response* or *audio response*. Figure 9.9 shows how both recognition and response facilities are integrated into the same product.

As an example, with the NEC SAR-10 plug-in board a menu-driven utility program is provided to digitise input audio signals at a rate of 24, 28 or 32 kbit/s. Words or messages are stored under filenames defined by the user and are output either by voice input control or by application program control. In this case the high bit rates available allow quite high quality sound to be produced.

9.5 *Sources of further information*

No attempt has been made in this chapter to conduct a quantitative comparison of current recognition products, because such an analysis would not stand the test of time. Instead, the current use of the techniques described in the first section of this book has been explored.

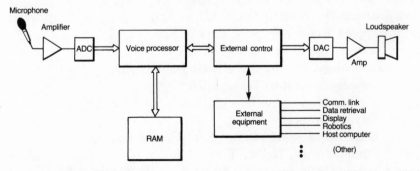

Figure 9.9 Example of voice response integrated into a Votan speech recognition system

From time to time various workers in the field have published comparative evaluations, probably the first major exercise of this sort being that conducted by Doddington and Shalk in 1982[1]. The reader is advised to seek out the most recent of these articles in the speech journals before committing to any major design expenditure, as well as contacting the vendors directly.

Although the field of vendors of recognition products is rapidly changing, the following list represents those companies that, to the author's knowledge, were operating at the end of 1985:

Active Voice, Seattle, Washington, USA.
Alpha Products, Woodhaven, New York, USA.
CGD International, Richmond, Surrey, UK.
Cascade, Santa Ana, California, USA.
Covox, Eugene, Oregon, USA.
Centigram, Sunnyvale, California, USA.
Dragon Systems, Newton, Massachusetts, USA.
Heuristics, Sunnyvale, California, USA.
Infovox, Stockholm, Sweden.
Interstate Voice Products, Orange, California, USA.
Keytronics, Spokane, Washington, USA.
Kurzweil Applied Intelligence, Waltham, Massachusetts, USA.
Lokersystems, Beltsville, Maryland, USA.
Logica, London, UK.
Logical Business Machines, Sunnyvale, California, USA.
Marconi, Portsmouth, UK.
Marketing Consultants International, Hagerstown, Maryland, USA.
Microsignal, Santa Barbara, California, USA.
NEC, Tokyo, Japan. *NEC America*, Melville, New York, USA.
Proximity Technology, Fort Lauderdale, Florida, USA.
Recognition Associates, Brooklyn, New York, USA.
Scott Instruments, Denton, Texas, USA.
Spectraphonics, Rochester, New York, USA.
Speech Systems, Tarzana, California, USA.
Sphere Technology, Providence, Rhode Island, USA.
Texas Instruments, Austin, Texas, USA.
Threshold Technology, New Jersey, USA. (Ceased trading.)
Vecsys, Bièvres, France.
Verbex, Bedford, Massachusetts, USA. (Ceased trading.)
Voice Control Systems, Dallas, Texas, USA.
Voice Machine Communications, Santa Ana, California, USA.
Voice Recognition Systems, San Francisco, California, USA.

Voice Systems International, Cambridge, UK.
Voice Works, Toronto, Canada.
Votan, Fremont, California, USA.

9.6 *References*

1. Doddington, George R., Schalk, Thomas B. (1981) 'Speech recognition: turning theory into practice'. *IEEE Spectrum*, Sept. 1981, 26–32.

CHAPTER 10

LINKING RECOGNISERS TO COMPUTERS

Tom Ivall

In this chapter, the use of currently available recognisers as peripherals to host computers is explored.

10.1 *The recogniser as a computer peripheral*

Many of the commercial speech recognisers now available (see Chapter 10) are designed essentially as computer peripherals, for the particular task of voice data entry. They provide an alternative to keyboards, bar-code readers or other devices for data entry, and they emulate these devices by giving outputs of binary-encoded alphanumeric characters in exactly the same format. The characters are commonly encoded as 7-bit numbers in the International Standards Organisation (ISO) data code or its American Standard Code for Information Interchange (ASCII) version. So as far as the host computer is concerned, it does not 'know' whether its input data is coming from a keyboard or from a speech recogniser.

The host computer may be anything from a single-board microcomputer close at hand to a large main-frame, housed in a building some distance away. But now that the personal computer has become so popular in industry and commerce, many automatic speech recogniser (ASR) products are designed as peripherals for this kind of machine. As explained in Chapter 9, the speech recogniser can be a physically separate unit – say, a desk-top cabinet plus microphone – or a printed-circuit board module which plugs into a spare socket inside a personal computer.

Broadly, the host computer 'drives' the ASR peripheral. In its operational role the computer runs a program to perform a particular

234

information processing task, perhaps in an automation system – an application program. This program calls for voice data entry at certain points. Thus the application program and the ensuing events in the computer's hardware determine the order and timing (protocol) of the information flow between the speech recogniser and the computer. This also means that the internal functioning of the recogniser is controlled to a greater or lesser extent by the computer.

In the case of ASR products which are essentially software packages designed to be run on particular computers (see Chapter 9), virtually all the speech recognition processing is done by the computer, and therefore this control is total. The host has almost completely absorbed the peripheral, both physically and functionally. In other ASR products the speech recognition processing is controlled by a built-in single-chip microcomputer or microprocessor (e.g. Intel 8086) and this runs a fixed program held as firmware, usually in a ROM or EPROM. Here the firmware program has to be coordinated with the host computer's particular application program that has been written to include voice data entry.

However, the overall control by the computer is no different in principle from that applied to other kinds of peripherals. So in practical operations it does not impose any great restriction on the user. To all intents and purposes the ASR peripheral works in real time. There is in fact a slight delay due to the ASR processing time and the transmission time of data flowing to the computer, but this is normally to be measured in a few tenths of a second.

USE WITH COMPUTER TERMINALS

In some applications the ASR peripheral is required to work in conjunction with a conventional computer terminal with keyboard and display screen – for example, to allow simultaneous voice and manual data entry. This is shown in simplified form in Fig. 10.1, with the speech recogniser interposed between the terminal and the host computer. In theory any kind of communications interface compatible with the three units can be used to interconnect them and convey data and control signals. But in practice there is widespread use of the well-known *V24/RS-232C* bit-serial two-way interface. (V24 is the designation of the International Telegraph and Telephone Consultative Committee (CCITT) while RS-232C is the American Electronics Industry Association's (EIA) designation for essentially the same interface standard, then only difference being in pulse shape.)

When the recogniser is operating, sequences of encoded characters in a standard data transmission code (see above), corresponding to the

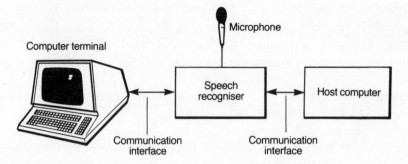

Figure 10.1   Speech recogniser used as voice data entry computer peripheral, in conjunction with conventional terminal and host computer

spoken words recognised, are sent over the duplex interface to the host computer. From the computer they are transmitted back to the terminal and displayed on its screen as text in letters and numerals. Alternatively, the recogniser's encoded output characters may be sent directly to the terminal and displayed. The terminal's keyboard and screen provide the user with input/output for communicating with the recogniser, through prompts, commands and responses, when programming it for the application concerned (see below).

A slightly more specific illustration of an arrangement for using a speech recogniser with a host computer is shown in Fig. 10.2. The ASR product is assumed to be speaker-dependent, so it has to be 'trained' (see Chapter 9). This training, in which the user supplies reference voice patterns, is done through a personal computer or computer terminal. Vocabulary words for the reference patterns are spoken in response to prompts appearing on the screen. A second personal computer allows the user to compile and edit specific vocabularies for particular applications.

10.2   *Controlling the speech peripheral*

For the digital system of the recogniser to operate as a peripheral of a host computer, several distinct groups of functions have to be performed and therefore programmed from the computer. First is the basic recognition process as outlined in the previous chapter and described in detail elsewhere in this book. For this the peripheral has to receive an instruction to function in the *recognise* mode. If the ASR product is speaker-dependent it has to be previously 'trained', and for this it has to receive an instruction to work in the *train* mode. A further group of functions is concerned with input/output transfers of information

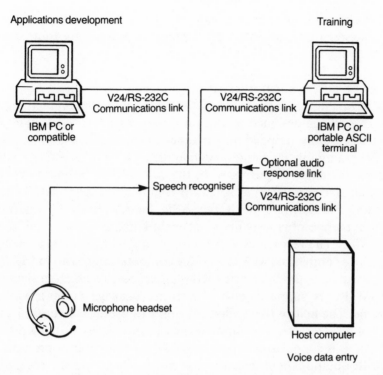

Applications development

Training

V24/RS-232C Communications link

V24/RS-232C Communications link

IBM PC or compatible

IBM PC or portable ASCII terminal

Optional audio response link

Speech recogniser

V24/RS-232C Communications link

Microphone headset

Host computer

Voice data entry

Figure 10.2 Elaboration of Figure 10.1 basic arrangement, using personal computers for training and applications development in addition to the host computer

between the recogniser and the host computer. This is a matter of transmitting groups of binary data along the interfaces between input/output registers in the recogniser and the host.

To provide speech recognition for a particular application program, a specific set of digital reference patterns has to be loaded, as an active vocabulary, into a working memory, usually RAM, in the recogniser unit. The data for these patterns is transferred from a large-capacity vocabulary file (e.g. on magnetic disk) located either in the host computer or in the recogniser itself. Conversely, at some point the active vocabulary may have to be returned to the vocabulary file and replaced by another. Some means is also required of editing and updating the stored vocabulary.

Yet another group of functions is for the purpose of setting the recogniser to operate in accordance with certain parameters, such as microphone amplifier gain, acceptance/rejection threshold and syntax control (see Chapter 9). The equipment must provide means for the user to select and enter these data or values. Finally, if the ASR peripheral is to operate reliably, the system must provide for a testing routine to be applied to it.

SOFTWARE FOR SPEECH RECOGNITION

All these functions are provided by the ASR product manufacturer as a software package designed to run on a particular host computer. This software is usually supplied on a magnetic disk (e.g. diskette) in a high-level programming language and comprises a number of specialised programs for different purposes. In the case of plug-in board products for personal computers the software is obviously designed for these machines. Furthermore, with the ASR board physically inside the computer there is obviously no need for the communications link shown in Fig. 10.1. The recogniser can communicate with the computer via a parallel bus compatible with that of the computer, as shown in Fig. 10.3.

As an example, the Interstate SRB plug-in speech recogniser board for the IBM PC is supplied with a software package comprising three programs. The first of these allows the user to produce a vocabulary by means of an interactive, menu-driven set of instructions. It is written in BASIC and is supplied in source code. When runnning, it prompts the user with questions and instructions, which appear on the computer's display screen.

Compilation of the vocabulary provides for storing the information in the host computer's magnetic disk memory, training the recogniser by uttering the vocabulary words, switching to the recognition mode, storing voice reference patterns on disk, loading them into the ASR's working memory from the disk, setting performance parameters and self-testing.

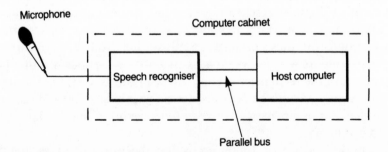

Figure 10.3 When a recogniser module is housed inside a computer, the communication between them can be via a parallel bus compatible with that of the computer

The second program is for rapid loading of vocabulary and reference voice patterns from the disk to the working memory, while the third program is for testing the module board after installation or at regular maintenance intervals.

10.3 *The software set of a typical recogniser*

The detailed interrelationship between the voice data entry peripheral and the host computer can best be explained by describing a particular set-up as an illustration. A suitable example is the CGD plug-in board speech recogniser designed to provide voice data entry for the Apple II and IIe and other compatible microcomputers. This is an isolated-word recogniser and has an active vocabulary of 80 words, drawn as a subset from a large-capacity vocabulary file in the computer. When the recogniser, called the *Voice Input Module*, is plugged into a spare slot it communicates with the computer via a parallel bus interface. Pre-processing is done by a 16-channel spectrum analyser.

To enable the computer to 'drive' the voice data entry board the ASR manufacturer supplies utility software on magnetic disk (diskette). This allows the user to program the recogniser module through its instruction set, which can be thought of as something like the instruction set of a microprocessor. Programming is provided for four distinct functions. The first is to compile and edit whatever *vocabulary* is required, the second is to *train* the recogniser to work with this vocabulary, the third is to make the module *recognise* the input spoken words, while the fourth function is to *test* various aspects of the recogniser's performance.

COMPILING A VOCABULARY

The first stage in preparing the recogniser for operational use is to compile a written text vocabulary of all the words (up to 80) that will have to be recognised as voice data entries for a particular application program run on the Apple computer. This is done by manually entering the words and/or decimal digits as alphanumeric characters, using the computer's keyboard and display screen. As a result, strings of binary-encoded characters are stored in the computer. Each of these character strings is assigned an index number, as a code to identify it.

In this system the user has to define two distinct groups of such character sequences. Each group has a specific purpose in the overall process. One group is used in training and recognition. During training it provides text words on the computer display screen to prompt the user to utter the corresponding spoken words. Thus, each text word is linked to a corresponding acoustic pattern that will form a reference pattern for the system. During recognition this group is used in the pattern classification process (see Fig. 9.5 in Chapter 9).

When an utterance has been classified as a pattern during the recognition mode, the second group of character sequences is brought into play by a *recognise* instruction to the ASR module. This causes a sequence of encoded characters to be transmitted as if they had originated from manual operation of a keyboard.

For each text word in the vocabulary the user enters two sequences of characters for the purposes described. These are separated by a typed semicolon, given a typed index number and terminated by typed symbols for *carriage return*, thus forming a complete line in the vocabulary for that text word.

TRAINING INSTRUCTIONS
Once the text vocabulary is defined in this way and stored, the training procedure – associating acoustic reference patterns with the already written words – can begin. In this mode, the working memory area that holds digital representations of the acoustic reference patterns is first cleared, ready for a new set of digital patterns to be generated and stored. The *train* instruction to the ASR module has the format:

$$1, FW, LW, TP$$

where 1 is the identification number of the *train* instruction from the instruction set, FW is the index number of the first word selected, LW is the index number of the last word selected, and TP is the number of training 'passes' (see Chapter 9).

The user utters each word in response to a text prompt on the computer display. After each word is spoken, the ASR module responds by transmitting data in the following format:

$$WD\#, TDS, NBA, NP$$

Here, $WD\#$ is a code number indicating one of several things. One code verifies that the display-prompted word has been accepted. Another code indicates that the word has been rejected. Yet another signals that training has been completed. Next, TDS gives the training difference 'score' between the previous reference pattern and the new reference pattern. NBA shows the number of bits in the current reference pattern, while NP gives the current number of training passes for the word spoken.

The trained reference pattern can be augmented by the use of an *update* instruction (no. 2 in the set). This is similar to the *train* instruction, and after a word is spoken the module transmits data to the computer in the same format as the *train* instruction.

RECOGNITION INSTRUCTIONS

Now the ASR module is ready to be switched into the 'recognise' mode of operation. This is done by a *recognise* instruction. It puts the user in complete control of the selection of reference patterns to be active at any time. Any order of the word patterns stored in the module may be chosen, so that syntax nodes (see Chapter 9) may be defined in this way.

The ASR module compares each input utterance with the defined reference patterns. Assuming the rejection threshold value is exceeded, the output information sent to the computer is the index number of the word with the highest 'score'. The *recognise* instruction has the following format:

$$8, \text{ word numbers and/or word ranges, } 255$$

Here, *8* is the identification number of the *recognise* instruction from the set. The word numbers and word ranges defined are restricted to a maximum of 40 bytes. Each individual word number specified needs only one byte. Each word range is specified by three bytes. The first byte is the beginning word number, *BW*, of the word range, while the second byte is used to mark the fact that a word range is being specified. By convention this second byte is always 252. The third byte in the word range specification is the ending word number, *EW*. Multiple word ranges may be specified. Thus the word range format is:

$$BW, 252, EW$$

For example, let us assume that the indexed words 1 to 5, word 10 and words 20 to 30 have to be recognised at some point. The *recognise* instruction sent from the host computer to the ASR module would then be:

$$8, 1, 252, 5, 10, 20, 252, 30, 255$$

When the module has been switched to the *recognise* mode, it responds to each utterance and transmits data describing this recognised word to the computer in the following format:

$$WD\#, RDS, SCORE, 2nd \ WD\#$$

Here, *WD#* can indicate one of three things. It can give the index number of the word with the highest score; it can show that the word duration is too long (more than 1.25 s); or it can indicate that the utterance has been rejected. *RDS* gives the recognition difference – the highest score minus the next highest score. Then, *SCORE* means the actual highest score, up to a maximum of 128, and finally *2nd WD#* is the index number of the word with the next highest score.

TRANSFER INSTRUCTIONS

In addition to instruction no. 1 for *train*, no. 2 for *update* and no. 8 for *recognise*, the ASR modules' instruction set contains over twenty more instructions for controlling various functions in its interaction with the Apple computer. For example, one group is concerned with input/output transfer of bytes of data between the two. These communications instructions centre on transmitting and receiving registers and also a status register in the ASR module. Information is transferred between them and the application program running on the computer.

Other instructions in the set are concerned with setting performance parameters, such as rejection threshold and word boundaries; with uploading and downloading reference patterns between the module and computer; and with testing the system and the self-diagnosis of faults in the module. Overall, this speech recognition module works with several well-known high-level languages that can be used on the computer, such as *Pascal*, the operating system *CP/M*, and the Apple version of *BASIC*.

Another ASR product designed for operation with the Apple II as host computer is the Microsignal SR-32 module. Like the CGD product, this is a plug-in, isolated-word, speaker-dependent printed-circuit board and is supplied with suitable voice data entry software on diskette. It has a smaller vocabulary of 32 words or short phrases, however, and also differs in other apsects of performance.

Apart from the special software supplied by the ASR product manufacturer, there may be a need for other, standard software to achieve successful interfacing of the recogniser to the host computer. This could include a text editor, such as the IBM *EDLIN*, to edit the text of the vocabulary file, and a host computer operating system such as the *VMS* operating system of the DEC *VAX* machine or the *DOS* (disk operating system) of the IBM PC.

Where the ASR product is housed in a separate cabinet and requires a communications interface to its host computer, there are options for other interface standards besides V24/RS-232C. These include the 20-mA current loop, the *IEEE-488* or *GPIB* (General Purpose Interface Bus) and the *RS-422* for long-distance communication over distances of 1000 ft or more. Usually the ASR product manufacturer specifies the interface transmission rate appropriate to the product. The V24/RS-232C interface, for example, has standard transmission rates ranging from 50 to 19 600 baud.

Transfers of vocabulary data between the ASR product and the host computer are normally controlled by the central processing unit (CPU) of the computer. There is, however, an alternative method of transfer called *direct memory access* (DMA) which does not require intervention from the CPU and is consequently faster and more efficient. Some recognisers provide this facility but the transfers are usually only available in one direction, from the computer memory to the recogniser's memory. This is because it is not normally necessary to move blocks of vocabulary data quickly from the recogniser to the computer, but transfers in the opposite direction may be required frequently, for changing the reference patterns.

Once a voice data entry peripheral has been set up as outlined above, it may be used at the same time as the keyboard in any associated computer terminal (see Fig. 10.1). When the user utters a word from the active vocabulary the ASR peripheral sends data equivalent to that generated by keystrokes to the host computer.

For example, the utterance *Help* could be previously defined, when preparing the vocabulary, to be equivalent to pressing the sequence of keys *H, E, CR* on the keyboard (where *CR* indicates 'carriage return' at the termination of the vocabulary line – see above). Every time *Help* is spoken, data equivalent to these keystrokes is transmitted to the computer as an entry to the application program being run. Thus, data entries that normally might require quite long or complicated sequences of keystrokes from a computer terminal can be achieved by utterance of simple, monosyllabic key-words.

CHAPTER 11

INTERFACING STANDARDS FOR RECOGNISERS

Jeff Tecosky

In this chapter, a method of generating a standard application interface for driving speech recognisers with computer software is proposed.

11.1 *The need for a standard interface*

In every discipline the need for well thought out standards is clear, and the field of speech recognition is no exception. Unfortunately, most technological standards do not appear until the technology in question is relatively mature. Sometimes partial standards are put into effect, as in the case of magnetic media whose physical dimensions are standard but whose methods of formatting are not.

Although speech recognition has been studied and highly developed over the past 20 years, the emergence of small, inexpensive recognisers is a new occurrence. Programmers are just now beginning to try to adapt old applications to speech and to design new ones. As the technology grows and better recognisers become available, application designers will have more functionality at their disposal. If we wait until the emergence of, say, a true voice typewriter before discussing and proposing standards for application interfaces, then an undesirable situation is likely to develop: it will require complete redesign to transport an application from one recogniser to another. Early development of standards for interfacing to recognisers can help prevent this situation and, more important, can have an important influence on the direction of the technological growth.

In this chapter we shall look at the problem of interfacing an application to a speech recogniser and suggest some ways in which the interface might be standardised. There are two interdependent parts of our discussion: a *grammar compiler* for interfacing to an application's language, and a set of functions called a *speech driver*. The speech driver is a collection of high-level hardware-independent routines that complete the interface between the application and the recogniser. Before treating these topics we examine the nature of the interfaces that are part of a speech recognition system.

THE INTERFACES

A speech recognition system is a dynamic interconnection of information resources that includes the recogniser, a host computer running an application program, and a human speaker. Each of these components must share information with the others during the operation of the system. There are three important pathways, or interfaces, over which information must be passed (see Fig. 11.1). Below we discuss some of the issues involved in standardisation of these interfaces.

The human–recogniser interface
Utterances must be converted from their origins as vibrations of vocal cords to some kind of digital representation suitable for processing by the recogniser. This interface typically consists of a microphone connected to some analogue-to-digital devices.

There are many human factors to be considered in the design of the microphone interface, and these will necessarily depend upon the application. Should the microphone be of a headset type, hand-held, or built in to some external structure (see Chapter 12)? Should the recogniser be able to respond to a wide range of sound levels, or only those above a certain threshold? How is the user to know when the microphone is receiving acceptable signals? There are not too many

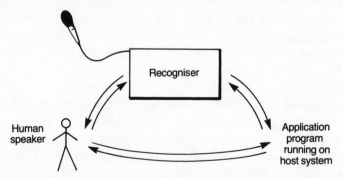

Figure 11.1   The three important pathways over which information must be passed

places (other than the size of the microphone connector) where it would be fruitful to develop standards for this interface.

The human–application interface

The human speaker uses speech to interact with the application program. This interface consists, in one direction, of the user controlling the application by uttering suitable sentences (and possibly through other input means, e.g. a keyboard). In the other direction, the application must communicate which words are appropriate at which points in the operation of the program.

While the details of this interface are, by definition, dependent on the nature of the application, there are several areas where standardisation could increase the efficiency of the interaction by increasing the confidence of the user.

To see why, consider the keyboard when used as an input device. It is a good example of a mode of interaction with an application for which there have developed many *de facto* standard idioms: press RETURN to terminate command, BACKSPACE to erase last keystroke, etc. Most people familiar with using a keyboard to interface to one application program can easily and confidently use it for another. We believe that applications that use speech as an input mode should strive to develop many of the same kinds of standards, so that users can approach a microphone with the same confidence as they do a computer keyboard. Features such as a user always being able to say *delete* or *erase* to remove the last entry, or saying *enter* to complete a command, would be desirable.

The application–recogniser interface

The bulk of the functionality of the system lies in the establishment of a clean mesh between the application and the recogniser. The application must be able to direct the recogniser to begin or stop listening, as well as which utterances to listen for. In the other direction, the recogniser needs to be able to communicate to the application which word was just recognised, as well as some statistical information on the reliability of the recognition.

The remainder of this chapter will address the problem of interfacing an application program to a speech recogniser. We shall present a high-level compiled language for encoding most of the application-specific information in a grammar (hence, *grammar compiler*). Together with this language we will discuss a package of hardware-independent routines (the *Speech Driver*) that provides an application with hooks into the gramar as the recognition of a sequence of utterances proceeds.

For simplicity we shall assume throughout that the recognition system to which we are interfacing is of the isolated-word, speaker-dependent type. The ideas presented, however, can easily be extended to speech recognition systems with more sophisticated capability.

11.2 *The grammar compiler*

The program designer who wishes to incorporate speech into an application needs to consider several questions:

(1) *How large* is the application vocabulary?
(2) Are there any potentially *confusable words* in the application language?
(3) Who are the *potential users?* Will they be casual or highly trained?

Clearly, the answers to these questions may not be obvious at the inception of the programming stage – the application vocabulary will probably evolve as it is use-tested. Therefore, any interfacing scheme should allow maximum flexibility in the design and refinement of the vocabulary/grammar. Our standard interface will involve the use of an adjunct tool, a grammar compiler, which will accept as its input a grammar specification. Its output is a set of tables that are used to drive the recognition process (see Fig. 11.2).

Why should we impose a grammar structure on the application language? The answer is twofold. First, and perhaps most important, there is usually no need for the recogniser to have to match a given utterance against all the words in the application vocabulary. At any given time in the progress of the application program, only certain words in the vocabulary will be acceptable for input. For example, if the application is menu-driven, then only those words in the current menu need to be 'listened for'. Part of the work of the grammar compiler is to distill from the grammar specification which subsets of utterances will be legal, when.

The advantages of working with currently active or legal vocabulary subsets should be clear: not only can recognition be faster (fewer models

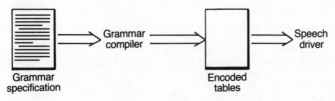

Figure 11.2   Operation of the grammar compiler

to compare against) but it can be more accurate. This last feature can come about since acoustically similar utterances (e.g. *no* and *go*) may never be legal at the same point in the application, and so cannot be confused by the recogniser.

The compiler provides the following services:

Generation of tables for managing active vocabularies. The compiler builds a sequence of finite state machines that accept the given (regular) grammar. (For the theory of grammars and finite state machines see[1].) The speech driver has functions for beginning recognition at any state in the grammar.

Assignment of identification (ID) numbers to words in the vocabulary. The speech driver functions all refer to vocabulary words by ID number. Ordinarily, the compiler chooses the mapping of IDs to words, although an explicit assignment of numbers can be arranged. To facilitate the interaction between an application and the driver functions, the compiler generates an 'include' file that is written in the same language as the application (e.g. C or assembly). This file contains symbolic definitions for each word in the vocabulary which in C would look like this:

$$\#\,define \qquad word\_name \qquad ID\_number$$

Here, *word_name* is the name of an utterance in the vocabulary and *ID_number* is the ID assigned to the word by the grammar compiler. By including such a file in the application source program, the programmer may refer to utterances by their symbolic names instead of their (artificial and possibly changing) ID numbers.

Attachment of output strings to each utterance or groups of utterances in the language. Keyboard emulation forms one of the major applications of recognisers: the applications designer uses speech to interact with an off-the-shelf program that expects its input from the keyboard. There are speech driver functions that can access the output string associated with any vocabulary word, and these strings can be inserted into the keyboard buffer of the host system as if they had been typed by the user at the keyboard.

Completed production lists. The grammar accepted by the compiler is 'phrase structured', which means that utterances can be grouped together into phrases (called *productions*). Each production is given a symbolic name, to which, like the words that correspond to single utterances, can be attached an output string. These phrases or productions can be defined in terms of other productions (see example below).

Whenever an utterance is recognised, the speech driver makes available a list of those productions that have been completed by the utterance. The application program can scan this list and perform any actions (i.e. subroutines) appropriate to the termination of any of the productions.

Initial deactivation of utterances. While an application is running, the speech driver can dynamically change the active vocabulary by removing or adding words. Words can only be added, however, if appropriate 'slots' have been reserved by the grammar compiler. This is accomplished by including the words as usual in the source for the grammar compiler (so that they are assigned ID numbers) but declaring them initially inactive (by preceding their names with exclamation points). Thus the compiler/speech driver interface allows some runtime customisation, as the user may add words to the application by activating initially inactive words.

Always active utterances. There may be certain utterances that the application designer wishes to be active in all grammar states, e.g. *quit* or *erase*. While these can be embedded in the grammar specification, it is usually awkward to do so. The compiler allows a list of always active utterances to be attached to each production, and arranges for these words to be legal in any state of the recognition of that production.

A listing of the finite state machines. The grammar compiler will produce a detailed listing of the finite state machine built for each production. This will provide the application programmer with complete knowledge of the composition of the active vocabulary at every state in the grammar.

11.3 *An example using a grammar compiler*

Let us now look at a simple example of the ideas discussed above. We shall call a complete sequence of legal utterances a sentence. To give a grammar that controls the application, we need to specify what constitutes a sentence. Table 11.1 gives a specification for a simple airline reservation transaction. It is not intended to be a realistic application – it is used only to fix the ideas.

The grammar is specified as a sequence of production definitions, beginning with the definition of a **SENTENCE**. A production is simply a name followed by an equals sign and the body of the definition. The body of a production definition consists of production names, names of utterances and operators. Each production definition is terminated by a semicolon. For the sake of clarity, we have used upper-case letters in the

Table 11.1 The grammar for a simple airline reservation transaction

SENTENCE =	**PREAMBLE REQUEST ITINERARY DATE;**
PREAMBLE =	*I need,* *I want,* *Please give me;*
REQUEST =	*information on flights,* *your schedule on flights,* *a ticket,* *a reservation;*
ITINERARY =	*from* **CITY** *to* **CITY** (*via* **CITY**) #;
DATE =	*next* **WEEKDAY,** *in* **MONTH,** *on* **WEEK WEEKDAY** *in* **MONTH;**
CITY =	(**CITY_NAME** delete)* **CITY_NAME;**
WEEKDAY =	(**DAY-NAME** delete)* **DAY_NAME;**
MONTH =	(**MONTH_NAME** delete)* **MONTH_NAME;**
WEEK =	*the first, the second, the third, the fourth;*
CITY_NAME =	*New_York, San_Francisco, Philadelphia, Baltimore, Atlanta, Ft_Lauderdale, Chicago, Toronto, Boston;*
DAY_NAME =	*Sunday, Monday, Tuesday, Wednesday, Thursday, Friday, Saturday;*
MONTH_NAME =	*January, February, March, April, May, June, July, August, September, October, November, December;*

names of productions (which correspond to groups of utterances) and lower-case letters in the names of vocabulary words.

The operators used in constructing the production definitions are:

SYMBOL * – repeat **SYMBOL** zero or more times

SYMBOL # – repeat **SYMBOL** zero or one time

SYMBOLA , **SYMBOLB** – either **SYMBOLA** or **SYMBOLB**

SYMBOLA   SYMBOLB – **SYMBOLA** followed by **SYMBOLB**

where **SYMBOL** is either a production name, a terminal symbol, or a compound expression enclosed in parentheses. Thus some legal sentences produced by this grammar are:

I need a ticket from New York to San Francisco next Sunday

Please give me a reservation from Chicago to Toronto via Boston in January

I want a ticket from New York delete Chicago delete Atlanta delete Boston to Baltimore on the first Monday delete Tuesday in February

In the last example, the application program is supposed to interpret the word delete as meaning *erase the last utterance*.

Now it is clear that at a given stage in the recognition of a sentence the active vocabulary is going to be significantly smaller than the total vocabulary of 53 words. For instance, when the recognition of **SENTENCE** begins, the active vocabulary consists of the models for *I* and *Please*. Once a word is recognised (say, *I*), the active vocabulary changes to *need* and *want*. Again, it is up to the driver to manage the building of the active vocabulary at any stage in the recognition.

COMPLETED PRODUCTIONS
As described above, the grammar compiler computes a list of productions that are completed in each state of the application grammar. Suppose, for example, that the following sentence is recognised:

Please give me a reservation from Chicago to Toronto via Boston in January

When *Please give me* has been recognised, the driver reports that the **PREAMBLE** production has been completed. When *January* is recognised, the driver reports that the productions **MONTH, DATE** and **SENTENCE** have all been finished. Any actions associated with the completion of these productions may be called by the application at this point.

11.4 *The speech driver*

After designing the application grammar, the programmer must write the application. Whether the application is as simple as a keyboard emulator or as complex as a reservation system, the programmer is going to need to have access to the information encoded in the grammar. The speech driver provides this functionality, together with many other housekeeping operations. We shall describe this other component of the proposed interface standard below.

We call the routines a *driver* because we feel that speech should be treated in the same fashion as any other input device, such as a keyboard or mouse. Such devices usually require a driver program to intermediate between themselves and an application program or operating system.

Let us describe some of the features of the speech driver by pointing out some parallels between keyboard and speech input:

- **The keyboard responds to external events** known as keystrokes; the speech input device responds to 'utterances'. An utterance is a spoken word or phrase, preceded and terminated by a brief period of silence.

- **Most keyboard interfaces support a typeahead queue**, where keystrokes are stored until the system is ready to process them. Likewise, the speech driver provides a 'talkahead' queue for utterances.

- On many computer systems, **the keyboard driver translates the internal representation of a keystroke** to a conventional encoding, such as an ASCII character code. Similarly, the speech driver maps an utterance into an ID number that is known to the application program.

AN OVERVIEW OF DRIVER OPERATION

Before we get into the details of the speech driver functions, it is a good idea first to get an overall picture of the operation of a typical recognition system, as well as to fix some terminology (see Fig. 11.3). The major components are:

- **The token source.** A *token* is what we will call the internal, digitised form of an utterance. The token source could be a human speaker connected to a digitising front end or an already digitised stream of utterances that have been recorded on an external storage device.

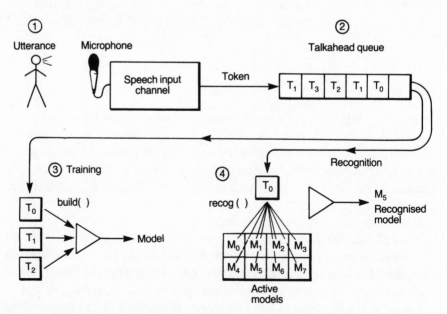

Figure 11.3　Overview of the operation of a typical speech recognition system

- **The talkahead queue.** Tokens are collected by a driver function in the talkahead queue, a first-in first-out data structure, where they await further processing. Tokens are removed from the queue by driver functions for one of two distinct operations: training and recognising.

- **In training, the user is prompted to say each word** or phrase in the application vocabulary a certain number of times. The driver enqueues a token for each rendition of the word. When all tokens for that word have been collected, the driver removes them from the queue and uses them to build a model, averaging the acoustic information from the tokens into a single representation of the word.

- **In recognition, the user says words for which the driver has already built models.** These tokens are again collected in the talkahead queue. When the application program is ready to recognise an utterance, it directs the driver to remove a token from the queue, whence the token is compared against the previously built models. The driver returns a number which identifies the model which most closely matches the token. In addition, the driver returns a measure of the statistical confidence of the closeness of the match.

SPEECH DRIVER FUNCTIONS

The actual driver functions, which we will briefly describe, fall into five major categories: *memory management, listening, training, recognition,* and *symbol table access.* Instead of providing full specifications for each function (parameters and output) we shall just give an indication of the full functionality. We would hope that this short list can serve as the foundation for a set of standard driver routines to be used in interfacing to many different recognisers.

Memory management: heap, models, tokens

The driver functions in this group are responsible for grabbing and releasing memory from the host computer for various tasks. We shall call the total memory space used by the driver a *heap*. The heap contains the information output by the grammar compiler: finite state machine tables, symbol tables, etc. It is used for the talkahead queue, as well as as a storage area for any tokens being saved during recognition or training. Finally, the heap contains all the word models that are built from tokens during training.

The memory management routines need to be able to manipulate models and tokens: they must be able to read them into memory from files or to save them from memory to files. Tokens and models need to be given some kind of handle so as to be efficiently manipulated by the memory management routines.

Listening

The listening functions control the speech channel, which is the front end for the queue. Listening routines include calibration of input levels, which allows the recogniser to be used in different environments or with different input transducers. Using the listening functions, an application may temporarily refrain from accepting audio input into the queue during a time when speech input is inappropriate.

Training

The training functions include *collect()*, *build()*, and *adapt()*. The *collect()* function initiates the collection of tokens from the queue to the heap for subsequent model building. Calling *build()* actuates the construction of a model using specified tokens. *Build()* can return an error code signifying that one or more of the tokens was sufficiently different from the others to reject it in building the word model. Models built previously can be averaged in with newly collected training tokens through the use of *adapt()* which, like *build()*, returns an indication of how closely the new tokens matched with the model.

Recognition

This is, of course, the heart of the matter, and the *recog()* function of the speech driver provides a great deal of functionality. In its simplest form, *recog()* removes the next available utterance from the queue and tries to match it against any models active in the current grammar state. If a good match is found, the ID number of the matched word is returned and the finite state machine is advanced to the next appropriate state. *Recog()* returns a pointer to a list of productions completed by the utterance, as well as a statistical index of confidence in the recognition. If there is a problem with the recognition (e.g. if it cannot recognise the utterance as being close to any of the active models) then *recog()* returns an appropriate error code to the application program.

Recog() can be set to recognise starting at the initial state for any production, or any intermediate state in a production. After a successful recognition, *recog()* returns the state just stepped into.

Symbol table access

The driver provides many functions which allow an application to have access to information encoded in the grammar. There is a *listsyms()* function, which when called with a grammar state as an argument returns a list of active models in that state. This could be used to print prompts on the screen at each point where speech input is desired: *Please say one of the following ....* Other functions, which allow access to the output strings associated with utterances or productions, look up names corresponding to ID numbers and vice versa. Finally, there are functions which activate and deactivate models, and which test to see if a given model is active.

11.5 *Conclusions*

Technology is often spurred to growth in response to market demand. The market for speech recognition is just now being tested, as inexpensive recognisers designed for use with microcomputers become available. To be appreciated by potential users, software applications will have to fully integrate speech into their user interface. Any set of interface standards, like those proposed herein, will undoubtedly make speech applications easier to design, implement and debug. Application programs will be more portable across product lines, and will make better use of the input means available. Application/recogniser interface standards can thus provide a secure framework for the growth of speech recognition technology. We expect that, as users begin to enjoy the fruits of speech technology, they will demand more.

11.6 *Acknowledgements*

Acknowledgements are given to Dragon Systems, Inc., for the original copyright on this material.

11.7 *References*

1. Aho, A., and Ullman, J. (1972) *The Theory of Parsing, Translation, and Compiling.* **Vols I & II**. Englewood Cliffs NJ: Prentice Hall.
2. *Speech Application Designer's Handbook*. Newton, MA: Dragon Systems, Inc.

CHAPTER 12

AUDIO AND ACOUSTICAL ASPECTS

Martin Jones

In this chapter, the reader is introduced to the design issues relating to the task of capturing the speech wave and presenting it to the recognition circuits.

12.1 *Capturing speech*

Science fiction has long imagined the listening computer. Such a machine is usually portrayed as responding to an instruction spoken from some distance away in a large, noisy, reverberant control room. Whilst the human ear/brain combination has a remarkable ability to recognise intelligible speech in such a situation, the inherent difficulty of electronic recognition can be appreciated simply by listening to a recording made through a distant microphone in such circumstances. The speech is barely audible above the reverberation and noise. Even in the relatively benign circumstances of a domestic party, casual attempts at tape recording usually produce disappointingly unintelligible results: the human ear's remarkable ability to distinguish an interesting conversation from the general hubbub is denied to the relatively crude microphone. It seems that there is no audio equivalent of the quick flash photograph, and the resulting reproduced signal is often of little value. A computer required to perform a speech recognition task on such a signal would obviously begin with a major handicap.

The aim of this chapter is to review the techniques of room acoustics, microphone applications and audio signal processing which have been found valuable in overcoming such acoustical difficulties in professional recording and broadcasting. The excellent quality of speech normally received via radio and television is the result of the application of established acoustical principles and accumulated experience which can be employed with advantage at the input of a speech recognition system.

12.2 *Room acoustics – strengths and weaknesses*

REVERBERATION

The appreciation of the acoustical characteristics of buildings has a long history. Vitruvius[1], a Roman architect of the first century BC, gave a graphic description of difficult acoustics: 'The circumsonants are those in which the voice spreads all round and then is forced into the middle where it dissolves, the case endings are not heard, and it dies away there in sounds of indistinct meaning'.

It is the appropriate handling of sound reflections which provides the key to successful room acoustics. In capturing speech with a microphone, the correct microphone position is a further factor which gives useful control.

The modern quantitative understanding of room acoustics began with W. C. Sabine in 1895. Sabine tackled the very practical problem of rendering a Harvard lecture room usable for intelligible speech by the deliberate addition of absorbent material. He began by defining *reverberation time* (r.t.) as the time taken for sound to decay to one millionth of its original intensity (-60 dB)[2]. Experiments led him to discover the inverse relationship between r.t. and the total acoustical absorption in the room, and to propose the empirical Sabine formula:

$$T = \frac{0.161V}{S\alpha} \qquad (12.1)$$

where T is r.t.(s)

V is room volume (m³)

$S\alpha = \sum S_j \alpha_j$ is total absorption,

where S_j is total exposed area of each type of material in m², and

α_j is the acoustical absorption coefficient of the material.

The original experiments of reverberation time were made using a pistol and stopwatch, but electronic methods using a high-speed level recorder or a microcomputer-based decay slope measuring instrument are used today to achieve acceptable accuracy[3].

A limitation in the applicability of the Sabine formula to relatively dead conditions is revealed by considering an anechoic room, where α is everywhere unity. Under these conditions the actual r.t. falls to zero but, on substituting $\alpha = 1$ in the Sabine equation, T takes on the incorrect value of $\dfrac{0.161V}{S}$.

Eyring[4] further developed reverberation theory, replacing Sabine's assumption of continuous absorption by the model of a process of discontinuous drops in intensity during the decay. The resulting formula remains the most useful general-purpose tool for reverberation calculations today:

$$\boxed{\begin{array}{c} \textbf{EYRING REVERBERATION EQUATION} \\[4pt] T = \dfrac{0.161V}{-S \ln(1 - \bar{\alpha})} \end{array}} \tag{12.2}$$

where V is room volume (m³),

   T is reverberation time (s),

   S is total surface area (m²), and

   $\bar{\alpha}$ is mean absorption coefficient.

The relationship between the Sabine and Eyring equations is revealed by setting $\bar{\alpha}$ small in equation (12.2), when $-\ln(1 - \bar{\alpha}) \to \bar{\alpha}$, thus giving Sabine's equation (12.1).

Knudsen[5] introduced a correction for atmospheric absorption into Eyring's equation to give more accurate prediction at frequencies above 1 kHz:

$$T = \dfrac{0.161V}{-S \ln(1 - \bar{\alpha}) + 4mV} \tag{12.3}$$

where m is the attenuation constant for plane waves in air (m⁻¹) and depends on frequency, humidity and temperature.

SPEECH INTELLIGIBILITY AND REVERBERATION TIME

Whilst excessive reverberation can have the undesirable effect of slurring speech syllables, completely dead acoustics sound unnatural. The presence of reflecting surfaces has the advantage of contributing to loudness and assisting uniform sound distribution. The design of rooms and studios for good speech intelligibility is not therefore concerned with the total suppression of reverberation, but rather with producing an optimum compromise value which is dependent on room size and application. Typical optimum r.t. figures for a theatre or lecture room for clear speech would be 0.7 s for a room volume around 300 m³, increasing to 0.9 s for volumes up to 3000 m³ and 1.0 s up to 10 000 m³. In a recording or broadcasting studio, electronic amplification provides the necessary loudness. This fact, together with the inherent limitations of microphones, leads to a much shorter optimum r.t. for small speech studios, typically around 0.3 s for volumes up to 100 m^3 [6].

As a guide, a typical domestic living room will exhibit an r.t. in the region of 0.5 s, whilst the sparseness of absorbent soft furnishing in the average laboratory often leads to r.t. values around one second – an unsatisfactory recording environment.

The single-frequency figures quoted for r.t. so far refer to the value at mid-frequencies between 500 and 1000 Hz. Most absorbent materials of a porous nature show a marked decrease in absorbing power at low frequencies and the exclusive use of this type of absorbent in a room leads to a rise in r.t. at low frequencies. Such effects can lead to 'boom', marring speech clarity, particularly in small rooms. It is advisable to aim for a flat r.t./frequency curve down to 100 Hz. The extra low-frequency absorption may be achieved by thin panel material, resonant cavities or large cavities hung with curtains of absorbent ('bass traps').

At high frequencies, above 2 kHz, air absorption begins to be significant in large rooms and hard, reflecting surfaces are often required to maintain a flat r.t. curve at these upper frequencies, so important for intelligibility.

REFLECTION DENSITY

If a room is excited by a sound impulse and the sound pressure at the microphone is recorded with a wide frequency bandwidth as a function of time, then after the reception of the direct sound wave the reverberation arrives as a vast number of discrete reflections. The reflection density increases with time until it becomes a statistical 'clutter' when the reflected impulses overlap in time and the concept of the individual echo loses its significance. Cremer[7] has indicated that, in a room where sound is well diffused, reflection density at any instant is proportional to the square of the elapsed time:

CREMER'S EQUATION FOR REFLECTION DENSITY

$$\text{Number of reflections per second} = \left(\frac{4\pi c^3}{v}\right) t^2 \qquad (12.4)$$

---

where c is velocity of sound in air (m/s),
$\quad$ t is elapsed time (s), and
$\quad$ v is room volume (m^3).

A salient reflection which is prominent above the exponential reverberation decay is often perceived as a discrete 'slap-back' echo which may seriously upset intelligibility[8]. Echoes usually arise from strong individual reflections arriving 80–200 ms later than the direct sound, an re often caused by the focusing effect of curved surfaces in larger auditoria, which provide longer sound transit times (approximately 3 ms delay per metre travelled). A disturbing echo effect sometimes observed even in small rooms is the *flutter echo*. This is the repetitive reflection pattern caused by sound bouncing back and forth between two parallel surfaces which are more highly reflective than the remainder of the room boundaries. This defect prevents a well-diffused statistical clutter of reflections from developing. The resulting comb filter effect can result in severe frequency coloration in the reverberant sound.

RESONANT MODES

Our discussion of sound decay so far has generally assumed that sound waves in a room may be treated geometrically as though they were rays of light. In practice, at low frequencies, sound wavelengths in air are comparable with room dimensions ($\lambda = 3.3$ m at 100 Hz). A more appropriate model, therefore, at these lower frequencies is to consider reverberation as the decay of a large number of standing waves in the room.

Rayleigh[9] has shown by solving the general wave equation in a rectangular chamber that standing waves exist such that:

$$k^2 = \pi^2 \left(\frac{n_x^2}{l_x^2} + \frac{n_y^2}{l_y^2} + \frac{n_z^2}{l_z^2} \right) \tag{12.5}$$

where k is the wave number $\dfrac{2\pi}{\lambda}$,

l_x, l_y, l_z are the room dimensions, and
n_x, n_y, n_z are integers.

Hence the possible frequencies of standing waves are given by:

$$f = \frac{c}{2} \sqrt{\left(\frac{n_x^2}{l_x} + \frac{n_y^2}{l_y} + \frac{n_z^2}{l_z} \right)} \tag{12.6}$$

where c is velocity of sound in air.

The standing waves (*eigentones*) described by equation 12.6 can be divided into three classes: those for which only one integer is non-zero are axial modes; those for which one integer is zero are tangential modes; and those for which no integer is zero are oblique modes.

In general it is axial modes which produce the strongest coloration in rooms and it is desirable to avoid shapes and dimensions of rooms which result in mode coincidence at specific frequencies[10]. The resulting perceived resonance can seriously degrade intelligibility and impart a strong 'bathroom' flavour to any recorded speech. It is clear from equation 12.6 that a cube is a disastrous room shape from the resonant mode point of view.

In addition to ensuring a short r.t., it is advisable in any room used for speech recording to avoid large plane reflecting surfaces by ensuring that absorbent material is well-scattered round all room boundaries. By this means, prominent modes and flutter echoes can be avoided and a well-diffused, natural sound distribution obtained which will make microphone positioning much less critical. One reflecting surface which can cause problems commonly lies between the voice and the microphone – a prominent specular reflection from the table can cause serious coloration due to interference with the direct sound wave. This problem is usually solved in broadcasting studios by the use of an acoustically absorbent table top.

SOUND LEVELS AND BACKGROUND NOISE

Background noise is a significant risk to good speech intelligibility. The common measurement of noise level is the decibel (dB), a logarithmic unit of relative measure capable of encompassing on a meaningful numerical scale the tremendous $1:10^6$ range of commonly encountered sound pressures.

$$\boxed{\begin{array}{c} \textbf{THE DECIBEL SOUND LEVEL SCALE} \\ \text{Sound pressure level } L = 20 \log_{10} \frac{P}{P_0} \text{ dB} \end{array}} \qquad (12.7)$$

where P is the measured sound pressure (N/m^2 or Pa), and

P_0 is the reference sound pressure ($20 \times 10^{-6} \text{ N/m}^2$ or $20 \, \mu\text{Pa}$).

P_0, the agreed reference sound pressure, corresponds roughly to the average human threshold of hearing perception at mid-frequencies.

Acoustic background noise levels are measured with a *sound level meter* which consists of a calibrated microphone, amplifier and voltmeter. It is common to use an electrical frequency *weighting network* in the chain to approximate the response of the human ear at moderate sound levels. The 'A' weighting network is common, giving rise to the dBA unit of sound level, with a response rolling off at frequencies below 1000 Hz, being 20 dB down at 100 Hz.

Table 12.1 shows some common sound levels, together with their average decibel ratings, to give a feel for the decibel scale.

Table 12.1 Decibel ratings of some common sound levels

Quiet studio background	10–20 dBA
Office or laboratory background	40–60 dBA
Whispered/muttered speech at 1 metre	35–55 dBA
Conversational speech at 1 metre	55–70 dBA
Busy traffic at kerbside	80–90 dBA
Full symphony orchestra in reverberant hall	100–110 dBA
Jet aircraft at takeoff	110–120 dBA
Loud shout at 10 cm	120–140 dBA

In recording and broadcasting practice, it is usual to aim for very low background noise to avoid any distraction to the critical listener. Where we are only concerned with speech intelligibility, however, some audible background pick-up is not usually a problem. Masking of the wanted speech is avoided if the background level lies at least 15 dB below average speech level at the microphone. It is sometimes an advantage to use filters to limit the bandwidth of the microphone and its amplifier to the speech band of 300 Hz to 6 kHz, or possibly to the 3 kHz telephone limit, in order to minimise disturbance from out-of-band noise.

12.3 *Microphones*

BASIC PRINCIPLES

Given the number of variables involved in the hazardous acoustical passage of speech sound from voice to microphone, the reader will be relieved to know that there is a good deal of scope in the choice of different microphones to alleviate acoustical difficulties.

The two most common types of microphone used for good quality speech are the *dynamic* or *moving coil* type and the *capacitor* or *condenser* type. Both of these microphones employ a small light diaphragm which is set in motion by the fluctuating air pressure of the sound wave. The diaphragm movement then results in an alternating voltage output.

In the dynamic microphone a small coil is caused to vibrate in the field of a permanent magnet – like a tiny loudspeaker working in reverse – and a voltage, e, is induced in the coil.

$$e = Blu \tag{12.8}$$

where B = flux density in field (T),
$\quad l$ = length of wire in coil (m), and
$\quad u$ = velocity of coil (m/s).

The design of a high-quality dynamic microphone involves the control and damping of the various resonances in the system in order to maintain constant coil velocity for a given sound pressure over the working frequency range. A good dynamic microphone achieves an axial frequency response flat to within ± 2 dB from 70 Hz to 15 kHz. Some dynamic microphones specifically designed for clear speech have a deliberate inherent rise in sensitivity of some 6 dB over the 'presence' region of the band from 2 kHz to 8 kHz. Such a frequency response, whilst strictly inaccurate, is often found to give increased intelligibility without the need for electrical equalisation.

The *ribbon* microphone is an elegant, though somewhat fragile, and therefore uncommon, dynamic type, where the 'coil' is simply a light, flexible corrugated aluminium foil ribbon suspended between the poles of a powerful magnet. The output signal is taken from between the ends of the ribbon. The simplicity of the moving system thus ensures a freedom from undamped resonances within the audio range, the fundamental resonance of the ribbon being only a few hertz. The ribbon microphone is also termed a *velocity* microphone. The very lightness and flexibility of its diaphragm, which is open back and front, enable its movement to be directly proportional to particle velocity in the sound wave over a wide frequency band.

The capacitor microphone depends for its operation on the variation of capacitance between a tightly stretched, thin metallic membrane diaphragm mounted close to a rigid metal backplate. The capacitance variations are turned into a voltage output by the application of a polarising voltage between backplate and diaphragm (typically 50–200 V).

As the diaphragm vibrates, its spacing, s, from the backplate varies by, say, $\pm \Delta s$. Since capacitance is inversely proportional to spacing:

$$C \pm \Delta C = \frac{K}{s \pm \Delta s} \tag{12.9}$$

where K is a constant, and C is capacitance.

The polarising voltage is applied via a high resistance, R, so that the time constant, RC, is long compared with the period of the lowest audio frequencies. Therefore at any instant the charge, Q, on the microphone capacitance is constant.

In the absence of sound pressure, voltage V across the capacitance is given by:

$$V = \frac{Q}{C}$$

and for constant charge, Q, variations $\pm\Delta C$ in capacitance C cause corresponding variations in V:

hence $$V \pm \Delta V = QK(s \pm \Delta s)$$

or $$\Delta V \propto \Delta s$$

The capacitor microphone designer therefore aims that diaphragm displacement should be proportional to sound pressure over the audio frequency band. As the diaphragm is simply uncomplicated light foil, excellent performance is obtained as long as the main resonance is well-controlled (typical frequency response 20 Hz–20 kHz $\pm$ 1 dB).

In recent years the use of permanently charged polyester *electret* material for the diaphragm has further simplified the capacitor microphone by eliminating the need for the polarising voltage. A thin metallised layer on the polyester forms the capacitor plate, whilst the presence of the insulating electret dielectric removes the risk of short circuits to the backplate and reduces the precision required in manufacture. Electret microphones are mass-produced cheaply and can give excellent quality at low price.

MICROPHONE DIRECTIVITY

Microphones are very rarely omnidirectional. As pressure is a scalar (non-directional) quantity it might be expected that the basic dynamic and capacitor microphones would respond equally to sound arriving from any direction. This is true for low frequencies, where the dimensions of the microphone are negligible compared with a wavelength. At the higher frequencies, however (above 3 kHz or so), *diffraction* effects occur due to the obstacle effect of the microphone as its dimensions become comparable with a wavelength. In the region of 10 kHz, where the wavelength is only 3 cm, the wave reflected from the diaphragm is typically of sufficient amplitude to double the sound pressure (6 dB increase) for an incident wave on axis. Conversely, for a sound wave incident at 90° to the axis, no reinforcement is obtained from the reflection, whilst for a wave incident from behind the microphone the obstacle effect attenuates the incident wave itself. Thus, at high frequencies most microphones become noticeably directional and the larger the microphone, the more serious its high frequency directionality (Fig. 12.1(a)).

In fact, directional microphones can be extremely useful in reducing background noise and acoustical problems[11]. Unfortunately, most of these problems occur at the middle and lower frequencies where diffraction effects are no help. However, we have already considered the

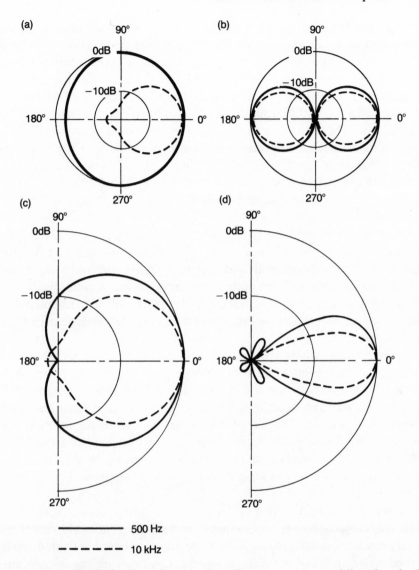

Figure 12.1 Typical microphone polar diagrams; (a) omnidirectional; (b) figure 8 (pressure gradient); (c) cardioid; (d) directional 'gun'

velocity (ribbon) microphone which depends for its operation on the *pressure gradient* in the sound wave, the diaphragm being open to the air on both sides. Such a microphone has zero response to a sound arriving from the side because no pressure difference is created and the polar diagram is of cosine 'figure of eight' form (Fig. 12.1(b))[12].

A pressure microphone such as a capacitor type may be converted to pressure gradient operation by using a perforated backplate to allow sound access to the rear of the diaphragm. The most generally useful directional response is obtained by introducing a deliberately tortuous path between the rear of the microphone and the back of the diaphragm so that rear sounds take just as long to reach the back of the diaphragm as they take to travel round the microphone to the front of the microphone. This produces cancellation in rear sound and the resulting heart-shaped *cardioid* response is shown in Fig. 12.1(c). Careful design can arrange that the low-frequency directivity obtained in this way matches the high-frequency directivity resulting from diffraction so that the frequency response is substantially flat over a wide range of angles of incidence.

A well-designed cardioid microphone will exhibit at least 20 dB front to back ratio in its polar diagram. This gives typically around 5 dB better rejection of omnidirectional wide band background noise or reverberation, compared with an equivalent microphone of omnidirectional characteristics. Cardioid microphones are commonly used with public address systems to minimise the problem of acoustic feedback from the loudspeakers.

In applications where the microphone cannot be close to the person speaking, so that even a cardioid reponse gives insufficient rejection of ambient sound, the highly-directional 'gun' microphone is common[13]. This uses a long tube, up to a metre long, on the front of the diaphragm. Apertures down the length of the tube are arranged so that the contributions from sounds on axis are in phase but that the arrival time differences at the diaphragm for sounds off axis cause phase cancellation, thus giving a very sharply directional polar diagram (Fig. 12.1(d)).

MICROPHONE APPLICATIONS

Most speech recognition applications are similar to the requirement for good broadcast-quality speech. In order to minimise unwanted background noise and reverberation, it is usual to work with the microphone close to the mouth (typically, 10–50 cm distance). It is advisable when speaking within about 20 cm to fit a windshield to the microphone to avoid uncharacteristic explosive effects from the puff of breath associated with plosive consonants such as 'P'. Sibilants can also become overemphasised due to the 'perspective' change at close range.

Pressure gradient microphones, and some cardioid microphones, suffer a low-frequency lift when used close to the mouth. This is because the mouth is acting as a source of spherical waves rather than the plane waves assumed in microphone theory. The pressure gradient in a spherical wave at distance r from the source is greater than the pressure gradient in a plane wave by the factor:

$$\left[1 + \left(\frac{c}{2\pi f r}\right)^2\right]^{\frac{1}{2}}$$

Thus, at low frequencies close to the source the pressure gradient gets a significant boost which in practice amounts to about 18 dB at 100 Hz for a microphone distance of 10 cm. This phenomenon can be exploited in very noisy surroundings by electrically equalising the microphone output to roll off the lower frequencies, thus removing any troublesome low frequency background noise at the same time as restoring natural speech. This principle is utilised in the *anti-noise* microphones.

If successful results are required at relatively long range (2 m–5 m), highly directional microphones are invaluable. The 'gun' microphone has become standard for 'electronic news gathering' (ENG) sound pickup in difficult circumstances.

Tiny electret microphones are extensively used as 'necktie' microphones in conjunction with a small VHF radio transmitter as a *radio mike*, thus allowing complete freedom of movement for the wearer, whether performing on stage or addressing a computer in an industrial control room. Sophisticated systems use diversity reception with several receivers and a 'voting' system to achieve optimum reception, free from blank spots. Microphones intended for use in the 'necktie' position are usually designed with a rising response at high frequencies to compensate for their disadvantaged location well below the speaker's mouth, with a speech input strong on vowels but weak on consonants.

12.4 Audio amplification and processing

MICROPHONE AMPLIFIERS

The output signal voltage from a microphone with normal speech input is typically between 1 mV and 10 mV. The voltage amplification required to reach the 10 V or so needed for digitising for computer input is therefore between 1000 and 10 000 times (60–80 dB).

Capacitor microphone capsules have an inherently high internal impedance at the lower audio frequencies because of their low inherent capacitance. It is therefore usual to incorporate a field-effect transistor (FET) source-follower amplifier within the microphone casing to present a low impedance (usually $< 200\,\Omega$) to the cable and main amplifier. Power requirements for the FET are modest and in the case of electret microphones are sometimes supplied by an internal 1.5 V battery. Studio grade capacitor microphones usually have the internal amplifier fed along with the polarising voltage supply from a 'phantom powering' system of $+12$ V to $+48$ V connected between the earth rail and a derived centre tap on the balanced line audio feed.

Dynamic microphones usually have a source impedance of 200 Ω, which is suitable for direct connection to the microphone cable. Because of the low signal level, it is worth paying attention to the first amplifier stage to achieve good low-noise performance[14]. A low-noise IC amplifier is common practice. Such chips generally give their best noise performance with a source impedance in the region of 5000 Ω, so it is common to step up the microphone output with a transformer of about 1:5 turns ratio to give the necessary 1:25 impedance change (square of turns ratio). The transformer also gives the advantage of an electrically balanced and floating input circuit with good interference rejection properties, and is suitable for phantom power feeding of capacitor microphones. A well-designed input circuit should be capable of an equivalent input noise (EIN) better than -125 dB, referred to 0.775 V r.m.s. using a 200 Ω source resistance and measured over a bandwidth of 22.5 Hz–22.5 kHz; this corresponds to a noise figure (NF) of less than 5 dB compared with the theoretical thermal noise in a 200 Ω resistor.

A sensitive microphone input is prey to any electrical or magnetic interference which may be around. Proximity to digital processing circuits is a particular hazard because of the wide band RF radiation from the fast pulse trains. Excessive bandwidth at the microphone input is therefore to be avoided and filters using small series chokes and shunt capacitors are usually included between microphone and transformer primary. The whole input stage should be shielded with an earthed metal case and it is also advisable for the transformer to have its own magnetic mu-metal shield. Particular care should be taken to avoid the high stray electric and magnetic fields emanating from display monitor timebase circuits.

FILTERING AND EQUALISATION

Whilst circuit details lie beyond the scope of this chapter, it is useful to note the considerable scope afforded by filters and by equalisation circuits in correcting for microphone deficiencies, acoustical defects and ambient noise.

Filters[15] are used for rapid roll-off at low frequencies (high-pass) and high frequencies (low-pass). Filter cut-off slope may be 12 or 18 dB per octave, with the high-pass filter giving a typical range of cut-off frequencies from 31.5 Hz to 315 Hz and the low-pass from 2 kHz to 15 kHz. A notch filter can be of particular value in cases where a discrete tone background noise, such as a 1-kHz whistle, is present: it enables the

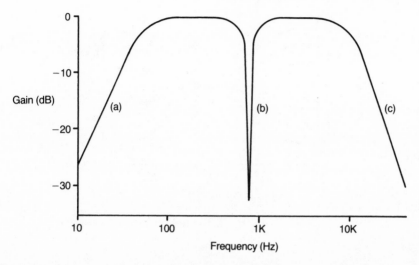

Figure 12.2 Typical audio filter frequency response curves; (a) high pass; (b) notch; (c) low pass

interfering signal to be rejected without losing a significant amount of the surrounding spectral speech content. Figure 12.2 shows response curves for typical filters.

Equalisers generally operate at more gentle slopes than filters and are widely used in broadcasting and recording for the tonal correction and enhancement of speech and music. Hi-fi amplifier-style bass and treble controls form the basis of most equalisers and are usually enhanced by one or two mid-range boost/cut (peak/dip) controls, usually of variable frequency from 100 Hz to 8 kHz and at least 12 dB range. It is common for the LF and HF controls to be switchable to a peaking characteristic as an alternative to the usual *shelving* curves. Peaking/shelving frequencies are usually continuously variable over a wide range. Figure 12.3 shows some typical shelving equaliser response curves.

Whilst some equalisers rely on LC tuned circuits, most present-day circuits are *active*, avoiding the use of expensive inductors. Most are based on the second-order state variable circuit (two-integrator loop) using operational amplifier ICs. Such circuits not only give the advantages of lower cost but also facilitate continuously variable frequency tuning (*'parametric'*) instead of the steps produced by switched inductors.

The *graphic equaliser* is a useful alternative to continuous frequency tuning. Here, the spectrum is split into typically 26 separate frequency bands: each has its own boost/cut control over a range of about ±15 dB. The frequencies are usually at third-octave intervals and overlap so that

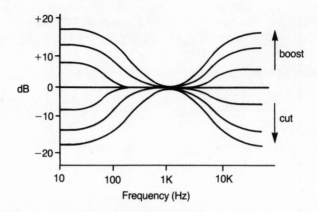

Figure 12.3 Shelving HF/LF equaliser response curves

the whole audio band is covered, enabling the user to synthesise almost any frequency response shape required.

The use of equalisers in audio processing is like the use of face make-up in a television studio in the correction or enhancement of the original source material. Unwanted features can be removed and the overall impression improved considerably. A comprehensively adjustable equaliser can be of great value in the experimental stages leading to the design of a commercial speech recognition system. Once the optimum frequency characteristic has been selected for maximum intelligibility, then the appropriate fixed filter/equaliser network can be cheaply built into the design. In some cases it may be worth providing several different networks, either manually or automatically selected, for different ambient conditions.

METERING AND DYNAMIC RANGE CONTROL

The measurement of audio signals presents many challenges because the short-term transient peak levels may well be at least 20 dB higher than the average level being measured at the time. Whilst this fact is readily understood in the case of orchestral music with its cymbal crashes and trumpet fortissimos, it is perhaps less obvious that speech too is of a very peaky character and requires care in level measurement and signal handling.

The simplest measurement of audio level is provided by the VU (volume unit) meter, which consists of a full-wave bridge signal rectifier feeding a voltmeter of standardised dynamic characteristics. The scale is calibrated in dB, from − 20 to + 3, and also in 0% to 100% modulation. The 0 dB mark (100%) is normally calibrated to correspond to a signal voltage level of 1.23 V r.m.s., which is $+4$ dB relative to 0.775 V r.m.s. The reason for these apparently curious calibration levels is derived from the history of telecommunications. The reference level of 0.775 V r.m.s. is common in professional audio measurement and corresponds to a power of 1 mW in a 600 Ω load, defined as 0 dBm. Why 600 Ω? That is the characteristic impedance of a long pair of telephone wires spaced 25 cm apart by ceramic insulators on telegraph poles – irrelevant today, but still used as a standard!

The rise and fall time constants inherent in the VU meter are entirely governed by the mechanical and electrical damping of the meter movement itself and are typically 300 ms for both rise and fall times. Thus the meter is too slow to respond to speech peaks, which typically have a duration less than 10 ms. It does, however, give a reasonably accurate indication of the subjective loudness of a signal. Modern VU meters are often used in conjunction with an electrically-driven peak warning LED in order to warn of those 'invisible' high peaks.

The BBC and other European broadcasters, anxious about risk of transmitter overload, have generally preferred the electronically-driven peak programme meter (PPM) to the VU meter. Time constants vary from organisation to organisation, but a fast rise time of 5 ms and a slow fall time of 3 s are typical and allow most audio peaks to be captured and displayed. Various different scales and calibrations are found, but a typical PPM calibration level is $+8$ dBm at the overload mark.

Today's digital recording technology with its inherent impressive (90 dB) signal to noise ratio has prompted the development of true peak meters to give the engineer a clear picture of the full dynamic range. These are usually digitally driven and have zero rise time to allow the capture of the fastest peak transient signals (always assuming that such signals travelled satisfactorily through the audio amplification and processing chain without overload). Electronic bar displays have no inertia.

Whilst well-designed electronics and digital recorders are capable of handling the wide dynamic range of natural speech, it is usually desirable to deliberately restrict the dynamic range to improve intelligibility in the ambient noise conditions of the average listener. This is achieved by manually or automatically increasing system gain on the quieter sections and reducing it on louder ones. Perhaps surprisingly, outside the professional broadcasting and recording field, the most common method of dynamic range control, whether intentional or not, is to clip off the peaks of the waveform (Fig. 12.4). This is very common in communications and public address systems and, provided the proper attention is paid to microphone technique and equalisation, even infinitely-clipped speech can achieve surprisingly high intelligibility[16].

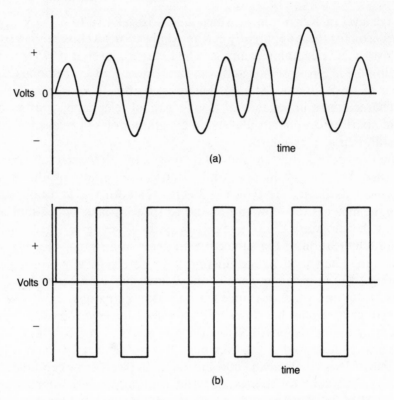

Figure 12.4 (a) Speech waveform; (b) hard clipped version

Unfortunately, despite the useful applications of clipped speech, much of the character is lost, and no listener would call it natural reproduction. It is therefore usual to use a *compressor* or *limiter* which has an electronic gain control element or *voltage-controlled amplifier* (VCA) controlled by a rectified version of the signal which has been smoothed out by time constants similar to those of the PPM. The VCA is arranged to reduce its gain in response to an increase in side chain signal so that high input levels are attenuated with respect to the quieter signals (see Fig. 12.5). Sometimes equalisation is included in the side chain – an HF boost gives extra compression at high frequencies for 'de-essing' an over-sibilant speech signal.

A typical attack time is 1 ms and an appropriate release time would be 100 ms for speech. In order to reduce the effect of background noise 'pumping' up and down, it is usual to begin compression only when the signal exceeds a pre-set threshold (say, 20 dBm). Typical compression ratios may range from 2:1 to 100:1. For a compression ratio of 2:1, an input signal dynamic range of 20 dB appears at the output with only

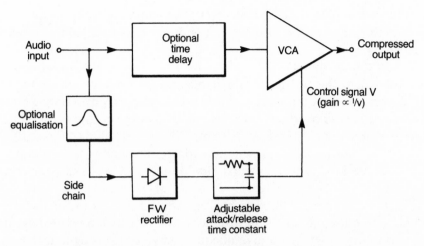

Figure 12.5 Outline schematic of limiter/compressor

10 dB dynamic range. The extreme condition of 100:1 is known as *limiting*, where all signals which exceed the preset threshold come out at the same level. Some sophisticated limiters and compressors include a signal time delay between the side chain input and the VCA. This gives the side chain 'advance notice' of each peak to give the time constants the opportunity to cut back the gain in readiness and thus avoid overshoot in the output on the initial transient.

12.5 *The overall speech audio channel*

Figure 12.6 shows a typical high-grade speech amplification channel starting with the microphone and ending with a line-level signal output

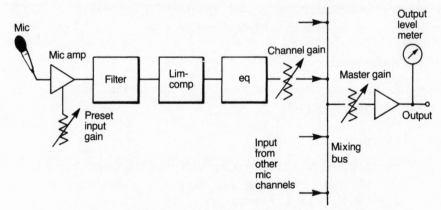

Figure 12.6 Outline schematic of overall speech audio channel

suitable for feeding an A/D converter. The audio digitising process lies outside the scope of this chapter, but is thoroughly covered in the cited literature[17, 18, 19].

For optimum quality, particular care is needed in the initial amplification where the full natural dynamic range is present prior to the limiter/compressor. It is useful to have a preset gain control on the input amplifier to avoid overload. The meter shown at the output is useful but it may be conveniently reduced to two LEDs – one to show overload and another to indicate signal present. An appropriate limiter setting may of course be used to control the maximum output and thus avoid metering altogether.

For completeness, a 'mixing bus' is shown bringing in inputs from other microphone channels for instances involving a number of speakers or a multi-mike set up to give adequate coverage throughout a large room. In many applications it is undesirable to employ an operator fading up and down microphones as required. In such cases 'automatic' mixing can be employed, where each channel is gated off until a preset threshold level is reached on the microphone[20]. Such a signal gate may conveniently be incorporated in the limiter-compressor circuitry by arranging that the VCA is turned off until the input signal exceeds a preset threshold.

Current digital signal processing technology (see Chapter 8) is now capable of implementing all the functions of the audio channel, the A/D converter being interposed immediately after the microphone amplifier[21, 22, 23, 24]. Although in general-purpose audio circuitry digital signal processing is more costly than analogue processing, it offers a precision and flexibility combined with remote digital control of all processing functions. The latter could usefully lead to further application of the intelligence within speech recognition software to provide itself with an optimally processed signal – a further step towards the intelligence of the human ear/brain combination.

12.6 *Further reading*

Borwick, J. (ed.) (1980) *Sound Recording Practice.* (2nd edn.). Oxford: Oxford University Press.

12.7 *References*

1. Vitruvius (c. 50 BC) Liber V Cap VIII; English translation Morris Hicky Morgan (1960) *The Ten Books on Architecture* Book 5 Chapter 8. New York: Dover.

2. Sabine, W.C. (1922) (Republished 1964) *Collected Papers on Acoustics*. p. 42. New York: Dover.
3. Livingstone, C.E., Base, T.E., and Hawtin, A.F. (1982) 'The design and testing of a "new" reverberation meter'. *J. Audio Eng. Soc.* **30** (9), 614–620.
4. Eyring, C.F. (1930) 'Reverberation time in dead rooms'. *J. Acoust. Soc. Amer.* **1** 217.
5. Knudsen, V.O. (1934) 'Recent developments in architectural acoustics'. *Rev. Mod. Phys.* **6** (1), 1.
6. Gilford, C.L.S. (1959) 'The acoustic design of talks studios and listening rooms'. *Proc. IEE* **106** (pt B) 245–258. (Reprinted 1979) *J. Audio Eng. Soc.* **27** (1/2), 17–31.
7. Cremer, L. (1948) 'Die wissenschaftlichen Grundlagen der Raumakustik'. *Geometrische Raumakustik* **1** 27. S. Hirzel Verlag.
8. Hass, H. (1949) Research report (reprinted 1972) 'The influence of a single echo on the audibility of speech'. *J. Audio Eng. Soc.* **20**, 146–159.
9. Rayleigh, Lord (1896) *The Theory of Sound* Vol. II, p. 69. (Republished 1945). New York: Dover.
10. Bonello, O.J. (1981) 'A new criterion for the distribution of normal room modes'. *J. Audio Eng. Soc.* **29** (9), 597–606.
11. Olsen, H.F. (1980) 'The quest for directional microphones at RCA'. *J. Audio Eng. Soc.* **28** (11), 776–786.
12. Robertson, A.E. (1963) *Microphones*. BBC Training Manual (2nd edn.) p. 67. London: Iliffe.
13. *ibid*, p. 201.
14. Jones, M.H. (1985) *A Practical Introduction to Electronic Circuits.* (2nd edn.) Chapter 5, p. 40. Cambridge: Cambridge University Press.
15. *ibid*, p. 162ff.
16. Licklider, J., Bindra, D., Pollack, I. (1948) 'The intelligibility of rectangular speech waves'. *Amer. J. Psychol.* **61**, 1–20.
17. Blesser, B.A. (1978) 'Digitization of audio: a comprehensive examination of theory, implementation and current practice'. *J. Audio Eng. Soc.* **26** (10), 739–771.
18. Stockham, T.G., Jr (1982) 'The promise of digital audio'. *Digital Audio.* Collected Papers from the AES Premiere Conference, Rye, New York, June 3–6.
19. Vanderkooy, J., and Lipshitz, S.P. (1984) 'Resolution below the least significant bit in digital systems with dither'. *J. Audio Eng. Soc.* **32** (3), 106–113.

20. Julstrom, S., and Tichy, T. (1984) 'Direction-sensitive gating: a new approach to automatic mixing'. *J. Audio Eng. Soc.* **32** (7/8), 490–506.
21. Jones, M.H. (1982) 'Processing systems for the digital audio studio'. *Digital Audio*. Collected Papers from the AES Premiere Conference, Rye, New York, June 3–6.
22. Jones, M.H. (1984) 'The digital sound mixer'. *International Broadcast Engineer*. March, **15** (194), 22–26.
23. McNally, G.W. (1984) 'Dynamic range control of digital audio signals'. *J. Audio Eng. Soc.* **32** (5), 316–327.
24. McNally, G.W. (1984) 'Audio processing for the BBC digital control vehicle'. *International Broadcast Engineer*. May, **15** (195), 67–76.

CHAPTER 13

ASSESSING THE PERFORMANCE OF RECOGNISERS

David Pallett

In this chapter, which is a reprint of a paper produced by the US National Bureau of Standards after extensive discussions with speech technologists from around the world, the reader is shown the main issues involved in assessing recogniser performance, and given a methodology to follow.

13.1 *The performance assessment problem*

In Part 2 of this book many technological 'solutions' to the speech recognition problem have been described, and the reader may be forgiven for thinking that the choice of a suitable Automatic Speech Recogniser could be made from the manufacturers' specification. In reality this is far from the case – not only will the optimum choice depend upon the exact nature of the application, but in addition the actual performance figures quoted will be dependent upon a large and complex set of factors. Accordingly, it is essential that every speech system designer be acquainted with the key elements that affect performance, and is able to conduct properly structured performance tests.

The science of performance assessment is, however, far from mature. Until automatic speech recognition technology is a well established element in the man–machine interface, therefore, continuing efforts must be made to identify the relative importance of factors influencing performance and to develop and specify definitive test procedures. Tests conducted using these procedures will then serve to clearly demonstrate appropriate uses of the technology and to document the associated productivity benefits.

The paper reprinted here as Chapter 13 of this book is a first report on the development of detailed and specific test procedures for performance assessment, compiled for the Institute for Computer Sciences and Technology at the National Bureau of Standards. The overall focus is towards assessing the performance of speech recognisers as system components, with emphasis on laboratory benchmark tests. Continuing attention to these issues, along with the contributions of consensus standards groups, will result in the development of detailed procedures for both benchmark tests of speech recognisers and for measuring human performance.

13.2 *Factors which influence recogniser performance*

Successful implementation of automatic speech recognition technology presents numerous challenges. In many cases these challenges are met through the selection and imposition of constraints on the many factors known to influence performance. Corresponding constraints must be imposed on the structure of performance tests if meaningful performance data is to be obtained. The need for these constraints arises, in large part, from the high inherent variability of unconstrained speech.

The inherent variability of speech arises from the nature of speech and the articulatory process. 'Speech is based on a sequence of discrete sound segments that are linked in time. These segments, called phonemes, are assumed to have unique articulatory and acoustic characteristics. When speech sounds are connected to form larger linguistic units, the acoustic characteristics of a given phoneme will change as a function of its immediate phonetic environment because of the interaction among various anatomical structures (such as the tongue, lips, and vocal chords) and their different degrees of sluggishness[1].' This variability in the articulatory gestures involved in the production of speech, and the interactions that arise from adjoining segments, are important factors contributing to the difficulty in successfully implementing automatic recognition of continuous speech.

Humans have well-developed abilities to adapt to and accommodate this variability, but at present it is a critical barrier to the automatic recognition of unconstrained speech. Automatic speech recognition systems have difficulty in discriminating between linguistically meaningful and insignificant variations. This variability significantly complicates the process of testing.

There are numerous other factors that further complicate the task of successfully implementing and testing automatic speech recognition technology. These factors make it desirable to clearly anticipate the effects they may cause when designing, implementing, and documenting performance assessment tests. Appropriate recognition of these factors will increase the value of the test results as benchmarks for comparative purposes and enhance the predictive power of the tests. The following factors describe the main sources of variability that should be considered when testing automatic speech recognition technology.

SPEECH-RELATED FACTORS

The form of the speech has a great effect on the difficulty of recognition. Isolated words or discrete utterances are easiest to recognise. Connected words, even if spoken carefully, are more difficult to recognise because the beginnings and ends of each word are affected by the adjacent words. Fluent or continuous speech is much more difficult to recognise because the sound segments (particularly those at the beginnings and ends of the words) tend to merge, and stress patterns affect the loudness and distinctiveness of vowels.

SPEAKER-RELATED FACTORS

There are important differences in the way different individuals speak. Factors contributing to these differences which may affect performance and which can be readily documented include:

Age. Voice quality in adolescence and old age often differs from that in mid-life.

Sex. Certain speech characteristics, such as pitch and vocal tract length, tend to be gender-specific for adults. Some speech recognition systems employ features that may have been optimised for user groups such as adult males, so that it is important to document age and sex data for the test speaker population.

Dialect history. Some speakers are dialect chameleons, and adapt quickly and convincingly to the dialect characteristics of a new region. Others retain some qualities of previous dialects while changing other qualities. Because pronunciation of many words depends strongly on dialect, documentation of dialect data may be particularly important in tests of speaker-independent recognisers.

Speech idiosyncracies. Speech-associated anomalies can be expected to affect recognition performance adversely. Stuttered, lisped, or slurred speech patterns and unusual characteristics should be identified and noted. For some individuals, speaker-generated noises such as lip smacks, tongue clicks, 'ums, ers, and ahs', etc., will degrade performance. Speech levels vary with changes in vocal effort and in the distance between the speaker's mouth and microphone.

Changes in rate of speech introduce additional complications. In words spoken rapidly, some of the sound segments may be shortened or deleted or altered in quality. A slow rate of speech may cause vowels to have drifting frequency spectra and extremely long silence gaps in plosive consonants (e.g., *p*, *t*, *d*, etc.).

When enrolling, testing, and using speech recognisers, the use of chewing gum and smoking should be noted and/or controlled. Care should be taken when selecting a test speaker population so that these characteristics are appropriately represented.

Speech variability. Individual speakers vary in the degree of consistency with which they repeat words. Some speakers produce nearly identical repetitions of individual words or utterances, even under stressful conditions. Others produce highly varied repetitions (e.g. words such as *eight* with the final consonant occasionally deleted, or with highly variable pitch). The former category will make a recogniser perform best, and is sometimes referred to as 'sheep'. The latter category is sometimes referred to as 'goats'.

Motivation and/or fatigue. Degradation of performance for speaker-dependent systems can be expected as motivation degrades or fatigue increases. It is useful to obtain samples of speech under these conditions in order to estimate the degree of performance degradation.

TASK-RELATED FACTORS
The design of vocabularies for successful application of this technology is an important consideration. Limited size vocabularies require careful planning. Vocabularies should be natural to the task and sufficiently distinct to ensure recognition with few substitution errors.

Performance is greatly improved by the imposition of syntactical constraints. In many task dialogues there are only a few possible choices at each point in the task, thus making the recognition task much simpler, faster, and more reliable.

Physical exertion, fatigue, and other stressing factors must be considered and documented in designing experiments and assessing performance. The voice pitch and loudness or vocal effort of the speaker change due to stress, as do the spectral components.

ENVIRONMENTAL FACTORS
The input speech signal to a speech recogniser is affected by background noise, reverberation, and transmission channel phenomena (e.g., the use of telephone lines or wireless microphones). These environmental factors may lead to spurious responses by the recogniser. The performance of speech recognisers will generally be lower when telephone lines are used for input than with direct microphone input because the frequency response is limited and noise artefacts make correct recognition more

difficult. The use of wireless microphones may lead to recognition errors due to transmission channel cross-talk, RF interference, signal fading, dropouts, etc.

OTHER FACTORS

Human recognition of speech involves an imperfectly known set of decision criteria. Automatic speech recognition devices apply specific, but (to some degree) arbitrarily chosen decision criteria in order to effect recognition. Optimum settings of these decision criteria, including the associated reject thresholds, are extremely important. However, the optimum settings of these decision criteria are controlled by the vocabulary, the design of applications software (i.e., the implementation of syntactic constraints, error-correction protocols, etc.), and the characteristics of the individual user's speech and personal preference. Experimentation is required in order to determine the optimum setting of the reject thresholds. As an alternative to the selection and use of optimum settings of the reject thresholds, the reject capability may be disabled, to simulate a forced choice response. This procedure is frequently chosen for benchmark tests.

In some cases, the system may also have the ability to return ordered word lists. Typically, these word lists are ordered according to the distance measure between the input word and the reference templates or word models, or in order of descending probability. The application of higher-level constraints such as syntax may then lead to correct identification of the utterance. While this process may emulate human decision criteria and typical decision trees, it can complicate assessment.

13.3 *Developing suitable test procedures*

The design and implementation of tests to define the performance of automatic speech recognisers requires that attention be paid to many of the previously described factors influencing performance. A systematic process of experimental design and testing is indicated in this section to account for these factors. This process includes:

- **Selecting an experimental design** that either:
  (a) models an application, or
  (b) provides benchmark data.
- **Selecting speakers to represent the user population** or some relevant subset.
- **Selecting a test vocabulary** that either:
  (a) exemplifies that used in an application, or
  (b) has been used by others for benchmark test purposes.

- **Training the system**, or constructing the reference patterns to be used by speaker-dependent recognisers.
- **Characterising the test environment** in order to document complicating factors such as factory noise, communications channel limitations, or task-related factors.
- **Recording the test material** to permit verification of the validity of the test results and re-use of the test material.
- **Scoring the test results**. Procedures are outlined for both isolated- and connected-word data.
- **Pragmatic considerations** to ensure that equipment is operating properly, that tests are conducted in a manner that is consistent with manufacturers' recommendations, and other related factors.
- **Statistical considerations** to indicate the statistical validity of performance data.
- **Documentation of test conditions and performance data** to allow evaluation of published data.

Tests designed and carried out accounting for these factors will be valuable in identifying the strengths and weaknesses of automatic speech recognition systems. The importance of performance assessment procedures has been emphasised in a recent study by the Committee on Computerized Speech Recognition Technologies of the US National Research Council. Their report[2] recommends that:

'... performance should be measured within a realistic task scenario, both within the laboratory and in actual operational settings, including worst case conditions. Laboratory benchmark tests using standard vocabularies, experienced users, and controlled environments, are useful for comparing recognizers, but they are not efficient for predicting actual performance in operational systems. Adequate methods are needed for measuring both human and recognizer performance under realistic conditions. The importance of performance measurement techniques cannot be over-emphasized since they provide the data for decisions about system design and effectiveness...'.

EXPERIMENTAL DESIGN

There are two complementary approaches to designing performance assessment tests. These approaches are summarised in Fig. 13.1.

In one approach, a set of benchmark test conditions is defined (e.g., use of a 'standard' speech vocabulary and database, and no use of syntax to actively control the recognition vocabulary). Little or no effort is taken to model an application. This approach provides valuable com-

Test Conditions	Benchmark Tests	Application Tests
Vocabulary	Benchmark or Reference Vocabulary	Applications Specific (Task) Vocabulary
Data Base	Widely Available Recorded Data Base	(Variable)
Use of Syntax	Little or No Use of Syntax	Syntactically Constrained Word Sequence or Imposed Task Grammar
User Interaction	None	(Variable)
Predictive Power	Very Limited	Less Limited
Data Analysis	Detailed	(Variable)
Documentation	Thorough	(Variable)

Figure 13.1   Alternative approaches to test design

parative performance information. It does not directly predict performance in real applications.

A second approach consists of carefully selecting test conditions in order to simulate a field application. The use of syntactically constrained word sequences may dramatically enhance performance and is acceptable for many user applications. The design of a test vocabulary should include specifying the structure of the grammar and the frequency of occurrence of each item. This approach may have greater predictive power in inferring performance in specific applications, but it complicates comparisons between differing applications. Because of the diverse applications proposed for recognisers, simulation of many different applications and the needs of differing users becomes very difficult and/or costly.

In both approaches to testing, simple averages such as error rates, recognition accuracy, etc., are often inadequate to indicate performance. It is important to determine and document the most frequently occurring confusion pairs (e.g., 'five-nine' confusion, when a spoken *five* is recognised incorrectly as *nine*) and, in many cases, to fully document the confusion matrix, representing the frequency with which each spoken word is recognised as another word. For an N-word vocabulary, the confusion matrix is an N-by-N matrix, with correct recognition data falling along a diagonal of the matrix.

SELECTING THE TEST SPEAKER POPULATION

The speakers selected for the test should be representative of the users of the recogniser. For example, if the application is to be in industrial quality control data entry systems, the test speakers should be quality control personnel. Representative sampling of all potential users may not be possible or necessary.

The characteristics of the test speakers and both their user training and system enrolment procedures should be documented. While all the documented factors may not significantly affect performance, the documentation will indicate to others whether the test group is of particular interest or relevance.

Some recognisers impose limitations on the duration of words, or of silence gaps within words considered as single words or strings. Other constraints may apply to the number of words which may constitute a connected string. These constraints may have important consequences in some applications and for some individual speakers (e.g., if the durations of the speaker's stop gaps are longer than a limit set by the manufacturer, the word or phrase may be segmented into two utterances, and will not be correctly recognised).

Because speech recognisers use enrolment data to build reference template sets, prototypes, or other internal representations of the words to be recognised, it is important that the enrolment data for speaker-dependent systems provide representative samples of the user's speech. The enrolment and test data should include speech that is characteristic of the application, possibly including fatigued or stressed speech. These requirements may complicate enrolment and test procedures and, when slighted, generally result in lower performance in an application. Other important factors include the degree of cooperation of the users and their familiarity with the equipment.

Automatic speech recognition algorithms and commercial systems perform best on systems trained for the intended user's voice. Such *speaker-dependent* recognisers provide some degree of language independence, depending on the type of acoustic-phonetic representation or pattern matching algorithm used by the device. They may perform equally well when used with several languages. However, speaker-independent recognisers are expected to be language- and dialect-dependent to the extent that they rely on phonological rules and specific databases for the development of internal representations. The issue of language- or dialect-independence may be very important for some applications.

Speaker-independent systems do not rely on the data obtained from the individual user's voice. Rather, they are designed using training or enrolment data from many speakers and incorporate internal representations (e.g., template sets derived by studying clusters of individual speakers' templates, or word models derived from statistical analysis of many individual speakers' word models) based on features which are presumed not to vary from individual to individual. This is a crucial assumption (that the system relies on features that are relatively consistent) and its successful implementation is the key to success in speaker-independent automatic speech recognition technology. It is essential to ensure that the most important variabilities and dialect-related factors have been accounted for when designing and testing such systems. These requirements become increasingly challenging if large vocabularies are required and response must be available in a time period comparable with the duration of an utterance (i.e., real-time recognition).

When selecting test speakers for speaker-independent systems there are a number of special concerns. Perhaps most importantly, a representative sampling of the intended user population should be obtained in order to appropriately represent regional dialect and/or transmission channel effects for the intended user and applications population. A statement describing the efforts taken to represent the user population should be included as part of the documentation. When conducting tests of these systems, it is important to exclude data from the test material that might have been used in constructing internal representations used by the recogniser. Casual recognition experiments using template sets generated from one person or a small number of people typically demonstrate highly variable performance. Sometimes recognition performance may be quite good or quite poor for some individuals, and frequently there will be good performance on some words and poor performance on others. For these reasons, casual experimentation to demonstrate speaker-independence for systems designed to be speaker-dependent is not recommended.

SELECTING THE TEST VOCABULARY

The actual performance of any given speech recognition system in both benchmark tests and applications is critically dependent upon the vocabulary items that must be distinguished at any given time. Both the number of items to be distinguished and the acoustic similarity or complexity of these items are critical factors.

Brief monosyllabic words (e.g., *yes*, *no*, *go*, the natural alphabet except for *w*, etc.) are more difficult to recognise than longer polysyllabic words or brief phrases spoken and intended to be recognised as single items (e.g., *Massachusetts*, *California*, *start printing*, *left bracket*). These more complex utterances contain much more acoustic information and redundancy than monosyllables. In actual applications, this fact is used to construct vocabularies that retain many of the qualities of a natural interaction while selecting somewhat more complex acoustical characteristics to maximise system performance. For these reasons it is necessary to explicity state the test vocabulary. It is, of course, desirable to use a test vocabulary that is identical to the intended vocabulary for the application.

One parameter often used to characterise recognition system performance is that of the vocabulary size. Vocabulary sizes ranging from approximately 40 to several hundred words are not unusual at present. However, in order to enhance performance, it is often appropriate to use syntactic constraints. This is implemented through the imposition of an artificial language grammar to constrain the vocabulary choices at each stage of a task in a given application. In many cases, this is not only appropriate but will lead to significantly enhanced productivity by imposing a desired order for completing the intended task.

Restricted vocabularies and formatted messages are widely used for speech communications in situations such as air traffic control and military tasks in which high-speech comprehension is required. Acceptance of these constraints in isolated- and connected-word speech recognition applications will result in higher performance, but must be explicity stated when documenting system performance.

It is important to distinguish between the total vocabulary capacity (typically a function of total memory available to the system) and other measures of the effective vocabulary size (typically functions of the structure of the imposed artificial language grammar). For artificially constrained tasks, the average number of alternative words that the system has to choose from at any time is given by the *perplexity*, or dynamic branching factor for the imposed artificial language.

A 10-word recogniser, requiring discrimination between the digits (0–9) with all transitions equally likely, is typically more difficult than a system with a several hundred word total vocabulary and branching factor of only 5. Even if the larger vocabulary has a branching factor of 10, the larger vocabulary may be easier than the 10-word digit vocabulary if the vocabulary words tend to be longer and more easily discriminated than the digits (eight of which are monosyllables).

The benefits achieved through the use of syntactic constraints may be better addressed in separately documented tests. In syntactically constrained tasks, performance results ought to be reported with the following information to describe the characteristics of the imposed grammar:

(a) Complete description of the task grammar including full specification of the vocabulary at each task state or menu choice.

(b) Frequencies of transitions from each task to successive states.
(c) Dynamic branching factor or perplexity.
(d) Frequency of occurrence in the test material of each vocabulary item.

TRAINING

Two meanings of the word *training* are sometimes found in the literature of current speech recognition technology. A clear distinction must be made between them.

In one meaning, the user's speech is used to 'train' the recogniser for the specific test or applications vocabulary. During this process, reference patterns ('template sets', 'voice patterns', 'voice prints, etc.) or more complex word models are developed and become the stored internal representations used for comparison with subsequently input speech in the recognition process. This process is referred to as *enrolment*, without ambiguity.

A second meaning of the term 'training' refers to that process in which the user of a recogniser becomes familiar with the device or system. During this *user training*, many factors may combine to influence the user's speech. Generally, familiarisation with the devices leads to improved performance, and the user learns to adapt to explicit as well as implicit constraints on the form of the input speech.

One factor in user training that tends to improve performance uses feedback provided to the user. To date, most recorded speech database material has not been obtained under circumstances allowing user feedback. The recorded speech database material has been obtained in response to prompts or in list-reading tasks. The nature of the feedback provided to the test speaker should be documented, along with a description of any prompts provided to the user or the tasks conducted by the user while providing test material.

In tests conducted on integrated systems (as opposed to tests on system components), time must be allowed for familiarisation with the system and to observe the nature of performance improvement or degradation. In most cases, after a period of initial user training, performance can be improved significantly by simply re-enrolling the user. The new internal representations should then be more representative of the experienced user's typical speech, and poor initial performance due to the lack of user familiarity will be improved. Documented performance ought to represent the data obtained with experienced or fully trained users.

CHARACTERISING THE ENVIRONMENT

Both the operational environment and the speech signal transmission system providing input to speech recognition systems are important environmental factors influencing performance. For example, in an industrial quality control voice data entry application, the talker's environment might be a noisy factory floor, while the speech signal transmission environment may be a wireless microphone. When modelling an application, the acoustic environment and signal transmission channel should closely simulate the intended operational environment.

When access to the actual intended operational environment is limited or costly (e.g., in tests of systems for use in operational aircraft), using accurate simulations can provide a cost-effective test environment. By accurately modelling the environment, the value of such tests is enhanced by increasing the correlation between the test data obtained in the simulation and the actual operational environment.

Because laboratory test data is often not applicable to the user's operational environment, the responsibility for tests in operational environments becomes a critical element in dialogues between vendors and users.

When an actual operational environment is used, as for laboratory tests, care must be taken to control and document all potentially relevant characteristics of the test environment. Environmental noise tends to interfere with communication between humans. It also tends to degrade speech recognition system performance and it is best to separately conduct certain benchmark tests in which all background and transmission noise is minimised. These tests tend to provide information on optimum system performance because acoustic-phonetic information is not obscured by the noise. Comparison of benchmark test data with operational data can indicate the existence of noise-related limitations on performance for which noise control measures or improved transmission channels can lead to improved performance.

There are at least three types of noise that can affect performance:

- **Ambient or background noise.** This noise originates with the operation of nearby machinery such as office equipment, with ventilation systems, with people conversing in the vicinity of the user, or within the applications environment such as the crewspace of an aircraft. When microphones are located some distance from the talker's mouth, reflections from nearby surfaces such as desk-tops and room walls constitute a form of multi-path interference that can be comparable to increased ambient noise in degrading system performance.

- **Transmission or channel noise.** Such noise is inherent in using wireless microphones or telephone lines, and (for long distance lines, in particular) may be due to signal processing devices such as echo suppression, multiplex, or satellite transmission systems.
- **Inadvertent test speaker noises.** These may originate in coughs, stammers, 'ers', 'ums', excessive breath noise, and speech extraneous to the selected recognition vocabulary.

Characterisation of noise is important in interpreting operational test results. Attention should be directed to performance limitations that may be due to the following factors:

1. *The noise experienced by the speaker.* Speakers may modify their speech significantly in the presence of high noise. Typical modifications include speaking more loudly or slowly and taking care to articulate more carefully than otherwise. Minimal characterisation provides the A-weighted sound level (dBA) experienced by the user. Because masks, helmets, and some headsets affect the perceived noise level, their use by the test speaker should be noted. More detailed characterisation should include spectral content (e.g., third-octave band analyses) and the temporal nature (e.g., steady-state, intermittent or impulsive). Impulsive noise can lead to substantial degradations in performance, but full characterisation of this noise is difficult to achieve without sophisticated instrumentation.
2. *The speech signal-to-noise input to the recogniser* (prior to any recognition system signal processing). The use of a noise-cancelling microphone can effectively eliminate much of the noise environment of the test speaker, even in a high noise environment. However, the signal-to-noise properties of the signal input to the recogniser may be a critical factor in limiting performance in noisy environments. The relative importance of the differing characteristics of speech emitted in a noisy environments vs. the degraded signal-to-noise properties is not yet well understood. Different algorithms and/or devices are probably affected to differing degrees.
3. *Type and characteristics of the microphone.* Useful characteristics to note include close-talking or noise-cancelling, directionality, whether push-to-talk or otherwise manually switched, distance from the speaker's mouth, etc. The effectiveness and frequency response of noise cancelling microphones are influenced by the distance from the sound sources. Thus placement of the microphones should be documented.
4. *Verbal characterisation and description of the origin of the noise.* Typical characterisations use terms such as 'buzzy', 'hum', 'static',

etc., and descriptions of the origin are 'office environment', 'package sorting machinery', 'receiving platform', etc.

If a speech signal transmission system other than direct microphone input is used, attention should be directed to these additional factors:

5. *Limitations on the transmission channel bandwidth and frequency response.* Cite the upper and lower cut-off frequencies and any significant deviations from flat frequency response over the cited bandwidth.
6. *Other limitations on the transmission channel.* Significant performance limitations may be due to other effects such as automatic volume control attack and release characteristics, signal compression and/or limiting, phase distortion, additive noise in transmission, etc. In general, these effects are difficult to characterise.

While it is possible and, in many cases, desirable to record speakers in sound isolated (low ambient noise) and anechoic (dead) environments in order to access subtle details of the speech signal, care must be taken in generalising these observations to infer the nature of speech in the presence of noise. A first-order procedure involves the addition of white, pink, or carefully shaped noise spectra to the speech data after it is collected. Factors associated with the acoustic environment that influence the speakers include both ambient noise level and the degree of reverberation.

Speakers may compensate for these factors by speaking more loudly or enunciating more clearly or slowly. It should be specified what ambient noise was audible to the speaker at the time of collection.

In addition to acoustic environmental influences on the speaker, the task environment modifies the speaker's performance. Different types of tasks will affect the speaker's speech to varying degrees. Routine speech tasks such as list-reading or responding to visual prompts displayed on terminals produce less word-to-word variations than speech produced when there are concurrent physical tasks or shifts in attentional focus usually associated with other cognitive activities such as inspection, measurement, etc. For these reasons, higher recognition system performance can be expected from speech obtained from list reading than when there is concurrent tasking, and the talker's task environment should be fully described in the results.

RECORDING THE TEST MATERIAL
Many performance assessment tests make use of recorded speech databases. Others are conducted 'live'. The general practice of recording

the test material, even for live testing, is recommended. The recorded material provides a means of replicating the results obtained and verifying that the test material was properly input to the system. It also provides material to be used in additional measurements on similar systems as well as for analysis of the input audio signal. Using recorded test material offers the advantage of providing samples of speech obtained on different occasions, separated by days or weeks. This can account for some of the day-to-day variation and may more accurately model potential applications.

Recorded speech databases exist in both digitally recorded and stored formats and analogue recorded formats. The digital formats have greater signal-to-noise ratio than the analogue format. Reference databases that are widely used in research and testing have been recorded with 16-bit samples at sample rates from 10.0 to 20.0 kHz. Signal-to-noise ratios in excess of 90 dB are feasible using this technology. A widely used format for analogue recordings is the use of quarter-inch magnetic tape at 7.5 inches per second, providing maximum signal-to-noise ratios of the order of 60 dB. The use of cassette tape recorders is not generally recommended for benchmark test purposes for a number of reasons, including increased print-through.

Another advantage of using digital storage for database material is that each speech token may readily be assigned an accompanying *header* to indicate the origin of that particular token. Comparable systems are feasible using analogue storage, storing the header information in an encoded analogue signal on the second channel of a two-channel tape recorder, but these systems may require specialised interfaces.

Newly developed recording technology includes use of 14- or 16-bit digital sampling and pulse code modulation systems to encode the signals for storage on Beta or VHS format video recorders, referred to as PCM/VCR recording technology. This technology offers many of the advantages of digital sampling and storage at lower costs for the storage medium than more traditional digital storage media, and offers the capability of copying the data with less degradation than for analogue recordings.

A number of speech databases have been widely used in testing and serve to provide benchmarks of test material. They are available in several recorded formats[3].

SCORING ISOLATED-WORD DATA
Scoring isolated-word recognition systems' performance presents fewer challenges than for connected-word systems. The relative ease in scoring isolated-word data arises from the fact that most errors tend to be

substitutions: deletions or insertions are easily identified when they do occur.

It is ordinarily presumed that the individual speech tokens (e.g., words or short phrases with minimal intra-word pauses) are separated in time by pauses that are long enough to permit the recognition system to respond. Indications that this may not be the case will be found if there is a high incidence of deletions or substitutions, and it should be noted that the origin of these errors may be due to a problem with the system's response time for the database used for these tests.

Prior to detailed data analysis, it is instructive to critically listen to the recorded test material, particularly for those portions of the test material where unusual numbers of errors may have occurred. These errors may be due to noise artefacts or departures from proper script-reading or responses to prompts. If this is the case, the recorded tokens or artefacts must be editorially deleted from the test material prior to testing. Objective analysis of the data must include full documentation of these decisions regarding certification of the test material. It is preferable not to delete any data if the process of obtaining and using the test material was carefully structured and monitored.

Preliminary analysis of the performance data should identify and tabulate words which were correctly recognised, words provided as input for which substitution errors occurred, words provided as input for which there was no response (deletion errors or rejections), and instances in which a response occurred without a corresponding appropriate input (insertion errors). The raw data should be summarised by determining the corresponding correct recognition percentage as well as the substitution, deletion, and insertion error percentage.

In comparative testing of differing systems, it is generally preferable to disable the reject capability, so that each system returns a forced choice response. In this case words provided as input for which there is no response are unambiguously classified as leading to deletion errors.

In performing benchmark tests to compare different recognisers, the removal of all syntax constraints may be preferable. These constraints, like the setting of a reject threshold, may affect systems differently. If, following data analysis, recognition errors are concentrated on several specific words or utterances, then re-enrolling the speaker on these words or substituting acoustically distinctive synonymous words may substantially improve performance.

In other tests, particularly those at the integrated system level or in modelling an application, the use of the reject capability is an important feature that should be included in the test program. Tests in this case should document the settings of the reject threshold and/or other decision criteria, identify and tabulate words input to the system for which the reject response occurred, and determine the rejection percentage. It is also valuable to determine and document the ratio of total errors to rejections, because this information may be useful in the design of applications software.

More detailed analysis of systems performance can be documented and easily reviewed by constructing a confusion matrix, tabulating the correct recognition response data along a diagonal element, with off-diagonal entries indicating the substitution errors. Analysis of this data will provide valuable insights into systems' performance and the design of successful vocabularies.

Another useful measure may be appropriate for those systems that present several ranked words for approval. In this case, recognition accuracy as a function of the word rank is a useful parameter, since it provides a measure of the probability that the second, third, ... Nth candidate is correct if the higher ranked candidate is incorrect. If it is known a priori that a recogniser will be implemented in an application that will impose higher-level constraints, such as a syntactically controlled (sub-) vocabulary, then it is appropriate to determine and report the probabilities that the correct word is to be found among the top N candidates on the ordered list. This practice is inappropriate if the imposition of higher-level constraints is impractical in a typical application.

It is sometimes desirable to have measures of a system's capacity to reject words that are not in its recognition vocabulary. This is particularly appropriate for those applications involving inexperienced users or those unaccustomed to using artificial grammars or syntactic constraints. For experienced users, it may be safe to assume that the input is limited to words in the recognition vocabulary, in which case out-of-vocabulary rejection capabilities are less critical.

In order to test a system's capability to reject out-of-vocabulary utterances, a secondary test can be performed using the same recognition database used for other tests. In this case, however, a subset of the recognition vocabulary is selected and the system is re-enrolled using only this subset of the entire test vocabulary. The entire database is then used for test purposes, with responses that occur for words that are not part of the active vocabulary (the selected subset) being classified as 'false acceptances'. Documentation in such a test must include the total test vocabulary and the specified active vocabulary.

SCORING CONNECTED-WORD DATA

There are several ways to score recognition performance on connected-word strings. The most stringent method is to record the percentage of strings completely recognised, i.e., the number of correct strings divided by the total number of strings tested. Another method is to calculate the percentage of individual words correctly recognised. The number of substitutions, deletions and insertions is calculated for each string, and the total error count is divided by the total number of words in the strings tested. The string scoring may be done by procedures involving strict left-to-right alignment or by a best-case pattern match.

Left-to-right alignment procedures involve matching each word in the input string with a corresponding word in the response string starting with the first (left-most) member of each string. Obviously, the occurrence of an insertion or deletion will shift the position of words in the response string so that succeeding responses will be compared with inappropriate members of the input string. For example, if the input string is *12345*, and a deletion error results in a response string *1345*, a left-to-right alignment procedure correctly scores the first digit as a correct recognition, but would cite the three following responses as substitution errors (e.g. *3* for *2*, *4* for *3*, *5* for *4*) and would detect the presence of a deletion error only at the last digit (e.g. no response for *5*). In this case, one correct recognition, three substitutions, and one deletion would be indicated, where in fact there were four correct recognitions, and one deletion (and the deletion error is, in fact, mis-identified). This left-to-right pattern match procedure, though well defined and easy to implement, is in many cases a very poor or worst-case pattern match.

When using best-case pattern match procedures, individual words are matched so as to minimise the number of errors within the string. That is, if the input string is *12345*, and the output string is *1345*, it is inferred that there were four correct recognitions and one deletion.

Selection of the most appropriate scoring method involves consideration of the relevant application, and particularly the manner of verification and correction by the speaker. Where the manner of correction involves repetition of an entire string, the string error rate may be most appropriate. The aligned word recognition scores would be appropriate measures for those cases in which correction may be possible by backing up one word at a time from the end of the string.

The use of best-case pattern match procedures tends to avoid some of these complications, but there are no generally agreed-upon procedures to uniquely define the best-case match criteria. Specific details of these procedures are beyond the scope of this book. Purchasers of systems for which these considerations are significant should discuss the scoring procedures used by vendors.

PRAGMATIC CONSIDERATIONS

Prior to conducting tests, care should be taken to make sure that the equipment is functioning properly. Because recognition systems are designed to perform with distorted and/or variable input, determining proper functioning is not a simple task. Malfunctioning components can masquerade as an imperceptible input distortion, and the system will appear to work, but not as well as it should. Check procedures should include tests to confirm consistency of recognition results with results obtained previously using recorded speech, checks of input amplitude settings and the use of any available software diagnostics. These tests should be routinely conducted at the time of testing.

In tests of commercially available systems, the manufacturer's recommendations should be followed in order to obtain optimum performance. If the manufacturer's recommendations are not followed, some degradation in performance may be expected.

Manufacturers may suggest procedures to use regarding:

- Recommended number of enrolment tokens.
- Presentation order of enrolment tokens.
- Required minimal interval pause duration.
- Amplitude and gain control settings (to accurately simulate live input if recorded input is used). Amplitude settings should not be readjusted, once set.
- Microphone position.

Specify if a *press-to-talk* switch is used. The use of press-to-talk microphones provides an input signal to the recogniser that has very little or no signal amplitude between words. Depending on the particular recogniser's procedure for accommodating input signals during inter-word pauses, this may lead to either improved or degraded performance, relative to the use of conventional unswitched microphones. Choice of open or press-to-talk microphones for test purposes should be determined by operational considerations (e.g. if it is an accepted practice in a proposed application or if it is required to activate a remote system) as well as whether the use of one or the other may lead to optimum performance with a given recogniser.

Proper connection of peripheral devices and electronic components should be checked before testing to eliminate ground loops and extraneous noise. The speech (audio) signal input to the recogniser should be monitored by the experimenter to verify that no extraneous noise is being introduced.

STATISTICAL CONSIDERATIONS

Performance assessment tests of any automatic speech recognition system require that a large number of speech tokens be input to the system by many users and that detailed analysis of the test data be conducted. Thorough testing requires the use of large test speech databases, substantial data storage, and time. Disregard for these facts inevitably leads to misleading conclusions regarding system performance.

Researchers, vendors, users and developers of automatic speech recognition technology each have different needs for performance data. The significance and interpretation of the data vary because of the different goals each group seeks to achieve. Consequently the degree of concern for the statistical validity of the performance data is variable.

Factors that need to be considered in structuring statistically valid performance tests include the size of the test speaker (user) group, the number of test tokens, and the amount of enrolment material provided to the system.

For benchmark testing, a concise statement of the number of test speakers, number of test utterances, and number of errors of each type should be given. It is recommended that the performance documentation should include a statement of the total error rate and the confidence level implied by each statistic. Statistical tables should be consulted to interpret the results, and the assumptions made in computing the statistics should be stated explicitly[4].

For tests that model an application, statistically-based considerations include sampling the intended user population and range of tasks to be implemented using speech recognition, and defining the variability in the noise environment.

For speaker-independent recognition technology, particular attention should be paid to sampling the intended user population and communications channels. Dialect-related effects and variations in the quality of telephone connections make it difficult to obtain consistent performance from current low-cost remote access speaker-independent recognition technology. Testing of this technology must be based on large speech databases.

To obtain optimal performance from each of the systems to be compared in a benchmark test, the appropriate vendor-recommended training procedure must be followed. Because some recognisers make use of single-token enrolment, whilst others build increasingly more reliable statistically-based word models in the process of enrolment (and, possibly, in operating in a speaker-adaptive mode), appropriate enrolment procedures often vary significantly from one system to another.

No generally-accepted rules have yet been developed for statistically reliable speech recognition system test procedures. In view of the many factors influencing performance, most researchers and vendors attempt to carefully control known sources of variable performance. Those researchers and vendors whose products build increasing accuracy with statistically large enrolment data are particularly conscious of the need for statistically large enrolment and test databases. Though no generally-accepted rules for adequate statistical sampling presently exist, data analysis should seek to define the distribution of performance data, as well as mean values. Decisions regarding apparent superiorities of algorithms or products cannot be reliably made if the differences in mean values are smaller than the associated variances. Reference to handbooks of experimental statistics can be valuable in avoiding misinterpretation of the test data.

In principle, extensive and statistically valid testing involves the use of a large database. However, the costs of testing and resources required for these tests are frequently regarded as prohibitive, and more limited testing is typical. Consequently, attempts should be made to determine the statistical validity of the tests as an important factor in performance assessment.

DOCUMENTATION

Proper documentation is an essential component in performance assessment. Information should be provided to document the relevant characteristics of the test speaker population, test vocabulary and other test data to establish the relevant context of the testing.

Test material obtained in accurate simulations of field applications may contain noise or speaker artefacts such as coughs, stammers, or false starts. Alternatively these artefacts may have been manually deleted or edited from the test and/or training material. The process of selection or preparation of the test material should be described.

Summary test data that should be documented includes:

Correct recognition per cent (*Recognition accuracy*)

$$= \frac{(\#\,\text{Correctly recognised words}) \times 100}{(\#\,\text{Test words})} \text{ (per cent)}$$

Substitution per cent

$$= \frac{(\#\,\text{Substituted words}) \times 100}{(\#\,\text{Test words})} \text{ (per cent)}$$

$$\text{Deletion per cent} = \frac{(\#\text{Deleted words}) \times 100}{(\#\text{Test words})} \text{ (per cent)}$$

$$\text{Insertion per cent} = \frac{(\#\text{Inserted words}) \times 100}{(\#\text{Test words})} \text{ (per cent)}$$

If the reject capability is employed, the following data are important:

Settings of the reject threshold or reject criteria:

$$\text{Rejection per cent} = \frac{(\#\text{Rejection responses}) \times 100}{(\#\text{Test words})} \text{ (per cent)}$$

Ratio of total errors to rejections

$$= \frac{(\#\text{Substitutions} + \#\text{Deletions} + \#\text{Insertions})}{(\#\text{Rejections})}$$

When the reject capability is employed, an unambiguous distinction cannot be made between deletion errors and rejections. Consequently, 'total errors' consists of substitutions and insertions, and the number of rejections includes words that would otherwise lead to deletion errors.

These results are the most frequently cited performance data; however, documentation of confusion pairs (e.g., *five* and *nine*) or confusion matrices is informative and provides useful information in designing applications vocabularies.

Response time is a critical factor in successful implementations of large vocabulary systems. There is no accepted procedure for precise measurement and specification of response time for connected-word systems. If the processing time is comparable to or less than the utterance duration, the system response time may be described as *real time*. A suggested comparative measure for other than real-time systems is a multiple of utterance duration, assuming processing is initiated at the beginning of the utterance and completed with display or return of the recognised word.

In view of the fact that processing times are finite, errors which arise from utterances spoken with insufficient pauses between words (for isolated-word systems, in particular) should be identified and noted in the performance documentation.

In view of the fact that processing times are finite, errors which arise from utterances spoken with insufficient pauses between words (for isolated-word systems, in particular) should be identified and noted in the performance documentation.

The *A-weighted* sound level (*dBA*) measured in the vicinity of the test speaker should be specified if environmental noise is believed to be a significant limitation on performance. More thorough documentation of the properties of the environmental noise may be appropriate.

Suggested documentation of the speech signal-to-noise properties of the test material should include the ratio of speech peak level to steady background noise level (in dB), measured according to ANSI S.3.59[5]. If this is not feasible, at the least, the range of typical maximum speech level to background level indication on the VU indicator of a conventional audio tape recorder should be noted and cited.

13.4 *Perspectives on testing*

As explained in the preceding material, there is no simple and completely objective way to test the performance of automatic speech recognition technology. The number and complexity of factors influencing performance is such that in many cases, the relative advantages offered by competing algorithms, commercial products, or integrated systems may be obscured.

The approach toward performance assessment in this chapter emphasises the value of benchmark tests and the need to carefully model applications. This is particularly important if the expenses of integrating speech technology into a particular well-defined application, and the benefits to be achieved, are appreciable. Attention to detail in planning an applications test should be reflected in greater confidence in the ability of the technology to provide the anticipated benefits. Here also, a poorly-structured applications test or one that does not adequately account for important factors influencing performance will invalidate the test results and may lead to costly and unsuccessful attempts to use this new technology.

There are, however, a number of other perspectives toward testing. It is useful to identify some of these perspectives:

INFORMAL DEVICE TESTING

Within the past several years, the emergence of low-cost commercial products has made an informal approach toward performance testing fairly widespread. Many individual purchasers of speech recognisers undertake an informal test programme that primarily consists of familiarisation of that purchaser or a designated individual with the technology. In many cases, the primary value of these tests appears to be that the experimenter learns to recognise the constraints imposed by the particular product on system enrolment, environmental factors, user interaction, interface design, etc. If informal testing of this sort results in development of a successful application, the experimenter gains valuable experience in the use of a new technology, and insights into the selection of improved second-generation or competitive products and the design of more formal and reliable tests.

However, there are real risks that the informal testing may not lead to the development of a successful application, that the purchaser may inappropriately conclude that the technology offers no promise for his application, and that the individuals involved in the testing and systems integration learn little of value in the process. Serious attention should be given to allocating adequate resources to carry out more formal tests to the point at which a serious and detailed investigation has taken place, and at which time the experimenter can demonstrate that he or she has developed an in-depth understanding of the relevant strengths and weaknesses.

WORKSTATION OR TASK REDESIGN

Another perspective toward studying the performance of this technology is based upon the desire to achieve the productivity benefits that might be offered by redesign of workstations or tasks, by using speech as an alternative or additional data entry or command/control modality. This is perhaps the implicit goal of all efforts to create successful applications. The design of tests to measure productivity benefits is beyond the scope of this book, but is extremely important. In tests to measure these productivity benefits, those benefits which are specifically due to the user of speech technology should be compared to those that might be primarily due to redesign of workstations or tasks.

HUMAN FACTORS RESEARCH

The design of successful human–machine dialogues is an active and important research topic at present (see Chapter 6). Not enough is known at present about the desired properties of automatic speech recognisers and the human–machine interaction to always lead to the design of successful applications. Further research on such issues as the design of optimal error correction protocols and user training and feedback is required and will serve to advance the technology. Attention to the factors contained in this report should serve to increase the value of these studies.

The differing perspectives are consistent with the different outlooks regarding the purpose of the tests. The testing, like the technology itself, may serve different purposes. Whatever approach is taken, however, there are many common concerns, including:

- **Recognised complicating factors** must be accounted for and carefully controlled. Failure to do so will invalidate the test data.
- **Detailed documentation** must be made available to indicate experimental design and to provide data and sufficiently detailed data analysis to indicate the significance of the test results to others. Detailed documentation should be part of reporting all performance tests. Failure to do so often leads to meaningless comparisons of product or system performance, or misleading citations.
- **Benchmark test data,** in which severe constraints have been imposed on the test conditions, is extremely valuable. Typical constraints limit the test vocabulary, the number of test talkers, the format of the input speech and the nature of environmental effects, and prohibit feedback between the user and the system. While it can be argued that under these conditions, it is possible to adapt or specially 'tune' algorithm or device characteristics to optimise test performance for a specified test database, benchmark tests provide data that is useful for initial comparisons of algorithm or device performance. Applications testing should reveal whether or not the particular device selected for this phase of testing is well suited to a particular application or user's needs.

Agreement should be reached at an early stage of interest in the technology on the purpose of testing and appropriate measures of performance. Once these issues are decided, the nature of the tests can be determined. In the absence of agreement on these issues, little progress can be made.

13.5 *Acknowledgements*

This chapter consists mainly of a reprint of a paper which originally appeared in the *National Bureau of Standards Journal of Research*, Volume 90, Number 5, September/October 1985, under the title: 'Performance Assessment of Automatic Speech Recognizers'. The paper was compiled by David S. Pallett, an employee of the US National Bureau of Standards, from material collected as follows:

An *ad hoc* group met at the National Bureau of Standards in June 1981, to discuss performance assessment of speech recognition systems, following discussions during the NBS/NADC sponsored Workshop on Standardization for Speech I/O Technology. Further discussions were held at the 1982 (Paris), 1983 (Boston) and the 1984 (San Diego) meetings of the IEEE International Conference on Acoustics, Speech and Signal Processing (ICASSP).

Following the 1982 ICASSP, the *ad hoc* group was constituted as the

Speech I/O Technology Performance Evaluation Working Group, sponsored by the Speech Processing Technical Committee of the IEEE Acoustics, Speech and Signal Processing Society. Material presented in Section 13.3 of this chapter is adapted from informal drafts circulated within this Working Group.

Particular appreciation is expressed to Dr. Janet M. Baker, Chairman of the IEEE Speech I/O Technology Performance Evaluation Working Group, for her enthusiastic support and constructive criticism of this material, as well as to many other individuals who have shared their perspectives and expertise in addressing these issues.

13.6 *Further reading*

Whilst there is a very limited literature on the topic of performance assessment *per se*, there are many valuable discussions of the issues that affect performance. The interested reader is encouraged to refer to the key papers described below (and the related literature cited therein) in order to develop a more thorough understanding of the process of performance assessment.

Baker, J.M. (1982) 'The performing arts – how to measure up!' *Proceedings of the Workshop on Standardization for Speech I/O Technology*, Pallett, D.S. (ed.), National Bureau of Standards, Gaithersburg, MD, March 18–19. p. 27–33.

Presents the results of a series of tests on isolated-word, speaker-dependent recognisers, and a discusssion of statistical factors in testing.

Baker, J.M., Pallett, D.S., and Bridle, J.S. (1983) 'Speech recognition performance assessment and available data bases', *Proceedings of ICASSP 83*, Boston, MA, April 14–16. p. 527–530.

Discusses databases used in some well-documented benchmark tests.

Chollet, G.F., and Gagnoulet, C. (1982) 'On the evaluation of speech recognizers and data bases using a reference system', *Proceedings of ICASSP 82*, Paris, May 3–5. p. 2026–2029.

Proposes the use of an openly published reference recognition algorithm to provide benchmarks of recogniser performance as well as of the relative difficulty of different speech vocabularies and databases. Chollett credits R. K. Moore with early advocacy of this approach.

Chollet, G.F., and Rossi, M. (1981) 'Evaluating the performance of speech recognizers and data bases at the acoustic-phonetic level', *Proceedings of ICASSP 81*, Atlanta, GA, March 30–April 1. p. 758–761.

Advocates comparison of measured confusibility for recognisers with that of humans.

Clark, J., Collins, P., and Lowerre, B. (1981) 'A formalization of performance specifications for discrete utterance recognition systems', *Proceedings of ICASSP 81*, Atlanta, GA, March 30–April 1. p. 753–757.
Discusses needs for objective procedures for comparing the performance of isolated-word recognisers.

DeMori, R. (1983) *Computer Models of Speech Using Fuzzy Algorithms* New York: Plenum Press. p. 382–386.
Proposes an experimental model for speech recognition and understanding using fuzzy-set theory and concepts of artificial intelligence. Includes a review of several procedures for evaluating language complexity.

Dixon, N.R., and Martin, T.B. (eds.) (1979) *Automatic-Speech and Speaker Recognition*, New York: IEEE Press p. 33.
An important collection of papers that documents the state-of-the-art just prior to widespread use of VLSI technology in automatic speech recognition technology.

Doddington, G.R., and Schalk, T.B. (1981) 'Speech recognition: turning theory into practice'. *IEEE Spectrum*, Sept. p. 26.
Describes the results of a series of benchmark tests on isolated-word, speaker-dependent recognisers, and presents a thoughtful discussion of factors complicating the performance assessment test procedure.

Goodman, R.G. (1976) *Analysis of Language for Man–Machine Communication* Ph.D. Dissertation, Stanford University, May.
An early study of the complexity of imposed grammars and the issues of phonetic ambiguity and measures of the similarity of acoustic events.

Jelinek, F., Mercer, R.L., Bahl, L.R., and Baker, J.K. (1977) 'Perplexity – a measure of the difficulty of speech recognition tasks' *J. Acoust Soc. Am.*, Vol. **62**, Suppl. No. 1, Fall p. S63.
The abstract of a paper given at the Autumn 1977 meeting of the Acoustical Society of America. This paper presented material summarised by Jelinek, Mercer, and Bahl, below.

Jelinek, F., Mercer, R.L., and Bahl, L.R. (1982) 'Continuous Speech Recognition: Statistical Methods', Chapter 25 in *Handbook of Statistics*, Vol. 2, Krishnaiah, P.R., and Kanal, L.N. (eds.), North-Holland Publishing Co. 549–573.
These papers describe methods of assessing the performance of continuous speech recognition systems and the relative difficulty of recognition tasks.

Lea, W.A. (1982) 'What causes speech recognizers to make mistakes?', *Proceedings of ICASSP 82*, Paris, May 3–5. p. 2030–2033.

Discusses factors that affect recognition accuracy and cites other papers by this author on related topics.

Leonard, R.G. (1984) 'A database for speaker-independent digit recognition', *Proceedings of ICASSP 84*, San Diego, Ca, March 19–21. p. 42.11.1–42.11.4.

Describes valuable database for research and test purposes that represents more than 20 dialects using approximately 100 adult males, 100 adult females and 100 children. Includes a discussion of an experimental procedure to 'certify' the database using human subjects.

Lerman, L. (ed.) (1984) *Proceedings of the Voice Data Entry Systems Applications Conference '84*, American Voice Input/Output Society, Arlington, VA, Sept. 11–13.

Most recent in a series of four Conferences addressing the design of applications of voice-interactive systems for data entry and other purposes.

Moore, R.K. (1977) 'Evaluating speech recognizers', *IEEE Transactions ASSP* Vol. **25**, No. 2.

A significant early contribution proposing a standard for comparing the performance of different recognisers based on a model of human word recognition.

Pallett, D.S. (ed.) (1982) *Proceedings of the Workshop on Standardization for Speech I/O Technology* National Bureau of Standards, Gaithersburg, MD, March 18–19.

Presents approximately thirty technical papers addressing the issue of performance assessment for speech I/O technology.

Peckham, J.B. (1985) 'Speech technology assessment activities in the UK', *Proceedings of Speech Tech '85*, New York, NY, April 22–24. pp. 165–169.

Describes the activities and goals of the Speech Technology Assessment Group formed in the UK within the Speech Group of the Institute for Acoustics.

Poock, G.K., Martin, B.J., and Roland, E.F. (1983) 'The effect of feedback to users of voice recognition equipment', *Naval Postgraduate School Report NPS55-83-003*, February.

One of a series of studies conducted by Poock and his colleagues addressed at measurement of the performance of integrated or interactive systems.

Rosenberg, A.E. (1984) 'A probabilistic model for the performance of word recognizers', *AT&T Technical Journal*, Vol. **63**, No. 1, Jan. pp. 1–32.
Develops analytic models of recogniser performance.

Sondhi, M.M., and Levinson, S.E. (1977) 'Relative difficulty and robustness of speech recognition tasks that use grammatical constraints', *J. Acoust. Soc. Am.*, Vol. **62**, Suppl. No. 1, Fall. p. S64.
The abstract of a paper given at the Autumn 1977 meeting of the Acoustical Society of America. This paper presented material summarised by Sondhi and Levinson, below.

Sondhi, M.M., and Levinson, S.E. (1978) 'Computing relative redundancy to measure grammatical constraint in speech recognition tasks', *Proceedings of ICASSP 78*, Tulsa, OK, May. pp. 409–412.
This paper develops algorithms for computing various statistical properties of finite languages and documents these properties for eight speech recognition task languages that have appeared in the literature.

Spine, T.M., Williges, B.H., and Maynard, J.F. (1984) 'An economical approach to modeling speech recognition accuracy', *Int. J. Man–Machine Studies* Vol. **21**. pp. 191–202.
Discusses the use of a central-composite design methodology as a means to develop empirical prediction equations for speech recogniser performance. Factors manipulated in the experimental design include number of training passes, reject threshold, difference score and size of the active vocabulary.

Wilpon, J.G., and Rabiner, L.R. (1983) 'On the recognition of isolated digits from a large telphone customer population,' *Bell System Technical Journal*, Vol. **62**, No. 7, September. pp. 1977–2000.
Describes the collection and use of an isolated digit database for use in research and development of speaker-independent speech recognition systems.

Wilpon, J.G. (1985) 'A study on the ability to automatically recognize telephone quality speech from large customer populations' *AT&T Technical Journal*, Vol. **64**, No. 2, February. pp. 423–451.
Provides an important and detailed analysis of procedures used in collecting speech databases over telephone lines. Together with the preceding paper by Wilpon and Rabiner, valuable information is presented on the complexity of successful implementation of speaker-independent automatic speech recognition over telephone lines.

13.7 *References*

1. Reddy, R., and Zue, V. (1983) 'Recognizing continuous speech remains an elusive goal', *IEEE Spectrum*, November.
2. *Automatic Speech Recognition in Severe Environments* (1984) Report of the Committee on Computerized Speech Recognition Technologies, National Research Council, National Academy Press (Washington, DC).
3. Baker, J.M., Pallett, D.S., and Bridle, J.S. (1983) 'Speech recognition performance assessments and available data bases', *Proceedings of ICASSP-83*, Boston, MA, April 14–16. p. 527–530.
4. See for example Burrington, R.S., and May, D.C. (1970) *Handbook of Statistics with Tables* (Second Edition) New York: McGraw-Hill. Sections 14.53–14.64.
5. *American National Standard Method of Measurement of Speaking Levels*, ANSI S.3.59 (pending).

PART 3
APPLICATIONS

CHAPTER 14

VOICE CONTROL FOR THE DISABLED

Mike Fisher

In this chapter, we discuss the remote control of equipment by disabled people, using speech recognition.

14.1 *Engineering a solution for the disabled*

The application of engineering to alleviate problems experienced by the disabled is certainly not new; a walking stick is a very basic example. However, such 'engineered solutions' have always suffered, and continue to do so, from two major difficulties.

The first can be broadly defined as the *perception of a suitable engineered solution*. This relates to functional requirements and does not include any sociological or psychological considerations. In particular, it concerns the ability to construct the solution from available or emerging technology.

Examples of what it is currently possible to engineer in terms of solutions include *myo-electric prostheses* (which use the signals in existing nerves to control the prosthesis), and cameras linked to pressure pads to provide some limited information as an alternative to total blindness. Both of these examples are leading edge technology and are extremely costly. This highlights the second major area of difficulty – the *cost of the engineered solution*.

KEEPING THE COSTS DOWN

Any solution which is not affordable to the potential user will at best benefit a very few and at worst engender feelings of extreme frustration among groups who might benefit from the solution, if only they could afford it. In order to make any product for the minimum cost the number of potential users of the product must be maximised. Ideally, the engineered solution should be the solution to many problems.

Within the United Kingdom, the number of registered disabled persons is approximately 420 000, representing about 10% to 20% of the actual total. Of the number of disabled, only a relatively small proportion will be in employment and only a small proportion will suffer from any one specific disability, although multiple disabilities are common. As an example of a group with a specific disability, the number of registered blind persons in the UK is 130 000, 65% of this total being over 65 years of age. These figures illustrate that any solution which must be specifically designed and manufactured to assist only those with a particular disability will never be produced in sufficient volume to gain the cost benefits of mass production.

The best approach, then, is to produce solutions which are not specific to a particular disability but which rather offer useful facilities to persons with a wide range of disabilities, and if possible to do so using technology which is readily available in the market place. This in effect means technology which is in widespread use by the majority, in this case the able-bodied. The solution should ideally be applicable in employment as well as in the home, in order to benefit the greatest possible number of users.

THE COMPUTER AS A BASIS FOR THE SOLUTION

An obvious candidate for inclusion in such a solution is the ubiquitous computer, which is probably the entity closest to being 'all things to all men'.

The next consideration, if a computer is to be used, is the user interface to the machine or, how can the user control the machine in order for it to perform some useful task? This consideration, whilst being particularly critical for the handicapped, is mirrored to an extent by the desire of the majority of computer users for a 'user-friendly interface'. Amongst the current range of available products for this purpose are touch-sensitive screens, 'mice' of various types (these use a ball which is rotated by the user to control the position of the cursor on the screen), special function keyboards and voice recognition.

From the available man–machine interfaces, voice recognition has the most to offer in that the user may be physically remote from the machine and the need for contact with the keyboard is removed.

Having selected a voice-controlled computer as the basis for solutions to a wide range of problems encountered by the disabled, the next question is, 'what functions might such a system perform?'. The answer is that the majority of functions which are controllable by a computer are in turn controllable by the user via speech. This leads to the production of systems employing speech control for able-bodied users which need minimal modification for use by the disabled. A description of two typical systems follows; the first is for a relatively specific application for use in industry and commerce, the second is relatively non-specific, and has application in the workplace and in the home. Both are usable by able-bodied and disabled persons.

14.2 *Personal telephone book with voice access*

This example shows how a personal list of telephone numbers can be stored and accessed using the voice, perhaps for use with the voice-activated telephone included in the next example. However, whilst a telephone book is the subject of this description, the reader should note that the same techniques and hardware could be used to access any other simple database – an address book, for example, or even a selection of recipes.

The system requires one of the following three configurations of hardware:

(1) IBM PCXT with asynchronous communication adaptor, 360 kbyte floppy drive and 10M fixed disk, Votan V5040 voice recognition/response system.
(2) IBM PCXT, or other micro, with asynchronous communication adaptor, floppy drive and fixed disk, Votan VTR6000 voice terminal.
(3) IBM PCXT with floppy drive and fixed disk, Votan VPC2000 voice card.

Figure 14.1 shows a block diagram of the system.

The voice recognition is speaker-dependent, i.e. the user must *teach* the system to recognise his/her voice patterns by speaking each word that he/she will subsequently use. Depending on which of the above configurations is used, the recognition may be isolated-word recognition or connected-word recognition.

To access a particular phone number the user must speak the name of the 'owner' of the number, but since the number of possible names exceeds the machine's capacity to hold voice patterns for names, a particular block of names within which the one that is required is resident must first be specified, so that the block of names can be loaded into memory in the recogniser. Depending on the total number of names in the directory, this is accomplished by the user speaking the first (or first two or first three) letters of the name, which is the equivalent of

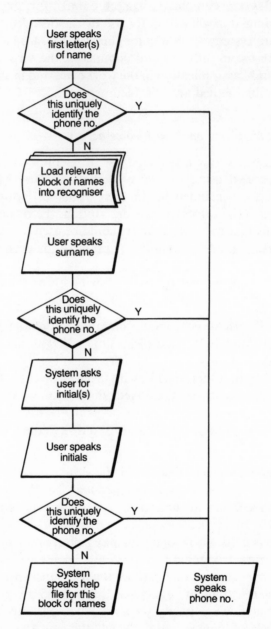

Figure 14.1 Block diagram of a voice controlled telephone book

searching for the correct page heading in a conventional paper telephone directory.

Once the relevant block of names is loaded and the user speaks the relevant surname, then the system will respond by speaking the telephone number. If the surname in question is duplicated then the system prompts for initials as appropriate. The user may also, by saying *help* or *description*, listen to a general help file for the block of names in memory, or a description of the user of the last phone number accessed, respectively.

The system uses the following files:

A file of names and telephone numbers which is a normal random access file.

A file of the user's voice templates speaking the phonetic alphabet, *help*, *description*, etc. This file is always resident in the recogniser during operation.

A separate vocabulary file for each block of names; for instance, in a small directory, possibly all names beginning with S might make up such a block. These files are loaded into the recogniser only as required.

The average transaction time for such a system depends on the configuration and the number of names in the directory but lies in the range 5s–10s.

The maximum number of names that any of the different configurations can access instantaneously is a few hundred. If this is sufficient to hold all the names in the directory then the first letter(s) of the name need not be spoken and transaction time drops to about 2s–3s. However, once this number of names is exceeded then the maximum number which can be accessed at one time is governed by the speed with which that number of names can be loaded. For instance, if the names must be restored over a serial interface then the restore time for 25 names would lie in the range 3s–6s.

The method which is used to link the recognition of spoken words to the random access file of telephone numbers is as follows:

When the user speaks the first 1 (or 2, or 3) letters of the name, a hashing technique is applied to the letters to generate a record number. If the record is the only record in that logical bucket then the system will speak that phone number; otherwise the vocabulary file for that group of names is loaded and the user speaks the surname (plus, possibly, some initials). This then provides a further value which, in conjunction with the first record number, generates the record number of the required phone number. The names are stored in the same file as phone numbers, merely for purposes of listing and updating.

The help files and description files are digitally recorded messages, the filenames of which are respectively the first 1 or 2 or 3 letters of a name and a phone number. Therefore a help file relates to a block of names and a description file to a single phone number. The number of such files that is needed is dependent on the application.

14.3 *Voice-activated domestic appliance system*

In this section an application that has been built and extensively demonstrated is described. The prototype was commissioned by the Department of Trade and Industry early in 1984 and was constructed by Voice Input Systems of St. Ives, UK. It first took the form of a travelling exhibition, the aim being to illustrate what could be done in terms of speech control of a user's environment (see Fig. 14.2). Later it was converted into a saleable product for the disabled.

OVERVIEW OF THE SYSTEM
Apart from the domestic appliances the system comprises the following hardware (see Fig. 14.3): Apple II with 2 asynchronous communication

Figure 14.2   The voice-activated domestic appliance. **1.** Turn the television on and off, change channels, select Teletext, adjust the volume. **2.** Turn the radio on and off and select stations. **3.** Play, fast-forward and re-wind the cassette player. **4.** Open and close the door. **5.** Open and close the curtains as desired. **6.** Control a security camera. **7.** Turn lights on or off. **8.** Activate the telephone and dial numbers. **9.** Turn on the Teasmaid. **10.** Accept dictation and print a letter. **11.** Activate an alarm signal. **12.** Control an electric fire. **13.** Speak foreign languages. (Hidden from view is a microcomputer, voice entry terminal, disc-drive and voice synthesiser. An Apple computer was used initially, to be replaced by a BBC Model B)

cards, 2 floppy drives, Silentype printer, Votrax synthesiser, Scott recognition card, device controller.

The speech recognition for this system is speaker-dependent isolated-word recognition. A block diagram is shown in Fig. 14.3.

Control of the domestic appliance is effected by the user speaking a command such as *heater*. This command is echoed to the monitor and repeated by the system via the speech synthesiser. The voice recognition

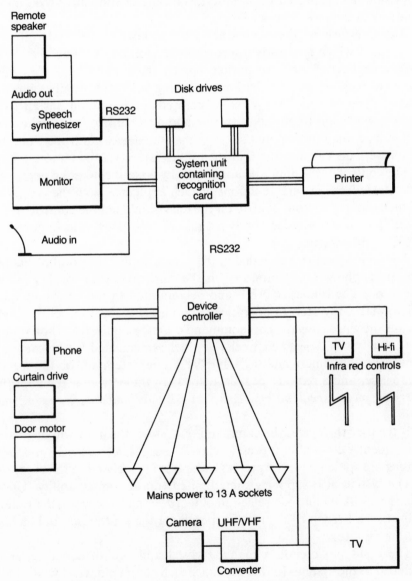

Figure 14.3   Block diagram of the VADAS system

card translates the spoken command into a numeric value plus H (high) or L (low). This is transmitted to the device controller via a serial interface. The device controller then latches the command so that it is not overwritten by subsequent commands and operates the relevant relay driver to turn on the required device, in this case the heater. (In the prototype version all mains power switching is accomplished via relay drives and hard wiring to the relevant devices, control of the hi-fi and television being effected via an interface to the existing infra-red remote controllers for these devices.)

The interface to the telephone is a special case. In order to use equipment which is already approved it is necessary to interface to the telephone keypad only such that signals from the device controller simulate picking up the telephone, pushing the recall number button, and entering the code for a previously stored number. In this instance the neatest solution is to provide a remote audio I/O link to the telephone to a standard, plug-in 'remote talker' so that the device controller initiates or answers the call and the user then talks/listens via the remote talker.

The control of the domestic appliances by voice includes the operation of almost all the normal functions of each appliance, with the exception of such things as colour control on the television and tone control on the hi-fi. These were excluded purely because of time constraints imposed on building the system.

The security camera included in the system supports an audio channel (the microphone being mounted in the camera) to the speaker in the television. The camera is VHF and is connected to the television via a UHF/VHF converter. In operation, upon hearing the doorbell, the user speaks the word *camera*. This command switches on the television (if it is not already on), selects channel 12 (which is dedicated to the camera), powers on the camera and the UHF/VHF converter and, via the speech synthesiser and a remote speaker, delivers to the person at the door the message, *please speak into the camera your name and the purpose of your visit.*

If the user then gives the command *front door;* the door will open and subsequently close after a preset delay. Messages *door opening* and *door closing* are spoken via the speech synthesiser and echoed to the monitor.

The system also supports some limited translation capability. Upon the user speaking one of a selection of words or short phrases, the system delivers the French equivalent as speech via the synthesiser and as text via the monitor.

The ability to dictate a highly stylised and pre-formatted letter is included in the system. In this example, each command word which may be used relates to a block of text held in memory in the computer or on disk. Within each group of such commands each related block of text contains the same number of characters so that the blocks of text are interchangeable within the letter without the need to re-format or edit. During construction of the letter the text is displayed on the monitor and is output to the printer on the user's command. Although in this prototype version the letter under construction was not read back to the user via the speech synthesiser, the ability to do so is inherent in the system.

Use of relatively few commands to produce a letter in this way is only possible when the content and format of the letter are confined within certain predefined parameters and when the constituent parts, and possibly some of the software, are user-defined. At its most basic level, a single spoken command could produce an entire letter, provided that the letter already exists as an entity in memory or on disk.

MODIFYING THE SYSTEM FOR PRODUCTION

Clearly, this prototype system requires much modification to bring it to a state suitable for sale to the disabled. The first offering of this system will not include any letter dictation capability, the reason being that while very *simple* letters can be generated by a simple, and therefore inexpensive, program, the extremely wide range of requirements for letter content dictates that any program catering for a reasonable range of content will be extremely complex, and therefore expensive. Should any user wish to create a 'dictation' program then the source code for the system program will be made available.

The English-French translation function in the prototype will also be dropped in the production model, the constraints mentioned in relation to letter creation also applying to translation.

All the other functions of the prototype will be included in the production version and some of the functions will be expanded. The words used to control the system will be user-definable and therefore independent of the user's language. Suitable commands would be, for example, *lamp on* or *switch lamp off*, and in appropriate cases, *lamp*, to toggle between the two possible states. The system will control up to 100 outputs, bearing in mind that twenty to thirty are required for adequate control of a teletext television. The two hardware configurations shown in Figs. 14.4 and 14.5 will be available.

All mains power switching will be accomplished by the device controller transmitting signals in infra-red to a receiver plugged into the mains power circuit, the receiver then generating signals which are transmitted through the mains and detected by addressable sockets into which the devices to be switched are plugged. This has the advantage

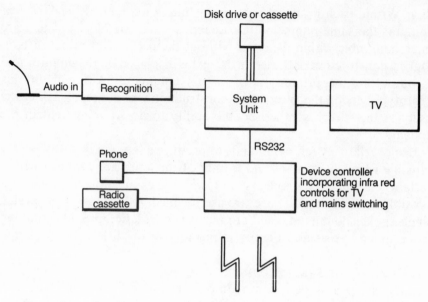

Figure 14.4   Production version of VADAS, with separate recogniser

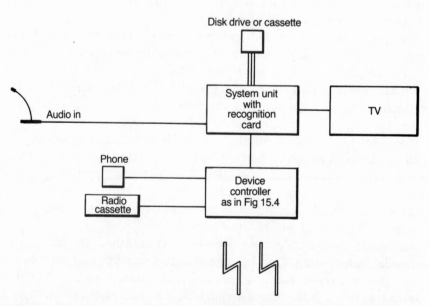

Figure 14.5   Production version of VADAS, with integrated recognisers

that devices in any part of the house or office may be switched from a single location, or, with the addition of an intercom system, or radio microphone, from many locations.

The interface between the telephone and the device controller will be hard-wired with control effected as in the prototype version, the telephone having a thirty-number memory. As an option, various other devices such as smoke detectors may be connected directly to the telephone.

The infra-red control of the hi-fi has been dropped in favour of a hard-wired interface to a radio cassette, remote control hi-fi systems being relatively expensive. As far as possible the total system will be modular in design and the addition of controls for such devices as door motors, curtain drives and solenoid latches will require minimal modification of the basic system. In the production system the television will double as monitor, although a separate monitor may be used, if required.

14.4 *Other design issues*

It may be seen from the description of these systems that although the voice control of the computer is readily available, the computer control of other systems, for example a radio cassette, is not always available in a form that is easy to integrate into the total system. Therefore any system or device which is currently computer-controlled can generally be adapted to voice control, whereas a system or device which is not already computer-controlled can only be adapted to voice control if the device or system is simultaneously adapted to computer control.

Over the next few years, certainly a proportion of consumer products, for example children's toys and telephones, will have speech recognition incorporated into them. However, the user will probably have to be physically close to any such product to operate it. If, for example, both a television and a reading lamp have incorporated within them a recognition chip which will respond to *turn on*, how will the user distinguish between the two? Although such products will have obvious benefits, there will still be a need, particularly for the disabled, for some centralised command facility for environmental control.

Returning to the present, for persons with certain specific disabilities there are some solutions already available as off-the-shelf packages, apart from those already mentioned. One example of such a package is voice recognition linked with voice response or speech synthesis. This is particularly suited to persons with severe speech impediments.

If the user is capable of consistent sound production, even if this speech is not intelligible to another human, it will be intelligible to a recognition device and may be used to control some action. Since, in this example, the user's speech may be unintelligible except to the machine, it would be useful to be able to control machine-produced speech. On recognition of perhaps a single word from the user, the system responds by speaking anything from one word to many sentences via speech synthesis.

Using voice response and assuming the user to be, say, a ten-year-old girl, then the words and messages to be spoken by the machine are previously digitally recorded, ideally by another ten-year-old girl. Systems offering this facility also offer the option of a telephone interface such that our ten-year-old user can carry on a limited conversation and make and receive telephone calls, using the voice of a ten-year-old girl.

The amount of storage required for digitally recorded messages lies in the range 500 bytes per second to 3 kbytes per second, depending on the required speech quality. Systems supporting voice store and forward can read such messages from disk and speak them without having first to read the whole message into memory. Comparing the storage capacity for digitally recorded speech with that of recognition templates (about 200 bytes per second), it is obvious that the ability to read messages from disk and at the same time to speak them is of primary importance in a voice response system.

The alternative method of producing spoken response, *speech synthesis from text*, uses a recognition to initiate the processing of a piece of previously stored text through a speech synthesiser, the output speech in this case sounding somewhat robotic. The major advantage of using the text-to-speech synthesiser method within the total speech system is the relatively small amount of storage needed for the text, although to achieve the best speech production the text must, in many cases, be purposely mis-spelt. In the case of both the digital voice response and the synthesis-from-text, the messages to be spoken by the system must be defined by the user and then digitally recorded or typed as appropriate. (The reader is referred to the companion book to this one, *Electronic Speech Synthesis*, for a full discussion of the subject of speech output.)

When the specific disability of a user is the inability to type on a keyboard then voice recognition, whether isolated word or continuous speech, may be used in many applications as a direct keyboard replacement, provided that the input to the computer from the recogniser is transparent to the computer. That is to say that any existing application program for the computer in question will run, without requiring any alterations, while it is receiving input from the recogniser. Recognition devices which function in this way allow the user to define a series of keystrokes to be associated with every word which is to be recognised. Subsequently, during operation, when a particular word is recognised, the keystrokes associated with that word are entered into the computer as if they had been typed on the keyboard. The number of keystrokes which may be associated with a spoken word usually lies in the range ten to forty, and may include more than one carriage return so that, for instance, one spoken command can duplicate a very complex keyboard command.

This last example illustrates the way in which a disabled person may use voice recognition to overcome his or her disability with no modification to a product which is already available for able-bodied users. As the use of voice recognition becomes more widespread throughout commerce and industry, so the capabilities of the systems which exist for able-bodied users will increasingly offer useful facilities to the disabled without the need for extensive modification. Furthermore, as such products proliferate they will, inevitably, decrease in price, to the benefit of all.

CHAPTER 15

VOICE INPUT APPLICATIONS IN AEROSPACE

Mike Taylor

In this chapter, the use of automatic speech recognition in the fields of avionics and space is explored.

15.1 *The man–machine interface in aerospace*

Shortly after man first showed it was possible to fly, advances in aircraft design enabled him to fly higher, faster and for longer periods of time. So rapid were these developments that it was not long before a stage was reached where pilots needed a more elaborate interpretation of the situation in which they were operating than was possible with their senses alone.

One of the earliest examples of a device which provided this interpretation was the length of string used by the Wright Brothers to indicate 'side slip', when flying their early aircraft. Devices were then developed with displays that were physically nearer to the pilot, such as the Smiths' tachometer in the 1912 B1 Blackburn aircraft (Fig. 15.1). Over the following years the performance of aircraft rapidly increased, giving rise to an even greater need for more information to be displayed to the aircrew.

An example of relatively recent high-density instrumentation may be seen on the flight deck (Fig. 15.2) of the Concorde supersonic transport. Although this is an advanced aircraft, the display methods are surprisingly conventional, being based on mechanical and electro-mechanical techniques.

MULTIFUNCTION KEYBOARDS AND DISPLAYS
With the advent of airborne *cathode ray tube* (CRT) displays, it has become possible to reduce the volume of information displayed at any

Figure 15.1 Cockpit instrumentation in a 1912 Blackburn B1 aircraft (*Reproduced by permission of Smiths Industries*)

Figure 15.2 Flight deck instrumentation in the Concorde supersonic transport (*Reproduced by permission of Smiths Industries*)

one time, while increasing the total spectrum of information which can be displayed. This has led to a new family of multifunction avionic 'flexible displays', such as the *Control Display Unit* (CDU) (Fig. 15.3), used in the Smiths Industries' Flight Management Computer System, on board the Airbus Industrie A310 commercial transport (Fig. 15.4). Another type of multifunction display is the *Electronic Flight Information System* (EFIS) now fitted to many of the world's commercial aircraft. A typical example is the EFIS (Fig. 15.5) fitted to the experimental BAC 1-11 operated by the Royal Aircraft Establishment (RAE) at Bedford, UK.

Whilst multifunction displays are recent additions to the civil flight deck, the American Space Shuttle has had *multifunction cathode ray tube display systems* (MCDS) fitted as standard equipment from its very inception.

Facilities for entering data and controlling displayed functions on multifunction displays have traditionally been in the form of edge keys,

Figure 15.3 Smiths Industries Control Display Unit (CDU) (*Reproduced by permission of Smiths Industries*)

Figure 15.4   Flight deck instrumentation in the A310 Airbus (*Reproduced by permission of Smiths Industries*)

Figure 15.5   Smiths Industries multifunction flight information displays as fitted to the experimental BAC 1-11 operated by RAE Bedford (*Reproduced by permission of Smiths Industries*)

often located close to the CRT display. In the case of the CDU, these keys are situated around the display face of the CRT (see Fig. 15.3).

As a flight progresses, or as keystrokes are executed, the functions attributable to each key may also change and are indicated to a user simply by a change of text displayed on the CRT near to each edge key.

The Space Shuttle MCDS, on the other hand, is currently controlled via oversize hexadecimal keyboards located remotely from the *Display Electronics Units* (DEU) (Fig. 15.6). This rather outmoded configuration is an attempt to overcome reduced manual dexterity caused by aircrew having to wear thick, bulky gloves as part of their space suit (Fig. 15.7).

OPERATIONAL DEFICIENCIES

Although multifunction keyboards such as the MCDS and CDU are finding increased usage, they can create problems of their own. These are largely because a system's response to a particular keystroke will generally depend on the previous sequence of keystroke entries. Likewise, the information in a particular field of a display will depend on the previous series of selections. Thus, whilst multifunction control/display devices can significantly reduce the tactile and visual search areas in

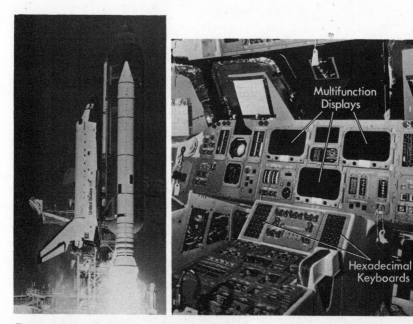

Figure 15.6 The flight deck of the American Space Shuttle showing the multifunction displays and hexadecimal keyboards. (*Inset: Space Shuttle Challenger.*) (*Reproduced by permission of Rockwell International and Smiths Industries*)

an aircraft cockpit, such devices can also create an increased mental workload through the need to remember both the correct sequence for information access and the means of controlling functions different to those already selected. Additionally, such devices are vulnerable in situations where short-term memory loss may be induced either through stress or extreme workloads.

The military are acutely aware of these problems, and are constantly searching for new techniques of command and control with particular emphasis on their possible integration into the tactical fighter aircraft cockpits of the 1990s. In this environment the probability of mission success and survival are being threatened by the excessive workloads which will be imposed on the pilots of single-crew aircraft. Ironically, some of this workload has been created by the very avionic subsystems which were designed to protect the pilot and aircraft. A need therefore exists for avionic companies and aerospace research organisations to explore ways of upgrading established techniques and to develop and prove new advanced concepts.

SPEECH – A NEW CHANNEL IN THE MAN–MACHINE INTERFACE

One of the most promising advanced concepts for controlling multifunction keys and displays is that of speech. Such a mode of control can lead to the concept of a 'virtual' keyboard where the number of individual

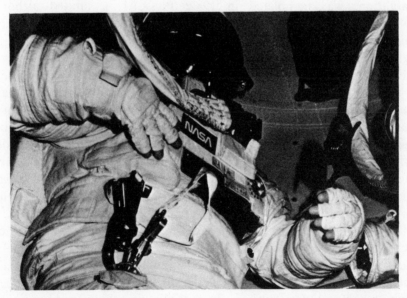

Figure 15.7   View of an astronaut wearing a space suit; note the bulky gloves. (*Reproduced by permission of NASA*)

keys is limited only by the size of the recogniser's vocabulary. The use of speech is not, however, only limited to multifunction key replacement, for it can be used in applications where ordinary keys or controls may not even be contemplated. Such applications are where the 'hands-on-stick' flying technique is fully utilised and no further hand movements may be contemplated, or where the 'head-up' concept rules out visual location of keys or switches.

15.2 *Applications in military avionics*

It is hardly surprising that defence applications have dominated the major avionic application trials of automatic speech recognition (ASR), or, as it is more commonly known in aviation circles, *direct voice input* (DVI).

AMERICAN PROJECTS

In America the combined US Air Force, Navy and NASA 'AFTI/F16' Advanced Fighter Technology Integrator has been spearheading trials of DVI. The US company, General Dynamics, for example, has been evaluating the use of DVI as an alternative method of interacting with the aircraft's on-board weapon systems[1]. They have structured an experimental programme consisting of three phases, of which the first two have already been completed. Phase 0, a laboratory simulation evaluation, was completed in 1982; Phase 1, a limited airborne environmental flight test which followed extensive ground simulations, was completed in August 1983, whilst Phase 2 will consist of functional flight tests.

Phase 1 verified the feasibility of using DVI in the harsh environment of a high-performance tactical fighter, and although the vocabulary consisted only of 34 words, these were sufficient to select the aircraft's four basic attack modes together with its navigation mode of operation. The edge keys surrounding the multifunction cockpit displays were also activated using vocal commands from the same 34-word vocabulary. The Phase 1 experiments additionally provided a rich source of speech data for future recogniser development and were recorded under varying noise levels of 96–110 dB and with varying load factors of 1–5 g.

Phase 2 of the experimental programme aims to optimise the pilot-cockpit interface to a stage where DVI is even more reliable and flexible than was demonstrated in Phase 1. This is an important step because the real value of DVI for the military will be when it is able to reduce critical function performance times, whilst still allowing the pilot to maintain the 'hands-on-stick', 'head-up' method of flying, and not just to replace a manual keystroke with a one-for-one vocal command. It has also become very clear from the AFTI studies that speech synthesis as well as recognition will be necessary if cockpit control is to be fully optimised.

EUROPEAN PROJECTS

In Europe, Crouzet[2] have been working on a system known as *Equipment Vocal pour Aéronef* (EVA). Development on the EVA began in 1978 and was supported by the Direction des Recherches Etudes et Techniques and the Service Technique des Télécommunications et Equipements Aéronautiques. This work was based on research carried out by the Centre National de Recherches Scientifiques for word recognition and voice synthesis.

Early studies at Crouzet were concerned with the laboratory analysis of airborne speech data which led to the development of the first EVA, which was subsequently evaluated during simulation tests at the Istres flight test centre (Fig. 15.8). The tests involved a partially simulated

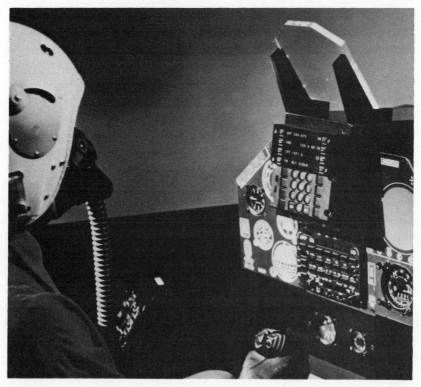

Figure 15.8 A mock-up of Crouzet's EVA (Equipment Vocal pour Aéronef or Aircraft Voice Command System) (*Reproduced with permission of Crouzet, Division 'Aérospatial'*)

interception mission, where the EVA system was used to test the voice command concept when applied to the pilot's management functions of radar and autopilot mode selection, *head-up display* (HUD) configuration, and system integration.

An isolated-word version of the EVA was first flown on 5th July 1982, on-board a single-seat French Air Force Dassault-Bréguet Mirage 3R fighter (see Fig. 15.9). This flight, from the Brétigny flight test centre, was considered to be a world-first using isolated-word DVI in a combat aircraft. The first phase of these flight tests was completed in July 1983 and included 40 missions flown by two French Air Force test pilots. The system was operated in flight conditions with airspeeds ranging from 180 knots to Mach 1.5 and with load factors approaching 5 g at altitudes up to 45 000 ft. At the end of the first series of tests, recognition rates of 95% to 96% were achieved with a system vocabulary consisting of a maximum of 30 words. This vocabulary was of sufficient size to allow the pilot to assess the value of DVI, when selecting UHF radio frequencies and commanding the Mirage's auto control system in the pitch and attitude modes. A later stage in the Crouzet programme is to have a connected-word version flying on-board a two-seat Mirage 3.

As with the US AFTI programme, all the French DVI speech data has been collected during the flight trials to provide a rich corpus for further research and development of airborne DVI systems.

UNITED KINGDOM PROJECTS

In the United Kingdom, automatic speech recognition trials are progressing at RAE Bedford and RAE Farnborough. Although the majority of military work is carried out at RAE Farnborough, the Wessex helicopter programme at RAE Bedford also has a military content and is described in greater detail in Section 15.3.

The research work at RAE Farnborough is concerned with DVI application trials and includes use in avionic system control and with advanced communications systems[3]. A flying test-bed is available to researchers at RAE Farnborough in the form of an experimental Buccaneer Mk. 2B aircraft. This aircraft has flown recently with a Marconi SR-128 connected-word recogniser which produced a 98% recognition success rate with isolated words, and 95% success with connected speech consisting of three digit strings. The trials were conducted at 550 knots at a height of 250 ft and in a cockpit noise-level of 115 dB.

During the forthcoming Phase 2 flying programme, the emphasis will be shifted from evaluation of recogniser performance to general in-flight applications of speech recognition.

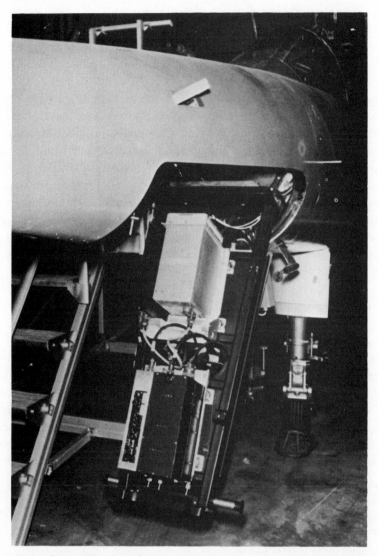

Figure 15.9   Crouzet's aircraft voice command system installed in the nose section of a French Air Force Dassault-Bréquet Mirage 3R. Included in the equipment is the system's voice interactive processor (bottom right on extended pallet), a test audio cassette recorder (bottom left on pallet) and a digital data recorder with power supply (top on pallet) (*Reproduced with permission of Crouzet, Division 'Aérospatial'*)

15.3 *Applications in civil avionics*

UNITED KINGDOM PROJECTS

Civil flight applications of DVI at the RAE have largely been focused on the work carried out at the Bedford site. Here, application trials include DVI experiments with a Wessex 2 helicopter and the RAE's experimental BAC 1-11.

The Operational Systems Division at RAE Bedford became involved in helicopter avionics through the need to investigate means of recovering helicopters to small ships in operationally stringent conditions. To this end they developed an integrated avionic helicopter cockpit suite, which in effect became a comprehensive prototype helicopter flight management system. The DVI component of the management system is used to control display formats, tune radio frequencies and select and change navigation waypoints. Using this system the pilot is able to control all systems from take-off to landing using only DVI, and is therefore able to keep his hands on the flight controls at all times. In operation the system has been shown to work well, and recoveries requiring the helicopter to hover alongside a manoeuvring ship in both simulated and actual visibilities down to 75 m have been successfully demonstrated during sea trials using the RAE Wessex helicopter.

The Civil Avionics Section at RAE Bedford operates the BAC 1-11 as a research aircraft, and has been running a DVI flight test programme since 1982. The aim of the programme is to assess the capabilities of DVI and its possible application to the civil flight deck. A significant milestone of the programme occurred on 26th August 1982 when the first flight took place in which connected-word DVI was used to control the Smiths Industries' EFIS. In this early application DVI was used to replace manual control of the 16 knobs and buttons associated with the navigation displays[4] (see Fig. 15.5). Recognition error rates of 2% using standard microphones have been reported; these are equivalent to those which may be expected from conventional keystroke methods of data entry and control.

Another application of DVI on the BAC 1-11 has been the operation of a Radio Management System in a real high-density Air Traffic Control environment. Recognition success rates of better than 90% for radio frequency instructions of the type *Box one – one two three decimal four five – enter* have been observed.

Work at Smiths Industries, Cheltenham, has focused on the development of an in-house speech recognition capability for both civil and military avionic applications. A demonstration rig has been built (Fig.

15.10) which has been used for assessment trials and for recogniser development[5]. The demonstrator uses a CDU as a means of controlling an Aircraft Navigation and Management System. Connected/continuous DVI is used as an enhancement to existing keyboard procedures and allows flight data pages to be accessed and data to be entered without the need for keystroke actions. Initial studies show that on the commercial flight deck, the greatest benefits may occur when multiple keystroke procedures are replaced by non-standard DVI procedures. Such procedures will bypass the multiple keystrokes required in the

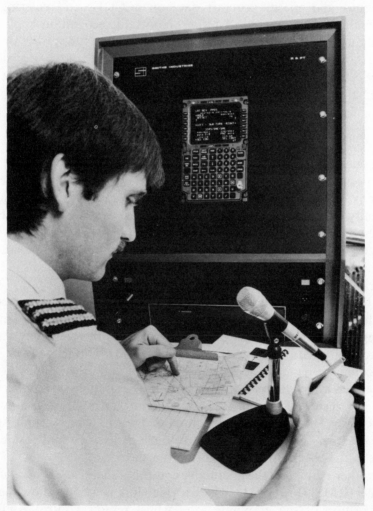

Figure 15.10 Smiths Industries Aircraft Navigation and Management System DVI demonstrator (*Reproduced by permission of Smiths Industries*)

manual mode of operation, hence giving rise to vastly improved transaction times.

AMERICAN PROJECTS

A recent study[6], conducted by the Boeing Aircraft Company and sponsored by the NASA Langley Research Center, investigated the potential application of speech recognition and synthesis/playback on the commercial flight deck. The researchers found that recognition systems could be rated as most beneficial when used to interrogate some of the more complex flight deck systems; examples include the selection of menus and specific aircraft data on a CDU, and entering new information when desired. Another important recognition application was thought to be that of entering necessary data to tune radios or to set navigation waypoints. Although speech was seen to provide a method for selecting switch or mode positions, it was thought to offer only marginal benefits when used on the civil flight deck.

15.4 *Applications in space*

UNITED STATES SPACE SHUTTLE

Two possible applications of DVI have already been identified in earlier sections of this chapter, namely the use of speech to overcome the difficulty of making accurate keystrokes whilst wearing bulky space suit gloves, and secondly, to allow a greater number of 'virtual' keys to be immediately available to the user. However, it is still worth examining specific high workload situations[7] where DVI could make a significant contribution to overall efficiency.

A typical example might be where a system failure had occurred and the shuttle crew had to consult the bulky flight data file for guidance on testing procedures. As part of these procedures the crew may have to extract information about the failed system via the MCDS. Such procedures on a conventional transport flight deck cause difficulties, but in the even more cramped environment of the shuttle's cockpit, coupled with the disadvantage of zero gravity, they may be severe or even intolerable. Therefore, if speech could be used to page system displays, crew members could rapidly complete check lists without losing their place in the check list or even losing the checklist itself!

Another example is the interactive control of the *Remote Manipulating System* (RMS) (Fig. 15.11), where a video link is used to show the crew the position of the grappling arm, whilst remote control is effected through an actuator situated in the shuttle's aft workstation. In this configuration it may prove beneficial to have the option of hands-free

Figure 15.11 A view of part of *Challenger's* Remote Manipulating System (RMS) (upper right portion of photo), viewed towards the rear of the Shuttle's cargo bay. An astronaut is also seen near the RMS using a Manned Manouvering Unit (MMU), conducting Extra Vehicular Activity (EVA) (*Reproduced by permission of NASA*)

interaction with the actuator using DVI, particularly if control is also to be achieved by an astronaut performing *extra vehicular activity* (EVA).

The proposed manned US space station may also have requirements for DVI, some of which have recently been described by researchers from Rockwell International[8]. The major advantage of using DVI in the space station would be to reduce transaction time between crew members and their respective workstations; a reduction here would provide clear financial benefits, as crew time has been estimated to cost in the region of $15 000 per hour.

An advanced DVI system for interacting with on-board systems and experiments has also been described, and consists of a microphone, headset and miniaturised head-up display (HUD) all mounted inside a helmet. Such a system is capable of providing both acoustic and visual cueing and feedback to the wearer. Furthermore, the wearer would not have to be tied to a particular location to use the system, as communication to the helmet could be effected through a radio frequency or infra-red link.

Another potential application for DVI in space is with the *Orbital Maneuvering Unit* (OMU) envisaged for development as part of the US space station. The purpose of the OMU is to enable tasks, including repairs, to be performed outside the space station. These tasks would be aided by the use of a dexterous manipulator attached to the OMU and controlled either by astronauts within the space station or by those performing EVA. In the case of EVA astronauts, it is possible that speech could be the only free channel available for control of the manipulator, particularly when their manual capacity for control is already overloaded in the guidance of their own manned manoeuvring units. A solution to the EVA problem of manipulator control therefore seems to be DVI, and if this was combined with the interactive helmet described earlier, it would also allow the astronaut to perform external interactive maintenance checks using DVI to access the space station's maintenance database.

15.5 *Conclusions*

Although electronic speech recognition remains at a very primitive stage, the last five years have witnessed significant leaps in the evolutionary process. No longer are recognition systems the sole preserve of research laboratories requiring massive main-frame computers, and no longer are recognisers limited to isolated-word performance. Algorithm development, coupled with new high-performance microprocessors and digital signal-processing devices, have enabled stand-alone real-time systems to be developed, some of which achieve real-time performance using a single 16/32-bit microprocessor[9]. However, perhaps more significant than the development of the hardware itself is the effort which has been channelled into identifying possible applications of DVI. This is particularly true in the field of Aerospace where additional effort by ergonomists and system designers has been used to match the recognition system to the needs of the aircrew[10].

The results of application trials to date show that DVI in Aerospace may be regarded as a successful additional and alternative mode of command and control, with virtually every aircrew participant reporting a positive and enthusiastic response to its use.

15.6 *Acknowledgements*

The author wishes to express his sincere gratitude for the helpful advice and abundant photographs provided by: the United States National Aeronautics and Space Administration (NASA), Rockwell International, Crouzet Division Aérospatial, the Royal Aircraft Establishments at Farnborough and Bedford, and Smiths Industries.

Particular thanks are also due to the staff at the Royal Aircraft Establishments at Bedford and Farnborough and to the staff within the Marketing Department at Smiths Industries for their constructive contributions towards the final script.

15.7 *References*

1. Moore, C.A., Moore, R.D., and Ruth, J.C. (1984) 'Applications of voice interactive systems – military flight test and the future'. *Proceedings AIAA/IEEE 6th Digital Avionics Systems Conference*, December 3–7, Baltimore, Maryland, USA. 301–308.
2. Melocco, J.M. (1984) 'Voice command on combat aircraft'. *Military Technology*. Electronics in Defence, MILTECH 6/84 44–46.
3. Anon (1985) 'UK flies voice-control'. *Flight International*. Avionics, February 9, 17.
4. Cooke, N. (1984) 'The flight testing and system integration of direct voice input devices in the civil flight deck'. *Colloquium on Speech Input/Speech Output*. March 30th, IERE, The Royal Institution, London.
5. Taylor, M.R. (1984) 'DVI and its role in future avionic systems', *Proceedings 1st International Conference on Speech Technology*. October 23–25, Brighton, UK. 113–120.
6. White, R.W., Parks, D.L., and Smith, W.D. (1984) 'Potential flight applications for voice recognition and synthesis systems'. *Proceedings AIAA/IEEE 6th Digital Avionics Systems Conference*. December 3–7, Baltimore, Maryland, USA. 1–5.
7. Hoskins, J.W. (1984) 'Voice I/O in the space shuttle'. *Speech Technology*. August/September, 13–18.
8. Castiglione, D., and Goldman, J. (1984) 'Voice I/O could dramatically improve the efficiency of a space station crew'. *Speech Technology*. August/September, 19–27.
9. Taylor, M.R. (1984) 'A microprocessor implementation of a speaker-trained isolated-word recognition system'. MPhil thesis, to be published by *University Microfilms International (UMI)*, White Swan House, Godstone, Surrey, RM9 8LW, UK.
10. Jones, D., Frankish, C., Starr, A., Taylor, M.R., and Richardson, I. (1985) 'Matching the machine to man – the human factor issues in voice input'. *Voice Processing Online Conference*. May 8–9, London, UK.

CHAPTER 16

TOWARDS THE 'TALKWRITER'

William S. Meisel

In this chapter, the feasibility of the voice-activated typewriter is examined in the light of the real needs and aspirations of the user.

16.1 *Market need and technical feasibility*

WHAT IS A TALKWRITER?

Much interest has been expressed in the possibility of producing a large-vocabulary speech-to-text system which can transcribe unrestricted natural speech into text, mainly for use within the business environment. A user might dictate a memo into such a system and see the text of the memo appear as he dictates. Various generic names have been proposed for such a system; 'voice-activated typewriter' has been a common term. Recently the term *talkwriter* has become popular; we will adopt this term.

Talkwriters are under development, but it is unlikely that any will be commercially available before this book is published. Since the characteristics users need in a talkwriter, the technology required to build a talkwriter, and the feasibility of that technology in the next few years, are all controversial, the conclusions of this chapter must be speculative.

This discussion will emphasise the application of talkwriter technology to the user's needs rather than the technology itself. It will, however, discuss how the application drives the technological requirements and distinguishes the requirements of a speech-to-text system from those of other speech recognition applications.

MOTIVATION FOR TALKWRITER DEVELOPMENT

Speech recognition industry market analysts believe that the user's most common motivation for buying and using a talkwriter will be to minimise the use of keyboards. Talkwriters are unlikely ever to *replace* keyboards, but they are likely to relieve the keyboard bottleneck for text input.

The most exciting benefit of talkwriter technology may be its potential to stimulate human productivity and creativity. Frederick Jelinek, who heads the continuous-speech recognition group at International Business Machines Corp.(IBM), made this point eloquently in a 1982 report:

'Speech recognition will eliminate the bottleneck between the conception of a task and its completion.

A person who has a letter to write or a book to publish dictates to a machine, which displays immediately its reaction to what it has heard. If there is an error, the speaker corrects it on the spot. Text generation is completed and recompleted at will, at the speaker's convenience. Privacy is total. Control is absolute. This particular mode of symbiosis with a machine will open horizons of efficiency, productivity and satisfaction, and expand human capacity for intellectual work.'

It is likely that the talkwriter will make substantial changes in the way we communicate, analyse, and create.

The talkwriter may encourage users to demand and use speech recognition in applications that, in themselves, do not seem cost-effective enough to exploit. A user of a talkwriter may wonder why he can't search his telephone directory by voice or enter an appointment on a computerised calendar (see Chapter 14). A talkwriter might provide unanticipated benefits in simple applications with minimal incremental cost and training.

FEASIBILITY

Is a talkwriter feasible? Some companies claim that they will be able to deliver units for testing in 1986, while other experts don't expect a practical unit until the 1990s or later. Part of the controversy results from different requirements and expectations for an acceptable talkwriter. The more extreme requirements include continuous speech, speaker-independence, an active vocabulary in excess of 20 000 words, and the ability to resolve ambiguities by understanding what was intended, much as a human secretary might.

While some of these objectives are useful long-term targets, they may not be prerequisites for commercial success. Later sections of this chapter will propose some of the tradeoffs involved in specifying a practical and technically achievable system. It is the author's contention that worthwhile products can be implemented at the current time by close analysis of the user's actual requirements.

Some sceptics also argue that success in applying speech recognition to simpler applications is a necessary prerequisite to success in the talkwriter application. They argue that applications such as Voice Data Entry (*VDE*) have been commercial, if not technical, failures, and they ask how a talkwriter can be expected to succeed where applications requiring only small vocabularies have failed.

We must separate the technical and commercial issues. Whilst the *technical* feasibility of VDE products and of talkwriters may be related, the *commercial* viability of each is independent of the other.

THE TALKWRITER PROBLEM COMPARED TO VOICE DATA ENTRY

The VDE problem is greater in several ways than the speech-to-text problem. The most significant difference is the acceptable error rate. If a user is asked the number of errors he will tolerate in a VDE application, he will typically reply, 'None!', because normally he has no context with which to judge which entries are wrong. Error rates as low as 0.1% are often targeted, but they are usually achieved only by audio or visual feedback to the user. It is arguable whether a user can speak with such accuracy over extended periods of time.

In a speech-to-text application, the system creates a rough draft of dictated speech which will usually be edited by the user or by an assistant (such as a secretary). The tolerable error rate is considerably higher, both because the user will normally expect to revise the text, and because errors can be found and corrected from context. In such an application, an error rate of 5% is probably acceptable, and there are some indications that even higher error rates will be tolerable[1]. The difference between the targeted error rate of the two applications could therefore be a factor of 50 or more.

The objective of a speech-to-text system without a real-time edit-as-you-go feature should be a rough draft. If interaction is allowed for correction, a 'first-time' final approach may be possible. In any case, accuracy objectives do not approach the accuracy limits of some VDE applications.

There are other important differences. For example, in industrial VDE applications, the end-user is often not motivated to make the application a success; VDE is often forced upon a worker who is accustomed to doing things differently. In the talkwriter application, we expect that the end-user will typically be motivated by self-interest.

On the other hand, the difficulties of the talkwriter approach are well known, particularly when features include continuous speech. Larger vocabularies make the discrimination problem more difficult, since they increase the number of similar words. In transcribing normal dictated speech, one cannot choose vocabularies to eliminate easily confused words, as is often done in VDE. For example, three of the most common words in the English language, *the*, *a*, and *of*, are all pronounced similarly when unstressed (/ðə/, /ə/, /əv/ – see Chapter 2 for details). Indeed, they are usually unstressed in continuous speech and are often co-articulated with adjacent words. Yet one can expect that at least one of every fifteen words in typical English speech will be one of these words.

VDE and talkwriter systems present different technical difficulties and address different markets. The feasibility or practicality of one is not directly related to the feasibility or practicality of the other.

16.2 *What type of recognisers should be used?*

ISOLATED-WORD VERSUS CONTINUOUS-SPEECH RECOGNITION
Isolated-word speech requires pauses between words; continuous speech is natural speech. Most people would prefer to be able to use continuous speech. Since this is significantly more difficult to recognise, however, the issue becomes that of whether the user will be willing to use isolated-word speech if it is the only option, or if it yields a cheaper or more accurate system.

Researchers at IBM[2] simulated a talkwriter in continuous and isolated-word mode. Their conclusions, in part, were that, 'Isolated-word speech with large vocabularies may be nearly as good as connected-speech systems for a listening typewriter'.

The tolerance of isolated-word speech by the potential users surveyed may be related to the fact that the major impediment to dictating material is the process of composition, and not the rate of speech, of the user[3]. Perhaps users can more easily tolerate pausing while speaking because they must already pause for thought while composing.

But the conclusions reached in the IBM paper must be put into context. First, the study dealt with letters, as opposed to longer memos. Interference with the composition process by isolated-word speech might present a less severe obstacle to the composition process in a short letter than it would in a longer document.

Second, the users in the study were asked to correct erroneous or unidentified words as they went along. In isolated-word mode, the user would correct a word immediately after speaking it. In continuous-speech mode, the user would have to backtrack, correct the erroneous word, and repeat the remainder of the sentence. This could have led to a bias against the continuous-speech mode that was not intrinsic to the mode of speaking.

Third, the study subjects were allowed to make written notes. The degree to which they composed a sentence or letter in writing before dictating was not reported. One could conceivably outline a brief letter to the extent that the process of dictating was close to reading.

Practical experience suggests a further objection to the conclusions of the IBM study. Even in VDE applications, where one might expect isolated-word speech to be quite appropriate, experience has suggested that speaking in isolated words for long periods is very tiring. As a result, vendors are moving towards continuous-speech systems for VDE, even at a cost penalty[4]. The fact that the subjects in the IBM study did not have to use the system on a continuing basis may have introduced another form of bias. One suspects that a user will tolerate considerably more inconvenience in a short-time test than in daily use.

Isolated-word speech is, of course, slower than continuous speech. Isolated-word speech is likely to force the user to think about *how he is speaking* rather than *what he is saying*. To be practical, then, an isolated-word system must provide a price and/or accuracy advantage to compensate for its ease-of-use disadvantages.

SPEAKER-DEPENDENT VERSUS SPEAKER-INDEPENDENT RECOGNISERS

A speaker-independent system would not require enrolment, but would pay a price in accuracy. Any speaker-dependent system requires some form of enrolment. There are several approaches:

(*1*) *Full enrolment*: Each user must say every word in the vocabulary, perhaps several times. Full enrolment may be required by some word-model (e.g. template-matching) approaches; any word spoken, but not enrolled, in word-model systems will result in an error or a blank.

(*2*) *Continuing enrolment*: Requirements for a long initial enrolment can be reduced by first enrolling a user on the most common words. As other words are needed, the user stops his dictation to enrol the needed word. (This approach would be consistent with a design that would allow the user to adjust the vocabulary as he uses the talkwriter – see Section 16.3.)

(*3*) *Extrapolative enrolment*: The system collects a representative set of words and phrases and then extrapolates from the limited enrolment vocabulary to a larger vocabulary. This does not require enrolling the speaker on all the words in the vocabulary. The ultimate extension of extrapolative enrolment is *vocabulary-independent* enrolment; in this approach, one initial enrolment process is all that is ever required, even if new words are later added to the vocabulary.

16.3 *Vocabulary and syntax*

CHOICE OF VOCABULARY SIZE

About 75% of typical text is covered by the 1000 most frequently used words. About 95% of text is covered by the most frequently used 5000 words. Beyond the most common 5000 words, the specific words used vary widely with the user's environment. The IBM study mentioned above[2] also measured user acceptance with 1000 words and with an unlimited number of words in the vocabulary. Letters could be dictated with 1000 words, but subjects preferred the unlimited vocabulary.

The vocabulary size issue is not simply one of picking a magic number that will provide 'enough' words. In a given memo, the user may need to use several times a word that he otherwise almost never uses; he will be frustrated if he can't use it. On the other hand, he will be annoyed if a word he does not expect to use often appears as an error in his text.

The relative frequency of words makes this problem worse. In an unpublished study at Speech Systems Inc., a corpus of 101 517 words of business text from representative sources was analysed. There were 9478 distinct words. The most frequent 2137 of these words accounted for 87.5% of the word occurrences in the corpus. Less-frequent words occurred no more than five times each – about once every 20 300 words, or once every 80 full pages of text. This rapid drop-off in frequency makes the choice of a fixed vocabulary difficult.

Keeping many words around for infrequent use lowers accuracy, as another IBM study[5] demonstrated. A body of text from business sources included 5000 distinct words. A 2000-word recogniser and a 5000-word recogniser were tested against this corpus. The 2000 words used by the 2000-word recogniser were the most frequent 2000 words in the corpus. The 2000-word recogniser was, of course, always incorrect when one of the 3000 words not in the 2000-word vocabulary occurred, but those 3000 words occurred much less frequently than the 2000 in the recogniser. The 5000-word recogniser had a chance to get all words correct, but made more errors on the 2000 most frequently occurring words. As a result, the overall accuracy was essentially the same. The study concluded that there would be no significant benefit in producing a 5000-word recogniser unless the accuracy of that recogniser was improved.

VARIABLE VOCABULARY SIZE

Several options could be offered which would have the effect of allowing a variable vocabulary size:

(1) Bias the recogniser by word frequency.

If the recogniser is biased to favour recognising words that occur most frequently, it will be difficult, but possible, to make the system recognise infrequently occurring words. Unfortunately, this may be equivalent to eliminating the less-frequent words as vocabulary size expands.

(2) Display a phonetic spelling of words not matching the vocabulary.

If no high-probability match to a word is found, make the recogniser analyse it phonetically and spell it as it sounds. Then a human editor can determine the intended word and insert it. While this in effect allows an infinite vocabulary size, it has the disadvantage of requiring editing. It also creates technical problems: for example, if syntax or statistical expectations of word order are used in the analysis, the unknown word may be difficult to deal with.

(3) Spelling.

If a 'spelling mode' is allowed, the infrequent word may be spelt.

(4) Temporary or permanent word addition.

The user, as he dictates, may be able to add a word to the permanent vocabulary or to a temporary vocabulary, using either oral spelling or a keyboard. This may be necessary to avoid user frustration, although it would certainly interfere to some degree with the creative process. It may also cause problems with a syntax or word-pattern analysis.

(5) Automatic vocabulary adaptation.

It is possible to make the system forget words not used frequently, and make it easier to recognise those that have been used or added recently.

The problem of vocabulary size and user control of vocabulary will be a challenging issue for talkwriter designers.

SYNTAX, SEMANTICS, AND WORD-ORDER EXPECTATIONS

No human language, including English, has *unrestricted* syntax, although natural English syntax is complex and poorly specified. Certain word sequences or sentence constructions are highly unlikely. We will refer to all forms of word-order expectation as 'syntax' for the sake of brevity.

Syntax is likely to be used by all designers of talkwriters in order to enhance accuracy and resolve ambiguities that cannot be resolved acoustically (e.g. *to*, *two*, *too*). The IBM case study testing accuracy with a 2000-word recogniser[5] provides an example of the enhanced accuracy syntax can provide. In that study, error rate was 20.3% without syntax and 2.5% with syntax.

Syntax cannot be ignored, but it poses difficult choices to talkwriter designers. Will a repeated word or bad grammar cause errors to propagate? How much discipline must be imposed on the user? Should sentence terminators (e.g. *full-stop, question mark*) be determined from context or delineated in some way (e.g. a button press)? Talkwriter performance will be significantly influenced by the approach designers take to the problem of syntax.

16.4 *Speed and accuracy*

WHAT ACCURACY DOES THE USER NEED?

It is difficult to compare accuracies of speech recognition systems (see Chapter 13). Accuracy depends on the speaker's characteristics, his motivation, his familiarity with the system, the vocabulary size and content, the mode of speaking (isolated versus continuous), the effectiveness of the enrolment strategy, background noise, the degree of restriction of the syntax, and the amount of time allowed for processing the speech. Thus, it may not be practical to compare speech recognition systems on the basis of *claimed* accuracy.

On the other hand, a user can observe the accuracy he is getting from a particular system under the conditions of his use. The accuracy he perceives must be sufficient to provide a benefit over alternative means of transforming thoughts to text.

The benefits can be speed, convenience, cost savings, or effectiveness. By 'effectiveness' I mean a lack of interference with the process of composition. The result of effective transcription may not be faster production of a document, but rather, a *better* document.

Alternative means of creating text include conventional dictation (face-to-face or with a tape recorder), handwriting and transcription, or typing directly. The disadvantages of each method will be differently weighted by different users. A poor typist will place a high premium on avoiding the keyboard. A user with poor handwriting will find alternatives to handwriting attractive. Standard dictation is usually an option only for those users having a secretary who can spare the time for transcription. Each method interferes with the composition process in a different way.

No alternative to a talkwriter produces error-free results, so a talkwriter need not be perfect to compete. At the same time, the proliferation of word-processing makes editing easier. Thus, the accuracy required of a talkwriter must be considered in the total context of the effectiveness and efficiency of the entire thought-to-text process and the totality of tools available for this process.

The task at hand also affects the accuracy required. A rough draft of meeting notes or ideas can be less accurate than a letter. Technically, it is possible to choose to some degree among speed, accuracy, and vocabulary size. Letting the user control these tradeoffs will allow him to choose the accuracy needed for a given task.

Answers to a question on a survey conducted by Speech Systems Inc. suggest another aspect of the acceptability of a system producing rough drafts. The question asked: 'If you could dictate your thoughts and notes, and have them transcribed by machine, would you use them in rough draft form?'. Eighty-seven per cent of the respondents indicated 'yes' to that question. It seems clear that an important application of a speech-to-text system would be to aid memory and composition by allowing the user to get a rough draft of facts or ideas down on paper. These rough notes would not necessarily even be retyped.

ACCEPTABLE ERROR RATES

The basic criteria for usefulness are, first, whether the resulting text can be read and understood and, second, whether it can be corrected easily and efficiently enough to make the talkwriter an attractive alternative to other thought-to-text systems. Speech Systems Inc. (SSI) performed a study[1] to attempt to estimate accuracy levels required for human correction of talkwriter-produced text, and to determine what level of error might cause a total inability to use context for correction. The study also examined how quickly different levels of error could be corrected.

The test was conducted using text with errors that might be created by machine transcription. Taking into account linguistic similarities among words, a linguist at SSI simulated the type of errors that might be caused by acoustic similarities among words. The text was a relatively difficult discussion of aspects of office automation and was not familiar to the transcribers. Seven transcriptionists were drawn from a temporary help agency. The agency estimated them to be evenly distributed over skill levels. Results were relatively consistent among all the transcriptionists: the error rate of the corrected text was roughly half the original error rate before correction. This was true even for very low error rates.

One would expect to find an error rate beyond which the errors became more difficult to correct because too much of the necessary context had disappeared. There was no clear evidence of such an effect up to the 15% error rate, the maximum included in the study.

The amount of time required to edit the material was also monitored. The editing time per 100 words of text tended to rise rather slowly through the 11% error-rate range, then rose more quickly between the 11% and 15% error rate. This figure suggests a possible disintegration-of-context effect, but not a pronounced one. Overall, the results suggest that a product may be feasible with an error rate of 15%; improvements beyond that figure improve its effectiveness to the user proportionately.

SPEED OF CONVERSION FROM SPEECH TO TEXT

It is often assumed that to be commercially successful a talkwriter must operate in real time. This assumes that the user can benefit from machine transcription only if he can see his dictation immediately – an assumption that does not seem wholly reasonable. Conventional dictation requires waiting for the result. Companies with large dictation pools or the equivalent would provide a market if they could avoid hiring additional personnel and still obtain comparable or better turnaround time from machine transcription than that required for human transcription. On the other hand, enabling the user to see the text shortly after speaking would give a talkwriter a major advantage over conventional dictation.

The time for a secretary to transcribe dictation on tape is typically 3–5 times the length of the material on the tape, allowing time for the transcriptionist to stop or rewind the tape. Since a machine is willing to work around the clock, it is reasonable to estimate that a machine working within ten times real time might be on the edge of commercial viability if other performance figures were acceptable.

As the transcription gets to within three times real time, it becomes practical to deliver the text immediately to the end-user. In dictation one pauses to think, and interruptions are part of any office environment. During these pauses and interruptions, the machine can catch up.

Real-time transcription is a desirable, but not absolute, requirement for a commercial speech-to-text system. A compromise would be to allow the user to choose between a quick 'rough draft' or a slower 'polished draft'.

16.5 *The evolving role of the talkwriter*

THE TALKWRITER AS A MULTI-FUNCTION DEVICE

The talkwriter application *justifies* a fairly costly system; it *requires* a high-performance speech recognition capability. A user who has this high-performance speech recogniser will want to be able to use it for applications other than transcribing text. Talkwriter designers can and should design systems which can support these other applications.

For example, Speech Systems Incorporated has designed a special handset for the talkwriter application which includes a 'command' button. When the command button is pressed, the system will interpret the spoken utterance as a command rather than as text. This button allows switching of applications by voice without requiring a syntactical analysis to decide if a command was spoken. This simple feature allows the smooth integration of several voice applications.

A key example of other likely applications for a talkwriter is in an Artificial Intelligence (AI) interface. Most AI systems use a natural language interface where the interaction is by keyboard. This allows relatively unstructured commands by the user, but can involve a great deal of typing. Since such systems typically also ask questions to resolve ambiguities, a user could become annoyed with the amount of typing required. A speech recognition component could minimise that problem.

16.6 *Conclusion*

This chapter has covered some of the technical and human-factor tradeoffs involved in satisfying the user's needs in a talkwriter product. Time will resolve most of the issues raised in this chapter – probably with the appearance of a multiplicity of approaches. Users will vote with their chequebooks for those that provide the greatest benefit. The author expects that many will vote to use the talkwriter as an important tool to enhance human creativity and effectiveness.

16.7 *References*

1. Meisel, W.S. (1984) 'Speech-to-text systems – the users' needs'. *Proceedings of the First International Conference on Speech Technology* 23–25 October, Brighton, UK.
2. Gould, J.D., Conti, J., and Hovanyecz, T. (1983) 'Composing letters with a simulated listening typewriter'. *Communications of the ACM* **26**(4) 295–308.
3. Gould, J.D. (1978) 'How experts dictate'. *Journal of Experimental Psychology; Human Perception and Performance* 4.4 648–661.
4. Ross, S., and MacAllister, J. (1984) 'Practical and continous speech recognition'. *Computer Design* 15 June 69–76.
5. Bahl, L.R. *et al.* (1984) 'Some experiments with large-vocabulary isolated-word sentence recognition'. *Proceedings of the 1984 International Conference on Acoustics, Speech and Signal Processing* (IEEE Cat. No. 84CH1945-5) March, 2 26.5, San Diego, California, USA.

CHAPTER 17

SPEECH INPUT TO COMPUTER SYSTEMS

G. Rigoll, B. Kornmesser and K. P. Faehnrich

In this chapter, an organisation with some experience of driving voice input/output systems from host computers presents some of the issues involved.

17.1 *Applications for computer systems with speech*

In many industrial applications where speech input or output may be advantageous, a large minicomputer or main-frame computer may already be present. This machine will probably be hosting the main application programs which are controlling the equipment, for example, in a manufacturing environment.

In such cases, it is most expedient to interface the speech sub-system directly to the host computer, and perhaps to integrate the use of speech prompts and input into the structure of the application program.

Some such applications that have been piloted at the *Fraunhofer-Institut für Arbeitswirtschaft und Organisation* in Stuttgart, Germany, are in quality control, numerically-controlled machine programming, and robotics.

QUALITY CONTROL
One application which has been studied is that of voice input/output technology in the quality control of car manufacture.

Before the introduction of speech I/O, the man concerned with the final acceptance used to walk around the vehicle and note all detected faults. This data was then entered through a standard terminal into the main computer system for further processing.

The decision was made to introduce a combined voice input/output device with wireless microphone. The voice output was used for acoustical feedback to the user. Detected faults were then entered directly into the main computer system using voice input. Detours to an extra terminal were no longer necessary.

NUMERICALLY-CONTROLLED MACHINE PROGRAMMING

Another application was concerned with the connection of voice input/output devices to NC (numerically-controlled) machine programming systems.

The software for programming NC machines is often menu-driven. Functions are selected by activating the proper fields in a menu which are stepped through successively using the cursor keys. A voice input system was introduced, which enabled the user to enter numerical data without having to look up from a list. Menu steps could also be controlled by voice. A speech synthesis board was used for error messages, not for repetition of entered commands, and the input and output data were transferred by separate channels.

ROBOT CONTROL

A *DEA PRAGMA 3000* robot was fitted with voice input for demonstration purposes.

The robot was connected to a voice input system. This was not difficult because the robot was controlled by a computer with an RS 232 interface. The robot then responded to verbal commands such as *turn right*, *up*, and *stop*. The required control sequences were entered into the recognition subsystem and were transferred to the robot after the corresponding word had been recognised. It was found that the application of a speech input unit to a robot improves the interaction when the person who controls the robot has to move away from the control panel. He can also always keep an eye on the robot while entering commands.

17.2 *The principles of interfacing speech to computers*

Modern computers are most useful when their computational capabilities are combined with powerful access methods. Therefore man–machine interaction in natural language has become an important subject in computer applications[1]. Speech input/output can assist casual users who are not acquainted with command syntax as well as experienced users, who then have an additional channel of access to the computer.

The eventual aim, then, is to provide for computer access for casual users with methods similar to those in interaction between human beings, whilst allowing more versatile access for experienced users.

A simple model of a natural language interface using visual and manual methods of interaction as well as speech input/output (without elaborate syntactic or semantic rules) is outlined in Fig. 17.1.

The host application programs for this task must be flexible in their command syntax. They must also have access to subsystems that enable communication with the outside world. These can be enhanced graphic displays combined with manual data entry devices (keyboard and/or mouse) as well as speech input/output systems[2, 3, 4].

The main problem is the translation of information between different representations, and so a common framework must exist or the information cannot be transferred between adjacent systems or subsystems (see Fig. 17.1). For speech recognition there are basically two translations that are necessary before the information from the outside world is available to the computer system.

First, speech signals must be mapped to certain codes representing a possible utterance in the communication framework between outside world and speech input system. This is a complex subject but has been treated in great detail in the earlier parts of this book. It includes the task of *enrolment* to allow the device to 'learn' the characteristics of the voice whose words it will have to recognise. A great deal of progress has been made in both techniques and technology since the first commercial

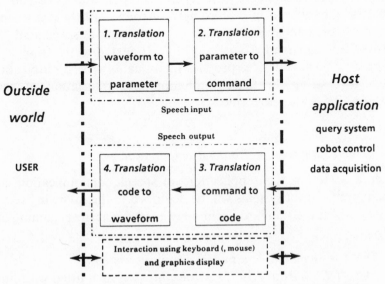

Figure 17.1 Simple model for an NL-system using speech I/O

devices were introduced around 1970, exploited mainly in industrial 'hands-free' environments and natural language query systems[5 – 13].

The second translation necessary for a computer to recognise words is between the recognising device and the application on a host computer. This is often a main problem in the commercial application and is the subject of this chapter.

Manufacturers of speech recognition hardware give support on interfacing to host computers on various levels. Many devices use a very simple protocol. The recognition device sends certain codes corresponding to the recognised speech input using a serial (RS 232), parallel, or other specialised interface. The user then has to alter his application program according to the protocol used by the speech input device.

Some recognition systems can be modified according to the needs of an application interface. Therefore the host application can remain unmodified and the second translation step is also performed in the recognition device. Various product descriptions are available in which interfacing procedures are explained in detail[12, 14, 15].

A third and fourth translation step may be required if the speech input is to be combined with speech output[14]. This can be useful for error messages to the user. Low-priced synthesiser chips, most often using an LPC synthesiser, can speak the limited vocabulary needed for error output[16] (see the companion book to this one, *Electronic Speech Synthesis*).

The output of an application program must be modified in such a way that it is understandable by the speech output chip. The chip then generates the waveform accordingly. Around 1980, text-to-speech converters became available that do not need a specialised input protocol but can read a string of ASCII text directly from a host computer[17]. These devices produce high-quality speech output of any ASCII text string. Sentence intonation and translation of certain abbreviations is also performed.

17.3 *Some examples of voice input/output systems*

To show some practical applications of speech communication, a few speech input/output systems will be described in the following sections. They represent the standard technology available at the beginning of the 1980s:

> The *Threshold 600* is a pure voice input system.
> The *ADES 1* from ANT is a voice input system fitted with limited voice output capabilities for feedback.

An LSI chip-set from NEC, capable of voice input.

A speech board from Texas Instruments, performing LPC voice synthesis, can be used for voice feedback to the user of a speech input system.

THE THRESHOLD 600

Description

The Threshold 600 is a versatile speech recognition device, the main elements of which are a processing unit, a tape drive and a microphone. The processing unit handles the recognition as well as all communication tasks with a host computer. The protocol can use standard host operating system commands. A terminal can also be used for independent command input and display of recognised words. The tape drive is the non-volatile storage device for the vocabulary and uses standard data cassettes. A small dynamic microphone is needed and can be linked to the Threshold 600 via a radio transmitter[15]. (Figure 17.2 shows the basic configuration.)

As mentioned, this recogniser only does the word recognition; it cannot take any action itself. The host receives the command corresponding to the word recognised and must decide itself what to do. The recogniser also depends on the host for information about the rejection threshold (which marks the point where two utterances are held apart) or the length of the pause between two words.

Interfacing the Threshold 600 to the host computer

This voice input device is specially equipped for interfacing with host computers. A number of facilities support the connection to the host operating system environment. The system can communicate with a

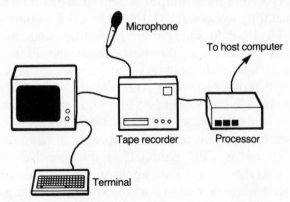

Figure 17.2 System configuration of the 'Threshold 600' voice input unit

wide variety of computers via a standard RS 232 interface. A parser for ASCII strings is built in for easy control by the host computer. An RS 232 software driver takes care of protocol and supports various handshake methods.

The host computer can communicate with this system using standard FORTRAN *READ* and *WRITE* statements. Predefined host control commands can be sent from the recogniser to the host depending on the recognised word.

The system is capable of polling a terminal at the same time as voice recognition is performed. Commands can be entered from the keyboard or through the microphone. More frequent commands can therefore be entered by voice input while the less frequent commands are typed at the keyboard.

The Threshold 600 reports its internal settings to the host, who can alter them according to the current application. Frequent recognition errors may prompt the user program to check what is wrong. Rejection threshold and length of pauses between words as well as other system parameters can then be modified by the host.

Application use

The Threshold 600 recognition system was used by the Fraunhofer-Institute for the voice input in two of the applications mentioned above – the numerically-controlled machine programming and the robotics application. In the former case, synthesis was required as well as recognition, but it was necessary to have these two communication processes dedicated to separate channels.

THE ADES-1 COMBINED SPEECH INPUT/OUTPUT SYSTEM

Description

The *ADES-1* is a voice input/output system. It is based on a *PDP 11/34* under the operating system *RSX 11/M* (Digital Equipment) with two floppy disks. The PDP does the pattern recognition and also handles the communication protocol to the host. Since the PDP is a multi-programming system, additional tasks can be installed that take care of specific communication necessities. ADES can be integrated into existing local area networks, e.g. DECnet (see Fig. 17.3 for usual configuration).

Voice input is via a headset with a dynamic microphone. An extra vocoder is used for voice output via loudspeaker. It has a limited output vocabulary (stored as LPC parameters) that consists of all words understood by ADES for a certain application, and a variety of system messages. A terminal is needed to start the system, but it can also display system status information as well as any user-specific output during

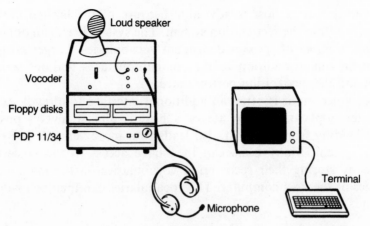

Figure 17.3 System configuration of the 'ADES-1' voice input/output system

operation. A powerful interface method can be installed using DECnet. Communication between ADES and host can then be achieved using symbolic node names. (Figure 17.4 shows a functional block diagram.)

Additional tasks that become active according to the recognised words can be installed. ADES can therefore be used as a stand-alone system. The PDP can also be upgraded by input/output ports to control appliances outside the ADES system. This can be complicated, so only a user familiar with both hardware and operating system should attempt to modify ADES.

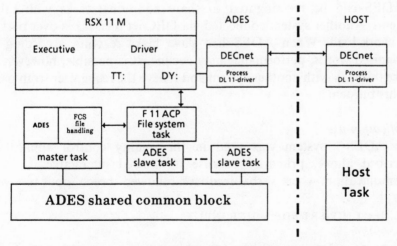

Figure 17.4 Software structure for data transfer between Host and ADES

Connection to a host is advisable because of the limited auxiliary resources within the recognition system. The system itself can only store a certain number of speaker-dependent vocabularies. Larger programs cannot be run in addition to the recognition tasks without seriously hampering the recognition performance.

Since voice input is often an additional interface to already existing computer applications, the use of a host is almost always possible. Down-loading from the host also leads to a more versatile use of the ADES system. Many users can then have access to the voice input system by storing their recognition vocabularies on the mass storage facilities of the host computer. The vocabularies can then be loaded on demand.

Interfacing the ADES-1 system to a host computer
Besides having an RS 232 interface for a terminal, ADES has a second RS 232 connecter for integration into any existing DECnet. One floppy disk is used for system and network tasks, and another floppy is used for the recognition software and vocabularies. The network software provides a wide variety of possibilities for communication. Any data can be exchanged through the network. ADES may be controlled remotely and can also use system facilities of other systems connected to the same DECnet.

When ADES recognises a word, a certain code (primarily consisting of the word-number) is sent to another task in the same system (network task, terminal driver, application task, etc.). The host can be prompted to act appropriately by sending user-definable commands to the application program.

ADES can be reconfigured to share additional tasks with other systems. Another system connected via DECnet then takes over part of the work-load. When ADES has slave tasks reacting according to recognised words, performance may decline. It is possible, however, to share this task with another system and relieve the recogniser from parts of this burden.

Application use
The ADES-1 system was used in the quality control application described above, primarily because it allowed interactive two-way communication, where verbal feedback followed speech input received.

THE NEC CHIP-SET FOR VOICE INPUT
Description
The NEC voice recognition LSI chip-set consists of an analogue

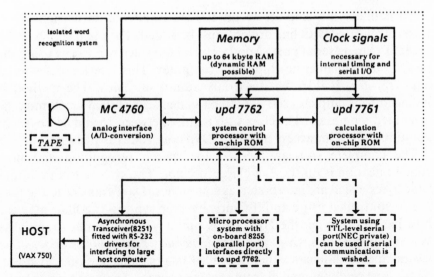

Figure 17.5 NEC speech recognition system – possible configurations

interface for connection of microphone or tape recorder, a signal processor performing spectral analysis and a single-chip computer that handles the matching algorithms as well as interfacing tasks (see Fig. 17.5). This system is designed for host interfacing but can also be integrated directly into a microprocessor system. The NEC chip-set performs speaker-dependent single-word recognition. It has a vocabulary of up to 512 words in 4 sets that can be selected by host control[12]. (See also Chapter 8.)

The NEC devices have three possible interfaces to other computers. The communication is only on a low level. Interfacing with standard terminal inputs of host computers is difficult because control characters that are often used for terminal control are misunderstood by the NEC chip-set. For instance, standard terminal interfaces often add CR/LF to start a new line after 80 characters (wrap-around), regardless of the initial intention. The host computer therefore must have driver software that allows a strict byte-at-a-time data transfer.

Interfacing facilities on the NEC chip-set
A parallel input port (8255) allows direct interfacing to a microcomputer system. The NEC chips can be connected to the peripheral side of a parallel port (i.e. the host connection is identical to an 8080-style bus interface connection). Depending on the bus-side connections of the parallel port, communication can even be interrupt-driven.

To connect the chip-set to an RS 232 interface, an asynchronous transceiver fitted with line drivers must be added. The main chip handles an 8251 chip as serial port. Another serial interface is possible using the on-chip port of the one-chip microcomputer. This interface uses serial data transfer. It does not need any additional chips. The method is intended for complete, self-contained systems. A system clock must be generated separately. The chips also require between 16 and 64 kbytes of additional random access memory. Dynamic RAM is possible.

The complete software needed for speech recognition and host communication is on the one-chip processor. The system awaits certain code bytes which are interpreted as commands. Data-transfer to the host is also controlled using an NEC-private code syntax. The first thing the host has to do to get the NEC chips running is send codes to initialise system parameters such as *input level, memory bank number* or *rejection values*. Speech data can either be loaded in a training session and stored on the host or down-loaded from existing sources. The host then tells the NEC chips to start scanning the voice input. When a word is recognised, the corresponding code is sent to the host as well as additional information on how well the word was matched to an internal template. The host can request the second decision if the recognised word doesn't fit into a certain syntax rule.

THE TEXAS INSTRUMENTS LPC VOICE OUTPUT BOARD
Description
The LPC voice output board from Texas Instruments has a fixed vocabulary stored in a set of EPROMs. Different languages are available. The board awaits a number from the host via a 16-bit parallel interface and routes the corresponding word to a loudspeaker. This board can also be integrated into a microprocessor system. It has all the necessary processing capabilities and the memory required to perform linear predictive coded speech synthesis[15].

Interfacing facilities on the TI LPC board
This LPC board can be accessed by a Texas-private bus built for interfacing directly to a microprocessor system. Another possibility is a 16-bit parallel port using a two-line handshake concept with busy and strobe signals. The speech synthesis system can communicate with any computer that has a parallel TTL-level 16-bit port and handshake lines. Additional software is needed to control the data transfer. Whenever the LPC board sets the busy line to false, a new code can be transferred to the voice output unit. Code sequences result in complete sentences.

17.4 *Conclusions*

The introduction of voice input to certain applications is somewhat hampered by the design of many older computers. They sometimes lack the interfacing facilities needed for easy connection of voice input systems. The second translation step (see Fig. 17.1) must then take place in the recogniser itself.

Because of missing interface-ports, speech input devices may have to be integrated into an existing communication protocol. The original data must then be passed on by the hardware of the speech recogniser and data concerning speech input inserted at appropriate places in the original data stream. The host computer application program may then have to demultiplex the incoming data stream. This is often difficult, and so most often a standard terminal connection is used and no distinction is made between keyboard- and voice-input data. The Threshold 600 is an example of this.

Several systems have been described which are all flexible enough to be used in many commercial environments, provided that adequate care is taken over the interfacing. In most cases, communication is by standard high-level language input and output. The examples given show only a brief glimpse of all the possible applications.

17.5 *References*

1. Schank, R.C. (1984) *The Cognitive Computer*. Reading, MA: Addison-Wesley Publishing Company, Inc.
2. Bullinger, H.J., and Faehnrich, K.P. 'Symbiotic man–computer interfaces and the user assistant concept'. *Human–Computer Interaction: Proc. of the 1st USA–Japan Conference on Human–Computer Interaction*. August 18–20, 1984, Honolulu, Hawaii.
3. Faehnrich, K.P., and Ziegler, J. 'Workstations using direct manipulation as interaction mode – aspects of design, application and evaluation'. *Interact 1984, 1st IFIP Conference on Human–Computer Interaction*, 4–7 September 1984, London.
4. Levinson, S.E., and Libermann, M.Y. (1981) 'Speech recognition by computer'. *Scientific American* **4**.
5. Kwok, H.L., Tai, L.C., and Fung, Y.M. (1983) 'Machine recognition of the Cantonese digits using band-pass filters'. *IEEE Transactions on Acoustics, Speech, and Signal Processing*, February.
6. Hiroaki Sakoe, and Seibi Chiba (1978) 'Dynamic programming algorithm optimization, for spoken word recognition', *IEEE Transactions on Acoustics, Speech and Signal Processing*, February.

7. Rabiner, L.R., and Schafer, R.W. (1978) *'Digital Processing of Speech Signals'* New York: Prentice Hall.
8. Rigoll, G., and Faehnrich, K.P. (1984) 'Some tools for speaker-independent, isolated-word recognition systems based on system theory and system dynamics algorithms'. *Proceedings of the Seventh International Conference on Pattern Recognition*, July 30–August 2. Montreal, Canada.
9. Levinson, S.E., Rabiner, L.R., and Sondhi, M.M. (1983) 'An introduction to the application of the theory of probabilistic functions of a Markov process to automatic speech recognition'. *Bell System Technical Journal* April.
10. Rabiner, L.R., Levinson, S.E., and Sondhi, M.M. (1983) 'On the application of vector quantization and hidden Markov models of speaker-independent, isolated-word recognition'. *Bell System Technical Journal* April.
11. Bui, N.C., Monbaron, J.J., and Michel, J.G. (1983) 'An integrated voice recognition system'. *IEEE Transactions on Acoustics, Speech, and Signal Processing*, February.
12. NEC *System Specification upd 7762, upd 7761, MC4760*. NEC Electronics.
13. Bucy, F., Anderson, W.W., McMahan, M.M., Tarrant, R.T., and Tennant, H.R. (1984) 'Ease-of-use features in the Texas Instruments professional computer'. *Proceedings of the IEEE*, March.
14. Texas Instruments TM 990/306 speech module, product description.
15. Threshold T 600 User Manual.
16. Soskuty, O. (1984) 'Phonem-synthesizer-IC ist uP-kompatibel'. *Elektronik* **17**/24.8.
17. Bruckert, E. (1984) 'A new text-to-speech product produces dynamic human quality voice'. *Speech Technology* January/February.

CHAPTER 18

VOICE INPUT FOR PERSONAL COMPUTERS

Kjell Elenius and Mats Blomberg

In this chapter, the design and use of one speech recognition peripheral for personal computers is explored.

18.1 *The advent of voice input for the PC*

As early as 1956, Harry F. Olson and Herbert Belar presented a *phonetic typewriter* that was capable of recognising the seven syllables *I can see you type this now* for one speaker[1]. The realisation of the system was, of course, influenced by the available technology, but it is interesting to see that their recognition principles are still (in 1984) actively exploited. They were using a filter bank of eight channels ranging from 200 to 6000 Hz, which was sampled every 40 ms. The amplitudes of the filters were used for tracing local spectral maxima after 'digitising' them into two levels using an array of forty electromechanical relays. They argued that the syllable was the optimal speech recognition unit. In this respect, they might seem somewhat old-fashioned compared to the contemporary researchers who rely on statistics and mathematics rather than on phonetics and linguistics.

The current trend may be explained to some extent by the fact that the researchers in the field are mainly recruited from persons with a background in engineering and computer science. But it is also true that techniques based on pattern matching, dynamic programming and Markov processes, to date, have been more successful than more phonetically-oriented approaches in which human speech processing is modelled. It simply seems that our current understanding of speech production and perception is too limited, making stochastic modelling of the speech process a better strategy, at least for the time being.

Such voice input technology – limited though it may appear at first sight – is now available to the user of a personal computer, and therefore to the population at large. This chapter explores the design and use of one such PC-based recognition system.

18.2 *A voice input board for personal computers*

The particular recognition board to be described in this chapter was derived from original work conducted at the Royal Institute of Technology in Stockholm, Sweden. Speech recognition research at the Department of Speech Communication and Music Acoustics at KTH, Stockholm, has been pursued since 1972 using both the technical and the 'human modelling' approach[2, 3, 4]. The rapid evolution of LSI-chips made it possible to realise a truly portable prototype word recognition device in April 1982 – a speaker-adaptive, pattern matching system using dynamic programming for time alignment of word patterns (Fig. 18.1). It included a Motorola *MC68000* microprocessor, a NEC *7720* signal processor, 16 kbyte ROM memory and 16 kbyte RAM, of which 12 kbyte were used to store a maximum of 48 reference words. This unit was later commercialised by the Swedish company, Infovox, as the Infovox *RA 101*[5].

The board of interest here, the *RA 201/PC*, is a recognition board for personal computers like the IBM PC, and is functionally the same system as RA 101, although major changes have been made to the implementation. The recognition board includes a speech amplifier, an anti-aliasing filter, a codec for A/D-conversion and a signal processor for speech analysis and the dynamic programming calculations. There is no microprocessor nor any memory on the board (Fig. 18.2). Instead it was found that it was possible to use the microprocessor of the PC to control the recognition process, and the memory of the PC to store the reference vocabulary: this reduces the cost of the device. The recognition program will, of course, take some memory and processing time from the applications program, but this will rarely be a problem.

TECHNICAL DESCRIPTION OF THE RA 201/PC
The Infovox RA 201/PC uses a signal-processing chip (NEC 7720) to digitally implement a 16-channel filter bank. The filter bank covers frequencies from 200 to 5000 Hz; the bands are spaced according to the frequency characteristics of the human auditory system using the psychoacoustically measured critical band scale[6]. The outputs of the filters for a male speaker saying *speech recognition* are shown in Fig. 18.3. Proprietary processing to increase the discrimination between

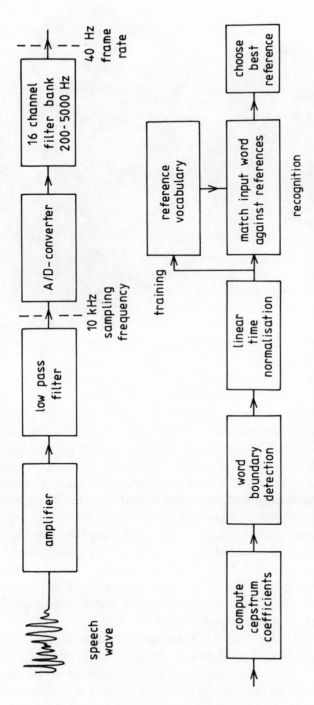

Figure 18.1 Block diagram of the Infovox RA 101 and RA 201/PC

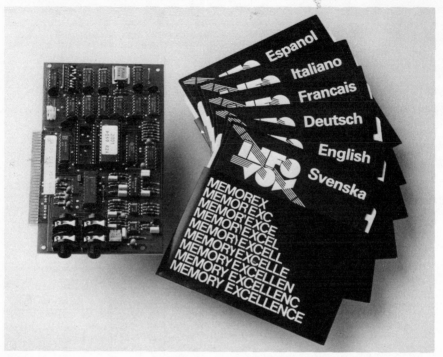

Figure 18.2   The Infovox RA 201/PC word recognition board. (*Reproduced by permission of Infovox AB, Danderyd, Sweden*)

speech sounds is included in the chip. The 16 filter outputs are converted into 6 cepstral coefficients sampled every 25 ms[7]. The maximum utterance length is 2.5 seconds. All input utterances are normalised to a nominal length of 32 sample points before the dynamic programming time alignment which is handled by the signal processor. The time taken to match one reference pattern is approximately 10 ms. Each vocabulary item requires 240 bytes of storage, of which $32 \times 6 = 192$ are used to store the speech parameter pattern. The remaining bytes are used to save specific information attached to each template, e.g., syntax markers and response string. In the training phase, it is recommended that each vocabulary entry be repeated three to five times. The corresponding reference template is calculated as a mean value of all the readings, taking the proper time warp into account.

When a word is recognised, the recognition program responds with a response string of up to 32 bytes. There is also a possibility of dividing the user vocabulary into subgroups using one or more of 16 'syntax' markers. The use of this feature will increase both the recognition speed and the accuracy. The maximum vocabulary size is 200 utterances. It is

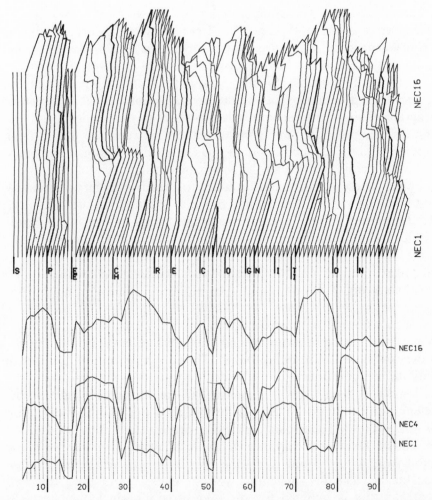

Figure 18.3 Two- and three-dimensional representation of the filter bank outputs of the RA 201/PC for the words '*speech recognition*'. Time in centiseconds. NEC1 is the lowest filter channel and NEC16 the highest

very easy to store (and load) vocabularies since they can easily be converted to files of the PC.

USAGE CONFIGURATIONS

The PC recognition unit may be used in essentially four different ways which will be described in detail below.

First, there is a basic recognition program which is used for training of vocabularies, calibration of levels and thresholds, testing of recognition accuracy, editing reference information and so forth.

Second, the same program may be used to voice control a device connected to an I/O-port of the PC. After recognising a word, a response string is sent to the device using the PC-interface. This makes it possible to use the PC as a stand-alone recognition unit.

Third, it is possible to fully integrate speech control into an applications program by calling different functions of the recognition program. This is the recommended method if you want to use the board's full potential. The communication between the applications program and the recognition program is handled by a special procedure making it possible to use all the commands of the device.

Fourth, speech control may be added to already existing programs by first invoking a special recognition program and then the user program. After initiating speech input, the response strings of recognised words will look like keyboard entries to the applications program.

The size of the recognition program is 32 kbyte and the data area needed is 16 kbyte plus 240 bytes for each reference up to a maximum vocabulary of 200 words.

SHARED USE OF THE PC PROCESSOR

When speech recognition is included in an applications program, the PC-processor is used as described below. The user program has full control until the recognition board is activated for input. A small fraction of the CPU-time is then used to monitor the speech input to detect the beginning of a word. When the beginning is found, the recognition program takes full control of the CPU to process the input speech. When the end of the utterance is detected, the recognition phase starts and the input word is compared to all the possible words in the recognition vocabulary. The best-matching word is chosen, and the associated control string is buffered for the user program which then resumes control of the processor. When a reject occurs, a reject string may be transferred. For a 20-word vocabulary the total interruption for word input and recognition would be about half a second.

PERFORMANCE

The evaluation of speech recognisers is commonly considered a very difficult problem (see Chapter 13). There are so many parameters that may vary between different tests, e.g., the vocabularies, the speakers, the influence of stress and background noise. Over the past years much effort has been put into attempting to create standardised test procedures, but the results are meagre so far[8]. While waiting for more controlled tests, the material recorded by Texas Instruments in 1981 has been used for making at least a qualitative comparison between word recognisers[9, 10]. It consists of a 20-word vocabulary read sixteen times by eight males and eight females without interfering noise. The results for the RA 201/PC without the proprietary speech processing were 1.9% errors, of which about half were *go* replaced by *no*. By including the proprietary processing, the errors were reduced to 0.7%, most of which were substitutions between *go* and *no*. A special feature of the device makes it possible to automatically create multiple reference patterns for a word when the training readings exhibit great variability. Including this feature, the error rate decreased to 0.4%. The number of templates increased by 15%, i.e., on the average, 3 extra templates were created per speaker.

18.3 *Applications for voice input on the PC*

Traditionally, the main field of applications has been in typical hands- or eyes-busy situations, such as the sorting of luggage at airports or inspection of products in the manufacturing industry. These applications can also be handled with the recognition integrated into a personal computer, perhaps at a cost lower than that for previously used devices.

However, we believe that in a PC or workstation environment the main interest for speech recognition will shift towards controlling applications programs such as word processing and computer-aided design (CAD). Voice commands will replace or complement the use of a keyboard or a mouse. As an example, it is easier when using a word processor to give a voice command like *search for*, *underline*, *superscript* or *mark block* than to enter an often arbitrary sequence of command keystrokes (Fig. 18.4).

Using the voice is also easier than using one hand to position a mouse for a menu choice. The voice commands are easy to learn and to remember because meaningful words or utterances may be chosen. This is especially true for the non-frequent commands which together may constitute the majority of a command vocabulary. In a CAD-environment it is an advantage to use the mouse for positioning of coordinates while the voice is used for selection of symbols, components or commands. This will make a natural division for the user and will facilitate his work.

One voice command may replace several keyboard commands. They need only to be concatenated in the response string of the command. Also, when changing from one word processor to another it is probably quite feasible to implement similar sets of voice commands.

Another more important advantage is that using voice will make the operator more independent of keyboard designs, especially considering

Figure 18.4   Using voice commands in word processing

the different layouts of function keys. The voice commands will not be affected at all when changing between computers or keyboards.

Naturally it is not always true that voice control is a superior means of input. On the contrary, there are many cases in which other means of input are a better choice. It would be truly awkward to use voice for moving the cursor seven steps to the left by repeating *left* seven times instead of pushing a button. Similarly, the use of a mouse for positioning or tracking is as advantageous as using a steering wheel to drive a car rather than using discrete commands like *left* and *right*.

LIMITATIONS

Though word recognition will make it possible to facilitate the handling of computers, it is important to bear in mind that there are limitations to the technique. The integration of voice must be effected carefully. It is essential to consider the ergonomic implications of introducing a new technique. Voice control should only be used when it renders absolute advantages for the operator. Speech recognition is not 100% accurate. This makes the use of commands like *delete file* and *abort program* somewhat hazardous. The traditional solution to this is to use feedback of recognised utterances followed by user approval or correction. This method will, however, reduce the advantage of voice input. It is our experience that when using voice for non-critical commands it is better not to use feedback, at least as long as the error rate is below a few per cent. A critical parameter in this respect is the reject threshold that rules out ambiguous utterances. It is generally true that no response is better than an erroneous response. When errors occur, they should be rare, and their effect should not be too harmful. This will reduce the irritation caused by them. However, we believe that there are many applications where the accuracy of many of today's recognisers is good enough to make them a real help for the user.

The selection of vocabulary words and utterances may cause problems. It is important to choose words that are easily connected to their usage, but they should also appear distinct to the recognition unit. In the above devices, it is possible to measure the similarity between vocabulary items in order to check whether there is a risk of confusion between some of them. Generally, short words are more prone to confusion than longer ones, e.g., compare *go* and *no*.

The limitations imposed by the fact that the utterances must be produced in isolation are not very severe when the voice option is mainly used for discrete commands.

Another kind of problem is the use of a headset for carrying the microphone. This is probably more of an inconvenience than it is generally considered to be. However, the positive effects of using a noise-cancelling microphone at the corner of your mouth are still necessary in order to get acceptable performance unless the device is used in a silent environment. This is an area in which further research is needed to find more satisfactory solutions.

An important option for the user is the possbility of turning on, or perhaps more essentially, of turning off the recognition device, making it possible to talk to other people without vast and unintentional consequences.

18.4 *Vocabulary training*

The use of voice control is most probably something totally new to the operator, and the introduction of it should be made accordingly. In user-adaptive systems, the training of the reference vocabulary easily stands out as something different from the actual application of the system. The differences between the two situations will be reflected in the acoustical properties of the words, and will cause misrecognitions. This may, in fact, be a major source of errors.

To reduce these differences between training and application, the Infovox devices described above have integrated the training of the vocabulary into the learning and operation of the applications program. One approach is called 'incremental training'. The idea is to enter the vocabulary words one by one as the user is actually using the applications program. When he enters a command by the keyboard, he will be notified that the option may be selected by voice as, e.g., *move block*. If he wants to train the command, he will be prompted to repeat it a few times, and then the corresponding command will be performed. Thus the user will incrementally train the vocabulary and the training will be done during the application.

Another approach to the training problem is to integrate the training of reference templates into a learning program of the application. In this case, the operator would be instructed to say *move block* at some phase in the learning. The corresponding command would be performed even if the word had not been trained earlier. The utterance is used as the first training sample of the command. The next few readings of the command will also be used for training. In this way the user will not be aware of the training. This 'training while learning' method may also be used to train the most frequent commands. Then the 'incremental learning' may be used for training the other commands.

One reason why an experienced user generally gets better performance than a naive one is that he does not produce as many lip smacks, hums and other sounds that will confuse the recogniser. Another important fact is that, through trial and error, he has achieved a more consistent articulation. This consistency will also make his reference templates more adequate in reflecting the utterances during the application.

One philosophy for training is thus to make an inexperienced user behave like an experienced one. Both of these training methods are now being explored in cooperation with some Swedish personal computer and software companies. The applications include word and document processing and computer-aided design. The feasibility of using a synthesis system for spoken messages to guide the learning of applications programs and the training of recognition vocabulary will also be explored.

18.5 *Conclusions*

When Harry F. Olson and Herbert Belar presented their Phonetic Typewriter almost 30 years ago, they were quite optimistic about the future of speech recognition. They would probably not be impressed by the fact that people are now talking to typewriters, not to say *what* to type, but rather *how* to type it. On the other hand, considering the complexity of human speech and the lack of correspondence between phonetic entities and their acoustic realisations, one could argue that something substantial has been achieved. However, it is our feeling that we need to know more about user experiences with voice input. This will help us take better advantage of this new technique.

18.6 *References*

1. Olson, H., and Belar, H. (1956) 'Phonetic Typewriter'. *J. Acoust. Soc. America* **28** 1072–1081.
2. Blomberg, M., and Elenius, K. (1978) 'A phonetically based isolated-word recognition system'. *J. Acoust. Soc. America* **64 (Suppl. 1)** 181.
3. Elenius, K., and Blomberg, M. (1982) 'Effects of emphasizing transitional or stationary parts of the speech signal in a discrete utterance recognition system'. *Proceedings of the IEEE International Conference on Acoustics, Speech and Signal Processing*, Paris, 535–538.
4. Blomberg, M., Carlson, R., Elenius, K., and Granström, B. (1984) 'Auditory models in isolated-word recognition'. *Proceedings of the IEEE International Conference on Acoustics, Speech and Signal Processing*, San Diego, paper 17.9.1.
5. Magnusson, L.-E., Blomberg, M., Carlson, R., Elenius, K., and Granström, B. (1984) 'Swedish speech researchers team up with electronic venture capitalists'. *Speech Technology* **2(2)** 15–24.
6. Zwicker, E., and Feldtkeller, R. (1967) *Das Ohr als Nachrichtenempfänger*. Stuttgart: S. Hirzel Verlag.
7. Davis, S., and Mermelstein, P. (1980) 'Comparison of parametric representations for monosyllabic word recognition in continuously spoken sentences'. *IEEE Trans. Acoustics, Speech and Signal Processing* **ASSP-28** 357–366.

8. Pallet, D., (ed.) (1982) *Proceedings of Workshop on Standardization for Speech I/O Technology.* Gaithersburg, Maryland: National Bureau of Standards.

9. Doddington, G., and Schalk, T. (1981) 'Speech recognition: turning theory to practice'. *IEEE Spectrum* September, 26–32.

10. Woodard, J., and Lea, W. (1984) 'New measures of performance for speech recognition systems'. *Proceedings of the IEEE International Conference on Acoustics, Speech and Signal Processing*, San Diego, paper 9.6.

CHAPTER 19

RECOGNITION PAST AND FUTURE

Sam Viglione

In this final chapter, the recent history of speech recognition is briefly summarised and the trends are discussed, leading to some conjecture as to how these trends will continue.

19.1 *The quest for natural communication*

Because of the inherent superiority of speech over other modes of human communication, and the growing need for better control of complex machines, speech recognition and speech response systems have begun to play a major role in man–machine communication.

Although technology has produced some spectacular aids to human communication, nothing can replace or equal speech. It is the most familiar and most convenient way for humans to communicate. In the past, man has been required to interact with machines in the language of those machines. With speech recognition and speech response systems, man can communicate with machines using natural-language human terminology. The use of voice processing systems for voice input and output provides a degree of freedom for mobility, alternative modalities for command and data communication, and the possibility of substantial reduction in training time to learn to interface with complex systems. These salient characteristics of speech, when incorporated into an effective voice control or voice data entry system, yield positive advantages over other methods of man–machine interaction.

A major goal of automated speech recognition is to use this natural means of communication to achieve direct human interaction with computers.

The commercial applications of automated speech recognition began in the early 1970s. Since that time many advances have been made in the development of more powerful algorithms for speech analysis and classification, the extraction of word features to permit improved performance in isolated- and connected-word recognition, and in the reduction of the cost of the hardware required to implement these speech processing methods. This latter has been most notable and has permitted board-level solutions to larger sizes of recognition vocabularies with an order of magnitude reduction in cost. Projections lead us to still further reduction in costs of the implementation function, with improving performance and expanded capabilities of the speech products, as the speech technology evolves into its next generation.

19.2 *A short chronology of developments to date*

COMMERCIAL PRODUCTS FROM 1969 TO 1985

One of the first commercial sales of a speech recognition system was made in late 1969 to United Airlines for a baggage-handling system at Chicago's O'Hare airport. A second system was initiated at the US Post Office in Philadelphia for entering Zip codes (post codes). These systems demonstrated limited success (85 to 95% recognition) and significant operational difficulty (i.e., noise, operator annoyance, and discomfort) and were discontinued in the early 1970s. But speech recognition continued in the US, under Department of Defense (ARPA Speech Understanding Program) and internal research funding, to make significant strides during the mid-1970s towards improving the accuracy and performance of word recognition and speech understanding systems. During the 1970s several companies became active in developing word recognition systems with limited vocabularies, and commercial applications began to emerge.

Since 1980 these and other companies have offered speech recognition systems ranging from isolated- and connected-word limited-vocabulary, speaker-dependent systems at $2000 to $20 000, to chip-sets capable of 100-word, trainable, isolated-word recognition at $100 to $200. W. Lea[1] in his Office of Naval Research report lists 24 vendors of speech recognition products. J. Michael Nye[2] in his report at the 1982 and 1983 Voice Users' Conference lists 50 vendors and researchers in the speech recognition area.

Threshold Technology, Inc., started in the early '70s by a spin-off group from RCA, pioneered the commercial applications of speech recognition. They developed and marketed an isolated-word recognition system and a voice-operated numerically-controlled machining system in the mid-70s. Their word recognition systems were selling for $15 000–

$20 000. They established a subsidiary company, 'Auricle, Inc.', in 1980–81 to introduce a board-level product at $2000, and developed a version of their larger system called 'Quick Talk' for more rapid data entry.

Interstate Voice Products first offered a speech recognition system in 1977 with the introduction of a multi-channel isolated-word recognition system built around a NOVA computer. Since that time they have pioneered the development of low-cost board- and chip-level products for speech recognition for both the commercial and the consumer marketplace.

Verbex had been a company traditionally involved with military R & D related to speech systems. Their founding company, Dialog, Inc., was funded by RADC to perform word spotting for communication intelligence applications. In 1980 they become a wholly-owned subsidiary of Exxon Enterprises. They have applied their hardware and analytic techniques to commercial speech recognition with a speaker-independent, limited-vocabulary system developed for Bell Illinois for a telephone transaction handling system, at a system cost of $65 000. In 1983 they announced a connected-speech recognition system, the Model 3000, capable of accepting large strings of utterances. It is a speaker-dependent system capable of handling a 360-word vocabulary, priced in the $15 000 to $20 000 range. In October 1984 Verbex announced the System 4000, to be used with any minicomputer, which offers continuous recognition for vocabularies up to 100 words at a price of $4500.

Votan, Inc. was formed in 1979 to address the voice store and forward market and has developed a product with both voice recognition and voice response capabiltiy. The basic system sells for $5000 and can be used to recognise speech, or digitise speech for recording and playback under software control. In 1984 they introduced a connected-word recognition board for the IBM PC for $2500.

Texas Instruments has been active in developments in speech recognition and speech response for over 15 years. Their principal thrust has been in the speech response area and they have offered a variety of products and chips using the LPC coding technique. Their 'Speak 'n' Spell' voice response product was the catalyst for the growth of interest in speech response in the consumer and commercial marketplace. Their speech recognition activity, like Verbex's, was principally directed at military R & D requirements. They were contracted for many years by the US Air Force to develop a speaker verification system for secure military installation facility access.

In 1981 TI formed a separate speech division with the purported intent of commercialising their speech product line. They announced an isolated-word recognition option to their personal computer in 1983.

This product uses the TMS320 signal-processing chip and extensive software developed for their personal computer. The system is marketed as an option to their computer and sold through their personal computer division.

Intel joined the community in 1984, offering speech recognition products using their 2920 signal-processing chip. The Intel system, called a 'speech transaction processor', is a complete turnkey product with a development system for vocabulary and reference pattern generation. The recognition algorithm permits isolated-word recognition with vocabularies of 100 words. The primary application of the transaction processor has been in quality control and inspection.

Nippon Electric Company was selected by MITI in Japan as the focal point for the Japanese attempt at solving the data entry problem for their fifth generation computers. NEC has been active in the speech recognition research area since 1972 with Japan's establishment of a national commitment to the machine solution of the pattern information processing problem. NEC has marketed their connected-word recognition product in the US since 1980, initially at a price of $100 000. They have since reduced the product price to about $20 000 and offered a board-level product at $2000. In 1983 they also introduced a chip-set using the 7920 signal-processing chip and a connected-word speech recognition board-level product.

The traditional leaders in the computer and communication product area have not undertaken commercial voice recognition product development; IBM maintains a research staff dedicated to the unlimited-vocabulary speech understanding and very large vocabulary dictation systems. Even in their successful personal computer market they are encouraging others to develop the voice peripherals and options. Bell Laboratories has been the traditional leader in speech encoding, speech compression, and speech response, with obvious telephone applications in mind. They are purchasers of other vendor speech recognition products, with their own research in speech recognition directed at speaker-independent telecommunications. ITT has a California-based and a New Jersey-based speech system group. The California operation is pursuing military applications, particularly for communications intelligence and aircraft cockpit applications, and in 1985 introduced a speech recognition board for the IBM PC.

General Instruments has a chip product (the SP1000) which can be used for either recognition or synthesis. The SP1000 uses an LPC approach and provides the filter coefficients as output for use in either recognition or synthesis. The SP1000 sells for under $10 in large quantities. In 1985 GI offered a limited vocabulary speech recognition chip-set combining the SP1000 with their PIC 7040 microcomputer programmed for isolated-word, speaker-dependent recognition and incorporating a version of the dynamic programming algorithm for speech classification.

Scott Instruments has marketed, since 1980, an isolated-word recogniser for the TRS80 computer. In October, 1984, they announced a chip product with phonetic code analysis. Its performance and utility are yet to be determined.

In 1984–85 some new companies emerged. Dragon Systems (Boston, Massachusetts), a spin-off from Verbex, offers consulting and technology licensing in connected-speech recognition. In a 1984 venture, Dragon Systems licensed ACT, a British firm, to use the Dragon Systems discrete recognition algorithm on the ACT personal computer (the Apricot). Voice Control Systems (Dallas, Texas) is comprised of spin-off technical staff from Texas Instruments and the Santa Barbara Speech and Communication Center. VCS offers licensing in limited-vocabulary, speaker-independent systems. Kurzweil Applied Intelligence, Inc. (Boston, Massachusetts), a division of Kurzweil, Inc., was funded by Xerox and Wang, to aid in the development a 5000-word vocabulary speech-to-text device with the ambitious schedule of test-marketing the unit in 1986. Speech Systems, Inc. (Tarzana, California), is developing a large-vocabulary (1000 words) dictation system targeting towards 'rough draft' near real-time dictation with a product introduction schedule of late 1985.

CHARACTERISTICS OF THE MARKET

The voice recognition product development and product supplier arena can be characterised as volatile, but not aggressively competitive. The potential applications have proven much too numerous, technologies varied, and the products innovative. The market is growing, and the spread of the product base will help to swell this growth.

Still coming into its own, the voice recognition marketplace and product development of 1985 can be characterised as shown in Table 19.1.

These conditions are typical of a developing market, and there is strong evidence that development is accelerating.

19.3 *The evolution of a voice recognition product family*

Making projections about the future is only possible in the light of a good understanding of the past, and a history of companies founded is not perhaps as useful as a tracing of the evolution of one general-purpose

Table 19.1 1985 market characteristics

Negative aspects
- No industry standards
- Distribution channels not settled
- Viewed by consumers and users as 'black art' versus science

Positive aspects
- Accuracy improving
- Cost is going down in conjunction with memory and processing cost reductions
- User-friendliness improving

Trends supporting market growth
- Applications and acceptance broadening
- OEM interest strengthening
- Bookings increasing
- Heavier recent investments

---

product family. In this section the gradual development of the Interstate product range is examined, to see why each change was made when it was.

EARLY WORD-RECOGNISERS

Initiated in April, 1976, Interstate Voice Products has developed isolated-word recognition systems in a variety of formats – voice recognition chip-sets, computer peripheral voice recognition boards, and turnkey systems using voice recognition for command, control, and data entry functions. The first product, the Voice Data Entry System (*VDES*), was developed initially for the Army Signal Communication Laboratory, and was modified in 1977 to serve the commercial marketplace.

The VDES, shown in Fig. 19.1, was a four-user system priced at $30 000 and directed at the quality control and inspection data acquisition market. It included a software language that permitted development of application software, including syntax processing and remote interaction with the optional telephone interface and voice response system. However, it became apparent that the voice data entry system, though justifiable with paybacks of 12 to 15 months, was too expensive and too complex for most data entry or command and control functions.

In 1979, a project was initiated to design a voice recognition board-level product targeted at the $2000 to $3000 price range. Introduced in

Figure 19.1 The multi-channel voice data entry system

November, 1979, the Voice Recognition Module, or *VRM* (Fig. 19.2), provided all voice processing, recognition, and computer output functions on a 6- by 12-inch printed-circuit board at a selling price of $2295. The VRM quickly replaced the VDES as the voice recognition product, and was instrumental in promulgating the use of voice for data entry in a host of applications.

Whilst the VRM was the price/performance leader of the year, its principal disadvantage appeared to be the software support required to put the system into a specific application. In addition, with the expanded customer base and more users – particularly the end user on the inspection and production line, the pathology laboratory, the office, and the computer-aided design station – operational constraints became apparent. User resistance to the microphone, and system performance degradation with environmental and operational conditions such as noise, operator mobility, variable operator speech characteristics, and microphone positioning inconsistencies, emerged as the critical obstacles to further rapid growth in the use of voice recognition.

Figure 19.2   The Interstate 'Voice Recognition Module'

THE VLSI REVOLUTION

Clearly, further product innovation was needed to counter these obstacles in the professional applications, but in addition, new markets were burgeoning around 1981 where speech recognition could only be employed if the cost was very low – particularly the video game, home computer, personal computer, and toy marketplaces. The answer had to be VLSI.

In 1979–80 Interstate had invested in the development of a custom VLSI semi-conductor to perform the frequency analysis of the speech data. This single chip, the 16-channel ASA-16 shown in Fig. 19.3, was directed at replacing 240 discrete components, then on the VRM board, with substantial savings in both material and production costs. With the use of this chip it also became practical to offer the VRM in virtually any form factor. With the availability of more advanced microprocessors, lower cost and higher density ROM and RAM, it also became feasible to improve system performance with added features and to continue to reduce costs.

To address the need for a base component to be used in computer-oriented turnkey applications, an intelligent terminal was introduced in 1981 which had a combined voice input and keyboard capability (the

Figure 19.3 ASA-16 Spectrum Analysis Chip

VRT101). The voice recognition board was packaged to plug inside the terminal. The VRT101 included a user-utility software package to enable even the novice user to quickly incorporate speech recognition into his application.

To satisfy the need for low-cost recognition in consumer applications, the ASA-16 frequency analyser chip was released as part of a voice

Figure 19.4 Voice-controlled toy robot, using the VRC008 single-chip recogniser

recognition chip-set, the VRC100, along with an EPROM containing the company's patented speech recognition algorithm*. The VRC100 attracted customers particularly interested in adding voice to the video game and personal computer markets.

Even such a chip-set, however, is not suitable in itself to infiltrate cost-sensitive markets such as that of toys (see the voice-controlled robot in Fig. 19.4). In 1982 Interstate introduced a single microcomputer chip with a new patented algorithm** to meet this demand. The chip, the VRC008, was capable of speaker-independent recognition of a vocabulary of six to eight words, and this was offered at less than $10 in large quantities.

* US Patents 3,582,559; 4,292,470; 4,297,528.
** US Patent 4,388,495.

Figure 19.5 The VRT300 plug-compatible recognition board for the DEC VT100 terminal

A further market was apparent for the addition of speech recognition capability to standard terminals and personal computers. Again, the same chips and techniques were exploited, but this time modified to produce single-board recognition products designed to be plug-in compatible with the popular DEC VT100 computer terminal and with the IBM PC.

The former, the VRT300 (see Fig. 19.5), incorporated additional features for more convenient user operation and with software, hardware, and algorithm improvements to help overcome operational, environmental, and noise problems. The VRT300 also saw applications as a stand-alone unit in its own powered enclosure as the SYS300.

The speech recognition board which is designed to be plug-in compatible with the IBM PC, the SRB, (Fig. 19.6), incorporates a 16-bit INTEL 80186 microprocessor, 128 kbytes of dynamic RAM, and 32 kbytes of EPROM. It provides a 240-word vocabulary and executes a speech recognition algorithm incorporating the dynamic programming technique for connected-word recognition. The SRB also uses the ASA-16 spectrum analysis chip described above.

The SRB is supplied with a menu-based utility program, including a set of subroutines, written in BASIC, and supplied in source code. This greatly simplifies the utilisation of voice input for the user. The program prompts the user with questions and instructions via the PC's display. A *HELP* display is available at each menu level. Combined with a system of simplified keystrokes, the menu allows the uninitiated user to quickly become familiar with the speech input method of data entry, and permits a user to add voice to any existing software package.

Finally, the trend towards VLSI for size- and cost-reduction is exemplified by a speaker-independent digit-recognition system intro-

Figure 19.6 The SRB speech recognition board for the IBM PC

duced in 1985. This utilises a coding algorithm extracting speaker-independent features from a sample population of the digit-vocabulary. The feature set is then combined with the spectrally encoded data which tracks the formant frequency amplitude and position (peaks and valleys) information. A set of reference patterns (one or more for each word) comprised of these features is stored and compared with the incoming utterances using a Euclidian distance metric.

A block diagram of the speech-processing chip offered in 1985 is shown in Fig. 19.7. This CMOS VLSI product incorporates all the analogue processing required to take a low-level speech signal from the microphone, do the amplification, spectrum equalisation and filtering required, then digitise the sampled spectrum and output the digitised samples onto the bus of the speech system's microprocessor. The speech preprocessor chip is designed with switched capacitor filter technology. It permits continued reduction of the cost of implementing speech recognition on board- and chip-level products.

19.4 *Future projections*
Future products that will emerge from the speech community will address the continued need for larger vocabularies and more natural

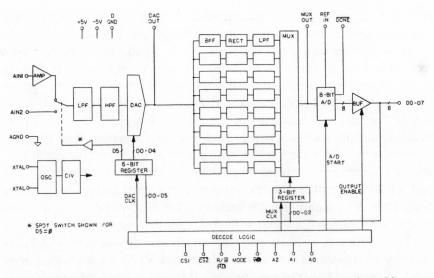

Figure 19.7 Block diagram of CMOS speech pre-processing chip

discourse with the user. With the expected advances in knowledge-based systems (Artificial Intelligence), word and sentence structure can be addressed, leading to more natural conversational systems. These systems have extensive computational and memory requirements and for the immediate future will be limited in application and scope. The rules for implementing the grammar and language structure are available, and this implementation will not be long in coming. These advances, along with the utilisation of signal processing and statistical signal communication methods for enhancement of signal-to-noise ratio, should permit the user-friendliness that has been long sought after and usher in a new area of man–machine communication.

What we have seen emerge in the last decade is not a wealth of new knowledge on speech analysis, or insight into the key features that permit recognition of speech – or even of words. Rather, what has occurred is that the computational tools have been made available that have permitted implementation of techniques developed in the '60s and '70s, in a cost-effective fashion, and encouraged the development of low-cost speech products and the integration of these products into useful applications. With the cost reduction, and the spread of voice recognition products into the user arena, limitations of the technology have become apparent. Now in the mid-80s we find ourselves at the threshold of a challenge – that is, to advance further our understanding of the basic structure of the speech signal that conveys the meaning, the linguistic information, necessary for recognition – even in the presence of noise, talker variability and changing environmental conditions.

Introduced around 1984/5 were products capable of connected-word recognition on vocabularies of 20–30 words. The implication is that the effects of co-articulation and word length variability are not insurmountable with restricted vocabularies. Even with vocabularies of 100–200 words, the major concern is not the recognition performance, but the implementation cost to provide real-time performance. The dynamic programming algorithm, used so successfully to permit connected-speech recognition, requires large memory arrays for pattern storage, and ultra-fast processors for sample frame correlation with stored templates. As vocabulary size increases we find ourselves in non-real time operation – or are faced with costly implementation solutions.

These obstacles will be partially overcome as the semi-conductor industry continues its assault on sub-micron VLSI integration. Larger memory chips at lower prices are inevitable, as are faster processors with built-in hardware computational capabilities such as array processing. These hardware advances will permit larger vocabulary connected-word recognition systems to emerge, such as the 1000–5000-word dictation machines currently in the research labs. They do not by themselves, however, permit the extension of speech recognition out of the realm of a forced learning, template-matching machine, with its inherent limitations, into the speech recogniser that will allow true man–machine communication.

Speech recognition is an ongoing interaction between the talker and the listener and involves language structure, semantic, syntactic and pragmatic information exchange. Many cues are provided to the listener to permit his successful interpretation of the discourse, even in the presence of noise, stress, and other distractions. Current research into the basic elements of the speech waveform, invariant under the changing environmental, physiological and psychological conditions, will lead to the specification of word or language primitives that can form a lexicon for word recognition. Digital signal-processing devices will permit reliable extraction of these word features, and will provide background noise rejection. The rules for combining these features into meaningful words and phrases, followed by higher-level rule-based systems to permit sentences to be constructed, will be the basis for the true man–machine discourse system.

Such will be the gradual evolution of voice input technology. In the near-term, larger vocabulary connected-word recognisers will be offered to the user community. As lexicons of word primitives emerge, and 'expert systems' are constructed with an inherent rule-based knowledge structure, limited-vocabulary speaker-independent versions will be implemented. Advances in microcomputer and digital signal-processor speed, instruction sets and built-in functions – combined with further reduction in cost of memory and peripheral chips – will permit cost-effective integration of larger primitive libraries, large resident knowledge bases and more detailed search strategies. This will foster speech recognisers with still larger vocabularies and speaker-independent, connected-speech capability.

However, I would concur with J.S. Bridle in his comment made at the September 1984 European Speech Technology Conference in Brighton, UK,

'... machines are likely to fall far short of human performance with large vocabularies and unknown speakers until it is possible to acquire and use far more knowledge of speech structure than seems possible with current recognition approaches. Several speech research laboratories are attempting to formalise speech structure knowledge at many levels, and hope to use a variety of techniques to apply this knowledge in automatic speech recognition.

Perhaps "real" automatic speech recognition will elude us until the pattern processing in our machines is equivalent to the perceptual processing performed by the brain.'

19.5 *References*

1. Lea, W. (1980) *Trends in Speech Processing*. New York: Prentice Hall.
2. Nye, J.M., 'Voice integration – the critical mass'. *Proceedings of Conference on Voice Data Entry*, San Mateo, California, September, 1982; Chicago, Illinois, 1983.

GLOSSARY

Notes on the glossary

Whilst many technical terms have been used in this book, in general each term has been defined at the first time it was used. The reader who is puzzled by any particular reference is encouraged to seek any earlier reference by use of the index.

However, since some ambiguity can be found within the industry about some definitions, particularly in the context of objective assessments of speech recognition products, this book would not be complete without including the definition of terms that has been published by the National Bureau of Standards in the United States of America. This glossary was produced by the NBS out of contributions received from the 'Speech I/O Performance Assesment' Working Group of the IEEE Acoustics, Speech and Signal Processing Society.

Readers who would like to assist in the further development of this standard glossary should contact David Pallett of the National Bureau of Standards.

NBS standard glossary of speech recognition terms

Active vocabulary: see *vocabulary*.

Adaptation: the automatic modification of existing internal machine representations (e.g., template sets, word models, etc.) of specific utterances and/or noise.

Artificial language: see *Constrained language*.

Automatic speech recogniser: a device implementing algorithms for accepting speech as input, determining what was spoken, and providing potentially useful output depending on word(s) recognised.

Automatic speech recognition: the process or technology which accepts speech as input and determines what was spoken.

Automatic speech recognition system: an implementation of algorithms accepting speech as input and determining what was spoken.

Connected words: words spoken carefully, but with no explicit pauses between them.

Constrained language: lexically and syntactically constrained word sequences (e.g., telephone numbers).

Continuous speech: words spoken fluently and rapidly as in conversational speech.

Deletion: an instance in which a spoken word is ignored, and for which the recogniser or system provides no response (e.g., in recognising a string of digits, if the recogniser returns one less digit than has been input).

Discrete utterance recognition: the process of recognising a word or several words spoken as a single entry.

Enrolment: the process of constructing representations of speech, such as template sets or word models, to be used by a recogniser. Also referred to as 'system training', as distinct from 'user training'.

Enrolment data: see *Training data*.

False acceptance: an example of failure to reject properly spoken input utterances that are not part of the active vocabulary, resulting in selection of a word in the active vocabulary.

Grammar: in general, a grammar of a language is a scheme for specifying the sentences allowed in the language, indicating the rules for combining words into phrases and clauses. In automatic speech recognition, task grammars specify the active vocabularies and the transition rules that define the sets of valid statements to complete the tasks. The task grammar and structured vocabulary provide syntactic control of the speech recognition process that can greatly enhance performance.

Insertion: an instance of a recognition response occurring due to spurious noise or an utterance other than those that are legitimate on syntactic considerations. In the former case, some input other than an utterance (typically some ambient or electrical noise artefact) is not properly rejected and the system response indicates that some utterance in the recognition vocabulary occurred. In the latter case, a word that has been uttered (but which is not part of the active recognition vocabulary because of current syntactic constraints) is falsely accepted as an utterance from the active recognition vocabulary.

Isolated words: words spoken with pauses (typically with duration in excess of 200 ms) before and after each word.

Isolated-word recognition: see *discrete-utterance recognition*.

Natural language: syntactically unconstrained word sequences, typically drawn from a large lexicon and complying with conventional usage.

Practice data: any speech material (utterances) used in developing a recognition system prior to a test of that particular recogniser.

Recogniser: see *Automatic speech recogniser*.

Recognition systems: see *Automatic speech recognition systems*.

Recognition unit: the basic unit of speech on which recognition is being performed, often presumed to be the word. The actual unit used may be smaller (e.g., phones, demisyllables, syllables or features) or larger (e.g., multi-word phrases or utterances).

Recognition vocabulary: see *Vocabulary*.

Rejection: the property of rejecting inputs. There are three general classes of system response involving rejection: (i) noise rejection, (ii) rejection of improperly spoken input utterances, (iii) rejection of properly spoken input utterances that are part of the active vocabulary, sometimes termed false rejection.

Speaker-dependent recognition: a procedure for speech recognition which depends on enrolment data from the individual speaker who is to use the device.

Speaker-independent recognition: a procedure for speech recognition which requires no previous enrolment data from the individual speaker who is to use the device.

Speech level: a logarithmically-based measure of the amplitude of a speech waveform. Accurate specification of speech level is important in specifying the input signal amplitude when testing recognisers and when specifying signal-to-noise ratio. American National Standard ANSI S3.59 provides a well-specified procedure for measurement of speech level.

String: a sequence of spoken words or phrases, often spoken as connected words or continuous speech and intended to provide a single useful input to a recogniser, e.g., a five-digit ZIP Code (or postcode) or a seven-digit telephone number.

Substitution: an instance in which one word in the recognition vocabulary is incorrectly recognised as another word in the recognition vocabulary.

Syntax: structure by which grammatical word sequences are specified.

Test data: any speech material (utterances) used in a particular test of a recogniser not previously used in developing or modifying that recogniser. The same set of test data may be used repeatedly for tests of different recognisers or in production testing, but not for continuing tests of an algorithm or recogniser in development.

Token: a sample speech utterance.

Training: see *Enrolment*. System training is preferably referred to as enrolment. User training refers to the process of user familiarisation with speech technology (e.g., learning how to use an automatic speech recognition device).

Training data: speech material used to construct parametric representations of speech such as template sets or word models used by a recogniser. Also referred to as enrolment data. Not to be confused with performance data obtained in training potential users of the technology.

Utterance: a word or multi-word phrase spoken continuously as a single unit.

Vocabulary: the words or phrases to be recognised by a recogniser. Distinctions should be made between the complete set of all words or phrases that a recogniser has been trained or programmed to recognise, sometimes called the total *recognition vocabulary*, and the (instantaneously varying) subset of these that may be active at a given time because of an imposed task grammar or other syntactic constraint, called the *active vocabulary*.

Word: see *Recognition unit*.

Word model: a parametric (coded) representation of the sound patterns of words as a sequence of units such as phonetic units, syllables, or other speech parameters.

INDEX

−F , −LB , +Yel −3 white , F+
          (L)P.   Left lower